Maryland Mortalities

1876-1915

From

The (Baltimore) Sun Almanac

Walter E. Arps, Jr.

HERITAGE BOOKS
2008

HERITAGE BOOKS
AN IMPRINT OF HERITAGE BOOKS, INC.

Books, CDs, and more—Worldwide

For our listing of thousands of titles see our website at
www.heritagebooks.com

Published 2008 by
HERITAGE BOOKS, INC.
Publishing Division
100 Railroad Ave. #104
Westminster, Maryland 21157

Copyright © 1983 Walter E. Arps, Jr.

Other Heritage Books by the author:

Heirs and Orphans: Anne Arundel County Distributions 1788-1838
Before The Fire: Genealogical Gleanings from The Cambridge Chronicle *1830-1855*
Departed This Life: Death Notices from The Baltimore Sun, *Volume 1: 1851-1853*
Departed This Life: Death Notices From The Baltimore Sun, *Volume 2: 1854-56*
Departed This Life: Death Notices From The Baltimore Sun, *Volume 4: 1859-60*

Cover shows "The Sun" Iron building, at the S.E. corner of Baltimore and South Streets in Baltimore, Maryland - *circa* 1890

All rights reserved. No part of this book may be reproduced or transmitted in any form or by any means, electronic or mechanical, including photocopying, recording or by any information storage and retrieval system without written permission from the author, except for the inclusion of brief quotations in a review.

International Standard Book Numbers
Paperbound: 978-1-58549-254-1
Clothbound: 978-0-7884-8051-5

INTRODUCTION

The following death notices have been culled from the annual necrologies that were printed in The (Baltimore) Sun Almanac during the yearbook's entire 39-year lifetime. Established during the Centennial year, the Almanac, with its dusty blue and black cover, proved to be a highly popular home reference for Sun subscribers, to whom it was issued gratis.

For the current family researcher, however, the necrology is the only element in these yearbooks that is of any potential genealogical value. The hope is, however, that these death notices will assist family researchers to "push back" on Maryland matters. For a precise date of death represents the necessary key to obtaining a copy of an individual's death certificate. This form of vital record contains (theoretically, at least) information about a deceased individual's parents.

In 1876, when the Almanac was established, death records began to be systematically maintained by Baltimore City, which was then a considerably smaller geographical entity than it is today. For Maryland as a whole, the recording of deaths became a legal requirement only in 1898.

Basically, these reconstituted death notices consist of five elements: the name of the deceased, his age, occupation, residence and/or place of death (ambiguity reigns on this matter), and the deathdate itself.

If an entry fails to indicate a person's age, this compiler has employed the abbreviation n.a., i.e., no indicated age. Similarly, for the sake of editorial conformity and space, the convention "in his 91st year" has been trimmed to 90 (years). No other liberties have been taken, except to add a county name when a non-Baltimore City place has been cited (Laurel, Prince George's County).

We have here in Maryland Mortalities many persons whose lives encompassed most of the 19th century, as well as some individuals who were born during the Revolutionary War Era. There are a number of "Old Defenders" and a veteran of the Battle of Waterloo.

Credit for sparking this project is fully extended to the Annapolis genealogist, John Frazer, Jr., who discovered one of the necrologies in an Almanac purchased at a yard sale in Anne Arundel County.

My work on this project was undertaken at the Maryland State Law Library, where a complete run of the Almanac may be consulted for verification.

Painstaking care has been exercised to transcribe encountered information accurately—even to the incorporation of obvious original typos. In the course of compilation, some alphabetizing lapses have, unfortunately, occurred.

Walter E. Arps, Jr.

Annapolis, Maryland
15 August 1983

AARON, G_____ W_____, 62, former Captain, Baltimore City police, February 22, 1886.
ABBES, Francis H., 57, hatter, Baltimore City, October 19, 1894.
ABBOTT, Cornelius F., 66, manufacturer, Baltimore City, June 23, 1894.
ABBOTT, Horace, 81, retired, Baltimore City, August 8, 1887.
ABBOTT, James F., 72, merchant, Baltimore City, May 10, 1894.
ABELL, Arunah S., 81, founder of The Sun, Baltimore City, April 19, 1888.
ABELL, Arunah S., Baltimore City, July 28, 1914, aged 49.
ABELL, Edwin F., 63, The Sun, Baltimore City, February 28, 1904, shortly before the Great Fire.
ABELL, George W., 51, The Sun, Baltimore City, May 1, 1894.
ABELL, Walter, 42, one of the proprietors of The Sun, Baltimore City, January 3, 1891.
ABENDSCHEIN, Dr. Henry S., 52, Baltimore City, March 1, 1911.
ABERCROMBIE, John, 69, Baltimore City, January 7, 1911.
ABRAHAM, Brother, 67, November 26, 1908; he had been President of Rock Hill College for 10 years.
ABRAHAMS, J_____ J_____, 71, shipbuilder, Baltimore City, December 23, 1880.
ABRAHAMS, Louis W., 68, Baltimore City, October 27, 1909.
ABRAHAMS, Woodward, 78, Baltimore City, August 5, 1892.
ABRAHAMS, W_____ Woodward 56, secretary, ice company, Baltimore City, March 7, 1905.
ABRAMS, George W., 49, manufacturer, Baltimore City, March 8, 1902.
ACHEY, Charles F., 72, retired merchant, Baltimore City, May 29, 1904.
ACHEY, Frederick, 77, retired, Baltimore City, September 7, 1886.
ACKERMAN, Henry, 53, merchant, Baltimore City, July 21, 1901.
ACOSTA, Mrs. Mary Carroll, 76, March 27, 1902; she died at Washington, D.C.
ACTON, Harry C., 43, Brooklyn, Anne Arundel County, March 8, 1901.
ACTON, Samuel G., 74, Anne Arundel County, September 21, 1903.
ADAMS, Alexander M., 90, Cumberland, Allegany County, September 7, 1901.
ADAMS, C_____ W_____, 41, manufacturer, Baltimore City, March 14, 1893.
ADAMS, Charles S., 56, Maryland State Senator, Baltimore City, May 18, 1890.
ADAMS, Eliza, 96, Baltimore City, September 4, 1911.
ADAMS, Dr. Frederick A., n.a., Pocomoke City, Worcester County, October 28, 1904.
ADAMS, Dr. G_____ F_____, n.a., physician, Baltimore City, January 13, 1882.
ADAMS, G_____ F_____, 48, manufacturer, Baltimore City, September 14, 1893.
ADAMS, J_____ G_____, 70, Confederate veteran, Pikesville, Baltimore County, February 9, 1911.

-1-

ADAMS, Captain G____ W____, 42, mariner, Baltimore City October 4, 1884.
ADAMS, Herbert B., 51, professor, Baltimore City, July 30, 1901.
ADAMS, Isaac S., 56, Salisbury, Wicomico County, February 14, 1903.
ADAMS, J____ Frederick, 68, builder, Baltimore City, November 3, 1897.
ADAMS, J____ H____, 65, sail manufacturer, Baltimore City, July 18, 1893.
ADAMS, Jacob, 79, Hagerstown, Washington County, October 25, 1907.
ADAMS, Captain John D., 60, Baltimore City, August 2, 1913.
ADAMS, Captain John E., 58, Baltimore City, September 8, 1892.
ADAMS, John Quincy, 78, Baltimore City, October 10, 1905.
ADAMS, Reverend R____ H____, 70, Northeast, Cecil County, September 11, 1914.
ADAMS, Samuel H., 56, builder, Baltimore City, June 11, 1882.
ADAMS, Samuel T., 61, retired, Baltimore City, October 2, 1884.
ADAMS, Captain Thomas D., 74, August 6, 1911, at Washington, D.C.
ADAMS, Thomas Ira, 43, Baltimore City, December 16, 1897.
ADDISON, A____ E____, 76, merchant, Baltimore City, May 10, 1881.
ADDISON, George M., 75, court crier, Baltimore City, April 3, 1902.
ADDISON, John A., 58, machinist, Baltimore City, February 20, 1897.
ADDISON, Samuel S., 85, manufacturer, Baltimore City, June 18, 1892.
ADDISON, Samuel T., 48, merchant, Baltimore City, March 15, 1906.
ADDISON, Walter D., 52, Baltimore City, March 19, 1896.
ADDISON, William, 80, retired, Baltimore City, January 27, 1891.
ADDISON, William E., 56, ex-school commissioner, Baltimore City, December 14, 1902.
ADLER, Elias E., 73, retired, Baltimore City, May 11, 1898.
ADLER, Henry M., 62, manufacturer, Baltimore City, February 28, 1901.
ADLER, Michael, 59, merchant, Baltimore City, April 7, 1906.
ADLER, Seligman J., 85, n.p., March 26, 1914.
ADREON, Harrison, 50, ex-postmaster, Baltimore City, May 25, 1891.
ADREON, William, 80, auctioneer, Baltimore City, March 15, 1881.
ADREON, Major William T., 54, pension agent, Baltimore, December 10, 1885.
AFFELDER, Samuel, 59, Baltimore City, April 29, 1913.
AGER, Joseph B., 70, farmer, Prince George's County, December 29, 1913.

AGNEW, Thomas A., 57, merchant, Baltimore City, October 17, 1897.
AHRENDT, Henry, 72, iron founder, Baltimore City, December 30, 1890.
AHRENS, Adolf Hall, 37, poet and musician, died on November 20, 1909, at Minneapolis, Minnesota.
AIDT, Gustav F., 43, manufacturer, Baltimore City, June 19, 1902.
AIDT, Louis, 70, retired merchant, Baltimore City, June 10, 1899.
AIKEN, Dr. George B., 75, physician, Baltimore City, April 18, 1892.
AIKEN, W____ E____ A____, 80, chemist, Baltimore City, May 31, 1888.
AIREY, Captain Samuel J., n.a., Baltimore City, June 10, 1914.
AIREY, Thomas, 42, editor, Baltimore City, December 25, 1895.
AISQUITH, A____ H____, 50, Montgomery County, November 3, 1894.
AISQUITH, Henry, 59, Annapolis, Anne Arundel County, July 9, 1902.
AKER, T____ M____, n.a., Queenstown, Queen Anne's County, November 24, 1907.
AKERS, Rezen T., 63, retired, Baltimore City, December 9, 1901.
AKIN, John W., 49, judge, Catonsville, Baltimore County, October 18, 1907.
ALBAUGH, Edward W., 66, Baltimore City, December 1, 1897.
ALBAUGH, J____ W____, Jr., 43, actor, Baltimore City, April 7, 1910.
ALBAUGH, James A., n.a., Woodbine, Carroll County, September 26, 1909.
ALBAUGH, John, 71, manufacturer, Baltimore City, February 16, 1901.
ALBERS, Captain Charles F., 55, Fifth Regiment, Baltimore City, January 9, 1900.
ALBERS, Dr. Henry, 70, physician, Baltimore City, October 7, 1882.
ALBERT, Augustus, 84, Baltimore City, November 4, 1912.
ALBERT, Augustus J., 75, retired, Baltimore City, September 10, 1886.
ALBERT, Charles, 32, physician, Baltimore City, June 30, 1882.
ALBERT, Francis, 73, merchant, Baltimore City, April 6, 1906.
ALBERT, Mrs. H____, 62, Owings Mills, Baltimore County, December 31, 1909.
ALBERT, J____ Erwin, 28, merchant, Baltimore City, October 30, 1882.
ALBERT, Rev. Richard H. (R.C.), 43, July 27, 1902.
ALBERT, William J., 62, retired merchant, Baltimore City, February 29, 1879.
ALBERTON, Dr. George A., 68, physician, Baltimore City, July 24, 1906.
ALBERTSON, Isaac, 76, hotel proprietor, Baltimore City, March 24, 1895.
ALCORN, Rebecca, 101, black, Baltimore City, December 16, 1885.

ALDERDICE, Eugene, 45, manufacturer, Baltimore City, September 18, 1901.
ALDRIDGE, Dr. John H., 57, physician, Baltimore City, March 21, 1889.
ALER, Jeremiah, 76, machinist, Baltimore City, July 15, 1899.
ALEXANDER, Columbus S., 58, civil engineer, Baltimore City, May 15, 1901.
ALEXANDER, Francis, 65, Baltimore City, September 10, 1910.
ALEXANDER, Colonel George W., 66, Laurel, Prince George's County, February 20, 1895.
ALEXANDER, Colonel Mark, 82, retired lawyer, Baltimore City, November 11, 1906.
ALEXANDER, W_____ M_____, 83, artist, Cumberland, Allegany County, April 21, 1910.
ALFORD, James E., 75, insurance agent, Baltimore City, June 21, 1902.
ALGER, Major P_____ R_____, n.a., veteran, died at Hampton, Virginia, on December 12, 1908.
ALLAN, William, 52, principal, McDonogh Educational Institution, September 17, 1889.
ALLEN, Edward M., 80, ex-Senator, Bel Air, Harford County, July 18, 1907.
ALLEN, Geraldus S., Adams Exp., Baltimore City, November 11, 1898.
ALLEN, Henry, 84, mechanic, Baltimore City, January 19, 1883.
ALLEN, Henry A., 87, composer, Baltimore City, April 5, 1902.
ALLEN, John E., 66, librarian, Baltimore City, November 22, 1899.
ALLEN, Joseph S., 69, builder, Baltimore City, November 5, 1902.
ALLEN, Luther P., 56, merchant, Baltimore City, November 14, 1904.
ALLEN, Dr. Robert G., n.a., Darlington, Harford County, June 24, 1906.
ALLEN, William H., 58, builder, Baltimore City, August 27, 1881.
ALLERS, John H. (of H_____), 45, merchant, Baltimore City, July 8, 1901.
ALLISON, James W., 62, on December 30, 1911, at Washington, D.C.
ALLISON, Major Richard T., 75, Confederate veteran, Phoenix, Baltimore County, April 10, 1909.
ALLNUTT, Mrs. Charlotte A., 69, Baltimore City, September 5, 1910.
ALLSTON, Joseph S., 37, former State Senator, at Leonardtown, St. Mary's County, December 8, 1885.
ALMAND, J_____ O'G_____, 84, Baltimore City, September 3, 1909.
ALMONEY, Mordecai A., 70, retired, Baltimore City, October 2, 1902.
ALMOSS, Winfield F., 41, attorney, Baltimore City, September 23, 1900.
ALPHONSUS, The Very Reverend., n.a., Passionist priest, Baltimore City, April 1, 1906.

ALREY, J_____ Z_____, 61, Baltimore City, August 11, 1910.
ALT, John, 65, merchant, Baltimore City, January 14, 1904.
ALVEY, R_____ H_____, 81, judge, Hagerstown, Washington County, September 14, 1906.
ALVEY, Thomas H., 32, Frederick, Frederick County, December 5, 1906.
AMBACH, David, 71, Baltimore City, November 8, 1908.
AMBACH, Max, 54, manufacturer, Baltimore City, October 23, 1904.
AMENDT, Jacob P., 73, retired, Baltimore City, July 11, 1899.
AMES, Captain Edward R., 37, U.S. Army, Baltimore City, September 24, 1882.
AMES, Edward Raymond, 73, bishop, Baltimore City, April 24, 1879.
AMMEDON, John P., n.a., manufacturer, Baltimore City, September 4, 1906.
AMMIDON, Sarah E., 88, Baltimore City, May 22, 1913.
AMOLSKY, 48, saloon keeper, December 27, 1895, in the Front Street Theater panic.
AMOS, Calvin, 43, Bel Air, Harford County, June 28, 1911.
AMOS, J. Jarrett, 79, merchant, Baltimore City, February 17, 1888.
AMOS, Thomas A., 79, Harford County, July 21, 1899.
AMOSS, Garrett, 80, Bel Air, Harford County, February 7, 1901.
AMOSS, James E., 63, Baltimore City, July 15, 1898.
ANCKER, Walter W., 60, Roland Park, Baltimore City, _____ __, 1913.
ANDERS, J_____ A_____, 71, Frederick, Frederick County, February 8, 1910.
ANDERS, John E., 53, contractor, Baltimore City, December 30, 1911.
ANDERSON, Benjamin T., 75, merchant, Baltimore City, January 15, 1903.
ANDERSON, C_____ Thomas, 70, inventor, Clarksburg, Montgomery County, January 26, 1898.
ANDERSON, Clifford C., 67, court clerk, Baltimore City, February 6, 1906.
ANDERSON, Ed_____ F., 78, Baltimore City, November 25, 1909.
ANDERSON, Captain Isaac J., 70, Baltimore City, October 24, 1892.
ANDERSON, J_____ D_____, 59, Deal Island, Somerset County, July 6, 1911.
ANDERSON, General James M., 87, Baltimore City, December 2, 1899.
ANDERSON, Mrs. Mary Taney, wife of Winfield S. Anderson and granddaughter of the late Chief Justice, Baltimore City, May 6, 1880.
ANDERSON, S_____ E_____, 58, hotelier, Baltimore City, February 15, 1893.
ANDERSON, T_____ D_____, 79, merchant, Baltimore City, March 22, 1893.
ANDERSON, T_____ W_____, 78, merchant, Cambridge, Dorchester County, December __, 1893.

-5-

ANDERSON, Thomas, 64, attorney, Rockville, Montgomery County, January 19, 1900.
ANDERSON, Captain W____ S____, 49, Fifth Regiment, Baltimore City, June 3, 1886.
ANDERSON, Dr. William A., 32, physician, Baltimore City, December 10, 1882.
ANDERSON, William C., 60, Cambridge, Dorchester County, August 25, 1910.
ANDRE, Dr. T____ Ridgeway, 84, Baltimore City, December 13, 1907.
ANDREWS, Hercules R. W., 73, retired, Baltimore City, September 11, 1884.
ANDREWS, John, n.a., clerk, Baltimore City, June 17, 1905.
ANDREWS, Joseph, 80, Cumberland, Allegany County, August 6, 1907.
ANDREWS, Olivera, 85, Baltimore City, August 17, 1914.
ANDREWS, R____ Snowden, 70, architect, Baltimore City, January 6, 1903.
ANDREWS, Thomas F., 89, physician, Baltimore City, January 31, 1886.
ANDRIES, Rev. Joseph L. (R.C.), 69, Baltimore City, July 20, 1903.
ANGERMANN, Henry, 76, manufacturer, Baltimore City, January 7, 1883.
ANKENEY, Charles, 54, Clear Spring, Washington County, October 25, 1913.
ANN, Sister, 93, Baltimore City, January 25, 1913.
ANNAN, Dr. A____, 92, Emmitsburg, Frederick County, July 7, 1896.
ANNAN, Isaac S., 74, Emmitsburg, Frederick County, November 10, 1909.
ANNAN, James R., 77, retired, Baltimore City, December 8, 1890.
ANTHONY, Henry A., 81, retired merchant, Baltimore City, August 22, 1905.
APPEL, George, 84, retired, Baltimore City, November 13, 1900.
APPLEBY, George R., 82, compositor, *The Sun*, Baltimore City, January 19, 1894.
APPLEBY, William H., 74, Baltimore City, July 13, 1909.
APPLEGARTH, Alexander, 88, retired, Baltimore City, October 10, 1899.
APPLEGARTH, Charles L., 63, Baltimore City, December 14, 1914.
APPLEGARTH, H____ C____, n.a., retired, Baltimore City, December 6, 1906.
APPLEGARTH, Captain John L., 58, mariner, Baltimore City, February 6, 1900.
APPLEGARTH, Nath____, 79, retired, Baltimore City, May 13, 1898.
APPLEGARTH, Nath____ J., n.a., retired, Baltimore City, December 11, 1898.
APPLEGARTH, Robert, 74, retired, Baltimore City, August 8, 1895.
APPLEMAN, Elizabeth, 101, Middletown, Frederick County, February 15, 1893.
APPOLD, George J., 77, merchant, Baltimore City, November 23, 1897.

APPOLD, George N., n.a., merchant, Baltimore City, June 18, 1892.
APPOLD, Samuel, 78, Lutherville, Baltimore County, June 13, 1893.
ARCHER, Dr. G_____ W_____, 83, Harford County, February 16, 1907.
ARCHER, H_____ W_____, 43, attorney, Bel Air, Harford County, January 19, 1898.
ARCHER, Henry W., 74, Bel Air, Harford County, July 8, 1887.
ARCHER, Sarah E., n.a., Baltimore City, July 1, 1913.
ARCHER, Stevenson, 82, Cecil County, May 11, 1901.
ARCHER, Stevenson, 70, former Treasurer of Maryland, Baltimore City, August 2, 1898.
ARENDT, Charles, 39, pharmacist, Baltimore City, March 8, 1901.
ARMBRUST, J_____ D_____ A_____, 91, Cumberland, Allegany County, May 14, 1910.
ARMCOST, D_____, 92, Westminster, Carroll County, July 4, 1904.
ARMIGER, James R., 60, jeweler, Baltimore City, February 23, 1896.
ARMIGER, John W., 80, retired, Baltimore City, June 13, 1901.
ARMIGER, Richard, 69, manufacturer, Baltimore City, December 10, 1893.
ARMISTEAD, S. Gordon, 53, Baltimore City, October 25, 1912.
ARMITAGE, Dr. James, 85, physician, Baltimore City, February 23, 1896.
ARMOR, George F., 77, Baltimore City, November 27, 1897.
ARMSTRONG, Alexander, 58, Hagerstown, Washington County, October 26, 1905.
ARMSTRONG, James, 66, manufacturer, Baltimore City, March 7, 1905.
ARMSTRONG, Rev. James E., D.D., 71, well-known clergyman and author, Baltimore City, April 7, 1908.
ARMSTRONG, John A., 65, retired, Baltimore City, March 27, 1884.
ARMSTRONG, Robert W., 73, merchant, Baltimore City, December 12, 1902.
ARMSTRONG, T_____ D_____, 86, Frostburg, Allegany County, July 21, 1893.
ARMSTRONG, Thomas, 71, manufacturer, Baltimore City, February 4, 1905.
ARNETT, Rev. Charles S., n.a., Baltimore City, February 4, 1913.
ARNOLD, Dr. A_____ B_____, 85, physician, Baltimore City, March 28, 1904.
ARNOLD, Francis, 77, manufacturer, Baltimore City, November 30, 1891.
ARNOLD, George W., 82, Baltimore City, May 16, 1911.
ARNOLD, Samuel, 82, merchant, Baltimore City, April 7, 1902.
ARNOLD, Dr. William T., 67, Baltimore City, April 1, 1912.
ARNOLD, Samuel B., 72, who was implicated in the alleged conspirancy against President Lincoln, on September 21, 1906.

ARRINGTON, Captain Daniel, 67, Baltimore City, April 25, 1910.
ARTHUR, John F., 65, educator, Baltimore City, May 24, 1906.
ARTHUR, Robert, 60, dentist, Baltimore City, June 22, 1880.
ARTHUR, William S., 35, physician, Baltimore City, March 29, 1880.
ASCHERFELD, Theodore, 86, musician, Havre de Grace, Harford County, December 28, 1905.
ASHMAN, William, 40, photographer, Baltimore City, February 15, 1902.
ASKEW, John, 70, engineer, Baltimore City, September 24, 1905.
ASH, Louis, n.a., realtor, Baltimore City, September 29, 1906.
ASHBAUGH, W_____ H_____, 75, Emmitsburg, Frederick County, April 27, 1912.
ASHBURNER, Charles H., 75, manufacturer, Baltimore City, May 22, 1901.
ASHBURY, Joseph M., 57, retired, Baltimore City, January 20, 1895.
ASHCOM, John L., 75, pilot, Baltimore City, March 14, 1901.
ASHCROFT, Robert, 71, retired, Baltimore City, July 10, 1883.
ASKEW, Jehu B., 56, retired, Baltimore City, November 15, 1886.
ATKINSON, Dr. A_____ S_____, 31, physician, Baltimore City, February 24, 1902.
ATKINSON, Dr. Archibald, 72, physician, Baltimore City, October 29, 1903.
ATKINSON, Dr. I_____ E____, n.a., physician, Baltimore City, November 24, 1906.
ATKINSON, James, 71, barber, Baltimore City, July 25, 1884.
ATKINSON, Dr. Robert, 79, educator, Baltimore City, May 22, 1911.
ATKINSON, Judge W_____ M_____, 63, Winchester, Anne Arundel County, April 3, 1911.
ATVATER, Dr. Edward W., 68, physician, May 15, 1905.
ATWELL, Mrs. Annie, 100, Baltimore City, June 8, 1886.
AUBRY, Arthur Louis Julain, 85, Baltimore City, May 17, 1892.
AUDOUN, Joseph H., 61, former judge, Baltimore City, August 23, 1884.
AUDOUN, Oliver, 77, builder, Baltimore City, October 14, 1892.
AUGHINBAUGH, D_____ C_____, 77, Hagerstown, Washington County, November 21, 1908.
AUGUR, Dr. Ralph H., 32, Baltimore City, November 26, 1914.
AULD, Benjamin F., 69, former police captain, Baltimore City, March 21, 1898.
AULT, Albert M., 41, Baltimore City, October 22, 1913.
AUSTEN, E_____, 64, farmer, Baltimore County, December 6, 1893.
AUSTEN, Dr. Philip H., 56, Baltimore City, October 28, 1878.
AUSTEN, Sidney F., 60, merchant, Baltimore City, January 25, 1901.
AUSTIN, John, 66, machinist, Baltimore City, December 16, 1905.
AUSTIN, Sister Mary, n.a., Mount Washington, Baltimore County, July 13, 1913.

AUSTIN, R____, 58, Hagerstown, Washington County, November 5, 1911.
AUSTIN, Theodore S., 58, retired, Baltimore City, June 4, 1898.
AUSTIN, Thomas, 85, Baltimore City, April 27, 1912.
AUSTIN, Rev. William (Presbyterian), 47, Baltimore City, September 11, 1896.
AUZMANN, Anthony A., 64, merchant, Baltimore City, December 19, 1904.
AVERY, Samuel, 82, Hagerstown, Washington County, October 22, 1911.
AVIRETT, Colonel John W., 50, Cumberland, Allegany County, May 29, 1914.
AVIRETT, Philip W., 36, Cumberland, Allegany County, July 31, 1902.
AX, Christian, 62, merchant, Baltimore City, March 20, 1887.
AYRES, Colonel C____ G____, 49, Baltimore City, September 25, 1909.
AYRES, Captain Samuel, 73, mariner, Baltimore City, August 1, 1883.
AYTON, J____ E____, 63, Rockville, Montgomery County, August 20, 1910.

BABCOCK, Rev. Maltbie D. (Presbyterian), 43, Baltimore City, May 18, 1901.
BABCOCK, Dr. P____, 93, Burkeville (Burkittsville, Frederick County?), February 14, 1912.
BABYLON, Jesse, 86, Carroll County, September 16, 1900.
BACHMAN, Rev. Dr. Marcus, 79, Baltimore City, March 10, 1914.
BACHMANN, H____ W____, 47, confectioner, Baltimore City, May 16, 1902.
BACHRACH, David, Sr., 83, retired, Baltimore City, February 17, 1895.
BACKUS, Rev. John C., 74, pastor emeritus of the First Presbyterian Church of Baltimore, in Baltimore City, April 9, 1884.
BACKUS, Mrs. Letitia C., 77, Baltimore City, April 4, 1892.
BACON, John, 82, Baltimore County, November 9, 1898.
BACON, Rev. Dr. Leonard W. (Congregationalist), 79, (Yale College), Baltimore City, December 24, 1881.
BACON, Rev. Thomas S. (P.E.), 80, Frederick, Frederick County, September 13, 1904.
BADEN, Dr. F____ A____, 36, dentist, n.p., November 18, 1902.
BADEN, Dr. Joseph Abell, 68, physician, Baltimore City, January 20, 1902.
BAER, Bankard, 81, retired, Baltimore City, January 29, 1897.
BAER, C____ W____, n.a., Baltimore City, July 16, 1910.
BAER, Dr. Edward R., 73, Baltimore City, August 7, 1900.
BAER, George H., 61, secretary of the Western Maryland Railroad, Baltimore City, January 3, 1896.
BAER, Rev. John, 83, Baltimore City, March 11, 1878.
BAER, Dr. Rort N. (M.E.), 48, Baltimore City, September 28, 1888.
BAER, Rosa Schley, 65, Frederick, Frederick County, January 9, 1913.

BAER, Thomas S., 64 (possibly a judge), Baltimore City, July 18, 1906.
BAER, William H., n.a., retired paymaster, U.S. Navy, January 10, 1906.
BAILEY, Dr. G____ W____, 90, physician, Baltimore City, February 29, 1892.
BAILEY, James, 75, pharmacist, Baltimore City, May 2, 1906.
BAILEY, Lewis E., 74, bookseller, Baltimore City, January 4, 1899.
BAILEY, Captain Thomas, 64, mariner, Baltimore City, April 14, 1897.
BAILEY, W____ A____, 75, retired, Baltimore City, January 3, 1888.
BAILEY, William, 86, retired, Baltimore City, September 2, 1895.
BAILEY, William S., 86, retired, Baltimore City, August 12, 1895.
BAIRD, Rev. Dr. James H. (Presbyterian), 76, Baltimore City, March 22, 1900.
BAJANOWSKI, Mrs. C____, 81, Baltimore City, July 30, 1909.
BAKER, C____ M____, 42, Cumberland, Allegany County, October 12, 1910.
BAKER, Charles G., 83, Aberdeen, Harford County, January 31, 1905.
BAKER, Charles J., 73, merchant, Baltimore City, September 24, 1894.
BAKER, Rev. Daniel, 80, Hagerstown, Washington County, February 27, 1911.
BAKER, George A., 83, educator, Baltimore City, March 9, 1901.
BAKER, George B., 60, died at Asbury Park, New Jersey, July 24, 1910.
BAKER, George C., 58, painter, Baltimore City, August 29, 1905.
BAKER, Rev. George G. (M.E.), 56, Baltimore City, January 16, 1894.
BAKER, George M., 74, retired banker, Baltimore City, November 2, 1905.
BAKER, Henry, 79, retired, Baltimore City, February 21, 1896.
BAKER, James M., 77, builder, Baltimore City, December 4, 1893.
BAKER, Rev. John H. (M.E.), 71, December 8, 1894.
BAKER, Jonathan W., 74, Rockville, Montgomery County, March 31, 1910.
BAKER, N____, 64, former school commissioner, Baltimore City, September 30, 1897.
BAKER, Richard J., 82, retired, Baltimore City, January 8, 1896.
BAKER, William, 87, merchant, Baltimore City, August 6, 1884.
BAKER, William B., 71, Aberdeen, Harford County, May 15, 1911.
BAKER, William W., 54, merchant, Baltimore City, March 19, 1898.
BALCH, Professor H____ H____, 45, Talbot County, February 19, 1902.

BALDERSTON, Dr. Isaiah, 78, dentist, Baltimore City, March 20, 1883.
BALDERSTON, J____, 71, manufacturer, Baltimore City, August 25, 1881.
BALDERSTON, O____ H____, 37, civil engineer, Baltimore City, April 27, 1893.
BALDWIN, C____ A____, n.a., physician, Smithsburg, Washington County, January 21, 1893.
BALDWIN, Captain Charles B., 48, Baltimore City, March 24, 1913.
BALDWIN, David, 87, Baltimore City, April 4, 1908.
BALDWIN, Edward, 82, Baltimore City, July 16, 1912.
BALDWIN, Dr. Edwin C., 87, physician, Baltimore City, March 29, 1901.
BALDWIN, Ernest, 47, Laurel, Prince George's County, September 20, 1897.
BALDWIN, Maurice, 82, Baltimore County, July 27, 1900.
BALDWIN, Oliver P., 65, editor, Baltimore City, July 17, 1878.
BALDWIN, Richard, 75, Waterbury, Anne Arundel County, February 20, 1903.
BALDWIN, Rignal W., 55, attorney, Baltimore City, January 4, 1891.
BALDWIN, Robert T., 67, bank president, Baltimore City, October 7, 1886.
BALDWIN, Silas E., n.a., n.p., October 21, 1914.
BALDWIN, Thomas, 60, auctioneer, Baltimore City, August 20, 1881.
BALDWIN, Thomas P., 61, merchant, Baltimore City, October 27, 1892.
BALDWIN, William H., Jr., 81, merchant, Baltimore City, October 20, 1902.
BALL, Charles H., 63, "U.S. Rev.," Baltimore City, September 10, 1901.
BALL, Rev. Dabney, 56, Baltimore City, February 15, 1878.
BALL, John H., 59, merchant, Baltimore City, November 27, 1902.
BALL, Philip A., 66, merchant, Baltimore City, April 21, 1895.
BALL, Thomas W., 67, manufacturer, Baltimore City, October 9, 1896.
BALL, Rev. Dr. Wayland D. (Congregationalist), 35, n.p., May 28, 1893.
BALLARD, Frederick, 63, carriage maker, Baltimore City, December 24, 1879.
BALLENTYNE, Thomas, 70, Baltimore City, October 29, 1898.
BALLOU, John W., 64, manufacturer, Baltimore City, February 1, 1904.
BALLY, Mrs. Frank, 88, Hagerstown, Washington County, March 23, 1910.
BALTZELL, Dr. William H., 67, physician, Frederick, Frederick County, September 19, 1899.
BAMBERGER, David, 70, retired, Baltimore City, March 28, 1895.
BAMBURGER, Elkaw, 87, Baltimore City, May 3, 1909.

BAMBURGER, Moses, 76, retired merchant, Baltimore City, December 17, 1903.
BAMBURGER, Mrs. T_____, 81, Baltimore City, October 3, 1909.
BANDEL, A_____ J_____, 73, insurance, Baltimore City, July 13, 1889.
BANDEL, Philip, 78, merchant, Baltimore City, September 16, 1896.
BANDELL, George W., 72, dyer, Baltimore City, December 3, 1882.
BANGERT, Philip, 70, retired, Baltimore City, August 18, 1887.
BANKARD, Dennis, 69, Baltimore City, March 29, 1907.
BANKARD, Henry N., 68, realtor, Baltimore City, July 13, 1903.
BANKS, Andrew, Sr., 71, Baltimore City, April 24, 1909.
BANKS, Horace, 35, insurance, Baltimore City, September 25, 1905.
BANKS, John, n.a., former Cecil County Treasurer, Elkton, April 19, 1906.
BANKS, Robert T., 79, former Mayor, Baltimore City, August 8, 1901.
BANKS, Robert T., Jr., 43, Baltimore City, February 16, 1890.
BANNAN, John, 62, Baltimore City, July 20, 1902.
BANNAN, John J., 46, cafe owner, Baltimore City, December 2, 1905.
BANNING, Alexander, 73, retired, Baltimore City, December 29, 1884.
BANNON, John C., n.a., Annapolis, Anne Arundel County, February 29, 1896.
BAPST, Rev. John (R.C.), 72, Baltimore City, November 2, 1887.
BARABASZ, Rev. Mieczyslaw, 51, Baltimore City, December 9, 1914.
BARBER, M_____ S_____, 77, Hagerstown, Washington County, January 31, 1893.
BARBER, Rev. Dr. Theodore P. (P.E.), 74, Cambridge, Dorchester County, January 1, 1893.
BARCLAY, Dr. Delancy H., 46, physician, Baltimore City, July 10, 1900.
BARCLAY, Rev. J_____ H_____ (Lutheran), 55, Baltimore City, October 13, 1887.
BARCLAY, Rev. T_____ P_____, 71, Baltimore City, September 19, 1910.
BARGER, Deeter, 86, builder, Baltimore City, January 28, 1879.
BARGER, Mrs. Margaret D., 85, Baltimore City, February 3, 1884.
BARKER, Alfred, 74, master mechanic, Baltimore City, December 14, 1882.
BARKER, Charles H., 29, merchant, Baltimore City, January 19, 1882.
BARKMAN, Jacob, 64, merchant, Baltimore City, December 16, 1883.

BARKSDALL, Dr. Randolph, 76, Petersburg (Virginia?), November 18, 1907.
BARNARD, Norris, 65, Kent County, March 13, 1892.
BARNES, Francis J., 70, Princess Anne, Somerset County, November 27, 1909.
BARNES, G____ W____, 69, Hagerstown, Washington County, January 1, 1908.
BARNES, George, 88, Lonaconing, Allegany County, October 28, 1911.
BARNES, Hanson P., 65, merchant, Baltimore City, January 18, 1898.
BARNES, Major J____ T____, 80, Baltimore City, January 28, 1913.
BARNES, John H., 75, inventor, Baltimore City, April 29, 1892.
BARNES, Dr. William M., 85, physician, Baltimore City, September 11, 1909.
BARNES, Dr. William S., 48, black physician, Baltimore City, October 19, 1882.
BARNEY, James H., 63, former Collector, Baltimore City, December 10, 1882.
BARNEY, William Chase, 77, Baltimore City, January 22, 1892.
BARNIE, William, 46, baseball manager, Baltimore City, July 15, 1900.
BARNITZ, Covington, 89, Baltimore City, May 13, 1911.
BARNUM, Allen S., 62, hotelier, Baltimore City, March 17, 1878.
BARNUM, Theron, 75, hotelier, Baltimore City, March 17, 1878.
BARNUM, Dr. Zenus, 27, physician, Baltimore City, March 23, 1882.
BARON, James, 80, retired, Baltimore City, May 20, 1905.
BARR, Rev. Hugh K. (R.C.), 60, Baltimore City, December 7, 1900.
BARRANGER, E____ B____, 65, butcher, Baltimore City, March 24, 1904.
BARRANGER, George W., n.a., butcher, Baltimore City, May 21, 1895.
BARRENGER, William, 63, merchant, Baltimore City, December 31, 1904.
BARRETT, George, 84, silversmith, (presumably Baltimore City), October 3, 1897.
BARRETT, George Bruce, 68, musician, Baltimore City, June 23, 1884.
BARRETT, Captain Gregory, 61, U.S. Navy, died of fever before Santiago de Cuba City, August 7, 1898.
BARRETT, Rev. John (P.E.), 63, retired, Baltimore City, December 23, 1900.
BARRETT, John I., 42, attorney, Baltimore City, June 7, 1895.
BARRETT, William D., 60, merchant, Baltimore City, January 2, 1887.
BARROLL, B____ C____, 88, Baltimore City, April 5, 1908.
BARRON, Dr. J____, 70, Baltimore City, August 3, 1912.
BARRON, J____ M____, 75, actor, Baltimore City, May 8, 1910.
BARRON, Thomas F., 73, animal surgeon, Baltimore City, February 15 1886.

BARRON, Thomas F., 58, veterinarian surgeon, Baltimore City, November 20, 1901.
BARRY, Rev. Joseph L. (R.C.), 64, Baltimore City, April 14, 1902.
BARRY, Robert C., 57, lawyer, Baltimore City, August 14, 1883.
BARRY, William R., 73, president, insurance company, Baltimore City, August 12, 1900.
BARTELL, Christopher, 60, retired, Baltimore City, April 15, 1885.
BARTLETT, David L., 82, manufacturer, Baltimore City, May 11, 1899.
BARTLETT, David L., 36, manufacturer, Baltimore City, February 22, 1904.
BARTLETT, Dr. Edward, 83, Oaklawn (?), October 2, 1913.
BARTLETT, Edward L., 59, manufacturer, Baltimore City, September 29, 1905.
BARTLETT, Mrs. Edward L., n.a., Baltimore City, October 27, 1914.
BARTLETT, J____ Kemp, 67, retired, Baltimore City, July 15, 1899.
BARTLETT, Judge John P., 68, Easton, Talbot County, November 3, 1907.
BARTLETT, Colonel Joseph R., n.a., Easton, Talbot County, September 28, 1906.
BARTLETT, Thomas, 73, retired, Baltimore City, May 25, 1901.
BARTLETT, Rev. William E. (R.C.), 56, Baltimore City, April 6, 1900.
BARTLETT, William E., Jr., 80, Baltimore City, March 11, 1895.
BARTOL, Mrs. Corrine M., n.a., wife of Judge ____ Bartol, Baltimore City, December 9, 1882.
BARTOL, H____ B____, 92, Baltimore City, December 27, 1909.
BARTOL, James L., 74, former judge, Baltimore City, June 23, 1887.
BARTOL, John D., 76, Baltimore City, March 13, 1912.
BARTON, Miss C____ M____, n.a., modiste, Baltimore City, July 30, 1902.
BARTON, Rev. George, 85, Church Hill, Queen Anne's County, March 18, 1893.
BARTON, Rev. Dr. J____ O____ (P.E.), 64, March 4, 1890.
BARTON, James I., 64, merchant tailor, Baltimore City, January 2, 1892.
BARWICK, Dr. George Irvin, 45, Baltimore City, October 27, 1914.
BASH, Henry M., 84, retired, Baltimore City, November 14, 1885.
BASIL, Joseph S____ M____, 64, merchant, Annapolis, Anne Arundel County, September 5, 1899.
BASSHOR, C____ Hazeltine, n.a., Cambridge, Dorchester County, August 22, 1914.
BASSHOR, Thomas C., 64, manufacturer, Baltimore City, February 13, 1900.
BATCHELOR, Dr. Kemp B. 32, Baltimore City, December 24, 1898.
BATCHELOR, William, 97, "Old Defender," Baltimore City, March 21, 1885.

BATEMAN, H____ E____, 85, Easton, Talbot County, November 30, 1892.
BATEMAN, Dr. James M., 63, Easton, Talbot County, August 2, 1907.
BATEMAN, John, 75, mariner, Baltimore City, December 5, 1882.
BATES, Dr. J____ W____ P____, 74, Baltimore City, July 9, 1910.
BATEMAN, John L., 80, Baltimore City, June 30, 1914.
BATES, Franklin L., n.a., retired, Baltimore City, March 30, 1906.
BATES, James, 79, foundry proprietor, Baltimore City, January 8, 1896.
BATES, John, 53, manufacturer, Baltimore City, February 14, 1901.
BATES, Rev. Laurence W. (M.P.), 81, Baltimore City, January 17, 1901.
BATONY, Ignatius, 88, retired, Baltimore City, May 11, 1906.
BATTEE, Richard R., 71, attorney, Baltimore City, January 28, 1894.
BAUER, John, 73, Bel Air, Harford County, October 12, 1907.
BAUERELS, G____ F____, 50, brewmaster, Baltimore City, August 2, 1902.
BAUERNSCHMIDT, George, 64, brewer, Baltimore City, April 12, 1899.
BAUERNSCHMIDT, John, 49, brewer, Baltimore City, June 28, 1879.
BAUERNSCHMIDT, John, 58, brewer, Baltimore City, March 3, 1897.
BAUGHER, John F., 69, educator, Baltimore City, August 10, 1901.
BAUGHMAN, Charles H., n.a., Frederick, Frederick County, September 18, 1913.
BAUGHMAN, Charles H., 52, statistician, Baltimore City, April 22, 1905.
BAUGHMAN, J____ William, 67, Frederick, Frederick County, July 28, 1914.
BAUGHMAN, Colonel L____ Victor, 63, farmer and journalist, Frederick, Frederick County, November 30, 1906.
BAUMANN, John T., 83, musician, Baltimore City, August 28, 1901.
BAUMBACH, Andrew, 78, Baltimore City, July 1, 1911.
BAUMGARTEN, Selig, 69, engraver, Baltimore City, March 19, 1883.
BAUSMAN, Charles 81, cattle dealer, Baltimore City, January 13, 1881.
BAWDEN, John H., 72, bank officer, Baltimore City, November 27, 1898.
BAXLEY, Dr. J____ Brown, 81, Baltimore City, March 30, 1896.
BAXLEY, J____ Brown, Jr., 35, physician, Baltimore City, July 12, 1891.
BAY, George E., 75, contractor, Baltimore City, August 19, 1903.
BAYER, George, 74, confectioner, Baltimore City, September 1, 1902.

BAYLEY, Dr. Alexander H., 78, Cambridge, Dorchester County, March 14, 1892.
BAYLEY, Charles, 73, merchant, Baltimore City, January 5, 1883.
BAYLEY, Henry, 87, missionary, Baltimore City, June 8, 1887.
BAYLEY, Robert F., 80, retired merchant, Baltimore City, December 4, 1905.
BAYLY, James F., 76, bookkeeper, Baltimore City, October 24, 1902.
BAYNARD, Mrs. Eliza, 90, Baltimore City, March 23, 1883.
BAYNE, Captain John A., n.a., n.p., January 30, 1914.
BAYNE, Lawrence P., 70, banker, Baltimore City, January 8, 1885.
BAYNES, W_____ W_____, 70, Baltimore City, February 27, 1911.
BAYZAND, William H., 80, magistrate, Baltimore City, June 1, 1887.
BEACH, Rev. Charles (Presbyterian), 62, Baltimore City, March 9, 1881.
BEACHAM, S_____ T_____, 73, shipbuilder, Baltimore City, May 5, 1893.
BEADENKOPF, George, 76, Mount Washington, Baltimore County, August 24, 1914.
BEAL, Emanuel, 64, Cumberland, Allegany County, December 17, 1914.
BEALL, Edward Sinclair, 40, cashier, Baltimore City, June 8, 1883.
BEALL, Henry D., 65, editor, Baltimore City, November 13, 1902.
BEALL, J_____ H_____, 82, Boyds, Montgomery County, October 12, 1911.
BEALL, O_____ W_____, 89, retired, Baltimore County, September 18, 1884.
BEALTY, Professor L_____ L_____, 56, teacher, Centreville, Queen Anne's County, November 17, 1906.
BEAM, Isaac R., 49, druggist, Baltimore City, October 23, 1878.
BEAN, Captain Robert M., 73, pilot, Baltimore City, December 4, 1881.
BEARD, George W., 77, Aberdeen, Harford County, October 6, 1909.
BEARD, Joseph, Sr., 69, retired, Baltimore City, April 22, 1884.
BEASTEN, Charles J., 47, lawyer, Baltimore City, January 11, 1889.
BEATSON, George H., 58, clerk, Baltimore City, December 22, 1901.
BEATTY, C_____ E_____, 62, judge of the Cecil County Orphan's Court, June 3, 1906.
BEATTY, James, 73, merchant, Baltimore City, June 24, 1896.
BEATTY, Dr. Joseph E., 75, Baltimore City, October 13, 1914.
BEAUCHAMP, Oliver, T., n.a., court clerk, Princess Anne, Somerset County, April 8, 1906.
BEAUMONT, Lewis, 77, builder, Baltimore City, March 15, 1910.
BEAVER, Rev. George F., 84, Hillsboro, Caroline County, January 10, 1909.

BEAVERS, Captain James S., 64, Baltimore City, January 19, 1895.
BECHHOFER, Alexander, 46, publisher, Baltimore City, May 7, 1897.
BECK, August, 58, brewer, Baltimore City, September 5, 1879.
BECK, August, 52, brewer, Baltimore City, January 23, 1902.
BECK, August T., 67, retired, Baltimore City, March 21, 1904.
BECK, Frederick W., 64, manufacturer, Baltimore City, May 23, 1895.
BECK, George, 53, furniture dealer, Baltimore City, July 1, 1881.
BECK, George W., 70, retired, Baltimore City, March 21, 1896.
BECK, John, 78, Baltimore City, July 8, 1911.
BECK, Louis, 60, manufacturer, Baltimore City, December 19, 1898.
BECK, Thomas, 86, brewer, Baltimore City, January 15, 1897.
BECK, William, 59, printer, Baltimore City, November 17, 1898.
BECKENBAUGH, Dr. T_____ L_____, 41, druggist, Baltimore City, February 15, 1881.
BECKER, August, Sr., 70, retired, Baltimore City, June 1, 1897.
BECKER, Frederick, 56, merchant, Baltimore City, August 16, 1899.
BECKER, George William, 66, merchant, Baltimore City, January 1, 1891.
BECKER, H_____, 68, manufacturer, Baltimore City, May 1, 1893.
BECKER, John A., 48, merchant, Baltimore City, January 1, 1898.
BECKER, Louis, 52, merchant, Baltimore City, March 17, 1899.
BECKLEY, Rev. George H. (Lutheran), 76, Baltimore City, June 1, 1905.
BECKLEY, Captain O_____ S_____ J_____, 52, Frederick, Frederick County, August 15, 1900.
BECKWITH, David G., 79, retired, Baltimore City, July 23, 1902.
BEECRAFT, Peter, 98, Baltimore City, November 16, 1883.
BEEHLER, F_____ T_____, 66, Baltimore City, August 2, 1910.
BEEHLER, Rev. Jacob M. (Lutheran), 64, Baltimore City, September 4, 1901.
BEER, Dr. G_____ B_____, 49, physician, Baltimore City, December 23, 1902.
BEER, Dr. Robert K., 62, The Sun, December 27, 1904.
BEERS, Captain William, 75, ship broker, January 10, 1899.
BEHMAN, Louis C., 47, theater manager, Baltimore City, February 27, 1902.
BEHREN, John, 35, merchant, Baltimore City, July 13, 1881.
BELL, Abraham, 100, retired, Baltimore City, August 14, 1904.
BELL, Alexander, 72, maltster, Baltimore City, November 17, 1880.
BELL, Alexander T., 77, Pikesville, Baltimore County, February 24, 1913.
BELL, Arthur E., 65, Baltimore County, November 8, 1905.
BELL, Edward G., 45, hotelier, Baltimore City, January 29, 1902.

BELL, Edwin, 87, Hagerstown, Washington County, December 9, 1907.
BELL, Dr. Samuel, 80, Baltimore City, July 23, 1913.
BELT, Eugene N., 73, merchant, Baltimore City, February 23, 1901.
BELT, J____ W____, 54, Prince George's County, December 11, 1896.
BELT, Stephen, 81, Prince George's County, March 10, 1902.
BENDANN, Daniel, n.a., Baltimore City, December 6, 1914.
BENEDICT, Brother A____, n.a., priest, (Baltimore City?), February 13, 1907.
BENESCH, I____, 68, merchant, Baltimore City, January 4, 1910.
BENESCH, Samuel, 40, Baltimore City, December 3, 1911.
BENHAM, Lieutenant Thomas W., 69, Baltimore City, April 12, 1914.
BENJAMIN, A____ J____, 63, railroad manager, Salisbury, Wicomico County, October 11, 1906.
BENJAMIN, Solomon, 79, broker, Baltimore City, May 24, 1894.
BENNETT, Alfred, 61, merchant, Baltimore City, October 23, 1881.
BENNETT, Benjamin F., 89, Baltimore City, April 24, 1913.
BENNETT, Captain Cleophas, n.a., Baltimore City, June 16, 1913.
BENNETT, David T., 60, builder, Baltimore City, October 2, 1889.
BENNETT, Edwin, 90, Baltimore City, June 13, 1908.
BENNETT, F____ W____, 61, auctioneer, Baltimore City, February 14, 1880.
BENNETT, George W., 78, pilot, Baltimore City, February 27, 1900.
BENNETT, Henry C., 72, Cockeysville, Baltimore County, January 12, 1912.
BENNETT, John E., 70, mariner, Baltimore City, May 20, 1900.
BENNETT, Mrs. Margaret, n.a., widow of F____ H____, Baltimore City, August 16, 1900.
BENNETT, Pinkney J., 49, Westminister, Carroll County, November 13, 1895.
BENNETT, Robert, 79, Baltimore City, April 16, 1892.
BENNETT, Rufus, 82, builder, Baltimore City, July 22, 1906.
BENNETT, Thomas C., 77, Cambridge, Dorchester County, May 7, 1894.
BENSON, Benjamin S., Sr., 80, inventor, Baltimore City, Sep- 8, 1896.
BENSON, Dr. C____ W____, 69, Baltimore City, February 10, 1907.
BENSON, Dr. George W., 62, physician, Baltimore City, August 22, 1893.
BENSON, John S., 75, retired, Baltimore City, February 4, 1897.
BENSON, John T., 87, Montgomery County, December 21, 1905.
BENTLEY, Charles W., 88, retired manufacturer, Baltimore City, July 23, 1902.
BENTLEY, Peter, 75, Baltimore City, July 16, 1898.
BENTON, Mrs. Luther B., n.a., Baltimore City, November 21, 1913.

BENZINGER, Frank de S_____, n.a., justice, Baltimore City, May 13, 1896.
BENZINGER, Frederick F., 63, attorney, Baltimore City, January 27, 1887.
BENZINGER, Dr. Joseph C., 70, Baltimore City, May 5, 1912.
BERG, Otto, 66, stock broker, Baltimore City, April 14, 1887.
BERGE, Henry, 55, manufacturer, Baltimore City, October 20, 1902.
BERGER, Rev. A_____ J_____ (P.E.), 65, Baltimore City, December 4, 1882.
BERGER, B_____, 47, brewer, Baltimore City, September 3, 1893.
BERGER, John M., 57, brewer, Baltimore City, June 21, 1883.
BERGER, Rev. John N. (R.C.), 45, Baltimore City, January 13, 1884.
BERGER, William M., 45, merchant, Baltimore City, July 31, 1902.
BERKELEY, Richard F., 66, physician, Baltimore City, May 25, 1886.
BERLINCKE, Christopher, 82, cigar manufacturer, Baltimore City, June 3, 1902.
BERNARD, Pierre, 45, musician, Baltimore City, August 15, 1883.
BERNARD, William A., 67, Frederick, Frederick County, April 10, 1914.
BERNEI, Philip, 49, merchant, Baltimore City, July 10, 1893.
BERNEI, Seligman, 62, merchant, Baltimore City, May 14, 1886.
BERNSTEIN, Gabriel, three years of age, Front Street Theater panic, December 27, 1895.
BERNSTEIN, Morris, 53, retired, Baltimore City, May 22, 1899.
BERNSTEIN, Samuel, 32, artist, Baltimore City, June 7, 1905.
BERNSTEIN, Teresa, six years of age, Front Street Theater panic, December 27, 1895.
BERRET, Julius B., 87, Carroll County, March 1, 1899.
BERRY, Dr. G_____ H_____, 84, Crisfield, Somerset County, September 6, 1909.
BERRY, George R., 78, manufacturer, Baltimore City, March 19, 1899.
BERRY, H_____ D_____, 41, Council page, Baltimore City, October 28, 1881.
BERRY, Jasper M., n.a., realtor, (presumably Baltimore City), October 16, 1906.
BERRY, Jesse L. C., 70, retired, Baltimore City, December 16, 1891.
BERRY, General John S., 78, merchant, Baltimore City, January 3, 1901.
BERRY, Walter W., 81, merchant, Baltimore City, October 27, 1884.
BERRYMAN, Charles E., 20, clerk, Baltimore City, October 4, 1902.
BERRYMAN, John B., 60, manufacturer, Baltimore City, January 21, 1899.
BERRYMAN, Mrs. Maria, 98, Baltimore City, September 2, 1909.
BERWANGER, Benjamin, n.a., clothier, Baltimore City, October 27, 1909.

BETTELHEIM, Rev. Dr. A_____ S_____ (Hebrew), 56, August 21, 1890.
BETZ, Christopher, 53, brewer, Baltimore City, October 31, 1882.
BETZ, Jacob, 70, Baltimore City, July 31, 1911.
BEVAN, Charles F., 65, merchant, Baltimore City, April 9, 1885.
BEVAN, Joseph, 79, jeweler, Baltimore City, November 22, 1894.
BEVAN, Thomas H., 51, attorney, Baltimore City, May 11, 1901.
BEVAN, William Francis, 76, retired, Baltimore City, March 27, 1897.
BEVAN, William J., 68, Baltimore City, August 11, 1892.
BEVANS, Joshua A., 55, Baltimore City, May 3, 1897.
BEVANS, R_____ A_____ L_____, 72, undertaker, Baltimore City, November 21, 1878.
BEVANS, Samuel, 76, merchant, Baltimore City, May 10, 1879.
BEVERIDGE, Robert, 72, Lonaconing, Allegany County, April 16, 1909.
BEYER, Frederick, 55, musician, Baltimore City, March 6, 1883.
BIANS, John, 97, retired, Baltimore City, November 19, 1901.
BIBB, Bentley C., 79, manufacturer, Baltimore City, June 23, 1894.
BIDDISON, Thomas C., 73, Gardenville, August 28, 1914.
BIDDLE, George, n.a., educator, Elkton, Cecil County, December 14, 1909.
BIDDLE, General James, 78, Berkeley Springs, Virginia, June 9, 1910.
BIDDLE, Jonathan S., 57, manufacturer, Baltimore City, June 18, 1882.
BIEDLER, William T., 51, merchant, Baltimore City, July 8, 1897.
BIEMILLER, E_____, 70, Baltimore City, November 5, 1893.
BIEMILLER, John B., 58, proprietor of an ice company, August 7, 1897.
BIERBOWER, Dr. C_____ E_____, 74, Baltimore City, November 10, 1914.
BIGELOW, W_____ O_____, 64, Civil War veteran, Baltimore City, September 16, 1902.
BIGGS, Joseph, 76, merchant, Baltimore City, January 23, 1892.
BILLINGSLEA, Dr. J_____ L_____, of Baltimore City but died in Carroll County, October 23, 1881.
BILLINGSLEA, James, 62, merchant, Baltimore City, January 30, 1903.
BILLINGSLEA, Dr. James, 47, physician, Baltimore City, March 2, 1904.
BILLINGSLEA, Dr. Martin B., 53, physician, December 8, 1902.
BILLINGSLEY, J_____ W_____, 42, merchant, Baltimore City, March 6, 1883.
BILLUPS, Captain John R., 50, mariner, Baltimore City, May 8, 1891.
BINGHAM, Rev. Dr. John S., 79, Baltimore City, April 3, 1914.
BINYON, T_____ W_____, 55, builder, Baltimore City, September 28, 1893.

BIRCH, Charles, 42, merchant, Baltimore City, August 4, 1879.
BIRD, Dr. Benjamin L., 60, Prince George's County, October 30, 1902.
BIRD, J____ Edward, 66, merchant, Baltimore City, September 30, 1882.
BIRD, Dr. S____ R____, 86, Baltimore City, August 17, 1914.
BIRD, W____ Bland, 24, physician, Baltimore City, April 4, 1898.
BIRD, W____ Edgeworth, 59, merchant, Baltimore City, January 19, 1910.
BIRELY, Lewis A., 71, retired, Baltimore City, December 28, 1890.
BIRELEY, William P., n.a., Funkstown, Washington County, February 28, 1914.
BIRKHEAD, James, Jr., 69, insurance, Baltimore City, January 17, 1895.
BIRCKHEAD, Lennox, 67, realtor, Baltimore City, January 27, 1905.
BISER, Daniel G., n.a., farmer, Frederick County, September 24, 1906.
BISER, Jonathan, 76, Frederick County, August 30, 1903.
BISHOP, Caleb, 83, retired, Baltimore City, February 19, 1885.
BISHOP, Dr. George W., 76, Snow Hill, Worcester County, March 6, 1903.
BISHOP, G____ W____, 71, Baltimore City, December 10, 1909.
BISHOP, George W., 41, clerk, Baltimore City, August 10, 1880.
BISHOP, Henry, 61, "Bird Man," Baltimore City, November 3, 1907.
BISHOP, John T., 82, builder, Baltimore City, December 6, 1896.
BISPHAM, Stacy B., 62, Baltimore City, April 29, 1909.
BISSING, W____ F____, 76, jeweler, Baltimore City, February 10, 1910.
BITTER, Justus, 50, singer, Baltimore City, January 14, 1894.
BITTING, Rev. Dr. C____ C____, of Baltimore City, in Philadelphia, December 24, 1898.
BITTING, L____ L____, 27, physician, Baltimore City, August 21, 1886.
BIXLER, Dr. S____ H____ C____, 69, Greencastler, March 28, 1914.
BIXLER, William H. H., 55, ship chandler, Baltimore City, March 5, 1897.
BLACK, Dr. Calvin, 82, physician, Baltimore City, May 16, 1883.
BLACK, Harry, 73, Elkton, Cecil County, July 5, 1912.
BLACK, James, 76, contractor, Baltimore City, February 2, 1904.
BLACK, Miss Margaret M., 93, Cumberland, Allegany County, January 24, 1901.
BLACK, Rev. Robert W. (M.E.), 71, Baltimore City. August 13, 1895.
BLACK, Samuel, 86, Glyndon, Baltimore County, August 30, 1910.
BLACK, William, 70, retired, Baltimore City, December 1, 1896.

BLACKFORD, Eugene, 68, Baltimore City, February 4, 1908.
BLACKFORD, William G., 34, Baltimore City, July 6, 1908.
BLACKFORD, W_____ H_____, 68, Baltimore City, October 7, 1910.
BLACKISTON, John B., 81, undertaker, Baltimore City, September 25, 1887.
BLACKISTONE, Dr. R_____ P_____, 91, River Springs, St. Mary's County, May 12, 1914.
BLACKISTONE, T_____ W_____, 62, Baltimore City, September 30, 1909.
BLACKISTONE, Walter R., 27, insurance agent, Baltimore City, October 13, 1902.
BLACKISTONE, William J., 78, lawyer, Baltimore City, January 29, 1882.
BLACKLOCK, John H., 48, accountant, Baltimore City, September 16, 1904.
BLACKSTON, Sarah, 98, Baltimore City, December 14, 1878.
BLACKWOOD, Rev. Dr. William (Presbyterian), 85, Baltimore City, November 13, 1893.
BLADDIS, B_____, 87, St. Michaels, Talbot County, August 9, 1911.
BLAIR, The Hon. Montgomery, 70, former U.S. Postmaster General, at Silver Spring, Montgomery County, July 27, 1883.
BLAKE, Charles D., 77, Baltimore City, April 1, 1912
BLAKE, Charles W., 59, accountant, Baltimore City, January 12, 1902.
BLAKE, Henry, 42, builder, Baltimore City, May 20, 1884.
BLAKE, John H., 62, Hagerstown, Washington County, November 26, 1902.
BLAKE, John R., 72, builder, Baltimore City, February 6, 1891.
BLAKE, Martin G., 86, builder, Baltimore City, April 12, 1883.
BLAKE, Solomon K., 72, Elkton, Cecil County, March 25, 1908.
BLAKISTON, George, 59, Baltimore City, July 7, 1914.
BLAKISTONE, Elizabeth, n.a., Riderwood, Baltimore County, September 25, 1913.
BLANCH, Jeremiah, 79, builder, Baltimore City, November 30, 1894.
BLAND, John B., 50, merchant, Baltimore City, November 16, 1895.
BLAND, Dr. William F., 77, Baltimore County, December 25, 1904.
BLANDIN, Lieutenant John J., U.S.S. Maine, died in Baltimore on July 16, 1898, five months and one day after the ship exploded in Havana harbor.
BLASS, Rev. Julius (Unitarian), 41, Baltimore City, April 5, 1902.
BLAYS, James P., 70, retired, Baltimore City, March 4, 1901.
BLISS, Major Horace, 77, U.S. Army, Baltimore City, November 6, 1878.
BLIZZARD, Elijah, n.a., "Sea Lion Man," November 1, 1908.
BLOCHER, W_____ L_____, 74, Cumberland, Allegany County, December 8, 1911.
BLOCK, Edward, 82, Baltimore City, December 26, 1911.

-22-

BLOCK, John, 61, druggist, Baltimore City, January 30, 1880.
BLOCK, Leopold, 83, retired merchant, Baltimore City, November 1, 1902.
BLOGG, Rev. Edward N.S. (M.E.), 61, Baltimore City, August 20, 1887.
BLOME, George, 69, confectioner, Baltimore City, February 12, 1902.
BLONDELL, William T., 74, retired, Baltimore City, February 12, 1896.
BLOODSWORTH, Jacob, 71, Baltimore Steam Packet Company, City, January 27, 1893.
BLOOM, Isaac, 73, merchant, Baltimore City, August 25, 1902.
BLOXHAM, John, 66, merchant, Baltimore City, September 3, 1891.
BLUM, Isaac, 79, retired, Baltimore City, March 23, 1899.
BLUM, Isaac, 81, merchant, Baltimore City, February 5, 1879.
BLUM, Samuel H., 73, retired, Baltimore City, June 21, 1902.
BLUMNER, Henry G., 35, realtor, October 3, 1911.
BLUNDON, Robert M., 58, merchant, Baltimore City, June 24, 1902.
BOARMAN, Dr. W_____ J_____, 66, Charles County, May 20, 1897.
BOARMAN, William W., 60, Maryland lawyer died at Washington, D.C., May 2, 1910.
BOBETH, Charles L, 80, piano manufacturer, Baltimore City, June 1, 1883.
BOBLITZ, Professor E_____ L_____, 63, educator, Frederick, Frederick County, November 30, 1906.
BODE, Selmer W., 39, druggist, Baltimore City, May 26, 1887.
BOEHM, Dr. A_____, 78, physician, Baltimore City, March 21, 1893.
BOGGS, F_____ Henry, 78, Baltimore City, January 13, 1912.
BOGGS, Samuel S., 68, merchant, Baltimore City, October 24, 1879.
BOGGS, William, 84, retired, Baltimore City, March 2, 1905.
BOGUE, Dr. Robert J., 66, retired, Baltimore City, June 3, 1899.
BOHANNON, W_____ J_____, 55, mariner, July 3, 1904.
BOHN, Rev. M_____ H_____, n.a., Ilchester, Howard County, July 15, 1914.
BOHRER, Dr. Benjamin F., 78, physician, Baltimore City, August 12, 1898.
BOKEL, J_____ G_____, 94, Baltimore City, May 19, 1908.
BOLAND, Rev. J_____ D_____, 52, Baltimore City, September 26, 1908.
BOLGIANO, John, 81, capitalist, Baltimore City, October 13, 1892.
BOLGIANO, Joseph, 77, Baltimore City, May 10, 1913.
BOLGIANO, W_____ H_____, 39, Baltimore City, May 14, 1913.
BOLGIANO, Dr. Walton, 40, Baltimore City, August 2, 1914.
BOLLMAN, Henry, n.a., merchant, Baltimore City, March 5, 1897.
BOLLMAN, Wendel, 70, bridge builder, Baltimore City, March 11, 1884.
BOLTE, Henry, 55, merchant, Baltimore City, October 10, 1897.

BOLTON, Daniel K., 66, merchant, Baltimore City, March 27, 1892.
BOLTON, Hugh W., 78, Baltimore City, April 22, 1909.
BOLTON, James T., 70, retired, Baltimore City, May 9, 1889.
BOLTON, William H., 62, merchant, Baltimore City, March 22, 1885.
BOMBAUGH, Dr. Charles C., 78, Baltimore City, May 24, 1906.
BONAPARTE, Jerome Napoleon, 62, died at Pride's Crossing, Massachusetts, September 3, 1893.
BONAPARTE, Mrs. Susan M., 69, Baltimore City, September 15, 1881.
BOND, B____ F____, 64, B. & O. Railroad, Baltimore City, April 19, 1909.
BOND, Hugh Lennox, 64, U.S. Judge, Baltimore City, October 24, 1893.
BOND, James A., 84, Calvert County, May 1, 1897.
BOND, James, 81, retired merchant, Baltimore City, January 4, 1902.
BOND, James H., 65, bookseller, Baltimore City, August 11, 1891.
BOND, Senator John J.B., 53, Calvert County, February 18, 1896.
BOND, John R., 74, Port Deposit, Cecil County, October 11, 1901.
BOND, John W., 80, bookseller, Baltimore City, September 14, 1880.
BOND, John W., 65, manufacturer, Baltimore City, April 11, 1899.
BOND, Margaret N., n.a., Jessup, Howard County, October 17, 1913.
BOND, Dr. S____ B____, n.a., physician, Baltimore City, December 21, 1911.
BOND, Thomas, 85, merchant, Baltimore City, January 26, 1885.
BOND, Thomas, 69, retired, Baltimore City, March 24, 1896.
BOND, Thomas C., Jr., 67, Port Deposit, Cecil County, July 14, 1900.
BOND, Thomas C., Jr., n.a., Port Deposit, Cecil County, December 21, 1913.
BOND, Thomas Davis, 71, Howard County, January 25, 1900.
BOND, William, 51, merchant, Baltimore City, February 3, 1879.
BONEBRAKE, Dr. Andrew S., n.a., Baltimore City, April 24, 1913.
BONIFANT, Washington, 90, former U.S. Marshal for Maryland, Montgomery County, April 8, 1899.
BONINGER, Edward, 54, merchant, Baltimore City, May 24, 1882.
BONN, H____ R____, 71, veteran, Pikesville, Baltimore County, February 6, 1909.
BONNER, Elijah, 67, mariner, Baltimore City, October 10, 1895.
BONNEY, Elias, 57, merchant, Baltimore City, January 8, 1881.
BONSAL, Stephen, 62, merchant, Baltimore City, February 13, 1893.
BOON, Joseph E., 55, Baltimore City, October 7, 1913.

BOONE, Daniel A., 70, merchant, Baltimore City, February 14, 1902.
BOONE, O____ A____, 60, Caroline County, May 30, 1893.
BOONE, Thomas Carroll, 24, of Annapolis, Anne Arundel County, died at Boston, March 19, 1899; he had been war balloon telegrapher at Santiago, Cuba.
BOONE, William M., 42, manufacturer, Baltimore City, January 23, 1879.
BOOTH, General Alfred E., 58, Baltimore City, May 10, 1914.
BOOTH, Junius Brutus, Jr., 62, actor, at Manchester, Massachusetts, September 17, 1883.
BOOTH, Washington, 77, merchant, Baltimore City, April 4, 1892.
BOOZ, Charles W., 66, shipbuilder, Baltimore City, December 13, 1900.
BOOZ, Daniel W., 66, contractor, Baltimore City, February 25, 1904.
BOOZ, Thomas, 57, shipbuilder, Baltimore City, July 28, 1878.
BOOZE, Joseph L., 62, lumber merchant, Baltimore City, October 18, 1891.
BOPP, John, Sr., 56, merchant, Baltimore City, December 25, 1899.
BORDLEY, Mrs. Blanche, 60, Baltimore City, August 13, 1911.
BORDLEY, Dr. James, 63, Centreville, Queen Anne's County, August 30, 1909.
BORDLEY, John, 77, Chestertown, Kent County, April 8, 1902.
BORDLEY, John B., 82, artist, Baltimore City, March 12, 1882.
BORDLEY, William C., 83, clerk, Baltimore City, April 16, 1883.
BORDLEY, William C., 63(?), tax department, Baltimore City, February 16, 1897.
BORNSCHEIN, T____ F____, 71, musician, Baltimore City, December 31, 1902.
BOSLEY, Charles, 72, Towson, Baltimore County, September 26, 1894.
BOSLEY, Mrs. Dorcas, 94, Philopolis, Baltimore County, June 18, 1909.
BOSLEY, Dr. Grafton M., 75, Baltimore County, January 25, 1901.
BOSLEY, John (of William), 64, former treasurer of Baltimore County, at Cockeysville there, December 22, 1885.
BOSLEY, John C., 77, Baltimore City, March 28, 1912.
BOSLEY, Dr. James, 60, Baltimore City, January 5, 1913.
BOSLEY, Rachel, 84, Cockeysville, Baltimore County, April 3, 1909.
BOSS, George, 92, "Old Defender," Baltimore City, December 4, 1886.
BOSSE, Anton, 65, merchant, Baltimore City, December 10, 1886.
BOSTON, J____ E____ H____, 61, merchant, Baltimore City, February 18, 1889.
BOSTON, Jacob, 84, librarian, Baltimore City, March 30, 1886.
BOSTON, Captain Robert H., 70, Baltimore City, June 25, 1913.
BOSTON, Mrs. Susan H., 82, Baltimore City, May 4, 1883.
BOSWELL, Edward, 80, Sandy Spring, Montgomery County, October 23, 1905.

BOTELER, Dr. E_____, 64, Washington County, October 21, 1892.
BOUCHELLE, John W., 92, Bohemia Manor, Cecil County, December 13, 1898.
BOUCHER, William, 77, retired, Baltimore City, March 8, 1899.
BOUIE (?), William Viers, 80, Rockville, Montgomery County, May 4, 1896.
BOULDEN, Dr. James E. P., 55, physician, Baltimore City, July 18, 1880.
BOULDIN, Augustus, 82, Baltimore City, February 4, 1912.
BOULDIN, Randolph J., 71, lawyer, Baltimore City, December 10, 1894.
BOULDIN, William, 73, railroad official, Baltimore City, April 29, 1893.
BOULT, Thomas H., 85, retired, Baltimore City, January 29, 1885.
BOWARD, Andrew, J., 76, Hagerstown, Washington County, April 2, 1905.
BOWDLE, William H., 64, Federalsburg, Caroline County, February 6, 1914.
BOWDOIN, George F., 76, grain merchant, Baltimore City, December 29, 1892.
BOWDOIN, W_____ Graham, 62, financier, Baltimore City, November 12, 1904.
BOWEN, Amos E., 59, railway conductor, Baltimore City, December 11, 1885.
BOWEN, Andrew J., 56, reporter, Baltimore City, October 6, 1885.
BOWEN, George W., 69, compositor, Baltimore City, January 25, 1886.
BOWEN, H_____ L_____, 79, Towson, Baltimore County, January 23, 1910.
BOWEN, J_____ L_____, 75, Sherwood, probably Baltimore County, February 14, 1910.
BOWEN, Dr. Robert, 87, Berlin, Worcester County, December 12, 1914.
BOWEN, William H., 74, merchant, Baltimore City, February 26, 1902.
BOWEN, W_____ H_____, 68, police sergeant, Baltimore City, August 28, 1902.
BOWERS, C_____ B_____, 61, Baltimore City, July 13, 1910.
BOWERS, Henry, 56, Hagerstown, Washington County, June 4, 1914.
BOWERS, Samuel H., 61, Hagerstown, Washington County, June 10, 1914.
BOWERS, William, 91, retired manufacturer, Baltimore City, August 23, 1902.
BOWES, John, 69, importer, Baltimore City, June 23, 1889.
BOWIE, Allen T., 53, Gaithersburg, Montgomery County, February 4, 1914.
BOWIE, David H., 69, Rockville, Montgomery County, March 31, 1900.
BOWIE, Edmund C., 62, Baltimore City, February 25, 1907.
BOWIE, F_____ M_____, 43, murdered on March 27, 1893, in Prince George's County.

BOWIE, Colonel H____ Brune, 62, twice-wounded Confederate veteran, Baltimore City, April 6, 1908.
BOWIE, Dr. Howard S., 56, physician, Baltimore City, February 26, 1900.
BOWIE, Oden, 68, ex-Governor of Maryland, December 4, 1894.
BOWIE, Oden, Jr., 47, Prince George's County, August 20, 1904.
BOWIE, Richard W. W., 74, Prince George's County, February 23, 1897.
BOWIE, Robert, 75, Annapolis, Anne Arundel County, August 5, 1901.
BOWIE, Mrs. Robert, 74, Annapolis, Anne Arundel County, November 5, 1913.
BOWIE, T____ J____, n.a., Anne Arundel County, September 3, 1898.
BOWIE, T____ T____ S____, 67, in Washington, D.C., February 12, 1910.
BOWIE, W____ D____, 55, retired, Baltimore City, February 2, 1888.
BOWIE, W____ W____, W____, 79, retired, Baltimore City, May 1, 1891.
BOWIE, William V., 60, attorney, Rockville, Montgomery County, October 12, 1906.
BOWLING, Alexander, 65, Confederate veteran, May 1, 1904.
BOWLING, Benjamin F., 74, Charles County, May 27, 1904.
BOWLING, Thomas, 80, pilot, Baltimore City, February 17, 1890.
BOWLING, William, 49, member of the Baltimore City police force, November 17, 1910.
BOWLUS, Dr. Edward, 69, Frederick, Frederick County, January 14, 1902.
BOWLUS, Noah, 74, of Frederick, Maryland, at Toledo, Ohio, August 9, 1904.
BOWMAN, David, 67, Hagerstown, Washington County, May 6, 1914.
BOWMAN, Richard H., 75, Rockville, Montgomery County, March 5, 1914.
BOYCE, A____ Page, 33, Baltimore City, December 27, 1912.
BOYCE, William, 77, Laurel, Delaware, March 23, 1910.
BOYD, Andrew G., 60, journalist, at Hagerstown, Washington County, October 2, 1885.
BOYD, David, 68, veteran, Baltimore City, January 8, 1909.
BOYD, John C., 72, insurance agent, Baltimore City, December 15, 1902.
BOYD, John E., 70, merchant, Baltimore City, January 17, 1899.
BOYD, John S., 48, electrician, Baltimore City, August 24, 1902.
BOYD, Joseph C., 49, attorney, Baltimore City, July 20, 1900.
BOYD, L____ McK____, 50, poet, Baltimore City, May 27, 1910.
BOYD, W____ A____, 74, Baltimore City, August 13, 1910.
BOYER, Professor W____ J____, 57, Millington, Kent County, April 8, 1910.

BOYD, William, 46, merchant, Baltimore City, April 29, 1898.
BOYD, William H., 66, merchant, Baltimore City, March 1, 1901.
BOYD, William H., 65, veteran fireman, Baltimore City, November 26, 1902.
BOYER, Captain J____ H____, 69, veteran, Baltimore City, June 4, 1910.
BOYER, Wilson S., 32, packer, Baltimore City, October 30, 1901.
BOYLE, Dr. Daniel S., 67, Westminster, Carroll County, February 4, 1901.
BOYLE, J____ B____, 84, Westminster, Carroll County, April 15, 1896.
BOYLE, James, 64, merchant, Baltimore City, June 9, 1885.
BOYLE, James W., 71, Baltimore City, August 24, 1907.
BOYLE, Dr. Samuel, 65, physician, Baltimore City, January 4, 1897.
BOYLE, Rev. W____ K____ (Methodist), 53, Hyattsville, Prince George's County, February 20, 1895.
BOYLE, William K., 67, printer, Baltimore City, October 15, 1883.
BOYLES, John, 65, Easton, Talbot County, June 9, 1914.
BOYNE, M____ W____, 66, civil engineer, Baltimore City, April 30, 1897.
BOYNTON, Austin C., n.a., Port Deposit, Cecil County, May 23, 1914.
BOYNTON, George E., 50, manufacturer, Baltimore City, June 17, 1899.
BRACKENRIDGE, W____ D____, 82, Govanstown, florist, February 3, 1894.
BRADFORD, Augustus Williamson, 76, Civil War Governor of Msryland (1862-66), March 1, 1881.
BRADFORD, Thomas K., n.a., attorney, July 14, 1906.
BRADLEY, Edward B., 69, merchant, Baltimore City, March 10, 1883.
BRADY, Edward, 70, contractor, Baltimore City, April 23, 1900.
BRADY, Rev. Francis Xavier, 51, president of Loyola College, Baltimore City, March 13, 1911.
BRADY, Henry H., 75, banker, Elkton, Cecil County, February 9, 1906.
BRADY, Henry I., n.a., attorney, Baltimore City, October 24, 1902.
BRADY, Hugh, 77, retired, Baltimore City, July 26, 1884.
BRADY, John K., 61, bookseller, Baltimore City, November 29, 1883.
BRADY, John W. S., 67, merchant, Baltimore City, March 11, 1899.
BRADY, P____, 75, Baltimore City, March 20, 1910.
BRADYHOUSE, Richard, 83, retired, Baltimore City, April 30, 1898.
BRAG, Simon, 76, retired, Baltimore City, October 23, 1896.
BRAGER, Charles G., 30, merchant, Baltimore City, October 8, 1897.
BRAINARD, B____, 81, manufacturer, Gardensville, January 2, 1893.

BRALEY, Elmer, 43, Cambridge, Dorchester County, May 26, 1904.
BRANCKER, J____ S____, 54, British vice-consul, Baltimore City, September 9, 1891.
BRAND, Rev. Dr. William R., 92, educator, Harford County, February 18, 1907.
BRANDT, Jacob, 70, retired, Baltimore City, January 13, 1882.
BRANDAU, Rev. G____ H____ (Lutheran), 83, Baltimore City, December 26, 1893.
BRANDT, John Duncan, 70, retired, Baltimore City, February 8, 1885.
BRANNAN, Charles H., 35, compositor, Baltimore City, June 24, 1890.
BRANDT, Samuel Reese, 83, founder of Oakland (Baltimore County?), died in Chicago, October 30, 1905.
BRANTLY, Rev. William T., Jr. (Baptist), 66, Baltimore City, March 6, 1882.
BRASHEAR, John A., 81, retired, Baltimore City, December 4, 1885.
BRASHEARS, J____ T____, 74, former Baltimore City police captain, May 6, 1886.
BRASHEARS, Robert T., 61, dentist, Baltimore City, November 28, 1882.
BRATTAN, Robert, 48, Congressman, Princess Anne, Somerset County, May 10, 1894.
BRATTEN, J____ H____, 58, marine engineer, Baltimore City, September 21, 1902.
BRATTON, Daniel, 40, (educator? editor?), Elkton, Cecil County, April 14, 1895.
BRAUNS, Rev. F____ William (Presbyterian), 64, Baltimore City, January 5, 1895.
BREHM, George, 72, brewer, Baltimore City, February 25, 1904.
BRENAN, Peter Edward, 84, merchant, Baltimore City, January 5, 1892.
BRENNAN, Rev. M____ J____ (R.C.), 35, Baltimore City, July 26, 1885.
BRENNEN, Rev. Michael J., 48, Cumberland, Allegany County, July 1, 1898.
BRENNAN, Rev. Edward (R.C.), 57, Baltimore City, December 6, 1884.
BRENNER, Moses, 63, retired merchant, Baltimore City, January 29, 1906.
BRENT, General Joseph Lancaster, 79, Confederate veteran, Baltimore City, November 27, 1905.
BRENTON, Daniel L., 48, attorney, Baltimore City, May 28, 1906.
BRESEE, Alfred A., 39, insurance, Baltimore City, June 24, 1891.
BRESEE, Louis O., 25, coal operator, Baltimore City, May 12, 1902.
BRESEE, Oscar F., 75, insurance agent, Baltimore City, December 16, 1901.

BREWER, Dr. George G., 59, physician, Baltimore City, April 8, 1895.
BREWER, J____ R____, 70, Baltimore City, November 6, 1911.
BREWER, Dr. Marbury, 72, physician. Baltimore City, January 24, 1903.
BREWER, Mrs. Maria T., 65, Annapolis, Anne Arundel Coutny, February 5, 1913.
BREWER, Nicholas, 91, "Old Defender," January 9, 1880.
BREWER, Nicholas, 68, Annapolis, Anne Arundel County, December 9, 1896.
BREWER, Richard H., 82, Annapolis, Anne Arundel County, November 15, 1905.
BREWER, Samuel R., 51, Annapolis, Anne Arundel County, June 25, 1901.
BREWER, William, n.a., senior editor of the Rockville (Montgomery County) Advocate, April 16, 1885.
BREWER, William R., 62, Baltimore City, November 15, 1907.
BREWINGTON, William L., 55, Salisbury, Wicomico County, December 18, 1903.
BRICE, John, 70, Chestertown, Kent County, October 20, 1900.
BRICE, Tilghman, 68, Anne Arundel County, June 13, 1903.
BRICKMAN, Rev. A____ O____ (Swedenborgian), 60, Baltimore City, January 5, 1886.
BRIDE, Cotter, 77, manufacturer, Baltimore City, October 9, 1887.
BRIDGES, John C., 75, merchant, Baltimore City, June 22, 1892.
BRIDGES, R____, 73, Hagerstown, Washington County, January 9, 1908.
BRIDGES, William, 87, merchant, Baltimore City, February 23, 1893.
BRIEL, George M., 53, contractor, Baltimore City, September 26, 1900.
BRIEL, John, 71, builder, Baltimore City, May 17, 1893.
BRIGGS, Rev. W____ H____ (M.E.), 88, December 22, 1902.
BRINKLEY, J____ B____, 71, oyster packer, Baltimore City, August 22, 1885.
BRISCOE, Alexander M., 57, justice, Baltimore City, November 9, 1901.
BRISCOE, George E., 66, manufacturer, Baltimore City, March 31, 1901.
BRISCOE, James T., 75, former Secretary of State of Maryland, of Calvert County in Baltimore City, April 22, 1903.
BRITTINGHAM, William J., 77, Princess Anne, Somerset County, April 18, 1900.
BROADBENT, Joseph F., 58, Baltimore City, October 16, 1897.
BROADBENT, Stephen, 70, retired, Baltimore City, February 22, 1882.
BROADERS, Henry, 73, stationer, Baltimore City, February 21, 1898.
BROCCHUS, P____ E____, 70, U.S. Judge, died in Utah, August 4, 1880.
BROCKENBROUGH, John B., 65, Baltimore City, November 15, 1901.
BRODERICK, John T., 48, merchant, Baltimore City, June 23, 1882.

BRODERICK, William E., 70, Baltimore City merchant, May 29, 1904.
BRODHEAD, Henry H., 57, restaurateur, Baltimore City, April 12, 1883.
BROLL, J____ H____, 80, Cumberland, Allegany County, December 26, 1909.
BROME, Dr. John M., in his 70th year, at St. Mary's City, July 28, 1887.
BROME, W____ H____, 68, pilot, Baltimore City, July 5, 1880.
BROMWELL, Hosea J., 62, butterman, Baltimore City, July 28, 1878.
BROMWELL, Dr. R____ E____, 83, Cecil County, March 21, 1906.
BROMWELL, Dr. William H., 52, physician, Port Deposit, Cecil County, September 30, 1898.
BROMWELL, William W., 68, retired, Baltimore City, November 8, 1899.
BROOKE, George E., 92, Sandy Spring, Montgomery County, October 6, 1905.
BROOKE, Horace L., 67, retired, Baltimore City, October 7, 1899.
BROOKE, John B., 78, former judge, Upper Marlboro, Prince George's County, December 22, 1905.
BROOKE, Dr. Roger, 62, Sandy Spring, Montgomery County, May 9, 1909.
BROOKS, Allen W., 75, retired, Baltimore City, March 12, 1902.
BROOKS, Dr. C____ C____, 56, scientist, Baltimore City, February 17, 1887.
BROOKS, Chauncey, 87, merchant, Baltimore City, May 18, 1880.
BROOKS, Chauncey, n.a., Baltimore City, March 11, 1908.
BROOKS, Edward W., 67, Baltimore City, February 3, 1912.
BROOKS, G____ R____, 44, merchant, Baltimore City, July 30, 1892.
BROOKS, Grafton S., 55, Baltimore County, February 5, 1901.
BROOKS, Dr. Horace A., 66, journalist, died at Alandale, Virginia, October 12, 1907.
BROOKS, Isaac, Jr., 70, Baltimore City, May 20, 1911.
BROOKS, J____ W____, 72, master mariner, Baltimore City, March 1, 1893.
BROOKS, John, 80, retired, Baltimore City, November 1, 1902.
BROOKS, John C., 71, retired merchant, Baltimore City, June 24, 1902.
BROOKS, Nathan C., 89, educator, Baltimore City, October 4, 1898.
BROOKS, Peter, Jr., n.a., Green Spring Valley, Baltimore County, April 5, 1913.
BROOKS, S____ W____, 50, Annapolis, Anne Arundel County, May 22, 1910.
BROOKS, Samuel M., 76, manufacturer, Baltimore City, April 8, 1895.

BROOKS, Walter B., n.a., president of the Canton Company, Baltimore City, January 17, 1896.
BROOKS, William, 62, customs inspector, Baltimore City, January 22, 1878.
BROOKS, Rev. Dr. William H. (P.E.), 69, February 19, 1900.
BROOKS, Dr. William Keith, 60, author and educator, Baltimore City, November 12, 1908.
BROSS, E____, 78, pioneer lithographer, Baltimore City, December 14, 1908.
BROTHERS, T____, 71, Westminster, Carroll County, April 4, 1908.
BROUMEL, James, 70, former Baltimore City Councilman, April 16, 1890.
BROWN, Alexander D., 68, Baltimore City, March 19, 1892.
BROWN, Andrew, 71, contractor, Baltimore City, July 5, 1898.
BROWN, Rev. B____ Peyton (Methodist), 66, August 26, 1896.
BROWN, Benjamin F., 78, manufacturer, Baltimore City, June 24, 1901.
BROWN, Charles, 82, shipmaster, Baltimore City, August 8, 1895.
BROWN, Charles H., 75, steamboat captain, Baltimore City, July 9, 1900.
BROWN, Charles H____ H____, 82, merchant, Baltimore City, December 14, 1881.
BROWN, Rev. Ebenezer (M.E.), 94, Baltimore City, January 3, 1889.
BROWN, Edward M., 52, merchant, Baltimore City, August 12, 1904.
BROWN, Judge Edwin H., n.a., Centreville, Queen Anne's County, March 25, 1906.
BROWN, Dr. Felix E., 52, dentist, Baltimore City, April 16, 1896.
BROWN, Mrs. Frank, 38, Baltimore City, May 11, 1895.
BROWN, Frederick J., 54, attorney, Baltimore City, June 9, 1900.
BROWN, George, 56, "Brooklandwood," Green Spring Valley, Baltimore County, May 17, 1902.
BROWN, George Alexander, 52, Baltimore City, March 2, 1905.
BROWN, George Allison, 47, of Baltimore City died in Norfolk, Virginia, July 22, 1900.
BROWN, George E., 50, clerk, Baltimore City, September 18, 1905.
BROWN, George S., 56, banker, Baltimore City, May 19, 1890.
BROWN, George William, 77, former judge, Baltimore City, September 5, 1890.
BROWN, Henry C., 63, manufacturer, Baltimore City, October 31, 1895.
BROWN, Mrs. Isabella, 86, Baltimore City, July 20, 1885.
BROWN, J____, 100, Ellicott City, Howard County, November 1, 1893.
BROWN, J____ B____, n.a., Confederate veteran, Baltimore City, April 20, 1907.
BROWN, J____ F____, 75, Baltimore City, January 15, 1911.
BROWN, Rev. J____ H____ (M.E.), 78, Baltimore City, March 15, 1886.

BROWN, J____ Harman, 71, Register of Wills, Baltimore City, November 23, 1879.
BROWN, J____ Robert, 73 (78?), builder, Baltimore City, August 16, 1899.
BROWN, Jacob, 88, publicist, Cumberland, Allegany County, October 12, 1912.
BROWN, Dr. James, 40, physician, Baltimore City, June 16, 1895.
BROWN, James H., 53, Annapolis, Anne Arundel County, September 14, 1894.
BROWN, John, 82, merchant, Baltimore City, December 14, 1904.
BROWN, John B., 62, lawyer, Centreville, Queen Anne's County, Mary 16, 1898.
BROWN, John N., 74, Baltimore City, January 31, 1881.
BROWN, John Pentland, 41, attorney, Baltimore City, January 22, 1899.
BROWN, John S., 67, librarian, Baltimore City, March 21, 1878.
BROWN, Matthew J., 70, merchant, Baltimore City, October 13, 1895.
BROWN, R____ D____, 86, Elkridge, Howard County, February 8, 1908.
BROWN, Robert, 84, watchmaker, Baltimore City, February 12, 1882.
BROWN, Captain Robert P., 54, Fifth Regiment, Baltimore City, April 26, 1895.
BROWN, Robert Riddell, 47, attorney, Baltimore City, July 8, 1898.
BROWN, Sebastian, n.a., Ellicott City, Howard County, August 31, 1909.
BROWN, Septimus, 56, physician, Baltimore City, January 31, 1883.
BROWN, Stewart H., 73, Baltimore City, March 19, 1905.
BROWN, Thomas, 78, Raspeburg, Baltimore County, August 4, 1909.
BROWN, Thomas, 74, jeweler, Baltimore City, May 3, 1886.
BROWN, Dr. Thomas R., 34, physician, Baltimore City, January 26, 1879.
BROWN, William, 89, retired jeweler, Baltimore City, September 16, 1903.
BROWN, William H., 65, merchant, Baltimore City, November 21, 1889.
BROWN, William N., Sr., 82, comptroller, August 8, 1892.
BROWN, William T., 71, builder, Baltimore City, April 4, 1892.
BROWNE, P____ A____, 38, audior, Circuit Court, Baltimore City, April 7, 1878.
BROWNE, William Hand, 82, scholar, Baltimore City, December 13, 1912.
BROWNING, Thomas, Sr., 90, Oakland (Baltimore County?), September 27, 1905.
BROWNING, Warfield T., n.a., attorney, Baltimore City, June 18, 1894.
BROWNING, William W., 56, ticket agent, Baltimore City, September 5, 1887.

BROWNOLD, Moses, 73, merchant, Baltimore City, February 26, 1905.
BROYLES, Perry, 92, of Maryland but died at Luray, Virginia, March 20, 1910.
BRUCE, David, 66, Baltimore City, October 8, 1900.
BRUCE, Edward B, 51, merchant, Baltimore City, December 14, 1900.
BRUCE, James A., 72, retired, Baltimore City, May 28, 1883.
BRUCE, W_____ C_____, Jr., n.a., Baltimore City, June 27, 1910.
BRUCE, William, 71, grocer, Baltimore City, January 28, 1884.
BRUCE, Dr. William W., n.a., Baltimore City, November 12, 1914.
BRUCHEY, D_____, 51, former police lieutenant, Baltimore City, November 6, 1892.
BRUMBAUGH, Judge N_____, 69, Hagerstown, Washington County, December 6, 1909.
BRUNDICE, W_____ H_____, 73, veteran, Baltimore City, February 7, 1910.
BRUNE, Frederick W., 63, attorney, Baltimore City, July 18, 1878.
BRUNE, Frederick W., 45, attorney, Baltimore City, February 27, 1899.
BRUNE, William H., 67, real estate, Baltimore City, October 22, 1887.
BRUNNER, Abel, 81, bookbinder, Baltimore City, June 11, 1903.
BRUNNER, John L., 69, tailor, Baltimore City, January 18, 1882.
BRUNNER, Lewis, 87, former mayor of Frederick City, January 26, 1898.
BRUNS, John, 85, Baltimore City, March 4, 1908.
BRUSSTAR, Henry, 88, shipbuilder, Baltimore City, February 13, 1885.
BRYAN, J_____ M_____, 80, miller, Baltimore City, February 13, 1893.
BRYAN, Rev. James L. (P.E.), 82, Cambridge, Dorchester County, November 6, 1904.
BRYAN, Samuel M., 55, former president of the telephone company, Baltimore City, January 23, 1903.
BRYAN, W_____ Shepard, 79, former judge, Baltimore City, December 9, 1906.
BRYAN, William S., Jr., n.a., former Attorney General of Maryland, April 3, 1914.
BRYANT, Colonel George Washington, 50, Baltimore City, August 7, 1901.
BRYANT, Colonel J_____ W_____, n.a., Caroline County, February 19, 1909.
BRYDON, William A., 69, Cumberland, Allegany County, March 27, 1907.
BUCHANAN, Charles A., 82, retired, Baltimore City, April 24, 1891.
BUCHANAN, J_____ H_____, 78, Baltimore City, May 22, 1911.
BUCHANAN, James A., 56, attorney, Baltimore City, January 24, 1895.

BUCHANAN, John M., 83, former judge, died at his residence near Cumberland, Allegany County, August 25, 1883.
BUCHANAN, John Rowan, 38, Baltimore City, November 18, 1880.
BUCHANAN, W____ M____, 43, B. & O. Railroad auditor, Baltimore City, October 20, 1891.
BUCHANAN, Wilson C., 60, manufacturer, Baltimore City, September 12, 1903.
BUCHER, A____ H____, 80, builder, Baltimore City, September 9, 1893.
BUCHHEIMER, Frederick, 55, vessel owner, Baltimore City, November 25, 1891.
BUCHHEIMER, John, 75, Baltimore City, December 25, 1892.
BUCHLER, Henry L., 88, retired, Baltimore City, June 14, 1897.
BUCK, G____ W____, 72, hotelier, Baltimore City, July 24, 1893.
BUCK, J____ M____, 75, retired, Baltimore City, June 25, 1889.
BUCK, John, 84, retired merchant, Baltimore City, July 7, 1893.
BUCK, John C., 66, contractor, Baltimore City, August 25, 1894.
BUCK, John H., 70, Baltimore City, May 9, 1910.
BUCK, Richard B., 45, merchant, Baltimore City, February 14, 1888.
BUCKEY, G____ P____, 80, Westminster, Carroll County, December 6, 1911.
BUCKINGHAM, J____ W____, 69, Baltimore City, November 4, 1893.
BUCKINGHAM, Perry G., 80, retired, Baltimore City, March 20, 1902.
BUCKLER, John H., n.a., St. Mary's County, January 22, 1904.
BUCKLER, Dr. Riggin, 52, physician, Baltimore City, August 31, 1884.
BUCKLER, Dr. Thomas H., 89, physician, Baltimore City, April 20, 1901.
BUCKLEY, David Z., 65, "ry. sup.," Baltimore City, November 26, 1904.
BUCKMILLER, Robert S., 78, retired, Baltimore City, February 4, 1884.
BUCKNER, Dr. Charles S., 78, physician, Baltimore City, March 2, 1899.
BUCKSBAUM, Julius, 90, retired, Baltimore City, February 26, 1899.
BULL, Dr. John F., 74, physician, Harford County, April 5, 1898.
BULL, Joshua L., 76, Foreston, April 21, 1909.
BULL, William C., 30, retired merchant, Baltimore City, February 3, 1879.
BULLOCK, John S., _5, merchant, Baltimore City, September 11, 1899.
BULLOCK, Rev. Dr. Joseph J., 79, Baltimore City, November 9, 1892.
BULLOCK, Joseph L., 58, merchant, Baltimore City, January 27, 1896.
BUMP, Charles Weather, 35, journalist and author, Baltimore City, March 30, 1908.

BUMP, Orlando F., 43, lawyer, Baltimore City, January 29, 1884.
BUNTING, William J., 85, retired, Baltimore City, December 8, 1882.
BURBAGE, John E., Sr., 64, founder of the Order of the Knights Golden Eagle, Baltimore City, January 21, 1903.
BURCH, Dr. J_____ C_____, 64, physician, Baltimore City, September 21, 1902.
BURCH, J_____ T_____, 63, Hyattsville, Prince George's County, November 20, 1908.
BURCHINAL, William D., 68, Chestertown, Kent County, May 18, 1899.
BURGER, S_____, 99, Hagerstown, Washington County, March 4, 1908.
BURGESS, Amos, 84, retired, Baltimore City, January 11, 1886.
BURGESS, J_____ A_____, 65, Confederate veteran, Baltimore City, January 8, 1910.
BURGESS, Neil, 63, actor, died in New York City, February 19, 1910.
BURGESS, Stephen F., 86, builder, Baltimore City, April 17, 1894.
BURGUNDER, Benjamin, 75, retired, Baltimore City, November 22, 1886.
BURGUNDER, Joseph, Jr., 60, Baltimore City, June 22, 1912.
BURK, Milton, 81, Frederick City, November 29, 1911.
BURKART, Rev. N_____, 76, Baltimore City, November 9, 1912.
BURKE, Rev. A_____ H_____, 72, Frederick City, March 28, 1914.
BURKE, Dr. A_____ J_____, n.a., physician, Whitehall, Baltimore County, January 17, 1893.
BURKE, Edward A., 42, school commissioner, Baltimore City, December 31, 1893.
BURKE, Nicholas, 69, property agent, Baltimore City, January 10, 1881.
BURKHART, Rev. J_____ (Lutheran), n.a., Baltimore City, November 20, 1902.
BURNESTON, Isaac B., 81, retired, Baltimore City, October 7, 1884.
BURNETT, E_____, 53, teacher, Baltimore City, October 20, 1893.
BURNETT, Joseph P., 72, retired, Baltimore City, December 6, 1899.
BURNS, Francis, Sr., 88, merchant, Baltimore City, December 28, 1879.
BURNS, Francis, Jr., n.a., manufacturer, Baltimore City, October 20, 1899.
BURNS, Francis, n.a., retired merchant and capitalist, November 2, 1906.
BURNS, Findley H., n.a., Baltimore City, January 21, 1912.
BURNS, Captain Hugh, 54, Cumberland, Allegany County, April 16, 1908.
BURNS, Colonel J_____ M_____, n.a., Cumberland, Allegany County, November 2, 1910.
BURNS, John, 45, shipbroker, Baltimore City, March 7, 1895.

BURNS, John T., 81, retired, Baltimore City, February 23, 1899.
BURNS, W____ Findley, 35, insurance, Baltimore City, April 14, 1905.
BURRUSS, Captain Nathaniel, 62, mariner, Baltimore City, October 6, 1905.
BURT, Alfred P., 88, Baltimore City, March 29, 1910.
BURT, Thomas, 78, bookkeeper, Baltimore City, September 3, 1883.
BURTON, C____ C____, 63, auctioneer, Baltimore City, September 3, 1883.
BURTON, Dr. J____ Wolff, 39, member-elect to the Maryland Legislature, Baltimore City, December 27, 1881.
BURTON, John, 76, Towson, Baltimore County, April 26, 1912.
BURTON, Dr. Orlando, 83, Sykesville, Carroll County, May 2, 1909.
BURTON, Thomas C., 91, Baltimore City, June 13, 1909.
BUSCH, George L., 69, manufacturer, Baltimore City, March 3, 1901.
BUSCHMAN, J____ D____ Ernest, 71, brewer, Baltimore City, January 27, 1901.
BUSEY, Ezra F., 63, clergyman, May 13, 1880.
BUSHELL, Edward, 75, professor, Baltimore City, December 5, 1888.
BUSICK, James H., 68, police lieutenant, Baltimore City, January 29, 1896.
BUSTEED, William W., 54, editor, Centreville, Queen Anne's County, February 14, 1898.
BUTCHER, Alexander, 80, retired, Baltimore City, October 3, 1884.
BUTLER, Charles, 88, retired merchant, Baltimore City, January 10, 1897.
BUTLER, Dr. Francis, 75, Westminster, Carroll County, May 31, 1883.
BUTLER, Dr. Frederick, 84, physician, Baltimore City, February 7, 1888.
BUTLER, John J., 47, lawyer, Baltimore City, October 9, 1884.
BUTLER, Colonel T____ H____, 70, Baltimore City, December 8, 1912.
BUTLER, Rev. William C., 81, Baltimore City, June 17, 1913.
BUTLER, William H., 21, clerk, Baltimore City, December 4, 1882.
BUTTLER, Thomas C., 69, lawyer, Baltimore City, July 8, 1897.
BUTTS, William M., 42, printer, Baltimore City, September 3, 1890.
BUXTON, Colonel John H., n.a., Baltimore City, November 19, 1914.
BUZBY, David T., 60, merchant, Baltimore City, May 27, 1899.
BYLES, M____ L____, 69, Hagerstown, Washington County, May 18, 1907.
BYRD, Colmore E., 73, merchant, Baltimore City, September 5, 1890.
BYRD, Dr. Harvey L., 64, physician, Baltimore City, November 29, 1884.

BYRD, John W. C., 74, merchant, Baltimore City, March 1, 1901.
BYRD, Lynn C., 42, pharmacist, Baltimore City, July 24, 1901.
BYRNE, William M., 48, superintendent of elections, Baltimore City, March 28, 1905.
BYRD, W____ S____, 65, merchant, Baltimore City, August 14, 1888.
BYRN, William M, 48, company secretary, Baltimore City, January 30, 1899.
BYRNES, Michael, 50, merchant, Baltimore City, December 6, 1882.

CADDEN, Dr. Charles W., n.a., Baltimore City, February 26, 1879.
CADDEN, Rev. James R., 78, Baltimore City, July 13, 1906.
CADWALLADER, J____ W____, 56, Cumberland, Allegany County, May 17, 1910.
CAHILL, John, 63 (68?), Baltimore City, December 23, 1896.
CAHILL, Patrick, 79, retired, Baltimore City, March 8, 1895.
CAHN, Bernard, 71, financier, Baltimore City, January 24, 1906.
CAHN, Edward, 25, merchant, Baltimore City, January 21, 1902.
CAIN, James M., n.a., judge of the Orphan's Court, Harford County, September 22, 1903.
CALDER, James, 73, Havre de Grace, Harford County, January 28, 1912.
CALDWELL, Henry A., 62, merchant, Baltimore City, September 24, 1904.
CALDWELL, James A., 75, retired, Baltimore City, September 23, 1883.
CALLAHAN, Mrs. Elizabeth, 93, Baltimore City, November 24, 1883.
CALLAHAN, Rev. P____ A____ (R.C.), 36, November 10, 1884.
CALLAWAY, Thomas C., 57, merchant, Baltimore City, December 22, 1900.
CALLEN, Michael, 77, banker, Baltimore City, January 11, 1899.
CALLIS, George R., 78, retired builder, Baltimore City, December 13, 1902.
CALLIS, James H., 83, retired merchant, Baltimore City, December 22, 1900.
CALLOW, William, 71, merchant, Baltimore City, April 15, 1882.
CALTRIDER, D____, 92, Westminster, Carroll County, January 19, 1908.
CALVERT, Cecilius Baltimore, 95, Prince George's County, March 13, 1901.
CALVERT, Charles, 63, merchant, College Park, Prince George's County, August 31, 1906.
CALVERT, John T., 56, mariner, Baltimore City, February 15, 1895.
CAMACHO, Louis, 56, retired, Baltimore City, November 14, 1890.
CAMALIER, John A., 70, Baltimore City, April 15, 1892.
CAMERON, Charles, 70, retired, Baltimore City, October 15, 1895.

CAMERON, John W., 73, attorney, Baltimore City, March 13, 1901.
CAMP, Joseph, 71, retired builder, Baltimore City, May 20, 1898.
CAMPBELL, Charles, 69, florist, Baltimore City, October 29, 1894.
CAMPBELL, Charles A., 55, machinist, Baltimore City, April 21, 1896.
CAMPBELL, G_____ S_____, 53, Baltimore City, December 18, 1912.
CAMPBELL, J_____ A_____, 78, former U.S. Justice, Baltimore City, March 12, 1889.
CAMPBELL, Rev. Richard C., 58, Oakland (Baltimore County?), August 19, 1914.
CAMPBELL, General Thomas W., 59, retired, Baltimore City, October 6, 1885.
CAMPER, J_____ Alexander, n.a., labor leader, Baltimore City, August 6, 1891.
CANBY, Samuel, 71, merchant, Baltimore City, August 21, 1878.
CANBY, Thomas Y., 80, banker, Baltimore City, March 5, 1886.
CANBY, William, 66, retired, Baltimore City, July 24, 1889.
CANFIELD, Ira C., Sr., 71, jeweler, Baltimore City, December 6, 1879.
CANFIELD, Ira C., Jr., 47, jeweler, Baltimore City, January 12, 1896.
CANFIELD, William B., Sr., 72, merchant, Baltimore City, January 10, 1883.
CANFIELD, Dr. William B., 42, physician of Baltimore City died in New York City, December 26, 1899.
CANN, Rev. Thomas M., 87, Frederick, Frederick County, December 27, 1906.
CANNON, Bertine A., 68, type foundryman, September 29, 1891.
CANNON, Richard H., 68, mariner, Baltimore City, October 29, 1895.
CANTER, Leonard H., 58, at his residence near Charlotte Hall, St. Mary's County, delegate from that county to the Legislature of 1882, September 23, 1883.
CAPRON, Francis B., 88, manufacturer, Baltimore City, October 1, 1904.
CARDER, John W., 72, Cumberland, Allegany County, July 24, 1909.
CARDWELL, Captain S_____ C_____, 34, Fort Howard, November 30, 1914.
CAREY, George G., 57, teacher, Baltimore City, May 26, 1894.
CAREY, James, 73, retired merchant, Baltimore City, October 18, 1894.
CAREY, Mrs. James, n.a., The Mount, June 16, 1913.
CAREY, Thomas I., 74, retired, Baltimore City, July 23, 1902.
CAREY, Thomas K., 55, retired, Baltimore City, May 29, 1906.
CARLIN, Frank, 66, court clerk, Baltimore City, February 8, 1906.
CARLING, Michael, 85, builder, Baltimore City, June 25, 1895.
CARMAN, Robert R., 48, sheriff of Harford County, at Bel Air, January 12, 1887.

CARMICHAEL, The Hon. Richard B., in his 77th year, Queen Anne's County, October 21, 1884.
CARMICHAEL, Thomas H., 65, former police marshal, Baltimore City, May 5, 1894.
CARMINE, Captain C_____ S_____, 77, Denton, Caroline County, February 11, 1908.
CARNES, Andrew J., n.a., accountant, Baltimore City, December 30, 1889.
CARNES, John, 67, merchant, Baltimore City, April 30, 1883.
CARPENTER, J_____ C_____, 72, litterateur, Baltimore City, September 24, 1911.
CARPENTER, J_____ Walter, 57, merchant, Baltimore City, January 2, 1898.
CARPENTER, L_____ B_____, 40, clergyman, Baltimore City, November 20, 1879.
CARPENTER, Professor William, 66, Baltimore City, September 1, 1896.
CARPENTER, William H., 85 (?), author and editor, Baltimore City, December 17, 1899.
CARR, Judge Arthur, 74, Hyattsville, Prince George's County, September 1, 1910.
CARR, J_____ G_____, Jr., n.a., court examiner, Baltimore City, April 3, 1910.
CARR, James E., 74, former police commissioner, Baltimore City, November 8, 1902.
CARR, Dr. Mortimer A. R. F., 47 (but probably should be 67), physician, Cumberland, Allegany County, March 24, 1898.
CARR, General R_____ K_____, 80, retired merchant, Baltimore City, February 4, 1902.
CARR, Samuel, 84, Annapolis, Anne Arundel County, April 13, 1909.
CARR, Wilson C. N., 59, attorney, Baltimore City, April 17, 1886.
CARRICK, Andrew F., 52, justice, Baltimore City, July 11, 1895.
CARRIGAN, James, 89, retired manufacturer, Baltimore City, July 12, 1894.
CARROLL, Albert H., 39, manufacturer, Baltimore City, September 15, 1882.
CARROLL, Dr. Dharles A., 60, physician, Baltimore City, July 14, 1905.
CALDWELL, Alonzo, 73, druggist, Baltimore City, September 15, 1902.
CARROLL, Charles, 65, of Baltimore City, at Aiken, North Carolina, February 20, 1895.
CARROLL, Charles P., 60, Baltimore City, January 12, 1907.
CARROLL, Charles Tucker, 55, retired, Baltimore City, January 27, 1883.
CARROLL, Dr. D_____ H_____, 72, Baltimore City, November 16, 1912.
CARROLL, David, 71, manufacturer, Baltimore City, July 30, 1881.
CARROLL, F_____ Howard, 29, merchant, Baltimore City, December 15, 1900.
CARROLL, George E., 33, attorney, Baltimore City, February 27, 1895.

CARROLL, Henry D. G., 63, retired, Baltimore City, July 12, 1882.
CARROLL, J____ Howell, 36, of Baltimore City, consul at Cadiz, Spain, February 7, 1903.
CARROLL, J____ K____, 87, former judge of the Orphan's Court, Baltimore City, May 9, 1888.
CARROLL, J____ W____, 68, Rockville, Montgomery County, January 6, 1910.
CARROLL, Jacob, 90, farmer, Baltimore City, January 12, 1881.
CARROLL, James, 74, merchant, Baltimore City, August 26, 1892.
CARROLL, James, 71, retired, Baltimore City, April 20, 1887.
CARROLL, James, 58, lawyer, Baltimore City, June 15, 1895.
CARROLL, John, n.a., retired hotelier, Baltimore City, February 5, 1897.
CARROLL, John B., 83, retired, Baltimore City, August 31, 1884.
CARROLL, John Lee, 80, former Governor of Maryland, at Washington, D.C., February 27, 1911.
CARROLL, Josiah, 76, Baltimore City, January 25, 1910.
CARROLL, Mrs. Mary C., 52, wife of the former Governor, in Washington, D.C., March 7, 1899.
CARROLL, Mrs. Susannah, 90, Baltimore City, December 11, 1882.
CARROLL, Captain T____, 76, Havre de Grace, Harford County, June 1, 1910.
CARROLL, Thomas, 70, merchant, Baltimore City, March 2, 1879.
CARROLL, William J., 53, merchant, Baltimore City, August 15, 1892.
CARRUTHERS, John S., 87, retired, Baltimore City, July 27, 1895.
CARRUTHERS, Richard, 67, Baltimore City, April 25, 1912.
CARSON, David, 57, builder, Baltimore City, May 27, 1878.
CARSON, John, 55, lawyer, Baltimore City, April 5, 1883.
CARSON, Rev. Thomas E. (M.E., South), 70, Baltimore City, October 13, 1902.
CARSON, W____ K____, 75, merchant, Baltimore City, June 3, 1893.
CARSON, William, 66, merchant, Baltimore City, February 28, 1887.
CARSON, William C., n.a., Port Deposit, Cecil County, May 18, 1913.
CARTER, A____ M____, 77, bank cashier, Baltimore City, May 28, 1893.
CARTER, A____ R____, 65, secretary, Baltimore City Health Department, August 25, 1893.
CARTER, Bernard, 78, Baltimore City, June 13, 1912.
CARTER, Desmus J., 79, retired, Baltimore City, August 16, 1896.
CARTER, Drurus, 82, retired, Baltimore City, August 4, 1897.
CARTER, Edward F., 81, retired, Baltimore City, January 28, 1897.
CARTER, Israel Day, 66, Cecil County, October 8, 1892.
CARTER, Rev. Dr. John Pym, 80, Baltimore City, January 6, 1892.

CARTER, John W., 55, merchant, Baltimore City, November 12, 1897.
CARTER, Captain T_____ F_____, 69, Baltimore City, April 4, 1912.
CARTER, Colonel T_____ H_____, 70, Baltimore City, July 9, 1912.
CARTER, William W., 71, retired, Baltimore City, November 29, 1883.
CARTERET, Rev. J_____ E_____, n.a., Hancock, Washington County, July 3, 1912.
CARUTHERS, Dr. J_____ A_____, n.a., physician, Baltimore City, September 16, 1897.
CARVER, William V., 64, builder, Baltimore City, March 16, 1881.
CARY, Wilson M., 75, died at Warrenton, Virginia, August 28, 1914.
CASEY, E_____, 72, Rockville, Montgomery County, December 5, 1911.
CASHMYER, Henry, 56, justice, Baltimore City, November 19, 1891.
CASPARI, William, 69, druggist, Baltimore City, August 14, 1886.
CASSARD, Frank W., n.a., retired merchant, Baltimore City, April 17, 1899.
CASSARD, George, 81, retired, Baltimore City, August 26, 1895.
CASSARD, John, 78, Baltimore city, May 21, 1911.
CASSARD, Lewis, 69, packer, Baltimore City, April 29, 1881.
CASSARD, Louis A., 65, retired, Baltimore City, April 17, 1899.
CASSARD, Louis R., 53, merchant, Baltimore City, April 22, 1894.
CASSARD, Thomas, 69, merchant, Baltimore City, December 13, 1892.
CASSELL, George R., 75, builder, Baltimore City, February 14, 1895.
CASSELL, Henry P., 77, mason, Baltimore City, May 28, 1900.
CASSELL, William H., 74, park superintendent, Baltimore City, February 14, 1904.
CASSIDY, Charles B., 34, captain, Fourth Regiment, Baltimore City, March 20, 1904.
CASSIDY, George, 51, retired, Baltimore City, April 2, 1899.
CASSIDY, Captain John, 84, former mariner, Baltimore City, February 22, 1884.
CASSIDAY, Luke, 42, merchant, Baltimore City, May 5, 1888.
CASTELBERG, Jacob, 84, Baltimore City, December 16, 1913.
CASTELBERG, Simon, 26, jeweler, Baltimore City, April 18, 1901.
CASTINE, Emmanuel, 67, theater manager, Baltimore City, January 9, 1903.
CASTLE, James L., n.a., Confederate veteran, Pikesville, Baltimore County, October 4, 1907.
CASTLE, Rev. Martin A., 74, Frederick, Frederick County, November 8, 1914.

CASWELL, Rear Admiral Thomas T., 73, Annapolis, Anne Arundel County, July 10, 1913.
CATE, Ammon, 77, retired, Baltimore City, April 5, 1886.
CATHCART, Robert. 72, electrical supervisor, Baltimore City, October 4, 1890.
CATHELL, George W., 68, chief judge of the Orphan's Court, Wicomico County, February 25, 1903.
CATHERINE, Sister, n.a., Cumberland, Allegany County, June 15, 1913.
CATOR, Mrs. Elizabeth B., 72, Baltimore City, November 21, 1898.
CATOR, James H., 52, merchant, Baltimore City, July 27, 1903.
CATOR, Robinson W., 75, merchant, Baltimore City, February 14, 1902.
CAUGHY, Noah W., 66, merchant, Baltimore City, September 2, 1891.
CAUGHY, S____ Hamilton, 74, merchant, Baltimore City, November 29, 1893.
CAULFIELD, Valentine, 39, organist, Baltimore City, April 16, 1887.
CAULK, James T., 70, former justice, Baltimore City, March 23, 1904.
CAUSEY, Uriah F., 79, Baltimore City, May 24, 1898.
CAVANAUGH, Maurice, 50, Baltimore City, August 19, 1914.
CAYE, Emil, n.a., barber, Baltimore City, September 26, 1910.
CAZENOVE, A____ Charles, 48, Baltimore City, May 4, 1897.
CESSNA, J____ B____ B____, 74, Centreville, Queen Anne's County, February 26, 1912.
CHABOT, Dr. G____ H____, 42, physician, Baltimore City, March 23, 1904.
CHAISTY, Dr. Edward J., 69, physician, Baltimore City, August 16, 1882.
CHALK, B____ R____, 71, Mount Washington, Baltimore County, April 7, 1910.
CHALK, Levi, 77, retired, Baltimore City, January 29, 1884.
CHAMBERLAINE, H____, 65, bank cashier, Baltimore City, December 12, 1881.
CHAMBERLAINE, Dr. Joseph E. M., 74, Easton, Talbot County, January 30, 1901.
CHAMBERLAINE, Joseph E. M., Jr., 51, Easton, Talbot County, August 27, 1900.
CHAMBERS, Robert M., 56, builder, Baltimore City, May 24, 1898.
CHANCELAUME, R____ P____, 64, hotel clerk, Baltimore City, May 27, 1886.
CHANCELLOR, Lorman, 77, lawyer, Baltimore City, February 9, 1894.
CHANDLEE, Henry P., 73, merchant, Baltimore City, September 26, 1901.
CHANDLEE, John S., 49, merchant, Baltimore City, January 12, 1905.
CHANDLER, Rev. Charles N., 61, Baltimore City, February 19, 1878.
CHANEY, Mareen D., 79, Anne Arundel County, October 2, 1905.

CHARLTON, Henry C., 43, mariner, Baltimore City, November 16, 1901.
CHANZ, Rev. Richard, 85, Baltimore City, April 25, 1909.
CHAPMAN, A_____ G_____, 53, Charles County, September 25, 1892.
CHAPMAN, Allan A., 76, retired, Baltimore City, March 4, 1890.
CHAPMAN, David Chase, 47, Baltimore City, May 11, 1892.
CHAPMAN, Dr. David T_____, 51, physician, Baltimore City, December 6, 1894.
CHAPMAN, James A., 66, La Plata, Charles County, August 23, 1909.
CHAPMAN, John Lee, 69, former mayor of Baltimore City, November 18, 1880.
CHAPMAN, Marshall, 67, Charles County, October 14, 1901.
CHARLES, Professor Thomas J., 52, musician, Baltimore City, December 1, 1889.
CHARLTON, Richard, 68, retired, Baltimore City, January 1, 1898.
CHASE, Algernon S., 69, merchant, Baltimore City, June 13, 1878.
CHASE, H_____ H_____, 72, bank president, Baltimore City, April 19, 1882.
CHASE, Richard M., 74, Annapolis, Anne Arundel County, July 4, 1901.
CHASE, William M., 82, retired, Baltimore City, November 21, 1901.
CHATARD, Mrs. Elizabeth A., 75, Baltimore City, January 11, 1883.
CHATARD, Dr. Ferdinand Edme, 83, physician, Baltimore City, October 18, 1888.
CHATARD, Dr. Ferdinand E., 60, physician, Baltimore City, August 27, 1900.
CHENOWETH, Arthur, 80, Pikesville, Baltimore County, July 3, 1914.
CHERBONNIER, Dr. Pierre Ovide, 66, in Talbot County but formerly of Baltimore City, June 12, 1883.
CHERRY, Edward, 70, cigar manufacturer, Baltimore City, March 9, 1890.
CHERRY, James W., 62, compositor, Baltimore City, October 17, 1890.
CHESTER, James, 40, surveyor, Baltimore City, June 11, 1895.
CHESTER, Rev. John A., 52, priest and educator, Baltimore City, December 20, 1906.
CHESTON, Dr. C_____ Morris, 49, Treasurer of Anne Arundel County, at Annapolis, December 1, 1898.
CHESTON, Galloway, 75, merchant, Baltimore City, March 9, 1881.
CHEW, James W., 74, clerk, Baltimore City, January 9, 1907.
CHEW, Richard B., 79, former judge, Ellerslie, Allegany County, May 31, 1907.
CHICHESTER, Rev. William J. (Presbyterian), 62, Baltimore City, March 23, 1903.

CHILD, Dr. George F., 87, physician, Baltimore City, February 28, 1897.
CHILD, Samuel, 63, merchant, Baltimore City, March 9, 1892.
CHILDS, Samuel, 64, Baltimore City, April 16, 1897.
CHILDS, Zachariah, Sr., 72, retired, Baltimore City, April 8, 1883.
CHILTON, Matthew, 94, Denton, Caroline County, March 20, 1912.
CHIPCHASE, Rev. James (P.E.), 75, Baltimore City, January 25, 1894.
CHIPLEY, General Charles A., 67, Talbot County, January 7, 1904.
CHIPMAN, George, 63, manufacturer, Baltimore City, June 3, 1882.
CHISM, Edward J., 58, Baltimore City, December 10, 1913.
CHISOLM, Dr. Julian J., 73, physician, Baltimore City, November 1, 1903.
CHOWANICE, Rev. Peter (R.C.), n.a., Baltimore City, May 2, 1892.
CHRIST, Rev. Ludwig (R.C.), 66, Baltimore City, February 21, 1902.
CHRISTHILF, George S., 69, Catonsville, Baltimore County, May 21, 1914.
CHRISTIAN, Rev. Edmund (P.E.), 80, Baltimore City, February 16, 1891.
CHRISTIAN, Dr. John H., 55 (?), physician, died at Richmond, Virginia, March 13, 1902.
CHRISTOPHER, Michael, 88, "Old Defender," Baltimore City, May 31, 1889.
CHRITZMAN, Dr. H_____ G_____, 71, Hagerstown, Washington County, August 13, 1909.
CHURCH, Thomas, 69, mechanic, Baltimore City, October 26, 1881.
CISSELL, G_____ O_____, n.a., Rockville, Montgomery County, September 23, 1910.
CISSEL, R_____ H_____, 61, Rockville, Montgomery County, December 6, 1911.
CLABAUGH, E_____ A_____, 64, merchant, Baltimore City, November 29, 1881.
CLABAUGH, Judge Harry M., 58, at Washington, March 6, 1914.
CLABAUGH, John H., 76, bridge builder, Baltimore City, January 30, 1894.
CLABAUGH, William H., 81, retired, Baltimore City, April 9, 1895.
CLACKNER, Mrs. Elizabeth, 96, Baltimore City, April 29, 1884.
CLAGETT, Charles T., n.a., Upper Marlboro, Prince George's County, March 23, 1892.
CLAGETT, Dr. Joseph Edward, 77, Baltimore City, April 4, 1908.
CLAGETT, Thomas, 76, of Maryland, died at Keokuk, Iowa, May 8, 1910.
CLAGGETT, Dr. Samuel, 41, Baltimore City, July 9, 1914.
CLAGGETT, William T., 61, dancing master, Baltimore City, November 6, 1896.
CLAPP, George C., 70, hatter, Baltimore City, October 17, 1884.
CLARE, Mary S., 67, Sister of Visitation Baltimore City, February 7, 1901.

CLARK, Charles L., 63, builder, Baltimore City, February 23, 1904.
CLARK, Daniel E., 53, Baltimore City Councilman, March 4, 1895.
CLARK, Dr. Ellery C., 69, physician, Baltimore City, October 3, 1905.
CLARK, Frank, 68, retired manufacturer, Baltimore City, October 18, 1901.
CLARK, Captain Frank P., 74, Baltimore City, January 3, 1912.
CLARK, Gabriel D., 83, retired, Baltimore City, December 8, 1896.
CLARK, Gabriel D., 73, of Maryland, died at Atlantic City, New Jersey, September 19, 1910.
CLARK, George, 89, architect, Baltimore City, January 7, 1890.
CLARK, Henry H., 84, retired, Baltimore City, November 24, 1899.
CLARK, Major J_____ A_____, 67, Baltimore City, October 17, 1908.
CLARK, James, 61, boiler maker, Baltimore City, May 22, 1880.
CLARK, James G., 70, cooper, Baltimore City, March 23, 1882.
CLARK, John, 72, Baltimore City merchant died at Jacksonville, Florida, September 27, 1898.
CLARK, John H., 44, mechanic, Baltimore City, January 20, 1882.
CLARK, John W., 75, retired manufacturer, Baltimore City, September 17, 1900.
CLARK, Levin P., 83, machinist, Baltimore City, March 26, 1882.
CLARK, Oliver H., 82, Rockville, Montgomery County, August 27, 1911.
CLARK, Philip R., 74, agent, Baltimore City, March 5, 1904.
CLARK, Dr. Thaddeus, n.a., Baltimore City, February 14, 1914.
CLARK, Thomas S., 80, merchant, Baltimore City, November 2, 1888.
CLARK, William H., 67, sailmaker, Baltimore City, June 18, 1900.
CLARK, William H., n.a., Clarksville, Howard County, November 30, 1910.
CLARK, Walter S., 81, Baltimore City, March 23, 1907.
CLARK, William J., n.a., former judge, Northeast, Cecil County, January 29, 1914.
CLARK, Zachariah, 84, pilot, Baltimore City, March 31, 1893.
CLARKE, Dr. Andrew P., 38, physician, Baltimore City, July 16, 1888.
CLARKE, George F., 34, funeral director, Baltimore City, September 5, 1899.
CLARKE, Dr. H_____ Lee, n.a., Glyndon, Baltimore County, August 18, 1913.
CLARKE, J_____ Lyle, 61, Baltimore City, January 6, 1898.
CLARKE, James, 66, manufacturer, Baltimore City, May 31, 1894.
CLARKE, General James C., 79, died at Chicago, December 9, 1902.
CLARKE, Rev. James C. (M.E.), 61, Baltimore City, March 26, 1899.

CLARKE, John G., 81, manufacturer, Baltimore City, September 24, 1904.
CLARKE, John T., 82, retired, Howard County, April 23, 1906.
CLARKE, Dr. Joseph, 78, physician, Baltimore City, November 27, 1902.
CLARKE, Joseph H., 95, educator, Baltimore City, September 10, 1885.
CLARKE, Joseph W., 62, Baltimore City, March 23, 1907.
CLARKE, Martin, 58, merchant, Baltimore City, May 8, 1881.
CLARKE, Robert W., 37, singer, Baltimore City, March 8, 1902.
CLARKE, Rev. S____ J____, 69, Frostburg, Allegany County, February 15, 1913.
CLARKE, William E., 49, merchant, Baltimore City, December 14, 1899.
CLARY, Thomas, 82, Mount Airy, Carroll County, September 19, 1912.
CLASH, Captain C____ H____, 83, Centreville, Queen Anne's County, May 2, 1911.
CLASH, W____ A____, 92, Cambridge, Dorchester County, March 12, 1911.
CLASSEN, Rev. Louis (R.C.), 68, Baltimore City, December 17, 1894.
CLAUDE, Dr. Abram, 82, Annapolis, Anne Arundel County, January 10, 1901.
CLAUSS, Rev. Joseph (R.C.), 55, Baltimore City, April 7, 1882.
CLAWSON, Dr. Jacob H., 35, physician, Baltimore City, January 24, 1884.
CLAYLAND, Samuel R., 82, retired, Baltimore City, January 21, 1886.
CLAYLAND, T____ McD., 57, veterinarian surgeon, Baltimore City, March 17, 1902.
CLAYPOLE, James, 55, politician, Baltimore City, July 11, 1892.
CLAYPOOLE, James Y., 56, clerk, Baltimore City, October 28, 1895.
CLAYPOOLE, Captain John, 81, retired, Baltimore City, August 13, 1883.
CLAYTON, J____ E____, 55, realtor, Baltimore City, June 18, 1902.
CLAYTON, James W., 45, Senate clerk, Baltimore City, February 8, 1880.
CLAYTON, R____ Vinton, 77, Annapolis, Anne Arundel County, October 13, 1907.
CLEARY, Edward M., 62, merchant, Baltimore City, February 28, 1902.
CLEGG, Dr. James R., 45, Baltimore City, July 17, 1884.
CLEMENS, Aug____ D____, 64, Baltimore City, November 10, 1909.
CLEMENT, Dr. Albert W., 44, veterinarian surgeon, Baltimore City, March 3, 1901.
CLEMENT, Clay, 46, actor, died at Kansas City, February 21, 1910.
CLEMENT, James 72, manufacturer, Baltimore City, December 29, 1904.

CLEMENTS, Captain J_____ W_____, 58, mariner, Baltimore City, March 22, 1883.
CLEMENTS, W_____ M_____, 73, Ruxton, Baltimore County, March 28, 1912.
CLEMM, Rev. T_____ D_____ (M.E.), 80, Baltimore City, February 12, 1895.
CLEMM, William E., 55, realtor, Baltimore City, January 6, 1896.
CLEMMENT, John B., 77, mariner, Baltimore City, August 15, 1891.
CLEMSON, Dr. H_____ E_____, 38, Elkton, Cecil County, March 21, 1910.
CLENDENIN, James W., 75, of Baltimore City, died in New York City, October 15, 1898.
CLENDENIN, Mrs. Susan R., 97, Baltimore City, November 6, 1898.
CLENDENIN, T_____ R_____, 62, Riverdale, Prince George's County, March 26, 1910.
CLENDENIN, William R., 69, Baltimore City, February 15, 1905.
CLENDENIN, Dr. William Hazlett, Jr., n.a., physician, Baltimore City, August 25, 1893.
CLIFTON, Robert D., 54, contractor, Baltimore City, January 20, 1903.
CLOGG, George S., 61, merchant, Baltimore City, May 3, 1886.
CLOKE, James, 61, former Baltimore City Councilman, January 27, 1890.
CLOTWORTHY, Colonel C_____ Baker, 46, February 11, 1914.
CLOTWORTHY, Colonel S_____ S_____, 63, Baltimore City, January 6, 1907.
CLOTWORTHY, William P., 72, chemical manufacturer, Baltimore City, June 12, 1902.
CLOUD, Charles F., 75, publisher, Baltimore City, February 3, 1882.
CLOUD, Daniel, 79, Baltimore City, March 16, 1908.
COAD, J_____ E_____, 87, Charlotte Hall, St. Mary's County, October 16, 1911.
COAKLEY, Daniel, n.a., merchant, Baltimore City, February 12, 1892.
COALE, A_____, 64, gatekeeper, Camden Station, Baltimore City, March 27, 1884.
COALE, George B., 68, insurance, Baltimore City, March 5, 1887.
COALE, James Carey, 65, insurance, April 13, 1891.
COALE, Lewis P., 64, Baltimore City, April 25, 1898.
COALE, Thomas E., 64, retired, Baltimore City, September 17, 1896.
COALE, William Ellis, 41, bank officer, Baltimore City, August 30, 1897.
COARTS, G_____ W_____, n.a., Catonsville, Baltimore County, September 12, 1910.
COATES, Dr. Charles E., 73, physician, Baltimore City, March 25, 1901.
COATS, Mrs. Anna, 72, Baltimore City, March 14, 1908.
COBB, Charles, 59, Baltimore City, June 15, 1913.
COBB, Edward R. E., 51, auctioneer, Baltimore City, December 27, 1887.

COCHRAN, Charles, Jr., 74, clerk, Baltimore City, July 5, 1881.
COCHRAN, John, 54, grocer, Baltimore City, January 23, 1897.
COCHRAN, Dr. John H., 66, Havre de Grace, Harford County, October 10, 1899.
COCHRAN, William B., 49, Treasurer of Baltimore County, Govanstown, May 1, 1903.
COCKERILL, Dr. James J., 63, Baltimore City, July 13, 1878.
COCKEY, Dr. C____ E____, 60, educator, Baltimore City, November 19, 1904.
COCKEY, J____ G____, 79, bank president, Lutherville, Baltimore County, March 20, 1893.
COCKEY, Dr. Joseph Cromwell, 72, physician, Baltimore City, October 18, 1881.
COCKEY, Judge Joshua F., 90, Cockeysville, Baltimore County, May 9, 1891.
COCKEY, Joshua T., 63, Baltimore County, August 23, 1905.
COCKRILL, Dr. Joseph M., 50, physician, Baltimore City, July 23, 1898.
CODD, John P., 36, Baltimore City, April 4, 1913.
CODD, Simon (age illegible), water department, Baltimore City, August 8, 1902.
COFFROTH, J____ R____, 85, Baltimore City, April 3, 1909.
COGGINS, Rev. J____, 72, local preacher, Baltimore City, February 3, 1881.
COGHLAN, Edward, 91, retired, Baltimore City, December 10, 1891.
COHEN, Rev. A____ D____ (Baptist), 83, Baltimore City, February 12, 1905.
COHEN, Emmanuel, 63, merchant, Baltimore City, December 17, 1881.
COHEN, Louis, nine years old, died on December 27, 1895, in the Front Street Theater panic.
COHEN, Mandel, 69, Baltimore City, February 18, 1907.
COHEN, Mendes I., 83, banker, Baltimore City, May 7, 1879.
COHEN, Rachel E., 88, Baltimore City, September 28, 1913.
COHEN, Simon, 93, Baltimore City, October 4, 1908.
COHN, Adolph, 50, merchant, Baltimore City, February 3, 1903.
COHN, Henry P., 72, merchant, Baltimore City, January 21, 1901.
COHN, Josiah, 53, merchant, Baltimore City, April 17, 1903.
COLBURN, Rev. Edward, 77, Baltimore City, April 28, 1907.
COLE, Abraham, 77, Waverly, suburb of Baltimore City, March 16, 1900.
COLE, Charles Edward, 58, Frederick, Frederick County, August 21, 1905.
COLE, George B., 63, merchant, Baltimore City, August 5, 1896.
COLE, Captain George H., 77, pilot, Baltimore City, May 20, 1887.
COLE, Colonel H____ A____, 75, Baltimore City, May 26, 1909.
COLE, Hiram, 74, hatter, Baltimore City, December 3, 1880.
COLE, James R., 64, merchant, Baltimore City, January 31, 1901.
COLE, J____ W____, 60, mail superintendent, <u>The Sun</u>, April 11, 1892.

COLE, Rev. Lewis (M.E.), 54, Baltimore City, September 7, 1887.
COLE, Louis M., 72, ticket agent, Baltimore City, June 4, 1889.
COLE, Robert C., 52, Baltimore City, December 16, 1914.
COLE, Thomas W., 70, Anne Arundel County, May 19, 1907.
COLE, Walter, 37, attorney, Baltimore City, August 7, 1902.
COLE, William H., 49, Congressman from Maryland died in Washington, D.C., July 8, 1886.
COLE, William H., n.a., merchant, Baltimore City, June 23, 1889.
COLE, William H., 89, Baltimore City, December 28, 1909.
COLE, William P., 78, manufacturer, Baltimore City, April 1, 1881.
COLEIN, John, 90, veteran of the War of 1812, Baltimore City, November 25, 1882.
COLEMAN, Charles R., 79, retired, Baltimore City, December 20, 1884.
COLEMAN, Major F_____ W_____, n.a., hotelier, Baltimore City, June 16, 1902.
COLEMAN, R_____ B_____, 76, hotelier, Baltimore City, November 1, 1881.
COLEMAN, Samuel, 82, retired, Baltimore City, June 13, 1902.
COLEMAN, Rev. T_____ K_____, 62, Baltimore City, March 11, 1881.
COLFLESH, G_____ B_____, 67, manufacturer, Baltimore City, July 28, 1893.
COLLEY, John W., 80, builder, Baltimore City, July 16, 1887.
COLLINS, Daniel, 69, Princess Anne, Somerset County, April 9, 1905.
COLLINS, Henry, 69, manufacturer, Baltimore City, August 6, 1881.
COLLINS, Captain James W., 70, Baltimore City, August 22, 1909.
COLLINS, Captain John, 66, retired conductor, Baltimore City, March 9, 1884.
COLLINS, Samuel, 78, Baltimore City, July 3, 1909.
COLLINS, William, 55, Easton, Talbot County, May 3, 1908.
COLLINS, William H., 80, attorney, Baltimore City, June 1, 1881.
COLLISON, Captain Charles W., 80, pilot, Baltimore City, August 13, 1900.
COLLISON, William H., 56, Easton, Talbot County, March 7, 1907.
COLLMUS, Solomon, 89, Baltimore City, April 26, 1910.
COLMARY, Captain A_____ I_____, 75, retired, Baltimore City, April 6, 1890.
COLSTON, J_____ M_____, 60, Church Creek, Dorchester County, January 16, 1910.
COLTON, George, 80, retired, Baltimore City, May 4, 1898.
COLTON, Luther, 39, retired, Baltimore City, November 16, 1884.
COLVIN, Frank D., 44, manufacturer, Baltimore City, April 20, 1901.
COMBS, J_____ S_____, 65, Cumberland, Allegany County, November 26, 1909.
COMEGYS, Benjamin, 92, Baltimore City, October 24, 1913.

COMEGYS, Edward T., 55, Baltimore City, February 13, 1910.
COMMES, William H., 73, Gaithersburg, Montgomery County, November 28, 1905.
COMPTON, Barnes, 68, Laurel, Prince George's County, December 2, 1898.
COMPTON, W____ P____, 68, Confederate veteran, Pikesville, Baltimore County, July 13, 1908.
CONDON, Levi Z., 82, Baltimore City, March 7, 1912.
CONE, Herbert, 68, merchant, Baltimore City, April 7, 1897.
CONE, Joseph M., 69, builder, Baltimore City, December 12, 1905.
CONDON, David, 85, contractor, Baltimore City, October 5, 1892.
CONGDON, S____ Hopkins, 52, retired, Baltimore City, February 1, 1898.
CONKLIN, Daniel E., 75, Karlsbad, Germany, August 2, 1910.
CONKLING, William H., 71, Baltimore City, January 18, 1907.
CONNELL, Thomas M (S.J.), 23, Baltimore City, January 13, 1892.
CONNELLY, William M., 68, journalist, Baltimore City, January 17, 1885.
CONNER, Captain Charles A., n.a., journalist, Baltimore City, December 25, 1901.
CONNER, Captain H____ F____, 67, Confederate veteran, Baltimore City, December 24, 1912.
CONNER, I____ B____, 90, Snow Hill, Worcester County, February 22, 1912.
CONNOLLY, Edward, 75, retired, Baltimore City, May 6, 1897.
CONNOLLY, Dr. Francis G., 81, physician, Baltimore City, January 10, 1901.
CONNOLLY, Hannah, 98, Baltimore City, December 6, 1878.
CONNOLLY, J____ T____, 102, Pikesville, Baltimore County, November 17, 1907.
CONNOLLY, James, 50, plumber, Baltimore City, January 1, 1902.
CONNOLLY, Michael, 84, oldest public school principal in Baltimore City, May 20, 1892.
CONRAD, Dr. J____ S____, 58, St. Denis, Howard County, December 7, 1896.
CONRAD, Joseph, 84, carpenter, Baltimore City, April 8, 1902.
CONRAD, Lawrence L., 44, lawyer, Baltimore City, August 7, 1883.
CONRADI, Rev. John P. (Lutheran), 85, Baltimore City, June 21, 1900.
CONROY, Captain Peter, 55, Baltimore City, April 21, 1909.
CONROY, Thomas, n.a., retired, Baltimore City, July 14, 1897.
CONSTABLE, Albert, 65, lawyer, Elkton, Cecil County, August 22, 1904.
CONSTANTINE, Captain Daniel, 75, naval constructor, Baltimore City, August 29, 1899.
CONTEE, John B., 39, Prince George's County, May 31, 1902.
CONTEE, Philip A. L., Sr., 58, Charles County Commissioner, La Plata, February 28, 1899.
CONTEE, Philip A. A., Jr., 30, La Plata, Charles County, January 22, 1899.

CONVERY, John P., 72, Baltimore City, February 7, 1913.
CONWAY, Henry J., 54, hotelier, Baltimore City, June 25, 1894.
CONWAY, Rev. J____ G____ (R.C.), 60, Baltimore City, October 27, 1893.
CONWAY, James, 59, merchant, Baltimore City, January 1, 1882.
CONWAY, James, 34, Ariel Club, Baltimore City, August 19, 1901.
COOK, Anthony, 90, florist, Baltimore City, May 13, 1906.
COOK, Arlington L., 40, hatter, Baltimore City, September 19, 1902.
COOK, Rev. Charles O. (M.E.), 53, October 11, 1899.
COOK, Columbus E., 82, auctioneer, Baltimore City, February 8, 1881.
COOK, Edward J., 47, auctioneer, Baltimore City, December 8, 1903.
COOK, F____, 81, former Baltimore City Councilman, November 12, 1893.
COOK, Frederick C., 54, attorney, Baltimore City, December 10, 1903.
COOK, Rev. Isaac P. (M.E.), 76, Baltimore City, February 15, 1884.
COOK, John, 80, merchant, Baltimore City, November 28, 1882.
COOK, John, 64, policeman, Baltimore City, August 4, 1893.
COOK, Newton S., 53, Hagerstown, Washington County, August 8, 1905.
COOK, Colonel R____ E____, 82, Hagerstown, Washington County, November 12, 1893.
COOK, Mrs. Susanna, 102, Havre de Grace, Harford County, February 10, 1905.
COOK, William I., 78, Baltimore City, December 17, 1909.
COOKE, Adolphus, 65, Baltimore County, July 30, 1905.
COOKE, Captain Isaac M., 63, retired, Baltimore City, January 20, 1885.
COOKE, Dr. O____ A____, 48, physician, Baltimore City, May 11, 1888.
COOKSEY, Captain W____ T____, 67, Baltimore City, June 18, 1912.
COOLEY, William L., 63, Bel Air, Harford County, February 10, 1905.
COOPER, Astley P., n.a., artist, Baltimore City, August 26, 1898.
COOPER, Captain E____ K____, 61, mariner, Baltimore City, February 14, 1883.
COOPER, Rev. G____ W____ (M.E.), 76, Baltimore City, January 22, 1902.
COOPER, Dr. J____ W____, 56, Elkton, Cecil County, March 10, 1906.
COOPER, Captain John H., 72, pilot, Baltimore City, April 9, 1900.
COOPER, John H., 73, retired, Baltimore City, August 19, 1901.
COOPER, Nelson, 76, Towson, Baltimore County, April 7, 1893.
COOPER, Samuel, 83, retired, Baltimore City, December 1, 1884.

COOPER, Captain T_____ J_____, 69, mariner, Baltimore City, December 20, 1906.
COPPER, Captain S_____ G_____, 78, Baltimore City, June 11, 1905.
CORDERY, William H., 77, retired, Baltimore City, August 5, 1897.
COREY, J_____ H_____, 70, Easton, Talbot County, March 11, 1907.
CORIELL, Alvin, 61, merchant, Baltimore City, September 1, 1904.
CORIELL, Isaac, 74, contractor, Baltimore City, November 4, 1882.
CORKRAN, F_____ S_____, 72, former naval officer, Baltimore City, November 13, 1886.
CORKRAN, William, 81, merchant, Baltimore City, April 2, 1898.
CORLIN, Dr. J_____ S_____, n.a., Boyds, Montgomery County, January 4, 1913.
CORNELIUS, Rev. J_____ W_____ (M.E.), 59, Baltimore City, September 23, 1894.
CORNELIUS, Rev. J_____ W_____ (M.E.), 58, Baltimore City, February 1, 1888.
CORNELIUS, John C., 53, veterinarian surgeon, Baltimore City, April 18, 1895.
CORNELIUS, Nicholas A., 85, merchant, Baltimore City, May 7, 1900.
CORNELIUS, Richard, 69, bank cashier, Baltimore City, January 4, 1897.
CORNELL, Michael, 78, builder, Baltimore City, August 30, 1888.
CORNER, Frank, 45, Baltimore City, May 19, 1899.
CORNER, George W., 84, retired merchant, Baltimore City, January 20, 1905.
CORNER, Theodore, 78, Anne Arundel County, May 10, 1904.
CORNER, W_____ H_____, 73, Blue Ridge Summit, Pennsylvania, September 23, 1911.
CORNING, Dr. A_____ J_____, 65, pharmacist, Baltimore City, August 17, 1907.
CORRELL, Dr. John W., 73, physician, Baltimore City, January 20, 1900.
CORTILLA, Sister Mary, n.a., Baltimore City, March 17, 1913.
CORTLAND, Colonel J_____, 87, Baltimore City, September 20, 1910.
CORUM, James C., 82, retired merchant, Baltimore City, January 26, 1902.
COSKERY, Dr. Oscar J., 46, physician, Baltimore City, July 5, 1889.
COST, Dr. Eugene F., 70, Baltimore City, August 27, 1913.
COSTER, Captain Jesse F., 78, Solomons, Calvert County, April 5, 1913.
COSTIN, Dr. Severn P., 26, physician, Baltimore City, January 30, 1883.
COTTAM, Dr. _____ S_____, 40, veterinarian surgeon, Baltimore City, November 13, 1902.
COTTEN, Lieutenant M_____ A_____, 72, Baltimore City, January 19, 1913.

COTTERELL, George, 54, merchant, Baltimore City, March 10, 1901.
COTTINGHAM, Peter D., 76, druggist, Snow Hill, Worcester County, October 5, 1897.
COTTON, Rev. Henry E., n.a., Hagerstown, Washington County, December 2, 1914.
COULBOURN, Augustus W., 66, physician, Baltimore City, April 20, 1886.
COULBOURN, Captain Joseph, 88, Crisfield, Somerset County, January 9, 1907.
COULBOURN, Rev. Thomas E., 37, Baltimore City, March 11, 1896.
COULSON, George J., 63, merchant, Baltimore City, October 27, 1882.
COULTER, Archibald B., 58, banker, Baltimore City, January 3, 1896.
COULTER, J_____ M_____, 87, Baltimore City, June 13, 1912.
COUNCELL, Joel F., 78, contractor, Baltimore City, April 11, 1900.
COUNCELL, Rhodes H., 30, pharmacist, Baltimore City, March 17, 1901.
COUNCILMAN, George, 94, Baltimore County, July 15, 1897.
COUNSELMAN, Jacob, 66, retired, Baltimore City, October 28, 1883.
COUNSELMAN, William H., 61, retired, Baltimore City, April 7, 1887.
COUPLAND, Richard, 82, merchant, Baltimore City, May 13, 1880.
COURLANDER, Bernard, 83, musician, Baltimore City, April 14, 1898.
COURTNEY, David S., 81, bank teller, Baltimore City, February 5, 1881.
COURTNEY, Hollis, Jr., 64, Havre de Grace, Harford County, March 12, 1908.
COURTNEY, Richard, 42, merchant, Baltimore City, June 17, 1886.
COURTNEY, Major T_____ L_____, 83, Confederate veteran died at Richmond, Virginia, January 9, 1908.
COURTNEY, William P., 40, Baltimore City, February 14, 1897.
COVER, Peter, 65, Carroll County, July 19, 1904.
COVER, Samuel, 80, Westminster, Carroll County, August 23, 1903.
COWAN, David, 72, bookkeeper, Baltimore City, March 25, 1901.
COWEN, John K., 59, lawyer and former president of the B. & O. Railroad, died at Chicago, April 25, 1904.
COWLES, Henry M., 83, educator, Baltimore City, December 25, 1905.
COWMAN, Edward, 78, grocer, Baltimore City, December 6, 1894.
COX, Dr. E_____ Gover, 63, physician, Baltimore City, August 19, 1883.
COX, Dr. Ernest Cleveland, 32, physician, Baltimore City, October 13, 1882.
COX, Isaac, 59, real estate, Baltimore City, December 5, 1884.
COX, James H., Sr., 71, Baltimore City, December 27, 1879.
COX, John R., 73, retired, Baltimore City, November 26, 1890.
COX, Luther J., 85, St. Michaels, Talbot County, September 3, 1904.
COX, Richard, 84, "Old Defender," Baltimore City, February 27, 1879.

COX, William, 55, merchant, Baltimore City, March 31, 1886.
COX, William G., n.a., teacher, Baltimore City, September 24, 1894.
COX, William H., 70, retired, Baltimore City, October 10, 1887.
COY, Byron F., 53, dentist, Baltimore City, July 26, 1881.
COYLE, Patrick A., 84, manufacturer, Baltimore City, December 17, 1905.
COYLE, Dr. T____ C____, 73, Baltimore City, January 27, 1914.
COYNE, Dudley, 37, manufacturer, Baltimore City, February 5, 1902.
CRAGGS, Dr. J____ H____, 75, physician, Anne Arundel County, February 11, 1893.
CRAIG, Dr. Philip E., 35, physician, Baltimore City, September 10, 1904.
CRAIG, Professor Thomas, 45, Johns Hopkins University, Baltimore City, May 8, 1900.
CRAIGHILL, General William P., 74, January 18, 1909.
CRAILE, Rev. A____ T____ (M.P.), 47, Baltimore City, February 18, 1886.
CRAIN, Peter, 86, former judge, Baltimore City, March 30, 1892.
CRAMER, D____, 80, Williamsport, Washington County, December 22, 1907.
CRAMER, E____ Lewis, 73, Frederick, Frederick County, July 19, 1900.
CRAMPTON, Rev. S____ W____ (P.E.), 87, January 19, 1898.
CRANE, A____ Fuller, 65, retired, Baltimore City, January 11, 1885.
CRANE, Henry H., 54, insurance, Baltimore City, July 30, 1899.
CRANE, Robert Brent, 70, Upper Falls (?), January 10, 1913.
CRAPSTER, Gustavus, 85, Westminster, Carroll County, February 15, 1907.
CRAPSTER, Thaddeus, 79, Ellicott City, Howard County, November 16, 1905.
CRAWFORD, Dr. Basil B., 75, Rockville, Montgomery County, May 4, 1906.
CRAWFORD, Dalrymple H., 55, Baltimore City, November 24, 1905.
CRAWFORD, William, 55, railroad agent, Baltimore City, October 8, 1882.
CRAWFORD, William H., 69, merchant, Baltimore City, July 28, 1898.
CREAGH, Peter, 66, grocer, Baltimore City, November 11, 1905.
CREAMER, Alexander, 83, retired, Baltimore City, October 24, 1905.
CREAMER, David, 74, retired, Baltimore City, April 8, 1887.
CREAMER, George B., 53, auctioneer, Baltimore City, September 16, 1894.
CREAMER, Joseph, 82, retired, Baltimore City, May 9, 1897.
CREIGHTON, Captain James, 80, mariner, Baltimore City, March 25, 1883.
CREMER, George H., 55, brewer, Baltimore City, October 7, 1900.
CRENSHAW, Professor T____ E____, n.a., Cambridge, Dorchester County, December 23, 1900.

CRESWELL, John A. J., 63, former Postmaster General, near Elkton, Cecil County, December 23, 1891.
CRICHTON, Malcolm, 49, distiller, Baltimore City, January 27, 1891.
CRIM, William Henry, 57, physician, Baltimore City, November 15, 1902.
CRISE, John L., 72, builder, Baltimore City, December 21, 1887.
CRISFIELD, John W., 88, Princess Anne, Somerset County, January 12, 1897.
CRISP, Joseph, 63, tobacconist, Baltimore City, June 8, 1891.
CRISP, Richard O., 51, farmer, Baltimore City, January 17, 1881.
CROCKETT, Captain H____, 72, Baltimore City, December 4, 1912.
CROFT, Henry C., n.a., pharmacist, Baltimore City, December 17, 1906.
CROMER, Thomas C., 65, merchant, Baltimore City, April 22, 1884.
CROMWELL, A____ T____, 75, Baltimore City, April 9, 1907.
CROMWELL, G____ W____, 83, Baltimore City, January 16, 1908.
CROMWELL, G____ W____, 65, Cumberland, Allegany County, March 19, 1910.
CROMWELL, R____, 75, Baltimore City, January 1, 1910.
CROMWELL, Richard, 84, retired, Baltimore City, November 28, 1890.
CROMWELL, Richard, Jr., 48, Baltimore City, June 12, 1912.
CROMWELL, Samuel, 79, Baltimore City, December 5, 1894.
CROMWELL, W____ H____, 76, Frederick, Frederick County, January 12, 1910.
CRONE, Michael, 70, Confederate veteran, April 11, 1902.
CRONE, William, 56, former detective, Baltimore City, February 26, 1887.
CRONENBERG, Peter, 71, clergyman, Baltimore City, May 3, 1880.
CRONMILLER, W____ W____, 85, Laurel, Prince George's County, April 17, 1908.
CROOK, Charles, 89, manufacturer, Baltimore City, October 14, 1882.
CROOK, Mrs. Frances A., 68, Baltimore City, November 20, 1891.
CROOK, Francis A., 86, merchant, Baltimore City, July 14, 1894.
CROOK, Philip P., 72, retired, Baltimore City, April 9, 1899.
CROOK, William, 70, Baltimore City merchant, February 11, 1892.
CROOKS, Francis M., 64, auditor, Baltimore City, June 6, 1895.
CROOKS, J____ H____, 69, Baltimore City, April 9, 1910.
CROSBY, S____ K____, 86, Baltimore County, March 7, 1911.
CROSBY, Captain Samuel, 50, mariner, Baltimore City, July 17, 1887.
CROSBY, Wilson, 70, civil engineer, December 18, 1904.
CROSS, Rev. A____ B____ (Presbyterian), 78, Baltimore City, September 6, 1889.
CROSS, Cyrus, 73, merchant, Baltimore City, August 20, 1893.
CROSS, E____ J____ D____, 65, attorney, Baltimore City, May 2, 1906.
CROSS, J____ T____, 64, Baltimore County, July 21, 1909.

CROSS, Joshua, 83, painter, Baltimore City, March 26, 1883.
CROSS, Rev. N_____ Baldwin, 77, Cumberland, Allegany County, November 21, 1914.
CROSS, R_____ K_____, 61, attorney, Baltimore City, September 5, 1909.
CROSS, Samuel B., 81, retired, Baltimore City, February 7, 1884.
CROSS, William Stewart, 63, merchant, Baltimore City, June 14, 1898.
CROTHERS, Alpheus, 76, Cecil County, March 26, 1897.
CROTHERS, Alpheus, 52, Cecil County, June 14, 1902.
CROTHERS, Austin Lane, 52, Governor (beginning 1908), Elkton, Cecil County, May 25, 1912.
CROTHERS, Senator Charles C., 40, Cecil County, September 28, 1898.
CROTHERS, Dr. Ransom R., n.a., Cecil County, November 8, 1902.
CROTHERS, Roman R., 28, Elkton, Cecil County, November 11, 1913.
CROUCH, F_____ W_____ Nichols, 88, of Baltimore City and author of Kathleen of Mavourneen, died at Portland, Maine, August 16, 1896.
CROUSE, B_____ F_____, 56, Westminster, Carroll County, November 8, 1910.
CROUSE, George, 83, Westminster, Carroll County, April 7, 1902.
CROUSE, Rev. William A., 81, Westminster, Carroll County, January 11, 1906.
CROUT, J_____ E_____, 73, Reisterstown, Baltimore County, May 31, 1908.
CROUT, Paul G., 40, former deputy sheriff, Baltimore City, February 13, 1884.
CROW, John T., 58, former Washington, D.C., bureau chief of The Sun, March 23, 1881.
CROWDER, Alexsnder N., 65, Baltimore City, January 25, 1897.
CROWE, Lawrence J., 26, machinist, Baltimore City, December 28, 1902.
CROWE, John, 43, railroad auditor, Baltimore City, April 12, 1884.
CROWELL, Michael W., 58, mariner, Baltimore City, January 9, 1898.
CROWL, Rev. Edward W., 55, Baltimore City, January 26, 1882.
CROWLEY, G_____ S_____., n.a., Millwood, December 19, 1909.
CROWTHER, Isaac, Sr., 77, builder, Baltimore City, August 15, 1894.
CROYEAU, Augustine, 78, retired, Baltimore City, February 23, 1897.
CROZIER, James, 75, molder, Baltimore City, November 4, 1893.
CROZIER, William W., 49, packer, Baltimore City, January 15, 1895.
CRUIKSHANK, George W., 64, clerk, Baltimore City, April 20, 1902.
CRUIKSHANK, Ward, 34, editor, Elkton, Cecil County, October 24, 1905.
CRUMMER, Alexander, 54, Stock Exchange, Baltimore City, January 7, 1897.
CRUMMER, Nathan, 74, retired, Baltimore City, February 14, 1885.

CRUSE, John H., 55, Baltimore City, May 2, 1897.
CRUTCHFIELD, Andrew P., 65, editor, Baltimore City, July 24, 1889.
CRUTCHFIELD, Dr. Eugene L., 50, Baltimore City, June 12, 1913.
CUDDY, John P., 87, Baltimore County, March 10, 1897.
CUGLE, Edwin, 36, bank teller, Baltimore City, September 23, 1881.
CULL, Edwin C., n.a., of Baltimore City, in Washington, D.C., December 26, 1900.
CULLUM, R_ev. J____ W____ (M.E.), 78, Baltimore City, April 30, 1886.
CULVER, George A., 68, Annapolis, Anne Arundel County, October 19, 1907.
CUMMING, James, 78, shipjoiner, Baltimore City, June 4, 1899.
CUMMINGS, John 73, distiller, Baltimore City, February 24, 1900.
CUMMINGS, Rev. Samuel H., 77, Baltimore City, June 1, 1914.
CUMMINGS, William J., 55, Baltimore City, December 8, 1897.
CUMMINS, J____ S____, 51, photographer, Baltimore City, March 3, 1895.
CUNDIFF, Albert T., 65, mariner, Baltimore City, November 30, 1903.
CUNNINGHAM, Edmund H., 57, merchant, Baltimore City, August 27, 1901.
CUNNINGHAM, John E. A., 65, merchant, Baltimore City, November 2, 1901.
CUNNINGHAM, Mortimer, 78, merchant, Baltimore City, October 30, 1880.
CUNNINGHAM, Thomas, 87, Cumberland, Allegany County, April 27, 1912.
CUNNINGHAM, William C., 76, merchant, Baltimore City, May 9, 1883.
CUNNINGHAM, William H., 68, merchant, Baltimore City, February 28, 1882.
CURLETT, John, 82, banker, Baltimore City, February 17, 1896.
CURLEY, Henry R., 86, builder, Baltimore City, March 19, 1896.
CURLEY, John 59, quarry proprietor, Baltimore City, October 29, 1891.
CURLEY, Rev. W____ E____, 62, Monkton, Baltimore County, October 9, 1910.
CURRAN, James A., 81, water engineer, Baltimore City, July 19, 1895.
CURRAN, John T., n.a., water engineer, Baltimore City, January 8, 1899.
CURRAN, Professor J____ H____, 34, Tome Institute, Port Deposit, Cecil County, November 14, 1905.
CURREY, Dr. James H., 55, physician, Baltimore City, April 30, 1887.
CURRY, Dr. Wilbur C., n.a., physician, Baltimore City, May 28, 1896.
CURRY, William R., 80, Westminster, Carroll County, April 23, 1905.
CURTIN, Lieutenant Commander Roland J., 39, Annapolis, Anne Arundel County, February 20, 1914.

CURTIS, Bishop A_____ A_____, 77, Baltimore City, July 11, 1908.
CURTIS, Henry A., n.a., retired, Baltimore City, July 14, 1897.
CUSHING, Rev. H_____ C_____, n.a., Westminster, Carroll County, September 2, 1908.
CUSHING, Henry M., 54, Baltimore City, July 6, 1896.
CUSHING, John, 82, fire insurance, Baltimore City, September 29, 1890.
CUSHING, Joseph, Jr., 73, bookseller, Baltimore City, July 5, 1879.
CUSHING, Wiley E., 60, retired, Baltimore City, December 31, 1903.
CUSHING, Joseph M., 67, merchant, Baltimore City, November 23, 1902.
CUSHWA, C_____ Frank, 34, Williamsport, Washington County, December 1, 1905.
CUSHWA, Isaac B., 87, Hagerstown, Washington County, January 23, 1898.
CUSHWA, Thomas B., 58, Hagerstown, Washington County, May 22, 1897.
CUSHWA, Victor, 79, Williamsport, Washington County, May 29, 1912.
CUSTIS, William Parke, n.a., merchant, Baltimore City, November 16, 1900.
CUTAIR, Francis, 71, cigar manufacturer, Baltimore City, November 11, 1903.

DABNEY, Colonel Thomas S., 87, retired, Baltimore City, February 28, 1885.
DAIGER, Frederick, 80, retired, Baltimore City, November 23, 1894.
DAIGER, Matthias A., 73, undertaker, Baltimore City, March 20, 1900.
DAILEY, Sergeant Thomas, 68, U.S. Army, Baltimore City, October 10, 1885.
DAILY, E_____ V_____, 63, manufacturer, Baltimore City, October 30, 1881.
DALBY, William T., 69, merchant, Baltimore City, January 17, 1881.
DALE, Rev. William, 85, Pocomoke, Worcester County, April 17, 1907.
DALLAM, Charles F., 79, Pikesville, Baltimore County, February 13, 1913.
DALLAM, H_____ Clay, 58, lawyer, Baltimore City, March 7, 1887.
DALLAM, John S., 82, Bel Air, Harford County, December 2, 1898.
DALLAM, Joseph W., 79, attorney, Baltimore City, December 4, 1902.
DALLAM, W_____ W_____, 34, merchant, Baltimore City, September 19, 1878.
DALLAM, Dr. William, 77, Harford County, August 31, 1899.
DALLAM, William H., n.a., dep(uty?) U.S. Collector, Baltimore City, February 21, 1883.
DALLAM, W_____ L_____, 44, lawyer, Baltimore City, October 21, 1890.
DALLY, Mrs. May, 93, Baltimore City, October 10, 1909.

DALRYMPLE, Dr. August J., 65, Baltimore City, July 24, 1895.
DALRYMPLE, Rev. Edwin A. (P.E.), 63, Baltimore City, October 30, 1881.
DALRYMPLE, George H., 34, Baltimore City, April 2, 1899.
DALRYMPLE, James A.D., 67, Baltimore City, November 7, 1913
DALRYMPLE, James C., 48, Baltimore City, September 26, 1905.
DALRYMPLE, Lewis, 42, cartoonist, Baltimore City, December 28, 1905.
DALRYMPLE, William H., 53, Baltimore City, November 22, 1881.
DALSHEIMER, David, 91, manufacturer, Baltimore City, March 18, 1901.
DALY, E____ M____, 55, restaurateur, Baltimore City, June 18, 1888.
DAMARON, Rev. C____ L____, 74, Baltimore City, November 20, 1914.
DAMBMANN, Gustav, 45, manufacturer, Baltimore City, February 23, 1881.
DAMER, Rev. C____ E____, n.a., Baltimore City, November 24, 1910.
DAMMANN, A____ E____, 82, Baltimore City, February 2, 1908.
DAMMANN, F____ W____, 77, merchant, Baltimore City, August 11, 1893.
DANDO, James, 68, judge of the Orphan's Court of Allegany County, Frostburg, December 18, 1905.
DANEKER, Ormond A., 84, retired manufacturer, Baltimore City, October 9, 1902.
DANENHOWER, John Wilson, 37, Arctic explorer, at the U.S.N.A., Annapolis, April 20, 1887; six years earlier, during the DeLong Arctic Expedition, he had survived the ice crush of the Jeannette.
DANIEL, William, 71, lawyer, Baltimore City, October 31, 1897.
DANIELS, Captain N____ C____, 63, mariner, Baltimore City, December 29, 1902.
DANEKER, John J., 85, veteran, Baltimore City, August 9, 1882.
DANENHAUER, Louis, 53, builder, Baltimore City, November 9, 1885.
DANNER, Wesley C., 59, manufacturer, Baltimore City, February 2, 1901.
DANSKIN, W____ A____, 69, merchant, Baltimore City, December 19, 1881.
DANZEGLOCK, Henry G., 62, Baltimore City, April 3, 1900.
DARBY, David, 66, retired manufacturer, Baltimore City, April 10, 1896.
DARBY, Francis M., 65, treasurer, Safe Deposit & Trust Co., Baltimore City, November 10, 1903.
DARBY, N____, 67, Gaithersburg, Montgomery County, January 10, 1910.
DARLEY, John W., 70, retired, Baltimore City, December 4, 1897.
DARLING, F____ Taylor, 67, merchant, Baltimore City, February 21, 1902.
DARLING, P____ P____, n.a., Salisbury, Wicomico County, November 28, 1893.
DARRELL, Stewart, 78, Baltimore City, March 19, 1908.
DASHIELL, Dr. Cadmus, 85, Princess Anne, Somerset County, July 9, 1898.

DASHIELL, Charles W., 40, editor, Baltimore City, August 6, 1898.
DASHIELL, Edwin, 72, Cambridge, Dorchester County, December 30, 1898.
DASHIEL(L), Dr. Erastus E., 67, Snow Hill, Worcester County, September 22, 1914.
DASHIELL, Dr. J_____ W_____, 93, Princess Anne, Somerset County, September 5, 1910.
DASHIELL, Rev. Dr. John H., 92, Annapolis, Anne Arundel County, January 21, 1914.
DASHIELL, Rev. Julius M. (M.E.), 68, Millersville, Anne Arundel County, January 3, 1895.
DASHIELL, Levin M., 85, Salisbury, Wicomico County, July 9, 1907.
DASHIELL, Dr. Nicholas L., 80, physician, Baltimore City, February 28, 1895.
DASHIELL, Dr. R_____ D_____, 61, Salisbury, Wicomico County, November 9, 1911.
DASHIELL, Rober K. W., 81, Somerset County, September 11, 1901.
DASHIELL, Dr. Rufus W., n.a., physician, Princess Anne, Somerset County, March 28, 1900.
DAUGHERTY, Rev. Beverly W. (Methodist), 58, Baltimore City, July 27, 1895.
DAUGHERTY, Captain William H., 67, Myersdale, March 8, 1914
DAUSCH, Rev. Michael (R.C.), 55, July 26, 1892.
DAVENPORT, J_____ C_____, 69, Baltimore City, December 25, 1909.
DAVIDS, Garrett B., 63, engineer, Baltimore City, January 7, 1885.
DAVIDSON, A_____ Brown, 80, merchant, Baltimore City, February 16, 1883.
DAVIDSON, Dr. Benjamin Reed, 64, Annapolis, Anne Arundel County, May 1, 1910
DAVIDSON, Clark Y., 61, manufacturer, Baltimore City, August 19, 1897.
DAVES, Edward G., 61, teacher, Baltimore City, August 1, 1894.
DAVIS, Aaron 90, Feagaville, Washington County, September 5, 1909.
DAVIS, Allen Bowie, 80, retired, Baltimore City, April 17, 1889
DAVIS, Dr. D_____ O_____, 53, physician, Baltimore City, August 3, 1899.
DAVIS, David P., 67, Orphan's Court judge, Cecil County, April 13, 1900.
DAVIS, Edwin, 64, builder, Baltimore City, April 3, 1897.
DAVIS, Franklin, 66, florist, Baltimore City, October 15, 1895.
DAVIS, Frisby, 71, Boonsboro, Washington County, July 11, 1909.
DAVIS, George A., 75, builder, Baltimore City, April 28, 1880.
DAVIS, Henry 53, assistant inspector of cruisers, Baltimore City, February 1, 1893.
DAVIS, J_____ C_____, 72, railroad machinist, Baltimore City, June 5, 1890.
DAVIS, J_____ M_____, 85, Towson, Baltimore County, July 21, 1908

DAVIS, J____ R____, 69, Pikesville, Montgomery County, July 5, 1911.
DAVIS, J____ Shelden, 32, black attorney, Baltimore City, December 6, 1892.
DAVIS, James, n.a., Baltimore City Councilman, February 28, 1909.
DAVIS, James A., 74, Port Deposit, Cecil County, November 12, 1894.
DAVIS, John C., 69, retired, Baltimore City, November 1, 1887.
DAVIS, John F., 78, builder, Baltimore City, March 2, 1887.
DAVIS, John W., 85, Baltimore City, November 8, 1888.
DAVIS, John W., 53, builder, Baltimore City, March 28, 1883.
DAVIS, Raphael, 78, Baltimore City, September 10, 1907.
DAVIS, Richard, 84, retired, Baltimore City, February 13, 1884.
DAVIS, U____ S____, 71, mariner, Baltimore City, September 16, 1910.
DAVIS, W____ H____, 71, physician, Baltimore City, January 24, 1881.
DAVIS, William W., 89, Cambridge, Dorchester County, October 29, 1905.
DAVIS, Wilson, 74, engineer, Baltimore City, November 6, 1892.
DAVISON, William, 71, manufacturer, Baltimore City, October 18, 1881.
DAVISON, Captain Wilmer, 60, Baltimore City, May 15, 1909.
DAVY, Henry, 83, Somerset County, August 19, 1893.
DAWES, Captain Joseph D., 47, mariner, Baltimore City, June 1, 1885.
DAY, Albert, 69, manufacturer, Baltimore City, November 7, 1904.
DAY, Rev. Hamilton (M.P.), 80, Baltimore City, June 15, 1900.
DAY, Ira, Sr., n.a., Baltimore City, March 5, 1896.
DAY, Robert O., 71, Gaithersburg, Montgomery County, December 17, 1913.
DAY, Washington, 81, Montgomery County, December 24, 1905.
DAY, Dr. William C., n.a., chemist, Baltimore City, August 11, 1905.
DAY, Judge William T., n.a., Ellicott City, Howard County, January 26, 1914.
DAYTON, C____ F____, 50, Cumberland, Allegany County, March 14, 1908.
DEACON, John, 75, grocer, Baltimore City, March 2, 1895.
DEALE, Rev. John S. (M.E.), 59, Baltimore City, April 19, 1885.
DEAN, George A., Sr., 57, manufacturer, Baltimore City, February 25, 1902.
DEAN, Morris M., 82, Baltimore City, August 21, 1909.
DEAN, Richard, 84, decorator, Baltimore City, January 8, 1904.
DEAN, Captain W____ H____, n.a., Cambridge, Dorchester County, August 18, 1912.
DEAVER, J____ S____, 36, druggist, black, Baltimore City, December 8, 1881.
DEAVER, S____ N____, 65, druggist, black, Baltimore City, February 20, 1884.

DEBARREDA, F____ L____, 58, of Baltimore City, died on February 15, 1883, at San Francisco.
DE BEER, Solomon, 62, retired merchant, Baltimore City, February 19, 1902.
DE BINNUM, Sister M____ P____, 74, Baltimore City, June 27, 1913.
DEBUTTS, Dr. John, 66, Queen Anne's County, May 19, 1894.
DECAMP, Henry, 88, bookbinder, Baltimore City, June 14, 1891.
DECKER, Alonzo, 44, manufacturer, Baltimore City, December 26, 1892.
DECOURCEY, Rev. W____ H____, 87, Baltimore City, April 6, 1911.
DEEFUR, George J., 70, manufacturer, Baltimore City, April 19, 1906.
DEEMS, General James M., 83, Baltimore City, April 18, 1901.
DERR, Dr. Hamilton K., 61, Hagerstown, Washington County, February 12, 1913.
DEETER, L____ A____, 59, decorator, Baltimore City, March 14, 1906.
DEFORD, Benjamin F., 61, merchant, Baltimore City, June 12, 1897.
DEFORD, George T., 60, merchant, Baltimore City, January 19, 1883.
DEFORD, Thomas, 68, manufacturer, Baltimore City, June 2, 1901.
DEFORD, William, 40, sugar executive, Baltimore City, November 6, 1893.
DEFORD, William Y., 60, merchant, Baltimore City, August 28, 1891.
DE GARMENDIA, C____ G____, 62, Baltimore City, November 27, 1894.
DEGOEY, Captain Charles C., n.a., mariner, Baltimore City, October 15, 1882.
DEIBEL, Peter, 66, merchant, Baltimore City, May 28, 1882.
DE KATOW, A____, 57, bookseller, Baltimore City, May 17, 1892.
DELACOUR, Lewis J., 48, Baltimore City, July 8, 1898.
DELAMATER, L____, 70, Hagerstown, Washington County, February 15, 1908.
DELANEY, Captain E____, 82, Baltimore City, November 7, 1911.
DELANEY, Right Rev. J____ B____, 41, R.C. bishop, died at Manchester, New Hampshire, on June 11, 1906.
DELANEY, Rev. John T. (R.C.), 52, Baltimore City, April 4, 1895.
DELANTY, William, 64, former police captain, Baltimore City, July 26, 1887.
DELAPLAINE, W____ T____, 35, ed____, Frederick, Frederick County, February 19, 1895.
DELAPLANE, J____ E____, 77, retired merchant, Baltimore City, January 24, 1902.
DELASHMUTT, J____ M____, 72, Frederick, Frederick County, October 2, 1908.

DELAWDER, George W., n.a., Garrett County, September 9, 1906.
DELCHER, E_____ W_____, 68, merchant, Baltimore City, December 3, 1893.
DELCHER, Dr. Edward W., Jr., 51, Shadyside, June 22, 1914.
DELLA, Charles M., n.a., clerk, Baltimore City, July 23, 1902.
DE LOUGHERY, Dr. Edward, 77(?), physician, Baltimore City, November 18, 1885.
DELPHEY, William, n.a., hotelier, Baltimore City, July 31, 1898.
DEMENT, Captain William F., 80, Confederate officer, LaPlata, Charles County, May 31, 1907.
DEMING, Captain Martin, 88, retired, Baltimore City, June 24, 1885.
DEMPSEY, John B., 45, court clerk, Baltimore City, February 21, 1887.
DEMPSEY, John F., n.a., clerk, Baltimore City, April 30, 1883.
DENIS, Rev. Peter P. (R.C.), 83, president, St. Charles College, Howard County, March 2, 1903.
DENISON, Captain D_____ S_____, 53, of Baltimore City, died in New York City, July 1, 1898.
DENISON, J_____ M_____, 80, Baltimore City, October 12, 1908.
DENKIN, William M., 54, pilot, Baltimore City, July 25, 1881.
DENMEAD, Adam, 44, attorney, presumably Baltimore City, July 29, 1898.
DENMEAD, Edward B., 62, Baltimore City, June 15, 1896.
DENMEAD, Francis, 62, maltster, Baltimore City, July 25, 1891.
DENNING, John N., 70, retired, Baltimore City, August 29, 1883.
DENNIS, Captain Edward P., 75, Howard County, June 23, 1904.
DENNIS, George R., 72, Frederick, Frederick County, August 23, 1902.
DENNIS, H_____ E_____, 82, Howard County, March 12, 1909.
DENNIS, James Upshur, 76, attorney, Princess Anne, Somerset County, June 22, 1900.
DENNIS, O_____, 87, former Baltimore City Councilman, August 20, 1892.
DENNIS, Dr. Stephen P., 73, Salisbury, Wicomico County, March 15, 1900.
DENNY, Alonzo D., 82, retired entertainer, Baltimore City, April 7, 1904.
DENNY, George B., 68, Baltimore City, November 27, 1902.
DENNY, John, 67, undertaker, Baltimore City, April 22, 1894.
DENSON, Alexander J., 63, builder, Baltimore City, September 23, 1902.
DENSON, Isaac M., 74, retired, Baltimore City, February 22, 1885.
DENT, John F., 84, St. Mary's County, January 7, 1898.
DENTRY, Dr. Henry H., 73, Baltimore City, November 17, 1913.
DEPKIN, Ernest A., 63, retired tailor, Baltimore City, May 6, 1906.
DEPKIN, Henry, 74, Baltimore City, November 24, 1907.
DERENBERGER, J_____ H_____, 80, retired manufacturer, Baltimore City, July 13, 1902.

DERR, Martin, 92, retired builder, Baltimore City, March 8, 1904.
DES FORGES, John P., 55, bookseller, Baltimore City.

DESH, John J., 45, hotelier, Baltimore City, November 28, 1895.
DETRICK, Louis F., 75, manufacturer, Baltimore City, October 12, 1906.
DEVRIES, Henry O., 77, Howard County, July 30, 1902.
DEVRIES, J____ O____, 74, Westminster, Carroll County, March 15, 1912.
DEVRIES, Samuel K. G., 51, merchant, Baltimore City, August 27, 1903.
DEVRIES, William R., 62, retired merchant, Baltimore City, February 21, 1902.
DEWLING, Dr. Isaiah, 54, U.S. Navy (Ret.), May 28, 1894.
DIAMOND, John, 40, reporter, Baltimore City, May 14, 1883.
DIAZ, Don Carlos, 45, Spanish Consul, Baltimore City, November 17, 1893.
DICE, Rev. John C., 71, Baltimore City, April 5, 1892.
DICKEL, H____ L____, n.a., Confederate veteran, Baltimore City, April 5, 1910.
DICKERSON, W____ H____, 74, Dickerson, Montgomery County, July 19, 1912.
DICKEY, Charles E., 72, retired, Baltimore City, February 4, 1905.
DICKEY, William J., 81, bank president, Baltimore City, August 13, 1896.
DICKINSON, Dr. Charles J., 22, physician, Baltimore City, December 10, 1894.
DICKSON, Rev. C____ (Presbyterian), 65, Baltimore City, September 11, 1881.
DICKSON, William 76, retired, Baltimore City, July 29, 1897.
DIDIER, Charles P., 30, artist, Baltimore City, March 24, 1900.
DIDIER, Rev. Edmund (R.C.), 70, Baltimore City, May 18, 1903.
DIDIER, Eugene L., 75, Baltimore City, September 8, 1913.
DIDIER, Henry A., 55, insurance agent, Baltimore City, July 3, 1883.
DIDUSCH, Joseph, 86, sculptor, Baltimore City, December 31, 1909.
DIEHL, John 76, Westminster, Carroll County, May 23, 1900.
DIETEL, George (The Fat Man), 37, Baltimore City, January 1, 1892.
DIETER, John A., 47, merchant, Baltimore City, November 13, 1899.
DIETRICH, John H., 40, merchant, Baltimore City, June 15, 1899.
DIETRICH, Leonard, 79, retired, Baltimore City, March 20, 1894.
DIETSCH, John, 68, tailor, Baltimore City, May 10, 1902.
DIFFENBAUGH, A____ H____, 54, teacher, Carroll County, February 14, 1894.
DIFFENBAUGH, J____ H____, 87, Carroll County, November 3, 1893.
DIFFENBAUGH, John T., 73, Carroll County, January 29, 1900.
DIFFENDERFER, James P., 79, Baltimore City, December 14, 1907.
DIFFENDERFER, Dr. William H., 75, physician, Baltimore City, July 7, 1897.
DIFFENDERFER, William, 58, Baltimore City, May 22, 1908.

DIGGS, Daniel E., 55, police sergeant, Baltimore City, March 3, 1890.
DIGGS, Eugene, 59, State Librarian of Texas, died at Austin, June 29, 1899; a native of Charles County.
DIGGS, J_____ Ross, n.a., Baltimore City, March 7, 1911.
DIGGS, John R., 69, merchant, Baltimore City, April 26, 1884.
DIGGS, Richard H., 73, retired, Baltimore City, October 31, 1885.
DIGGS, Ross Miles, 20, Baltimore City, December 5, 1910.
DIGGS, William J., 81, Baltimore City, January 24, 1909.
DILL, Frederick, 81, retiree, Baltimore City, March 27, 1906.
DILLEHUNT, John T., 60, Baltimore City, July 12, 1895.
DIMPFEL, W_____ O'Sullivan, 58, Talbot County, December 6, 1904.
DINGER, Rev. F_____ W_____ (Methodist), 74, Baltimore City, April 26, 1895.
DINNEEN, John H., 50, attorney, Baltimore City, April 7, 1903.
DINSMORE, Mrs. Margaret, 92, Baltimore City, August 21, 1882.
DIRICKSON, Dr. James C., n.a., Snow Hill, Worcester County, January 4, 1907.
DIRICKSON, Levin, n.a., Worcester County, August 31, 1894.
DISHAROON, E_____ W_____, 70, Salisbury, Wicomico County, October 3, 1905.
DISNEY, J_____ T_____, 60, Baltimore City, December 17, 1911.
DISNEY, O_____ M_____, 75, former Baltimore City Councilman, February 24, 1893.
DISNEY, Richard P., 70, merchant, Baltimore City, October 13, 1897.
DISSTON, Horace C., 46, Philadelphia manufacturer, died in Cecil County, June 13, 1900.
DITCH, John, 87, retired, Baltimore City, November 29, 1894.
DITMAN, Thomas M., 71, merchant, Baltimore City, July 23, 1891.
DITTUS, J_____ F_____, 63, Confederate veteran, Pikesville, Baltimore County, April 26, 1909.
DITTY, C_____ Irving, 50, lawyer, Baltimore City, October 3, 1887.
DIX, J_____ Franklin, 67, retired, Baltimore City, April 15, 1888.
DIX, William C., 46, Equitable Society, Baltimore City, April 15, 1901.
DIXON, John A., 85, Baltimore City, October 6, 1909.
DIXON, John B., 47, merchant, Baltimore City, April 10, 1892.
DIXON, R_____ W_____ K_____, 76, merchant, Baltimore City, October 19, 1898.
DIXON, Thomas, 67, architect, Baltimore City, July 25, 1886.
DIXON, Thomas J., 81, banker, Princess Anne, Somerset County, July 30, 1903.
DIXON, William T., 62, banker/merchant, Baltimore City, August 16, 1904.
DIPPEL, H_____ G_____, 33, undertaker, Baltimore City, April 16, 1902.
DOANE, Albert R., 47, mariner, Baltimore City, December 11, 1882.
DOBBIN, George, 81, former judge, Baltimore City, May 28, 1891.

DOBBIN, John, Sr., n.a., liveryman, Baltimore City, November 23, 1880.
DOBLER, Gustavus A., 64, paper merchant, Baltimore City, September 4, 1903.
DOBSON, Colonel George H., Mount Washington, Baltimore County, August 16, 1913.
DOBSON, John A., 53, merchant, Baltimore City, October 19, 1882.
DOCKERY, Colonel Oliver H., 77, Baltimore City, March 21, 1906.
DODD, General Levi A., 68, Baltimore City, August 5, 1901.
DODGE, Dr. Augustus W., 49, physician, Baltimore City, March __, 1887.
DODSON, Dr. J_____ F_____, n.a., physician, Baltimore City, October 29, 1893.
DODSON, Richard S., 58, retired hotelier, Baltimore City, March 23, 1897.
DOENJES, Andrew, 63, manufacturer, Baltimore City, October 28, 1882.
DOERKSEN, Dr. J_____ L_____, 25, physician, Baltimore City, December 9, 1883.
DOERKSEN, Rev. Jacob (United Brethren), 69, August 28, 1891.
DOHERTY, William, 85, retired, Baltimore City, January 16, 1886.
DOHME, Charles E., 78, Baltimore City, December 7, 1911.
DOHME, Cornelius P., 67, drug manufacturer, Baltimore City, February 17, 1906.
DOHME, Dr. G_____ C_____, 42, physician, Baltimore City, February 11, 1883.
DOHME, William F., 66, Baltimore City, March 18, 1913.
DOLBY, Augustus R., 66, Baltimore City, August 9, 1913.
DOLL, Melville E., 77, Frederick, Frederick County, April 7, 1914.
DOLL, Rev. Penfield, 62, Baltimore City, September 9, 1879.
DONAHUE, William 72, Confederate veteran, Pikesville, Baltimore County, May 1, 1912.
DONALDSON, Rear Admiral Edward, 72, Baltimore City, May 15, 1889.
DONALDSON, Dr. Francis, 68, physician, Baltimore City, December 9, 1891.
DONALDSON, Genral J_____ L_____, 72, U.S. Army (Ret.), Baltimore City, November 4, 1885.
DONALDSON, John, 80, retired, Baltimore City, November 14, 1886.
DONALDSON, Samuel C., n.a., librarian, Baltimore City, January 24, 1898.
DONALDSON, T_____, Jr., 67, Baltimore City, April 3, 1910.
DONALDSON, T_____ W_____, 70, Baltimore City, October 8, 1911.
DONALDSON, Walter A., 75, Union veteran, Baltimore City, February 7, 1903.
DONALLEN, Andrew, 93, retired, Baltimore City, October 18, 1902.
DONAVIN, Dr. M_____ W_____, 77, physician, Baltimore City, June 4, 1905.
DONELSON, James L., 77, manufacturer, Baltimore City, July 11, 1902.
DONNELL, Captain George S., 64, Light House Service, Baltimore City, July 25, 1904.
DONNELL, William, 77, retired, Baltimore City, October 20, 1887.
DONNELLY, James, 70, Baltimore City, June 10, 1896.

DONNELLY, James, 73, former super Baltimore City Hall, September 10, 1905.
DONNELLY, James P., 72, real estate, Baltimore City, November 22, 1882.
DONOHUE, Dennis, 81, late British Consul in Baltimore, died at San Francisco, December 11, 1896.
DONOHUE, James, 82, retired, Baltimore City, June 19, 1885.
DONOVAN, Rev. T____ B____, 44, Baltimore City, January 13, 1908.
DOREMUS, Peter B., 87, builder, Baltimore City, November 16, 1895.
DORMAN, J____ F____ W____, 57, manufacturer, Baltimore City, March 26, 1893.
DORR, Caspar, 67, retired, Baltimore City, August 26, 1884.
DORSETT, Josias H., 71, merchant, Baltimore City, August 26, 1902.
DORSEY, Allen, 87, retired, Baltimore City, June 28, 1903.
DORSEY, Colonel Aug____, 72, Rockville, Montgomery County, September 5, 1911.
DORSEY, C____ W____, 76, Confederate veteran, Pikesville, Baltimore County, December 10, 1908.
DORSEY, Colonel Daniel, n.a., hotelier, Baltimore City, September 14, 1885.
DORSEY, Edward B., 69, civil engineer, Baltimore City, February 6, 1900.
DORSEY, Franklin M., 59, Ellicott City, Howard County, April 3, 1901.
DORSEY, Hammond, 56, Howard County, January 9, 1898.
DORSEY, Dr. J____ O____, 67, Broome Island, Calvert County, January 9, 1910.
DORSEY, James I., 83, merchant, Baltimore City, August 30, 1892.
DORSEY, John 95, Laurel, Prince George's County, November 25, 1900.
DORSEY, John R., 79, Baltimore County, April 19, 1905.
DORSEY, John W., 24, clerk, Baltimore City, December 4, 1882.
DORSEY, Joseph, 57, hotelier, Baltimore City, May 10, 1895.
DORSEY, Nicholas, 84, Howard County, July 15, 1896.
DORSEY, Owen, 87, reaper inventor, Howard County, February 16, 1897.
DORSEY, Miss Priscilla M., 80, Ellicott City, Howard County, March 18, 1892.
DORSEY, R____ H____, 81, Frederick Frederick County, November 18, 1911.
DORSEY, Reuben M., 70, Howard County, February 3, 1899.
DORSEY, Richard, 60, Howard County, February 25, 1901.
DORSEY, Dr. Robert, 91, physician, Baltimore City, June 28, 1889.
DORSEY, Dr. Robert W., 66, physician, Baltimore City, February 4, 1900.
DORSEY, Dr. T____ R____, 60, physician, Calvert County, May 28, 1893.
DORSEY, Upton W., 64, Baltimore City, August 4, 1907.
DORSEY, W____ T____, 79, Glenwood, Howard County, October 12, 1912.

DORSEY, William H., 69, bank officer, Baltimore City, March 9, 1892.
DOSH, Rev. J____ H____ C____ (M.E.), 60, Baltimore City, April 16, 1881.
DOUB, D____ R____, 65, Hagerstown, Washington County, May 29, 1904.
DOUD, John S., 34, actor, Baltimore City, April 18, 1902.
DOUD, Oliver W., 36, actor, Baltimore City, December 10, 1891.
DOUGHERTY, Rev. J____ J____ (R.C.), 58, Baltimore City, April 14, 1885.
DOUGHERTY, Daniel, 55, contractor, Baltimore City, August 18, 1904.
DOUGHERTY, Reginald E. S., n.a., merchant, Baltimore City, June 2, 1904.
DOUGHERTY, Rev. Thomas (M.E.), 55, Baltimore City, September 15, 1885.
DOUGHERTY, Thomas, 79, merchant, Baltimore City, December 3, 1881.
DOUGHERTY, Thomas B., 63, printer, Baltimore City, February 24, 1901.
DOUGLAS, General Henry Kyd, 63, Hagerstown, Washington County, December 18, 1903.
DOVE, B____ F____, 75, B. & O. Railroad, Baltimore City, February 3, 1881.
DOWELL, John, 76, retired, Baltimore City, July 28, 1886.
DOWNS, Rev. Wilford (M.E.), 57, Baltimore City, October 12, 1884.
DOYLE, C____ C____, 24, Tivoli medalist, Baltimore City, June 1, 1884.
DOYLE, John F., 40, politician, Baltimore City, January 11, 1900.
DOYLE, Matthew, 65, contractor, Baltimore City, April 28, 1894.
DOYLE, Samuel B., 64, express messenger, Baltimore City, June 17, 1893.
DOYLE, Thomas G., 70, bookseller, Baltimore City, March 22, 1904.
DOWNING, Captain John, 103, at Dover, Delaware, November 30, 1909.
DOWNS, W____ H____, 83, Glen Burnie, Anne Arundel County, December 9, 1911.
DRANE, James, 71, grocer, Baltimore City, June 27, 1894.
DRAWBAUGH, Alexander C., 76, Cumberland, Allegany County, April 23, 1909.
DRESEL, Werner, 64, retired, Baltimore City, June 24, 1884.
DROESCHER, Adolph, 44, merchant, Baltimore City, May 8, 1880.
DROST, G____ A____, 77, merchant, Baltimore City, December 19, 1902.
DROSTE, William H., 54, deputy police marshal, Baltimore City, September 16, 1893.
DRYDEN, F____ H____, n.a., Pocomoke, Worcester County, March 11, 1908.
DRYDEN, George J., 76, Snow Hill, Worcester County, August 10, 1905.
DRYDEN, Joshua, 87, "Old Defender," Baltimore City, February 15, 1879.
DRYDEN, Joshua R., 84, retired merchant, February 1, 1903.

DRYDEN, Littleton T., 75, Crisfield, Somerset County, September 30, 1912.
DRYDEN, Robert W., 62, merchant, Baltimore City, October 20, 1882.
DRYDEN, William H., 63, merchant, Baltimore City, October 30, 1896.
DRYSDALE, Rev. Alexander J., 45, bishop-elect of Easton, Talbot County, died August 30, 1886, at Waukesha, Wisconsin.
DUBOIS, Edward S., 67, clerk, Baltimore City, September 19, 1905.
DUBOIS, Emil J., 78, barber, Baltimore City, November 20, 1882.
DUBREUL, Rev. Joseph Paul, 62, Baltimore City, April 20, 1878.
DUCKER, George E., 64, merchant, Baltimore City, July 20, 1895.
DUCKETT, Reuben G., 79, retired, Baltimore City, April 1, 1905.
DUER, Douglas H., 62, Baltimore City, May 16, 1913.
DUER, John 85, retired merchant, Baltimore City, October 29, 1901.
DUER, R_____ A_____, 64, steamboat captain, Baltimore City, September 12, 1904.
DUFFY, Charles, 73, Baltimore City hotelier died at Williamsport, Pennsylvania, February 20, 1893.
DUFFY, Daniel, 72, Baltimore City, July 29, 1898.
DUFFY, Edward, 61, judge, Baltimore City, July 1, 1892.
DUFFY, Michael, 72, merchant, Baltimore City, February 18, 1900.
DUGAN, Cumberland, 85, Ilchester, Howard County, December 12, 1914.
DUGAN, Hugh, n.a., merchant, Baltimore City, October 31, 1895.
DUGAN, Pierre C., 55, realtor, Baltimore City, October 6, 1893.
DUGDALE, William, 65, ship broker, Baltimore City, January 18, 1899.
DUGGAN, Rev. Francis P. (R.C.), 60, Baltimore City, July 31, 1903.
DUGGAN, Patrick, 85, retired, Baltimore City, March 1, 1905.
DUKE, Dr. Alexander, 98, Battle Creek, Calvert County, February 6, 1885.
DUKE, Dr. Augustin W., 76, Govanstown, June 8, 1904.
DUKE, J_____ E_____, 75, Cumberland, Allegany County, February 28, 1912.
DUKE, James B., 78, retired hotelier, Baltimore City, November 19, 1902.
DUKE, Jennie Abell, n.a., Baltimore City, August 1, 1912.
DUKEHART, Edward W., 81, manufacturer, Baltimore City, November 1, 1888.
DUKEHART, John, 78, Baltimore City, December 17, 1878.
DUKEHART, John P., 69, conductor, Baltimore City, September 27, 1892.
DUKEHART, Joseph R., 82, retired, Baltimore City, February 1, 1894.
DUKEHART, Robert W., 68, manufacturer, Baltimore City, January 20, 1879.
DUKEHART, Thomas M., 73, retired, Baltimore City, May 10, 1902.
DUDLEY, Hamilton L., 56, Confederate veteran, July 13, 1902.
DUKER, Herman O., 38, manufacturer, Baltimore City, October 16, 1902.
DUKER, John H., 64, manufacturer, Baltimore City, November 8, 1900.
DULANY, H_____ Rozier, 65, attorney, Baltimore City, April 25, 1899.

DULANY, Walter, 57, merchant, Baltimore City, November 19, 1897.
DULANY, William J. C., 58, publisher, Baltimore City, February 13, 1901.
DULSKI, Rev. Joseph J., 41, priest, Baltimore City, May 9, 1906.
DUMAR, Andrew G., 59, bookkeeper, Baltimore City, December 22, 1900.
DUNAN, Winfield S., 45, merchant, Baltimore City, January 10, 1885.
DUNCAN, Charles V., 71, realtor, Baltimore City, May 17, 1904.
DUNCAN, John G., 30, cattle dealer, Baltimore City, August 16, 1878.
DUNGAN, R____ E____, 54, engineer, Cumberland, Allegany County, December 16, 1908.
DUNLAP, Charles, 75, merchant, Baltimore City, February 23, 1881.
DUNLEVY, Andrew F., 68, auditor, B. & O. Railroad, Baltimore City, October 26, 1898.
DUNLOP, Joseph O., 38, copper mining, Baltimore City, September 8, 1880.
DUNN, Andrew, 77, tailor, Baltimore City, February 17, 1899.
DUNN, C____ J____, 65, Baltimore City, January 13, 1912.
DUNN, Charles, 60, builder, Baltimore City, December 9, 1890.
DUNN, Dr. E____ H____, n.a., physician, Mount Washington, Baltimore County, August 16, 1893.
DUNN, E____ T____, 77, paymaster general, U.S. Navy, Baltimore City, September 27, 1887.
DUNN, Captain Goerge H., shipmaster, February 27, 1902.
DUNN, Captain James R., 53, Baltimore City, March 24, 1914.
DUNN, James T., 34, policeman, Baltimore City, June 20, 1894.
DUNN, John, 67, retired, Baltimore City, March 19, 1903.
DUNNINGTON, William A., 79, retired, Baltimore City, March 15, 1896.
DURKEE, Henry H., 69, policeman, Baltimore City, November 30, 1901.
DUTROW, Samuel, 69, Frederick, Frederick County, May 26, 1905.
DUTTON, George H., 91, retired, Baltimore City, February 8, 1901.
DUVAL, Algernon S., 66, Baltimore City, September 29, 1913.
DUVAL, C____ F____ W____, 79, Annapolis, Anne Arundel County, October 11, 1912.
DUVAL, George W., 82, Carroll County, August 1, 1905.
DUVAL, James Hl, 48, insurance broker, Baltimore City, October 11, 1901.
DUVALL, Dr. E____ P____, 70, Annapolis, Anne Arundel County, September 5, 1901.
DUVALL, Charles, 68, merchant, Baltimore City, July 1, 1898.
DUVALL, Edward B., Sr., n.a., inspector, Baltimore City, July 29, 1881.
DUVALL, George W., 54, Baltimore City, April 18, 1897.
DUVALL, George W., 77, Prince George's County, November 15, 1902.
DUVALL, Grafton, 79, Baltimore City, November 7, 1909.
DUVALL, Henry, 74, justice of the peace, Baltimore City, May 29, 1894.
DUVALL, Jacob I., 66, agent, Baltimore City, May 20, 1899.
DUVALL, John H., 76, retired, Baltimore City, July 10, 1884.
DUVALL, L____ M____, 58, lawyer, Baltimore City, December 24, 1912.
DUVALL, Dr. Msrius, 73, U.S. Navy, February 21, 1891.

DUVALL, Richard, 93, Baltimore City, October 23, 1893.
DUVALL, Richard T., 70, Baltimore City, October 2, 1913.
DUVALL, S_____ T)____, 39, deputy Baltimore City register, May 6, 1884.
DUVALL, Thomas J., 78, merchant, Baltimore City, September 14, 1891.
DUVALL, Thomas J., n.a., Annapolis, Anne Arundel County, April 10, 1900.
DWINELLE, Dr. James Elliott, 72, physician, Baltimore City, July 18, 1902.
DWYER, John, 76, manufacturer, Baltimore City, August 4, 1899.

EADER, August, 87, Frederick, Frederick County, February 11, 1907.
EARECKSON, Charles F., 65, merchant, Baltimore City, December 25, 1899.
EARHART, George W., 60, former police captain, Baltimore City, December 13, 1900.
EARLE, Dr. John Charles, 78, Easton, Talbot County, May 17, 1902.
EARLE, Richard Tilghman, 78, Queen Anne's County, January 20, 1895.
EARLE, Samuel T., 86, Queen Anne's County, October 16, 1904.
EARLY, John D., 73, Baltimore City, November 26, 1913.
EARLY, T_____ J_____, 76, Hagerstown, Washington County, February 21, 1910.
EARNSHAW, Al_____, 52, president, Earn Line, Baltimore City, July 24, 1896.
EARNSHAW, G_____ W_____, 55, Hagerstown, Washington County, December 21, 1909.
EASTER, Charles E., 38, merchant, Baltimore City, July 25, 1880.
EASTER, Hamilton, 85, merchant, Baltimore City, April 12, 1895.
EASTER, Hamilton, 39, of Baltimore City died in California, March 23, 1903.
EASTER, James W., 70, retired merchant, Baltimore City, April 1, 1900.
EASTER, Mrs. Margaret Elizabeth, 55, poetess, Baltimore City, October 28, 1894.
EASTER, Philip C., 40, merchant, Baltimore City, January 20, 1897.
EASTMAN, Dr. Lewis M., Sr., 64, Baltimore City, June 27, 1901.
EASTON, George W., 41, Laurel, Prince George's County, February 22, 1905.
EATON, Charles J. M., 85, trustee, Peabody Institute, January 13, 1893.
EATON, Samuel, 76, Stablersville, Baltimore County, March 10, 1910.
EATON, William H., 60, retired, Baltimore City, February 1, 1895.
EAVEY, Henry S. 84, banker, Hagerstown, Washington County, December 23, 1903.
EBAUGH, Frank, 70, brass manufacturer, Baltimore City, December 26, 1904.
EBELING, Rev. George W. (Lutheran), 79, Baltimore City, September 25, 1901.
ECCLES, Samuel, n.a., ex-Councilman, Baltimore City, November 21, 1906.
ECCLESTON, Charles A., 31, Montgomery County, January 24, 1901.
ECCLESTON, Rev. J_____ H_____, n.a., Baltimore City, April 1, 1911.
ECKHARDT, Philip, 46, stereotyper, Baltimore City, July 11, 1902.
ECKHARDT, William, 62, manufacturer, Baltimore City, May 4(?), 1901.

EDELEN, Richard H., 66, lawyer, Charles County, May 2, 1898.
EDESON, George R., 60, actor of Baltimore died in Philadelphia, April 18, 1899.
EDGAR, John M., 74, attorney, Baltimore City, March 28, 1886.
EDMONDS, William H., n.a., editor, Baltimore City, March 29, 1898.
EDMONDSON, Joseph A., 73, retired, Baltimore City, May 16, 1891.
EDMUNDS, Professor J_____ R_____, 60, Baltimore City, March 27, 1910.
EDMUNDS, James R., 68, banker, Baltimore City, April 20, 1911.
EDMUNDS, Dr. Page, 65, physician, Baltimore City, December 4, 1893.
EDWARDS, Charles G., 40, professor, Baltimore City, October 12, 1884.
EDWARDS, James, 70, Rising Sun, Cecil County, February 24, 1912.
EDWARDS, John R., 66, manufacturer, Baltimore City, August 3, 1899.
EDWARDS, LeRoy, 80, retired merchant, Baltimore City, September 21, 1880.
EDWARDS, S_____ J_____, 68, Cumberland, Allegany County, April 18, 1908.
EDWARDS, Thomas J., 48, teacher, Baltimore City, December 4, 1888.
EGERTON, General C_____ C_____, 75, Baltimore County, January 19, 1893.
EGERTON, William A., n.a., packer, Baltimore City, September 21, 1900.
EGGLESTON, Joseph, 78, builder, Baltimore City, April 4, 1892.
EGGLESTON, Rev. W_____ S_____, 94, Winchester, Anne Arundel County, April 25, 1908.
EHLERS, H_____ C_____, 94, Baltimore City, November 7, 1910.
EHLERS, Captain J_____ D_____, 76, engraver, Baltimore City, January 2, 1910.
EHRMAN, Lewis, 75, Baltimore City, February 6, 1907.
EHRMAN, Charles H., 76, retired, Baltimore City, January 1, 1899.
EICHELBERGER, Albert G., 73, Prohibitionist leader, Baltimore City, February 17, 1906.
EICHELBERGER, B_____ G_____, n.a., Frederick, Frederick City, August 12, 1909.
EICHELBERGER, E_____ C_____, 55, attorney, Baltimore City, January 2, 1906.
EICHELBERGER, Dr. James W., 71, presumably Baltimore City, February 23, 1913.
EICHELBERGER, Otho W., 79, merchant, Baltimore City, January 30, 1879.
EIGENBROT, Henry, 60, brewer, Baltimore City, April 19, 1906.
EINWAECHTER, Adam W., 91, Baltimore City, July 21, 1910.
EISGELT, Mrs. Caroline, 100, Baltimore City, November 29, 1895.
EISMAN, John, 62, merchant, Baltimore City, August 15, 1902.
ELBRING, H_____ R_____, 58, former superintendent, Schutz Park, Baltimore City, October 7, 1883.
ELDER, Francis W., 81, retired, Baltimore City, August 13, 1889.
ELDER, Hillary J., 35, policeman, Baltimore City, December 31, 1900.
ELDER, James A., 68, Emmitsburg, Frederick County, September 10, 1898.
ELDER, Robert N., 35, banker, Baltimore City, January 14, 1903.

ELDER, Thomas S., 81, of Baltimore City died in New Orleans, November 3, 1898.
ELIASON, T_____ W_____, n.a., Kent County landowner, August 28, 1893.
ELLEGOOD, Robert D., 46, postmaster, Salisbury, Wicomico County, February 5, 1895.
ELLERBROCK, Dr. C_____ F_____, 27, physician, Baltimore City, September 2, 1905.
ELLERBROCK, John B., 56, organist, Baltimore City, November 11, 1901.
ELLICOTT, Henry W., n.a., retired, Baltimore City, March 19, 1895.
ELLICOTT, General John, 55, engineer, Baltimore City, January 11, 1890.
ELLICOTT, Jonathan H., 80, merchant, Baltimore City, March 3, 1881.
ELLICOTT, T_____ P_____, 78, Baltimore City, September 17, 1908.
ELLICOTT, Mrs. William M., n.a., Baltimore City, May 14, 1914.
ELLINGER, Jacob, 63, bank president, Baltimore City, April 13, 1882.
ELLINGER, Samuel, 79, realtor, Baltimore City, June 28, 1891.
ELLIOTT, Edward, 56, merchant, Baltimore City, December 16, 1892.
ELLIOTT, Joseph P., n.a., broker, Baltimore City, January 14, 1898.
ELLIOTT, Lewis, 84, Taneytown, Carroll County, May 21, 1893.
ELLIOTT, Robert, 91, Baltimore City, June 12, 1912.
ELLIOTT, Professor William, Jr., 68, Baltimore City College, July 1, 1890.
ELTERMAN, Frederick, 74, retired, Baltimore City, November 8, 1884.
ELY, Mahlon S., 88, retired, Baltimore City, January 31, 1885.
ELY, William T., 55, druggist, Baltimore City, September 15, 1881.
ELZEY, Ellen I, 77, widow of General Arnold Elzey, Baltimore City, February 23, 1902.
EMERSON, John L., n.a., fire chief, Baltimore City, November 17, 1914.
EMERY, Captain G_____ E_____, 68, mariner, Baltimore City, March 6, 1887.
EMERY, J_____ B_____, 83, past grandmaster, I.O.O.F., Baltimore City, November 25, 1889.
EMICH, Wesley, 78, Baltimore City, March 21, 1909.
EMMART, A_____ D_____, 74, Baltimore City, June 12, 1910.
EMMART, Frederick, 64, Baltimore City, July 24, 1912.
EMMART, Nelson, 81, Catonsville, Baltimore County, October 20, 1901.
EMMERICH, Christian, 84, retired, Baltimore City, February 16, 1904.
EMMERICH, J_____ S_____, 28, salesman, Baltimore City, April 10, 1904.
EMMERT, Samuel, n.a., State Senator, Hagerstown, Washington County, December 6, 1914.
EMMONS, D_____ W_____, 78, Kensington, Montgomery County, April 19, 1905.
EMMONS, Herman L., 64, attorney, Baltimore City, April 9, 1897.
EMORY, Arthur, 60, merchant, Baltimore City, January 29, 1901.
EMORY, Blanchard, 52, Centreville, Queen Anne's County, September 21, 1907.
EMORY, Daniel, n.a., insurance, Baltimore City, February 14, 1886.

EMORY, Frederick, 55, journalist, author, and former official of the U.S. Department of State, Queenstown, Queen Anne's County, September 20, 1908.
EMORY, John K. B., 66, druggist, Baltimore City, March 21, 1896.
EMORY, Captain Robert S., 74, farmer, Kent County, June 1, 1906.
EMORY, T____ R____, 72, Centreville, Queen Anne's County, April 28, 1910.
EMORY, William H. (of A____), 57, realtor, Baltimore City, February 25, 1901.
EMORY, Wilmer, 66, Baltimore City, October 4, 1913.
EMRICH, John P., 68, machinist, Baltimore City, December 11, 1884.
ENGEL, Gottlieb, 77, gardener, Baltimore City, October 25, 1883.
ENGELBRIGHT, M____, 68, Hagerstown, Washington County, March 18, 1910.
ENGELHARDT, J____, 53, brewmaster, Baltimore City, July 19, 1902.
ENGELHAUPT, John, 58, merchant, Baltimore City, April 8, 1903.
ENGLAND, James, 82, retired merchant, Baltimore City, March 12, 1906.
ENGLAND, John G., n.a., Rockville, Montgomery County, February 28, 1913.
ENGLAND, Joseph T., 79, Cecil County, October 23, 1900.
ENGLAND, William, 82, sea captain, Baltimore City, March 15, 1889.
ENGLE, Joseph, 88, retired, Baltimore City, October 31, 1905.
ENGLISH, John R., 64, Baltimore City, January 22, 1893.
ENNIS, James A., 70, Snow Hill, Worcester County, January 28, 1901.
ENSEY, Marcellus P., 65, Baltimore City, March 5, 1896.
ENSIGN, Howard B., 65, president of steamboat line, Baltimore City, June 28, 1891.
ENSOR, Abraham, 89, "Old Defender," Baltimore City, April 22, 1881.
ENSOR, J____ C____, 87, Baltimore City, December 28, 1908.
ENSOR, John, 77, Baltimore County, October 10, 1898.
ENSOR, John H., 80, Baltimore County, March 25, 1903.
EPPLER, John, 51, cooper, Baltimore City, October 4, 1905.
EPSTEIN, Isaac, 77, Baltimore City, December 25, 1912.
ERDMAN, John, 80, Baltimore City, December 13, 1909.
ERDMANN, Adam G., 70, gardener, Baltimore City, October 22, 1878.
ERICH, Dr. Augustus Frederick, 49, physician, Baltimore City, December 6, 1886.
ESCHBACH, Dr. Joseph A., 46, physician, Baltimore City, December 28, 1881.
ESPEY, S____ B____, 82, Catonsville, Baltimore County, August 11, 1912.
ESSENDER, Dr. James, 83, Baltimore City, December 27, 1883.
ESSEX, Captain W____ B____, 76, Baltimore City, June 21, 1910.
ESTES, Charles A., 82, Chestertown, Kent County, January 26, 1912.
ETCHBERGER, James, 88, mariner, Baltimore City, January 27, 1893.
ETCHISON, Frederick, 84, merchant, Baltimore City, November 15, 1902.
EUBANK, Robert W., 59, teacher, Baltimore City, February 17, 1884.

EUKER, William C., 64, cafe proprietor, Baltimore City, June 22, 1902.
EUPHEMIA, Sister Mary, 60, Baltimore City, March 21, 1913.
EVANS, General A_____ W_____, 76, U.S. Army (Ret.), Elkton, Cecil County, April 24, 1906.
EVANS, The Honorable Alexander, 73, former Congressman, Elkton, Cecil County, December 5, 1888.
EVANS, Charles R., 37, captain, Fourth Regiment, January 11, 1904.
EVANS, Daniel T., 67, pilot, Baltimore City, December 6, 1894.
EVANS, Rev. David (M.E.), 80, Baltimore City, July 11, 1890.
EVANS, George, 83, retired, Baltimore City, April 13, 1883.
EVANS, H_____ H_____, 84, Elkton, Cecil County, April 26, 1907.
EVANS, Henry, 80, retired packer, Baltimore City, May 13, 1904.
EVANS, Henry C., 74, Mount Washington, Baltimore County, November 24, 1908.
EVANS, J_____ M_____, 69, judge, Cecil County Orphan's Court, May 8, 1893.
EVANS, Rev. J_____ W_____, 40, Carroll County, November 8, 1902.
EVANS, Jacob H., 45, machinist, Baltimore City, August 1, 1880.
EVANS, John C., 76, Baltimore County, August 26, 1905.
EVANS, Sewell T., 51, supervisor of elections, Wicomico County, May 31, 1903.
EVANS, Thomas, 75, stage carpenter, Baltimore City, May 29, 1887.
EVANS, Dr. Thomas B., 58(?), physician, Baltimore City, October 30, 1891.
EVANS, Thomas G., 65, builder, Baltimore City, May 19, 1880.
EVANS, Thomas H., 65, merchant, Baltimore City, October 21, 1887.
EVANS, Dr. W_____ Roland, 43, druggist, Bel Air, Harford County, September 1, 1906.
EVANS, Dr. William J., 53, physician, Baltimore City, January 11, 1888.
EVANS, William T., 37, pilot, Baltimore City, June 5, 1895.
EVEREST, Joseph, 91, cooper, Baltimore City, December 4, 1882.
EVERIST, Frank S., 60, president, Cecil County School Board, January 13, 1897.
EVERITT, Rev. W_____ L_____ (Presbyterian), 35, Baltimore City, September 5, 1905.
EVERSFIELD, Dr. W_____ O_____, 67, College Park, Prince George's County, January 20, 1908.
EVERSMAN, Frederick, 40, musician, Baltimore City, March 30, 1890.
EWALDT, Augustus, 70, retired, Baltimore City, April 28, 1883.
EWALT, Samuel A., 58, manufacturer, Baltimore City, November 21, 1882.
EWELL, Rev. J_____ E_____ T_____ (M.P.), 68, Baltimore City, November 7, 1902.
EWELL, L_____ P_____, 78, Pocomoke City, Worcester County, November 23, 1912.
EWELL, Dr. L_____ S_____, 82, Cambridge, Dorchester County, January 8, 1909.
EWELL, Dr. Oscar B. B., 49, Crisfield, Somerset County, October 6, 1905.
EWING, Edward E., 77, editor, Cecil County, August 20, 1901.
EWING, William, 72, merchant, Baltimore City, January 28, 1900.
EWING, William P., 79, Elkton, Cecil County, September 5, 1907.

FAEHTZ, Colonel E____ F____ M____, 59, Baltimore City, April 24, 1882.
FAHEY, John T., 44, contractor, Baltimore City, February 13, 1900.
FAHEY, Martin, n.a., undertaker, Baltimore City, August 6, 1906.
FAHNESTOCK, Derick, 81, banker, Baltimore City, May 10, 1903.
FAHNESTOCK, Edward, 82, retired, Baltimore City, May 27, 1904.
FAHRNEY, Dr. Daniel P., 63, Hagerstown, Washington County, March 5, 1905.
FAHRNEY, Dr. Lewis, 48, Hagerstown, Washington County, August 22, 1906.
FAHRNEY, Dr. Peter, n.a., died in Chicago on March 6, 1905.
FAIRALL, William E., 39, grocer, Baltimore City, December 15, 1887.
FAIRBANK, Andrew J., 73, retired, Baltimore City, February 1, 1897
FAIRBANK, Henry T., 73, builder, Baltimore City, November 10, 1902.
FAIRBANK, John, 76, retired, Baltimore City, July 12, 1895.
FAIRBANKS, James A., 75, Baltimore County, February 23, 1898.
FAIRFAX, Donald McNeill, 72, Rear Admiral, U.S. Navy, Hagerstown, Washington County, January 10, 1894.
FAIRFAX, Dr. John Contee, 70, Prince George's County, September 28, 1900.
FAIRLEY, Thomas, n.a., florist, Baltimore City, December 14, 1895.
FAIT, John, 60, merchant, Baltimore City, February 7, 1881.
FALES, Captain Ebenezer C., 74, mariner, Baltimore City, December 6, 1883.
FALLS, J____ Wesley, 69, Elkton, Cecil County, February 17, 1905.
FANGMEYER, J____, 67, merchant, Baltimore City, March 3, 1893.
FANTON, James H., 87, retired, Baltimore City, May 7, 1902.
FARBER, Henry J., 60, merchant, Baltimore City, March 5, 1889.
FARBER, John H., 63, merchant, Baltimore City, October 28, 1900.
FARENHOLD, Captain W____ H____, 60, Baltimore City, October 18, 1905.
FARINGER, Charles H., 33, clerk, Baltimore City, December 10, 1882.
FARLAND, John F., 74, sailmaker, Baltimore City, January 9, 1897.
FARLOW, John T., 65, police justice, Baltimore City, April 12, 1880.
FARNANDIS, Dr. G____ S____, 80, Baltimore City, April 7, 1909.
FARNANDIS, Henry D., 82, attorney, Bel Air, Harford County, March 8, 1900.
FARNANDIS, James D., 79, Bel Air, Harford County, April 9, 1900.
FARNANDIS, Walter, 68, lawyer, Baltimore City, March 12, 1889.
FARQUHARSON, John D., 72, merchant, Baltimore City, April 19, 1882.
FAUL, August, 61, park superintendent, Baltimore City, August 25, 1884.
FAULKNER, John, 98, Tilghman's Island, Talbot County, April 12, 1902.
FAUTH, H____, 71, Catonsville, Baltimore County, May 2, 1909.
FAWCETT, Dr. Christopher, 81, Baltimore City, November 11, 1905.

FAWCETT, Harvey C., 71, Rockville, Montgomery County, February 19, 1907.
FAY, Professor William Wirt, 65, U.S.N.A., Annapolis, Anne Arundel County, April 23, 1898.
FEARHAKE, Adolphus, 73, Frederick, Frederick County, October 7, 1913.
FEAST, John, 85, florist, Baltimore City, June 7, 1885.
FEAST, John E., 60, florist, Baltimore City, January 30, 1888.
FEBIGER, Admiral John C., 77, Easton, Talbot County, October 9, 1898.
FECHTIG, C____ C____, 61, Hagerstown, Washington County, November 23, 1907.
FECKLY, Roger, 74, Elkton, Cecil County, July 20, 1905.
FEELEMYER, George W., 61, Baltimore County, August 5, 1905.
FEELEMYER, Rev. George W. (Methodist), 74, November 25, 1904.
FEELEMYER, Joseph, 84, Baltimore City, March 29, 1897.
FEIGNER, F____ W____, 69, tobacco manufacturer, September 18, 1879.
FEINOUR, Edward, 72, Baltimore City, October 5, 1883.
FELDHAUS, Bernard, n.a., Baltimore City, August 27, 1897.
FELDHAUS, Joseph C., 55, politician, Baltimore City, April 16, 1900.
FELDMAN, Henry, 78, Baltimore City, October 3, 1907.
FENBY, Mrs. Anna M., 72, Carroll County, April 25, 1900.
FENBY, William, 82, Carroll County, April 20, 1900.
FENDRICH, Charles, 54, retired merchant, Baltimore City, November 18, 1880.
FENTON, Aaron, 81, merchant, Baltimore City, April 30, 1880.
FENTON, Daniel A., 66, Confederate veteran, Baltimore City, September 23, 1905.
FENTON, David H., House of Delegates, Kensington, Montgomery County, March 25, 1906.
FENTON, Captain J____ J____, 66, Confederate veteran, Baltimore City, June 25, 1912.
FENTON, John, 73, tailor, Baltimore City, March 8, 1883.
FENTRESS, Rev. W____ H____ (Presbyterian), 28, Baltimore City, September 4, 1880.
FERGUSON, G____ H____, 83, Baltimore City, November 4, 1912.
FERGUSON, James I., 64, contractor, Baltimore City, November 27, 1901.
FERGUSON, Ralph S., 38, fire department, Baltimore City, October 18, 1895.
FERGUSON, William, 63, builder, Baltimore City, November 29, 1905.
FERGUSON, Rev. William M., 64, Libertytown, Worcester County, September 3, 1913.
FERNANDIS, Mary E., 81, Baltimore City, January 15, 1910.
FERRIS, William M., 74, Baltimore City, February 22, 1913.
FERRY, John, 83, retired, Baltimore City, January 1, 1887.
FIDDIS, Levi, 88, retired, Baltimore City, December 28, 1902.
FIELD, Abiathar, 89, retired, Baltimore City, September 8, 1883.
FIELDS, The Hon. Daniel, 71, former president of the Maryland Senate, Caroline County, September 16, 1883.
FIETCHALL, John T., 69, former superintendent, C. & O. Canal, Montgomery County, December 12, 1893.

FIFER, Godfrey, 74, manufacturer, Baltimore City, August 4, 1902.
FILES, Joseph, 56, veteran of the Mexican War, Baltimore City, December 2, 1879.
FILON, James L., 60, Baltimore City, September 11, 1909.
FINCH, John, 86, Baltimore City, November 26, 1909.
FINCK, John Henry, 66, printer, Baltimore City, November 17, 1884.
FINCKE, Professor Fritz, n.a., musician, Baltimore City, June 26, 1900.
FINDLAY, J____ V____ L____, 67, attorney, Baltimore City, April 19, 1907.
FINDLAY, Judge James, 77, Hagerstown, Washington County, November 2, 1914.
FINK, Henry, 59, retired, Baltimore City, September 6, 1884.
FINK, Henry S., 76, merchant, Baltimore City, December 31, 1902.
FINK, Joseph, 75, merchant, Baltimore City, March 11, 1898.
FINK, William Louis, 56, agent, Baltimore City, April 28, 1899.
FINLEY, French, n.a., Cambridge, Dorchester County, March 26, 1908.
FINLEY, Rev. George F., 84, Monrovia, Frederick County, July 12, 1913.
FINNEY, Rev. Ebenezer D., 78, Harford County, June 14, 1904.
FINNEY, Judge George J., n.a., of Harford County, died in Baltimore City, December 17, 1906.
FINNEY, Dr. J____ M____, 73, Harford County, June 25, 1896.
FINNEY, Colonel N____ S____, 74, Confederate veteran, Annapolis, Anne Arundel County, November 26, 1910.
FISCHER, Julius C., 64, druggist, Baltimore City, June 21, 1894.
FISCHER, Louis C., 66, secretary, Mercantile Trust Company, Baltimore City, November 29, 1899.
FISHER, Judge Abram H., n.a., Baltimore City, March 16, 1913.
FISHER, Charles D., 58, capitalist, Baltimore City, November 29, 1906.
FISHER, Frederick, 72, musician, Baltimore City, November 8, 1899.
FISHER, George F., 78, merchant, Baltimore City, March 13, 1883.
FISHER, George W., 67, packer, Baltimore City, November 24, 1897.
FISHER, Henry, 85, retired, Baltimore City, August 22, 1901.
FISHER, Henry C., 63, Caroline County, February 21, 1904.
FISHER, J____ C____, 77, Hagerstown, Washington County, June 14, 1910.
FISHER, James B., n.a., pilot, Baltimore City, June 6, 1894.
FISHER, R____ D____, 77, banker, Baltimore City, August 13, 1910.
FISHER, Robert, 48, president, Baltimore City Board of Trade, February 4, 1881.
FISHER, William, Sr., 75, Baltimore City, February 29, 1908.
FISHER, Dr. William, 86, Pikesville, Baltimore County, August 7, 1879.
FISHER, William A., 64, attorney, Baltimore City, September 26, 1901.
FISHER, Captain William L., 52, mariner, Baltimore City, April 24, 1883.

FITE, Conrad R., 82, merchant, Baltimore City, September 6, 1879.
FITZBERGER, Henry, 75, Baltimore City, November 24, 1893.
FITZGERALD, Edward D., 41, attorney, Baltimore City, November 17, 1899.
FITZGERALD, James H., 62, Baltimore City, July 25, 1905.
FITZGERALD, Captain Thomas, 72, retired, Baltimore City, August 10, 1883.
FITZGERALD, Thomas, 55, B. & O. Railroad, Baltimore City, March 28, 1909.
FITZGERALD, W____ B____, 42, clerk, Baltimore City, April 29, 1884.
FITZHUGH, Henry M., 83, retired, Baltimore City, March 3, 1898.
FITZPATRICK, James, 84, contractor, Baltimore City, March 9, 1900.
FITZPATRICK, Rev. P____ P____ (R.C.), 47, December 10, 1886.
FITZSIMMONS, J____ N____, 75, builder, Baltimore City, December 27, 1881.
FIZONE, Jacob, 55, coal dealer, Baltimore City, February 15, 1904.
FLACK, Benjamin W., 51, oil company, Baltimore City, August 22, 1895.
FLAHERTY, Edward, 64, builder, Baltimore City, May 14, 1881.
FLAHERTY, Edward F., n.a., justice of the peace, Baltimore City, March 10, 1894.
FLAHERTY, Joshua, 95, retired, Baltimore City, December 9, 1894.
FLANNERY, F____ J____, 48, police lieutenant, Baltimore City, September 22, 1892.
FLEDDERMAN, H____ S____, 69, Baltimore City, January 27, 1908.
FLEDDERMAN, J____ H____, 50, Baltimore City, December 22, 1912.
FLEDDERMAN, John H., 71, retired, Baltimore City, July 25, 1882.
FLEEHARTY, Samuel H., 78, Denton, Caroline County, February 25, 1905.
FLEET, Charles T., 43, publisher, Baltimore City, June 22, 1902.
FLETCHER, J____ H____, 68, merchant, Baltimore City, April 8, 1882.
FLETCHER, J____ W____, 67, Marshall Hall, Charles County, April 2, 1893.
FLOOD, James, 74, ferryman, Baltimore City, November 5, 1905.
FLOOD, Philip A., 57, Baltimore City, January 6, 1913.
FLORY, Alexander M., 82, Four Locks, May 2, 1913.
FLOYD, William, 62, printer, Baltimore City, January 15, 1893.
FLUEGEL, Dr. Maurice, 79, author, Baltimore City, February 9, 1911.
FLUHARTY, G____ T____, 62, Easton, Talbot County, January 29, 1908.
FLUSKEY, John B., Sr., 78, rigger, Baltimore City, December 22, 1904.
FLYNN, James, 80, manufacturer, Baltimore City, July 25, 1902.
FOARD, Addison K., 73, retired, Baltimore City, December 22, 1897.
FOARD, Addison K., 26, Baltimore City, November 1, 1907.
FOARD, Albert, 53, farmer, Baltimore County, September 26, 1906.
FOARD, James R., 57, Baltimore City, June 28, 1911.
FOARD, Norval E., 68, editor of *The Sun*, Baltimore City, March 26, 1906.

FOBES, G____ C____, 52, contractor, Baltimore City, June 14, 1893.
FOLEY, Daniel J., 86, retired merchant, Baltimore City, November 28, 1905.
FOLEY, Mrs. Elizabeth, 90, Baltimore City, May 22, 1882.
FOLEY, Miss Juliana, 67, Baltimore City, February 9, 1884.
FOLEY, R____ F____, 48, steamship captain, Baltimore City, March 3, 1884.
FOLEY, Rev. Thomas J. (R.C.), 31, Baltimore City, July 4, 1905.
FOLEY, Thomas J., n.a., Ellicott City, Howard County, March 14, 1914.
FONSHILL, Dr. A____ Balley, n.a., Baltimore City, May 16, 1913.
FONTAINE, J____ H____, 72, Princess Anne, Somerset County, June 13, 1912.
FONTENEAU, Rev. Augustus S. (R.C.), 64, St. Charles College, Howard County, December 19, 1905.
FOOKS, William N., 50, tugboat captain, Baltimore City, December 4, 1899.
FOOTE, David E., 74, packer, Baltimore City, May 28, 1903.
FORBES, Rev. M____ L____ (P.E.), 70, Baltimore City, January 21, 1883.
FORD, Alfred, 60, Cecil County, August 26, 1905.
FORD, Mrs. Anna (widow of Elias Ford), 83, Baltimore City, January 23, 1884.
FORD, Charles, 70, manufacturer, Cecil County, April 16, 1899.
FORD, Charles E., 67, retired theater manager, Baltimore City, May 7, 1898.
FORD, Charles E., Jr., 28, contractor, Baltimore City, December 31, 1906.
FORD, G____ T____, 57, Roland Park section of Baltimore City, July 7, 1912.
FORD, Dr. James B., 84, physician, Baltimore City, July 1, 1906.
FORD, John Thomson, 64, theater manager, Baltimore City, March 14, 1894.
FORD, Robert, n.a., former judge, St. Mary's County, August 10, 1884.
FORD, Samuel, 68, Cecil County, February 27, 1900.
FORD, W____ H____, 77, Baltimore City, April 12, 1893.
FOREMAN, Alfred R., n.a., printer, Baltimore City, December 11, 1881.
FOREMAN, Mrs. Bessie B., 57, died at Chester, Pennsylvania, December 31, 1912.
FOREMAN, George A., 47, contractor, Baltimore City, April 16, 1900.
FOREMAN, J____, 75, retired carpenter, Baltimore City, November 30, 1904.
FOREMAN, Leander, 73, Govans, December 16, 1912.
FORMAN, Alexander D., 68, merchant, Baltimore City, January 22, 1888.
FORNEY, Jacob S., 78, farmer, Baltimore City, November 1, 1882.
FORREST, J____ H____, 93, Baltimore City, December 18, 1912.
FORRESTER, Allen E., 60, attorney, Baltimore City, November 12, 1891.
FORRESTER, William H., 70, builder, Baltimore City, September 1, 1899.

FORSTER, D____ K____, 72, artist, Baltimore City, September 14, 1893.
FORSYTH, Franklin J., 46, conductor, Baltimore City, July 19, 1881.
FORSYTHE, A____ W____, 75, contractor, Baltimore City, January 31, 1880.
FORSYTHE, Abrah, 94, Washington County, June 18, 1900.
FORT, Rev. Edward S., n.a., Baltimore City, October 10, 1882.
FORT, Samuel W., 50, theater employee, Baltimore City, January 11, 1895.
FORWOOD, Dr. Francis F., 34, Bel Air, Harford County, December 9, 1902.
FORWOOD, Thomas G., 41, Bel Air, Harford County, July 29, 1903.
FORWOOD, W____ S____, 71, Bel Air, Harford County, February 28, 1905.
FOSSETT, Francis C., 87, Baltimore County, October 2, 1905.
FOSTER, David C., 74, printer, The Sun, Baltimore City, January 3, 1903.
FOSTER, James R., 29, Baltimore City, February 18, 1905.
FOSTER, James W., n.a., steamboat captain, Baltimore City, November 7, 1897.
FOSTER, John D., 90, retired, Baltimore City, February 21, 1884.
FOSTER, Dr. M____ W____, 77, Baltimore City, June 30, 1914.
FOSTER, Robert E., 60, merchant, Baltimore City, March 26, 1901.
FOSTER, William P., 28, weigher, Baltimore City, July 30, 1881.
FOSTER, William T., 75, retired broker, Baltimore City, June 4, 1901.
FOSTER, William T., 85, builder, Baltimore City, December 2, 1904.
FOUTZ, D____ E____, 40, cattle powders, Baltimore City, August 25, 1878.
FOUTZ, Joseph, 75, Westminster, Carroll County, January 8, 1910.
FOUTZ, R____ R____, 59, merchant, Baltimore City, February 13, 1884.
FOWBLE, Joseph M., 81, Baltimore County, July 2, 1905.
FOWLER, Captain C____ E____, 70, mariner, Baltimore City, March 19, 1910.
FOWLER, Charles H., 50, manufacturer, Baltimore City, September 30, 1901.
FOWLER, Rev. Francis M. (R.C.), 52, Baltimore City, July 19, 1901.
FOWLER, E____ H____, 70, police commissioner, Baltimore City, March 10, 1904.
FOWLER, George W., 59, Baltimore City, April 24, 1898.
FOWLER, John H., 66, justice, Baltimore City, September 18, 1901.
FOWLER, John L., n.a., builder, Baltimore City, August 24, 1897.
FOWLER, M____ J____, 73, Chaneyville, Calvert County, January 26, 1910.
FOWLER, Captain William C., 69, pilot, Baltimore City, February 12, 1886.
FOX, Charles J., 77, journalist, Baltimore City, June 17, 1896.
FOX, Dr. Fabius, 42, physician, Baltimore City, March 29, 1905.
FOX, John, 63, builder, Baltimore City, January 16, 1888.
FOX, M____, 61, horse dealer, Baltimore City, December 19, 1902.
FOX, Patrick, 101, Baltimore City, January 21, 1893.
FOX, Theodore B., 43, teacher, Baltimore City, November 28, 1905.

FOXWELL, Garrett, 69, Chestertown, Kent County, April 11, 1914.
FOXWELL, Captain W_____ W_____, 59, mariner, Baltimore City, November 4, 1892.
FRAMES, George T., 52, druggist, Baltimore City, October 23, 1888.
FRAMES, James P., 64, druggist, Baltimore City, June 27, 1898.
FRAMPTON, Rev. Richard B., 81, Royal Oak (probably Talbot County), February 25, 1913.
FRANCES, Agnes, Sister of Charity, Baltimore City, March 8, 1893.
FRANCES, Thomas, 90, retired, Baltimore City, May 21, 1901.
FRANCIS, Isaac H., 58, hat manufacturer, Baltimore City, September 25, 1905.
FRANCIS, William J., 59, merchant, Baltimore City, May 16, 1892.
FRANCK, George C., 72, cigar manufacturer, Baltimore City, October 8, 1878.
FRANK, Abram S., 51, merchant, Baltimore City, April 4, 1904.
FRANK, Alexander, 60, banker, Baltimore City, May 7, 1903.
FRANK, Henry, 71, merchant, Baltimore City, October 22, 1881.
FRANK, Moses, n.a., retired merchant, Baltimore City, December 27, 1901.
FRANK, Moses D., 67, Baltimore City, August 9, 1913.
FRANK, Dr. Samuel L., 64, philanthropist, Baltimore City, August 3, 1906.
FRANKFURTER, Manas, 77, merchant, Baltimore City, April 25, 1901.
FRANKLIN, Dr. Benjamin A., 64, Westminster, Carroll County, June 24, 1907.
FRANKLIN, Benjamin, 63, builder, Baltimore City, August 11, 1902.
FRANKLIN, Benjamin T., 47, butcher, Baltimore City, December 16, 1905.
FRANKLIN, Joseph P., 67, Confederate veteran, Pikesville, Baltimore County, November 4, 1910.
FRANKLIN, Mrs. R_____ L_____, 99, Frederick, Frederick County, January 7, 1910.
FRANKLIN, Dr. Thomas G., 80, Anne Arundel County, July 27, 1896.
FRANTZ, Dr. J_____ H_____, 43, U.S. Army, Baltimore City, March 2, 1882.
FRASER, Alexander, 53, florist, Baltimore City, July 15, 1891.
FRAZIER, Edward E., 73, Baltimore City, September 23, 1905.
FRAZIER, William E., 43, merchant, Baltimore City, October 2, 1902.
FRAZIER, W_____ H_____, 69, police lieutenant, Baltimore City, September 5, 1893.
FREDERICK, Adolph L., 50, Baltimore City, July 9, 1897.
FREDERICK, John, 55, pork packer, Baltimore City, July 11, 1903.
FREDERICK, John M., 84, retired, Baltimore City, July 19, 1898.
FREDERICK, John M., 39, Baltimore City Fire Department, May 14, 1901.
FREDERICK, William C., 77, retired, Baltimore City, August 2, 1897.
FREE, Dr. Eli W., 81, physician, Baltimore City, January 27, 1905.
FREEBURGER, Edward, 65, bricklayer, Baltimore City, September 26, 1903.
FREEBURGER, Jacob H., 84, merchant, Baltimore City, July 7, 1903.
FREEBURGER, Jesse, 36, carpenter, Baltimore City, December 11, 1903.

FREEBURGER, Samuel T., 50, elocutionist, Baltimore City. December 17, 1903.
FREELAND, Dr. Joseph E., 27, dentist, Baltimore City, August 13, 1894.
FREELAND, Robert, 78, retired, Baltimore City, January 18, 1886.
FREEMAN, Frederick L., 58, shipbroker, Baltimore City, May 8, 1888.
FREEMAN, Lucius W., 70, retired, Baltimore City, November 18, 1899.
FREEMAN, Mother Superior Mary Julia, n.a., Visitation Nuns, Mount de Sales, Catonsville, Baltimore County, December 15, 1891.
FREEMAN, William H_____, 53, Annapolis, Anne Arundel County, September 4, 1902.
FREENY, Elijah, 84, Wicomico County, May 14, 1907.
FREHN, C_____ W_____, n.a., druggist, Baltimore City, July 13, 1911.
FREUDENREICH, Faust, 76, merchant, Baltimore City, November 6, 1893.
FREY, Albert G., 52, Baltimore City, December 22, 1896.
FREY, Jacob, 75, police marshal, Baltimore City, January 1, 1911.
FREYBE, Frederick, 71, butcher, Baltimore City, March 25, 1895.
FRICK, E_____ A_____, 55, merchant, Baltimore City, January 2, 1885.
FRICK, Frank, 82, Baltimore City, December 26, 1910.
FRICK, Frederick, 41, butcher, Baltimore City, March 18, 1895.
FRICK, George P., 59, president, streetcar company, Baltimore City, June 9, 1885.
FRICK, James S., 64, Baltimore City, August 7, 1897.
FRICK, John, 73, Westminster, Carroll County, April 4, 1910.
FRICK, William F., 87, retired, Baltimore City, January 26, 1905.
FRIEDEL, George N., 76, confectioner, Baltimore City, March 28, 1894.
FRIEDENWALD, Dr. Aaron, 66, physician, Baltimore City, August 26, 1902.
FRIEDENWALD, Isaac, 73, publisher, Baltimore City, March 25, 1904.
FRIEDENWALD, J_____, 92, merchant, Baltimore City, September 2, 1893.
FRIEDENWALD, Joseph, 83, financier, Baltimore City, December 24, 1910.
FRIEDMAN, Ida, 14, Front Street Theater panic, December 27, 1895.
FRIEDMANN, Menka, 80, president of the Hebrew Asylum, June 21, 1903.
FRIEZE, John T., 71, Havre de Grace, Harford County, January 2, 1898.
FRINCKE, Rev. Charles H. F. (Lutheran), 81, Baltimore City, June 5, 1905.
FRISCH, Henry G., 55, postman, Baltimore City, January 23, 1900.

FRISS, Allen, 62, Hotel Westminster, Baltimore City, October 1, 1905.
FROEHLICH, John C., 50, manufacturer, Baltimore City, April 10, 1898.
FRUSH, William W., 55, merchant, Baltimore City, December 25, 1881.
FRY, Frederick G., 46, insurance agent, Baltimore City, December 18, 1904.
FRY, Rev. William 65, local preacher, Baltimore City, June 30, 1883.
FRYER, Thomas, 65, merchant, Baltimore City, July 14, 1891.
FUCHS, Professor Otto, principal, Maryland Institute, Baltimore City, March 13, 1906.
FULDA, F____, 85, veteran, Baltimore City, April 23, 1910.
FULLEM, John J., 59, policeman, Baltimore City, December 6, 1909.
FULKS, Dr. James S., 69, physician, Baltimore City, March 13, 1898.
FULLENKAMP, John H., 82, retired, Baltimore City, May 6, 1897.
FULTON, Albert K., 63, journalist, Baltimore City, January 31, 1900.
FULTON, Alexander, 79, journalist, Baltimore City, July 1, 1900.
FULTON, Charles C., 67, journalist, Baltimore City, June 7, 1883
FULTON, David C., 53, merchant, Baltimore City, August 1, 1880.
FULTON, E____ P____, 63, editor, Baltimore City, January 4, 1911.
FULTON, Edington, 59, editor, Baltimore City, May 13, 1878.
FULTON, J____, 78, Laurel, Prince George's County, April 26, 1912.
FULTON, Rev. Robert (R.C.), 69, of Baltimore, died in California, September 15, 1895.
FULTON, S____ Howard, 60, agent, Baltimore City, July 10, 1899.
FULTON, William N., 74, journalist, Baltimore City, September 26, 1888.
FUNK, Rev. E____ P____ (United Brethren), 35, Baltimore City, November 13, 1883.
FUNK, Samuel, 82, Washington County, June 8, 1900.
FUNK, William, 70, architect, Baltimore City, March 5, 1884.
FURESCHI, Demetrio, 69, artist, Baltimore City, February 20, 1904.
FURESCHI, Enrico, 72, Baltimore City, April 5, 1910.
FURRY, John, 62, veteran, Hagerstown, Washington County, November 16, 1909.
FURST, Joseph, 69, builder, Baltimore City, January 19, 1894.
FUSSELBAUGH, William H. B., 76, ex-police commissioner, Baltimore City, August 6, 1902.
FUSSELBAUGH, W____ H____ B____ (of J____), 50, merchant, Baltimore City, October 5, 1904.

GADDES, Charles W., n.a., merchant, Baltimore City, January 19, 1897.
GAEDE, Frederick J., 56, artisan, Baltimore City, August 30, 1882.
GAFF, William J., 63, shipbuilder, Baltimore City, May 3, 1903.
GAIERTY, P____, 84, Baltimore City, August 2, 1911.

GAIL, Emil, 65, Baltimore City, August 14, 1897
GAITHER, Alfred, 58, express manager, Baltimore City, November 25, 1880.
GAITHER, George R., 69, merchant, Baltimore City, May 11, 1899,
GAITHER, Howard E., 37, auctioneer, Baltimore City, July 7, 1903.
GAITHER, John D., 36, merchant, Baltimore City, September 25, 1902.
GAITHER, Thomas B., 75, court clerk, Baltimore City, November 3, 1902.
GAITLEY, Rev. J____ T____ (R.C.), 54, Baltimore City, December 8, 1892.
GALBREATH, Samuel, 69, Baltimore City, February 27, 1897.
GALE, Colonel George, 79, Still Pond, Kent County, April 3, 1884.
GALE, Joseph H., 70, clerk, Baltimore City, December 3, 1904.
GALE, Dr. William H., 76, Princess Anne, Somerset County, February 3, 1904.
GALL, George W., Sr., 77, merchant and manufacturer, Baltimore City, October 5, 1905.
GALLAGHER, Barclay, 65, journalist, Baltimore City, May 8, 1900.
GALLAGHER, Dr. Charles R., 79, insurance, Baltimore City, February 14, 1903.
GALLAGHER, James L., 69, magistrate, Baltimore City, February 15, 1887.
GALLAGHER, Joseph, 61, contractor, Baltimore City, November 6, 1902.
GALLEN, Rev. Joseph A. (R.C.), n.a., Baltimore City, November 24, 1898.
GALLIGHER, Dr. H____ P____, n.a., druggist, Baltimore City, January 2, 1893.
GALLOWAY, H____ J____, 36, ship chandler, Baltimore City, June 24, 1902.
GALLOWAY, James, 77, florist, Baltimore City, July 23, 1899.
GALLOWAY, Dr. Joseph B., 27, physician, Baltimore City, October 23, 1881.
GALLOWAY, Captain P____, 69, mariner, Baltimore City, April 23, 1910.
GALLOWAY, Mrs. Patty, 106, Baltimore City, August 2, 1890.
GALLOWAY, William, 81, railroad engineer, Baltimore City, April 7, 1890.
GALLUP, John Fenton, 83, retired, Baltimore City, April 10, 1884.
GALT, Captain Henry, 85, mariner, Baltimore City, August 2, 1890.
GALT, Dr. John M., 87, physician, Baltimore City, May 13, 1898.
GAMBEL, T____ B____, 66, railroad employee, Baltimore City, December 26, 1883.
GAMBRALL, Rev. Theodore C. (P.E.), 55, Baltimore City, May 18, 1897.
GAMBRILL, Albert, n.a., manufacturer, Baltimore City, May 29, 1900.
GAMBRILL, Charles A., 47, manufacturer, Baltimore City, August 23, 1885.

GAMBRILL, G____ A____, n.a., miller, Frederick County, November 30, 1898.
GAMBRILL, H____ N____, 70, cotton manufacturer, Baltimore City, August 30, 1880.
GAMBRILL, Launcelot, 62, merchant, Baltimore City, June 6, 1901.
GAMBRILL, William B., 52, manufacturer, Baltimore City, April 1, 1893.
GANDOLPHO, Rev. Hyppolite Angel (R.C.), 72, Emmittsburg, Frederick County, December 10, 1883.
GANS, Daniel, 81, former judge of the Orphan's Court, Baltimore City, August 27, 1903.
GANS, Edgar H., 57, Govans, September 20, 1914.
GANTT, Edward C., 65, State's Attorney, Anne Arundel County, at Annapolis, January 15, 1905.
GANTZ, George C., 67, Govanstown, June 7, 1909.
GARDEN, Alexander, 76, Pikesville, Baltimore County, August 2, 1909.
GARDENER, G____ R____, n.a, "ad" man, Baltimore City, September 13, 1908.
GARDINER, William B., 70, Annapolis, Anne Arundel County, May 5, 1909.
GARDNER, Christopher, 66, theatrical machinist, Baltimore City, March 7, 1884.
GARDNER, Dr. Frank B., 47, physician, Baltimore City, September 7, 1895.
GARDNER, Franz, 78, hotelier, Baltimore City, July 25, 1895.
GARDNER, George, 68, bank teller, Baltimore City, March 15, 1902.
GARDNER, George A., 64, stage manager, Baltimore City, December 7, 1906.
GARDNER, George W., 77, Westminster, Carroll County, August 26, 1905.
GARDNER, George W., 47, Baltimore City, February 25, 1899.
GARDNER, Joshua S., Sr., 73, retired, Baltimore City, October 30, 1901.
GARDNER, L____ N____, 67, merchant, Baltimore City, March 21, 1901.
GAREE, Dr. Ellis, 41, physician, Baltimore City, August 30, 1902.
GAREY, H____ F____, 71, ex-judge, Baltimore City, July 28, 1892.
GAREY, Henry F., 50, physician, Baltimore City, August 31, 1905.
GAREY, Thomas F., 65, former State Senator, Caroline County, May 2, 1886.
GARLINGER, Benjamin A., 71, judge of the Orphan's Court, Hagerstown, Washington County, January 20, 1897.
GARRETT, Horatio, 23, of Baltimore City died in England, October 2, 1896.
GARRETT, Mrs. John, 60, Baltimore City, November 15, 1883.
GARRETT, John W., 64, president, B. & O. Railroad, Deer Park, September 26, 1884.
GARRETT, Robert, 49, former president, B. & O. Railroad, July 29, 1896.

GARRETT, T_____ Harrison, 39, banker, Baltimore City, June 7, 1888.
GARRIGUES, H_____ H_____, 48, merchant, Baltimore City, November 19, 1888.
GARRISON, W_____ G_____, 46, pilot, Baltimore City, April 25, 1904.
GASKILL, Dr. E_____ C_____, 58, Allegany County, April 29, 1892.
GASKINS, Dr. J_____ H_____, 42, physician, Baltimore City, June 1, 1892.
GASSAWAY, Augustus, 59, clerk, Baltimore City Records Office, June 15, 1885.
GASSAWAY, J_____ H_____, 83, Rockville, Montgomery County, November 15, 1911.
GASSMAN, John, 68, Hagerstown, Washington County, August 13, 1913.
GATCH, Thomas A., 69, educator, Baltimore City, September 1, 1901.
GATCHELL, Hugh M., 46, bookkeeper, Baltimore City, November 10, 1889.
GATCHELL, Judge William H., 79, Baltimore City, April 27, 1878.
GAUL, George P., 50, musician, Baltimore City, January 23, 1885.
GAULT, Albert, 63, detective, Baltimore City, July 26, 1900.
GAULT, Cyrus, 74, stonecutter, Baltimore City, January 12, 1881.
GAULT, Captain Cyrus, Jr., 39, Baltimore City, August 10, 1878.
GAYLEY, Rev. Samuel A. (Presbyterian), 81, Cecil County, May 14, 1903.
GAYNER, Philip (Ch. Brother Vincent), 64, Baltimore City, February 13, 1883.
GEDDES, Adam, 91, retired, Baltimore City, November 5, 1897.
GEEKIE, Charles W., 73, Baltimore City, October 7, 1893.
GEER, Dr. Edwin, 41, physician, Baltimore City, February 25, 1906.
GEER, Herbert G., 30, electrical engineer, Baltimore City, March 7, 1900.
GEGAN, Joseph, 82, music teacher, Baltimore City, April 18, 1882.
GEHR, Dr. Daniel, 72, Smithsburg, Washington County, January 3, 1913.
GEHRING, John G., 70, jeweler, Baltimore City, October 14, 1895.
GEHRING, Joseph, 81, Baltimore City, July 1, 1909.
GEIGAN, John H., 57, Baltimore City, March 25, 1890.
GEIGER, John W., 45, druggist, Baltimore City, January 16, 1898.
GELBACH, George, Jr., 61, broker, Baltimore City, February 13, 1880.
GELSTON, Samuel P., 74, Baltimore City, February 20, 1892.
GELSTON, Victor D., 44, Baltimore City, December 14, 1882.
GEOGHAGON, Captain Joseph R., 66, Baltimore City, July 20, 1907.
GEOHEGAN, Robert, 42, Baltimore City, March 8, 1905.

GEOGHEGAN, S____ K____, 91, retired mariner, Baltimore City, December 2, 1904.
GEORGE, Andrew J., 74, retired merchant, Baltimore City, July 3, 1903.
GEORGE, Henry, 68, actor, Baltimore City, July 9, 1894.
GEORGE, Isaac S., 84, retired banker, Baltimore City, January 2, 1903.
GEORGE, J____ H____, 84, Denton, Caroline County, November 1, 1911.
GEORGE, James B., 36, merchant, Baltimore City, July 9, 1880.
GEORGE, John T., 74, Baltimore City, August 10, 1909.
GEORGE, Rev. Theodore, n.a., at Philadelphia, December 30, 1914.
GEORGE, Thomas I., 55, civil engineer, Towson, Baltimore County, September 4, 1898.
GEORGE, Thomas J., 63, merchant, Baltimore City, August 1, 1897.
GEPHARDT, John, 82, retired, Baltimore City, June 3, 1898.
GERDING, Henry H., 65, Baltimore City, March 13, 1905.
GERHARDT, Christopher, 62, jeweler, Baltimore City, January 30, 1897.
GERMAN, Captain Andrew W., 55, fireboat, Baltimore City, February 25, 1905.
GERMON, June, 88, actress, Baltimore City, August 10, 1909.
GERTRICK, J____, 94, Baltimore City, September 24, 1908.
GERWIG, William, 69, contractor, Catonsville, Baltimore County, March 26, 1905.
GESSFORD, Rev. T____ C____, 60 (Baptist), 60, Baltimore City, August 9, 1894.
GETTIER, Joseph A., 81, Baltimore City, February 10, 1912.
GETTY, George A., 44, merchant, Baltimore City, January 10, 1895.
GETTY, James, 92, financier, Baltimore City, February 16, 1903.
GETTY, William R., 70, Garrett County, September 12, 1902.
GETZ, Conrad, 80, retired, Baltimore City, April 1, 1895.
GETZ, John M., 64, builder, Baltimore City, January 26, 1897.
GHENT, Alred J., 77, Baltimore County, December 10, 1905.
GIBBON, General John, 70, U.S. Army (Ret.), Baltimore City, February 6, 1896.
GIBBONS, Dr. James E., 58, physician, Baltimore City, December 2, 1901.
GIBBONS, Stephen M., 51, hotelier, Baltimore City, August 9, 1891.
GIBBS, Edward A., 83, retired, Baltimore City, August 26, 1895.
GIBSON, Rev. Alexander (Methodist), 71, Baltimore City, January 10, 1897.
GIBSON, Rev. Frederick (P.E.), 77, Baltimore City, May 22, 1904.
GIBSON, James, 77, banker, Baltimore City, May 25, 1902.
GIBSON, Dr. Resin S., 79, retired, Baltimore City, January 30, 1885.
GIESE, J____ Henry, 83, Baltimore City, February 5, 1905.
GIFFORD, Hugh, 81, retired, Baltimore City, June 6, 1898.
GIFFORD, James J., 80, retired builder, Baltimore City, March 5, 1894.
GIFFORD, Thomas, 71, tax court assessor, Baltimore City, February 3, 1878.
GILBERT, A____ P____, 54, Bel Air, Harford County, August 14, 1893.

GILBERT, Aquilla, 86, builder, Baltimore City, December 17, 1893.
GILBERT, Rev. D____ N____ (Methodist), 31, Baltimore City, August 15, 1881.
GILBERT, James L., 54, lumber dealer, Baltimore City, August 7, 1906.
GILDEA, Francis D., 66, builder, Baltimore City, August 21, 1881.
GILDERSLEEVE, George, 78, broker, Baltimore City, December 31, 1900.
GILES, William Fell, 71, judge, Baltimore City, March 21, 1879.
GILES, William T., 72, Elkton, Cecil County, March 18, 1901.
GILL, C____ Lorraine, 59, merchant, Baltimore City, July 5, 1899.
GILL, Dr. Charles M., 68, dentist, Baltimore City, October 4, 1903.
GILL, Ernest C., 61, Baltimore City, April 3, 1909.
GILL, George M., 85, lawyer, Baltimore City, November 18, 1887.
GILL, Henry James, 42, Baltimore City, September 29, 1905.
GILL, Howard, n.a., aviator of Baltimore City died at Chicago, September 14, 1912.
GILL, General John, 71, died at Ventnor, New Jersey, July 2, 1912.
GILL, M____ Gillet, 69, Baltimore City, September 23, 1908.
GILL, N____ Rufus, 67, lawyer, Baltimore City, October 30, 1905.
GILL, T____ H____, 67, Baltimore City, May 4, 1911.
GILL, William D., Sr., 69, Mount Washington, Baltimore County, January 1, 1904.
GILL, William H., 64, realtor, Baltimore City, February 30, 1906.
GILL, William L., 83, bank cashier, Baltimore City, January 14, 1880.
GILLESPIE, Dr. Franklin, 39, Elkton, Cecil County, August 22, 1905.
GILLESPIE, W____ Edgar, 42, Baltimore City, April 7, 1905.
GILLESPIE, William, 77, engraver, Baltimore City, May 16, 1894.
GILLET, Joseph, 88, tea merchant, Baltimore City; died at New York City, July 21, 1904.
GILLINGHAM, Captain C____ R____, n.a., Baltimore City, December 16, 1911.
GILLIS, Dr. J____ A____, 62(?), physician, Baltimore City, June 2, 1905.
GILLOTT, G____ R____, 67, Baltimore City, May 1, 1910.
GILMAN, John S., 61, bank president, Baltimore City, November 16, 1889.
GILMAN, Dr. Judson, 65, physician, Baltimore City, August 1, 1883.
GILMOR, Charles, 64, retired, Baltimore City, October 3, 1899.
GILMOR, Ellen, 69, Baltimore City, September 20, 1880.
GILMOR, Colonel Harry, 45, Baltimore City, March 4, 1883.
GILMOR, Hoffman, 40, broker, Baltimore City, December 21, 1885.
GILMOR, Meredith, 56, Govanstown, September 21, 1900.
GILMOR, Lieutentant R____ T____, 68, Confederate veteran, Pikesville, Baltimore County, August 23, 1908.
GILMOR, Robert, 73, ex-judge, Baltimore City, April 19, 1906.

GILMOR, William, 72, railroad president, Baltimore City, November 13, 1904.
GILMOUR, Henry C., 52, hotel manager, Baltimore City, January 13, 1900.
GILMOUR, J_____ Madison, 43, Baltimore City, April 6, 1892.
GILMOUR, James D., 56, hotelier, Baltimore City, December 28, 1880.
GILPIN, A_____ G_____, 54, manufacturer, Baltimore City, January 26, 1893.
GILPIN, Bernard, 71, merchant, Baltimore City, May 7, 1897.
GILPIN, Bernard, 59, Baltimore City, March 1, 1914.
GILPIN, E_____ C_____, 89, Sandy Spring, Montgomery County, March 9, 1908.
GILSON, Charles H., 58, U.S. Senatory from Maryland, at Washington, D.C., March 31, 1900.
GIRVIN, John H., 43, merchant, Baltimore City, February 16, 1891.
GITTINGER, John C., 37, press (sic), Baltimore City, December 1, 1897.
GITTINGS, Dr. David S., 89, physician, Baltimore City, March 12, 1887.
GITTINGS, Major Erskine, 41, U.S. Army, Baltimore City, September 19, 1880.
GITTINGS, John S., 81, banker, Baltimore City, December 8, 1879.
GITTINGS, Lambert, 80, retired, Baltimore City, July 22, 1887.
GITTINGS, Richard J., 53, attorney, Baltimore City, August 2, 1882.
GITTINGS, Richard M., 49, Baltimore City, September 23, 1897.
GIUSTINIANI, Rev. Joseph (R.C.), 75, Baltimore City, October 20, 1886.
GLADDING, Captain S_____ B_____, 60, Baltimore City, May 22, 1913.
GLASS, David W., 56, merchant, Baltimore City, December 11, 1900.
GLEICHMANN, Frederick, 71, Baltimore City, August 24, 1907.
GLEN, Alexander, 71, retired merchant, Baltimore City, February 21, 1901.
GLEN, Captain James, 68, Baltimore City, July 4, 1912.
GLENN, Captain J_____ W_____, 70, Confederate veteran, Chestertown, Kent County, November 27, 1907.
GLENN, John, 67, realtor, Baltimore City, March 30, 1896.
GLENN, Joseph, 92, retired, Baltimore City, October 13, 1904.
GLENN (DEMSTER), Samuel W., 72, actor, Baltimore City, February 10, 1903.
GLICKMAN, Mrs. _____, 107, Baltimore City, April 5, 1909.
GLOCKER, Theodore, 72, lawyer, Baltimore City, July 16, 1884.
GLOCKER, Dr. Theodore W., 53, physician, Baltimore City, November 15, 1894.
GLOVER, Townsend, 71, naturalist, Baltimore City, September 7, 1883.
GMINDER, Jacob, 64, silversmith, Baltimore City, September 10, 1898.
GOING, Alvah, 94(?), retired, Baltimore City, September 15, 1889.

GOLA, Professor Charles, 80, musician, Baltimore City, November 28, 1889.
GOLDER, Mrs. Mary J., 92, Baltimore City, May 15, 1883.
GOLDER, Robert, 67, retired, Baltimore City, August 23, 1884.
GOLDSBOROUGH, Dr. C_____ W_____, 67, Frederick, Frederick County, February 6, 1908.
GOLDSBOROUGH, Colonel Charles, 64, merchant, Baltimore City, May 31, 1903.
GOLDSBOROUGH, Charles F., 62, associate judge, Cambridge, Dorchester County, June 23, 1892.
GOLDSBOROUGH, Captain Fitzhue, 47, Fifth Regiment, December 13, 1895.
GOLDSBOROUGH, George R., 78, Talbot County, August 18, 1899.
GOLDSBOROUGH, Dr. Griffin W., 81, Caroline County, June 14, 1902.
GOLDSBOROUGH, Henry H., 87, former judge, Baltimore City, November 30, 1899.
GOLDSBOROUGH, William, 55, educator, Talbot County; died in New York City, September 21, 1898.
GOLDSMITH, Herman, 76, Baltimore City, May 27, 1909.
GOLDSMITH, Jonas, 62, teacher, Baltimore City, May 4, 1886.
GOLDSMITH, Lewis, 64, merchant, Baltimore City, January 24, 1904.
GOLDSTROM, Emmanuel, 43, merchant, Baltimore City, May 17, 1905.
GOLDSTROM, Moses, 72, merchant, Baltimore City, November 25, 1894.
GONDER, A_____ B_____, n.a., justice of peace, Oakland, Garrett County, December 26, 1908.
GONTRUM, J_____ F_____, 54, Gardenville, December 27, 1909.
GONTRUM, John, 80, Baltimore County, April 5, 1903.
GOODING, Jesse, 77, Easton, Talbot County, August 15, 1909.
GOODWIN, Rev. B_____ A_____ (R.C.), 58, of Baltimore; died in Ireland, December 17, 1896.
GOODWIN, C_____ Ridgely, 52, Surveyor, Port of Baltimore, May 19, 1894.
GORDON, Basil B., 40, capitalist, Baltimore City, July 20, 1901.
GORDAN, Douglas H., 66, retired, Baltimore City, January 20, 1883.
GORDAN, Graham, 50, lawyer, Baltimore City, November 2, 1898.
GORDON, H_____ Skipworth, 43, Baltimore City, May 17, 1888.
GORDON, John M., 75, retired, Baltimore City, March 12, 1884.
GORDON, Josiah H., 71, former judge, Cumberland, Allegany County, August 13, 1887.
GORDON, Dr. L_____ Charles, 29, physician, Baltimore City, October 30, 1880.
GORDON, Rev. Samuel B. (P.E.), 70, rector, St. Thomas' Chruch, Croom, Prince George's County, August 23, 1883.
GORDON, Thomas W., 59, hotelier, Baltimore City, July 19, 1905.
GORDON, W_____ M_____, 68, Baltimore City, June 19, 1910.
GORDSELL, Dr. G_____ W_____, 68, Baltimore City, June 9, 1883.
GORDY, John T., 70, Wicomico County, November 27, 1904.

GORDY, Stephen P., 52, Pocomoke City, Worcester County, March 25, 1907.
GORGAS, Dr. Ferdinand J. S., 80, Baltimore City, April 8, 1914.
GORMAN, Arthur Pue (sic), 67, U.S. Senator from Maryland; died in Washington, D.C., June 4, 1906.
GORMAN, Richard P., 53, Baltimore City, March 2, 1893.
GORMAN, William, 78, Baltimore City, February 24, 1900.
GORMLEY, Matthew, 68, merchant, Baltimore City, February 1, 1883.
GORRELL, Andrew J., 83, Harford County, November 11, 1898.
GORRELL, James L., 81, Harford County, May 18, 1903.
GORSUCH, B____ Howsrd, 56, Baltimore County, January 2, 1902.
GORSUCH, Edward C., 39, broker, Baltimore City, October 24, 1903.
GORSUCH, Dr. J____ E____, 54, physician, Baltimore City, August 28, 1893.
GORSUCH, J____ T____, 78, Baltimore City, January 4, 1910.
GORSUCH, John, 77, merchant, Baltimore City, May 29, 1880.
GORSUCH, Nathan I., 81, Westminster, Carroll County, September 1, 1902.
GORSUCH, Noah, 86, Baltimore City, January 5, 1894.
GORSUCH, Rev. Rezin H. (Methodist), 80, Baltimore County, April 12, 1895.
GORSUCH, Dr. Silas N., 62, Westminster, Carroll County, October 3, 1907.
GORSUCH, Rev. T____, 89, Parkville (Parkton, Baltimore County?), May 9, 1911.
GORSUCH, Thomas, 77, bank president, Frederick, Frederick County, March 23, 1896.
GORSUCH, Thomas J., 91, retired, Baltimore City, November 17, 1905.
GORSUCH, William G., 83, builder, Baltimore City, October 7, 1887.
GORTER, G____ O____, 69, Belgian consul, Baltimore City, February 20, 1879.
GORTES, Albert L., 54, realtor, Baltimore City, February 4, 1906.
GOSLIN, Edward E., 55, Federalsburg, Caroline County, March 20, 1914.
GOSLIN, Edward R., 85, Federalsburg, Caroline County, April 24, 1905.
GOSNELL, Charles H., 66, Baltimore City, May 7, 1905.
GOSNELL, George W, 58, merchant, Baltimore City, April 4, 1894.
GOSNELL, John S., 53, miller, Baltimore City, October 7, 1900.
GOSNELL, M____ T____, 59, merchant, Baltimore City, June 30, 1885.
GOSSAGE, Captain James E., 73, Easton, Talbot County, February 14, 1905.
GOSWEILER, Daniel, 82, manufacturer, Baltimore City, December 11, 1881.
GOTT, Jackson C., 80, (no place indicated), July 8, 1909.

GOTTSCHALK, Albert, 63, manufacturer, Baltimore City, October 7, 1898
GOUDY, Stephen S., 71, magistrate, Baltimore City, September 10, 1884.
GOULD, Alexander, 71, Baltimore City, June 14, 1880.
GOULD, John H., 70, singer, died in Massachusetts, February 12, 1895.
GOULD, John R., 71, journalist, Baltimore City, February 19, 1900.
GOULD, William Wallace, 65, Baltimore City, November 22, 1894.
GOVE, James E., 44, teacher, Baltimore City, February 26, 1897.
GOVER, Henry T., 77, Baltimore City, October 24, 1896.
GOVER, Philip, 80, banker, Baltimore City, September 15, 1892.
GOVERNEUR, Mrs. Mary D., 88, Frederick, Frederick County, October 4, 1898.
GOWDEY, Captain James, 76, Halethorpe, Baltimore County, April 17, 1912.
GRACE, Henry, 67, Melrose, Frederick County, January 2, 1912.
GRADY, Professor Edward F., 35, musician, Baltimore City, June 26, 1883.
GRAFF, August N., n.a., Baltimore City, February 27, 1898.
GRAFF, E_____ Beatty, 75, lawyer, Baltimore County, June 25, 1897.
GRAFFLIN, Jacob W., 71, lumber dealer, Baltimore City, January 22, 1883.
GRAFFLIN, John C., 59, merchant, Baltimore City, September 6, 1888.
GRAHAM, Daniel, 70, Baltimore City, July 6, 1898.
GRAHAM, George, 36, Baltimore City, October 5, 1890.
GRAHAM, Captain George R., 68, mariner, Baltimore City, October 23, 1889.
GRAHAM, Israel, 75, Confederate veteran, Pikesville, Baltimore County, December 5, 1908.
GRAHAM, James T., 32, Elkton, Cecil County, February 24, 1896.
GRAHAM, John Van Lear, 53, attorney, Baltimore City, August 25, 1899.
GRAHAM, William, 95, St. Denis, Howard County, March 25, 1893.
GRAHAM, William H., 60, banker, Baltimore City, January 19, 1885.
GRAMMER, Rev. J_____ E_____ (P.E.), 71, Baltimore City, March 20, 1902.
GRANGER, A_____ J_____, 53, Baltimore City, September 2, 1907.
GRANGER, William H., 66, tabacconist, Baltimore City, May 16, 1891.
GRANT, General J_____ F_____, 61, Baltimore City, April 12, 1905.
GRANT, Rev. William M., n.a., Baltimore City, December 24, 1909.
GRANVILLE, Thomas, 56, contractor, Baltimore City, April 21, 1904.
GRAPE, George S., 63, teacher, Baltimore City, January 24, 1894.
GRAPE, Joseph, 58, secretary, Sheppard Asylum, May 11, 1903.
GRASON, R_____, 73, former judge, Towson, Baltimore County, September 21, 1893.

GRAVES, Dr. John James, 89, retired physician, Baltimore City, January 19, 1890.
GRAVES, Dr. Roswell H., 79, died in China, June 5, 1912.
GRAVES, Rev. Uriel (Lutheran), 47, Baltimore City, July 13, 1884.
GRAY, Dr. A____ W____, 58, physician, Baltimore City, October 18, 1889.
GRAY, D____ W____, 62, deputy U.S. Collector, Baltimore City, April 1, 1884.
GRAY, Ezekiel, 93, Carroll County, March 9, 1893.
GRAY, George, 83, retired, Baltimore City, June 6, 1883.
GRAY, Rev. John C. (P.E.), n.a., Baltimore City, July 4, 1903.
GRAY, John T., 67, court clerk, Baltimore City, November 13, 1895.
GRAY, Thomas F., 38, surveyor, Baltimore City, October 25, 1895.
GRAY, Captain Walter L., 57, mariner, Baltimore City, October 6, 1900.
GRAYBILL, Rev. J____ M____, 85, Clear Spring, Washington County, August 8, 1912.
GREACEN, Thomas, 76, retired, Baltimore City, April 5, 1884.
GREEN, Edward J., 72, businessman, Baltimore City, March 29, 1901.
GREEN, Elisha, 29, grocer, Baltimore City, October 22, 1878.
GREEN, G____ W____, 92, Baltimore City, September 28, 1908.
GREEN, George, 32, manufacturer, Baltimore City, August 22, 1881.
GREEN, H____ H____, 47, superintendent of job office, The Sun, June 8, 1890.
GREEN, Henry, Sr., 83, undertaker, Baltimore City, September 25, 1887.
GREEN, J____ A____, 65, Towson, Baltimore County, October 12, 1910.
GREEN, Jacob F., 42, tailor, Baltimore City, September 19, 1878.
GREEN, Joseph, 84, California pioneer; died in Baltimore City, February 19, 1901.
GREEN, Matthew, 69, Confederate veteran, Baltimore City, December 21, 1904.
GREEN, Dr. Richard, 64, Mayor, Annapolis, Anne Arundel County, January 21, 1899.
GREEN, Rudelph, 54, musician, Baltimore City, July 27, 1895.
GREEN, Samuel H., 80, retired, Baltimore City, November 19, 1900.
GREEN, T____ T____, 60, policeman, Baltimore City, April 24, 1910.
GREENBERG, Israel G., 86, merchant, Baltimore City, January 12, 1899.
GREENE, Rev. William Wallace, 92, Cambridge, Dorchester County, February 14, 1913.
GREENFELDER, Moses, 65, Baltimore City, December 21, 1897.
GREENSFELDER, S____, 69, merchant, Baltimore City, June 29, 1893.
GREENFIELD, Aquila H., 59, retired, Baltimore City, November 20, 1890.

GREENFIELD, Caleb W., 70, merchant, Baltimore City, December 14, 1893.
GREENTREE, Andrew, 63, detective, Baltimore City, April 17, 1897.
GREENTREE, Dr. Hiram, n.a., pharmacist, Baltimore City, October 28, 1900.
GREENTREE, Howard, 82, Baltimore City, June 8, 1909.
GREENTREE, Dr. Winslow, 34, physician, Baltimore City, April 28, 1883.
GREENWAY, E____ M____, 88, builder, Baltimore City, August 21, 1880.
GREENWAY, Edward McD____, Jr., 74, banker, Baltimore City, March 5, 1895.
GREENWAY, J____ Henry, 81, Havre de Grace, Harford County, December 29, 1902.
GREFE, Louis, 71, grocer, Baltimore City, February 19, 1899.
GREGG, H____ K____, 64, realtor, Baltimore City, April 2, 1884.
GREGG, James, 85, capitalist, Baltimore City, July 27, 1896.
GREGG, John, 81, retired, Baltimore City, February 11, 1890.
GREGG, Newton, 53, merchant, Baltimore City, April 21, 1894.
GRESHAM, H____ H____, 62, Kent County, January 28, 1907.
GRIEST, Moses, 77, retired, Baltimore City, December 19, 1885.
GRIFFIN, Rev. H____ F____, 81, Catholic University, Howard County, January 5, 1893.
GRIFFIN, M____ J____, 69, Baltimore City Water Department, December 14, 1905.
GRIFFISS, Edward, 48, attorney, Baltimore City, July 4, 1902.
GRIFFISS, John Irving, n.a., attorney, Baltimore City, February 19, 1894.
GRIFFITH, Rev. Abram, 62, Baltimore City, March 4, 1907.
GRIFFITH, Albert G., 72, retired, Baltimore City, July 7, 1883.
GRIFFITH, Rev. Charles C. (P.E.), 44, Baltimore City, May 8, 1901.
GRIFFITH, Dr. Edward, 90, Baltimore City, April 12, 1892.
GRIFFITH, Goldsborough S., 89, merchant, Baltimore City, February 24, 1904.
GRIFFITH, H____ Lee, 38, judge, Orphan's Court, Baltimore City, March 26, 1900.
GRIFFITH, Howard, 75, Montgomery County, March 5, 1897.
GRIFFITH, John A., 63, merchant, Baltimore City, June 21, 1880.
GRIFFITH, Joseph, 100, Denton, Caroline County, September 18, 1902.
GRIFFITH, R____ H____, 49, shipbuilder, Baltimore City, September 7, 1888.
GRIFFITH, Robert S., 35, printer, Baltimore City, October 25, 1898.
GRIFFITH, Romulus R., 76, retired, Baltimore City, October 15, 1906.
GRIFFITH, Captain Thomas, 81, Olney, Montgomery County, July 14, 1912.
GRIFFITH, Rev. W____ C____, 79, Hagerstown, Washington County, April 27, 1913.

GRIFFITH, Colonel W____ R____, 73, Baltimore City, October 22, 1910.
GRIFFITH, William, 78, Baltimore City, December 9, 1909.
GRIFFITH, William A. R., 67, merchant, Baltimore City, March 8, 1892.
GRIGGS, Captain J____ E____, 80, Baltimore City, February 12, 1908.
GRIGGS, John J., 69, Baltimore City, August 16, 1905.
GRIGGS, Dr. William O., 35, physician, Baltimore City, August 26, 1904.
GRIM, Emmanuel, 87, Baltimore County, November 21, 1905.
GRIMES, Dr. John W, n.a., Baltimore City, November 7, 1914.
GRIMES, Dr. W____ H____, 75, Washington County, May 19, 1892.
GRIMM, Rev. Jacob L., n.a., Baltimore City, August 20, 1905.
GRIMMELL, D____ M____, 70, manager, Westminster, Carroll County, February 7, 1906.
GRINDALL, John J., 42, justice, Baltimore City, August 1, 1895.
GRINDALL, John T., 73, builder, Baltimore City, May 17, 1885.
GRINDALL, Josiah J., 76, clerk, Baltimore City, December 29, 1900.
GRINE, Isaac, ten years old, Front Street Theater panic, December 27, 1895.
GRINSFELDER, Joseph, 69, merchant, Baltimore City, June 13, 1887.
GRISWOLD, Rev. Dr. Benjamin B. (P.E.), 73, Baltimore City, July 18, 1894.
GROLLMAN, Rev. Joseph, n.a., rabbi, Baltimore City, July 15, 1903.
GROOM, F____, 72, Towson, Baltimore County, May 19, 1908.
GROOME, Mrs. Elizabeth, 86, Elkton, Cecil County, September 10, 1902.
GROOME, James Black, 55, former State Governor, Baltimore City, October 4, 1893.
GROSCUP, William H., n.a., teacher, Baltimore City, February 25, 1897.
GROSS, J____ F____, 75, Baltimore City, June 4, 1909.
GROSS, Dr. John L., 60, physician, Baltimore City, December 14, 1900.
GROSS, William H., 61, Archbishop of Oregon died in Baltimore, November 14, 1898.
GROSSI, Angelo, 73, ballet master, Baltimore City, March 28, 1898.
GROTJAN, Thomas J., 67, auctioneer, Baltimore City, February 11, 1891
GROVE, Jacob F., 69, retired, Baltimore City, April 1, 1884.
GROVE, Manassas J., 83, Frederick, Frederick County, February 2, 1907.
GROVERMAN, Anthony, 86, retired merchant, Baltimore City, November 7, 1901.
GROVES, John A., n.a., Kent County, May 11, 1896.
GRUBB, Lillian, n.a., actress, Baltimore City, September 7, 1890.
GRUBE, C____ C____, 81, Baltimore City, January 29, 1910.
GRUBER, Isaac, 81, Williamsport, Washington County, February 6, 1900.

GRUVER, William H., 61, former police captain, Baltimore City, January 21, 1890.
GUARD, Rev. Thomas (M.E.), 51, Baltimore City, October 15, 1882.
GUEST, George, Sr., 74, ship owner, Baltimore City, July 2, 1879.
GUEST, J_____ Wesley, 67, cashier, Baltimore City, September 13, 1898.
GUEST, Captain John W., 70, mariner, Baltimore City, July 3, 1904.
GUEST, Samuel, 76, realtor, Baltimore City, July 9, 1879.
GUETHLER, M_____ W_____, 45, brewmaster, Baltimore City, July 13, 1902.
GUGGENHEIMER, Isaac, 63, publisher, Baltimore City, May 6, 1904.
GUGGENHEIMER, Max, 77, merchant, Baltimore City, October 27, 1898.
GUITEAU, Mrs. Jane, 69, Baltimore City, December 11, 1878.
GUNBY, Francis M., 24, Salisbury, Wicomico County, December 8, 1905.
GUNBY, Dr. H_____ N_____, 61, Crisfield, Somerset County, April 8, 1913.
GUNBY, Captain Stephen C., 58, mariner, Baltimore City, October 2, 1905.
GUNDERSDORFF, Christopher, 46, Baltimore City, August 7, 1895.
GUNDRY, Dr. Richard, 60, superintendent of Spring Grove, April 23, 1891.
GUNNELL, William H., 65, Montgomery County, August 20, 1904.
GUNNING, John, 80, Annapolis, Anne Arundel County, May 24, 1900.
GUNNING, Professor William, 64, Cumberland, Allegany County, February 13, 1913.
GUNNISON, William, 79, former Abolitionist, June 20, 1892.
GUNTHER, Dr. Conrad, 70, physician, Baltimore City, May 23, 1887.
GUNTHER, George, Sr., 84, Baltimore City, September 6, 1912.
GUNTHER, John, n.a., manufacturer, Baltimore City, June 27, 1895.
GUNTHER, L_____ W_____, Jr., 32, former member of the Maryland Legislature, Baltimore City, May 9, 1889.
GUNTHER, Ludolph W., 68, merchant, Baltimore City, July 10, 1889.
GURRY, Sister Mary L., 30, Baltimore City, November 11, 1913.
GUSTAVUS, Gerhard, 37, broker, Baltimore City, May 12, 1898.
GUTHRIE, Alexander, Sr., 73, Baltimore City, April 28, 1897.
GUTHRIE, Joseph, Sr., 68, mariner, Baltimore City, January 23, 1884.
GUTMAN, Isaac, 67, Baltimore City, April 9, 1911.
GUTMAN, Josel, 62, merchant, Baltimore City, February 23, 1892.
GUTMAN, Mrs. Joel, n.a., Baltimore City, December 12, 1912.
GUTMAN, John A., 62, Baltimore City, November 23, 1911.
GUTMAN, Loeg, 81, retired, Baltimore City, July 15, 1886.
GUTSCHALL, D_____, 90, Mercersburg, August 3, 1909.
GUY, E_____ K_____, 68, retired, Baltimore City, December 15, 1902.
GUYTON, W_____ L_____, 75, Glendale, Prince George's County, February 7, 1910.
GWALTNEY, Dr. James A., 35, Baltimore City, December 18, 1886.

GWINN, C_____ H_____, 67, retired, Baltimore City, December 28, 1902.
GWINN, Charles J. M., 71, former Attorney General, Baltimore City, February 11, 1894.
GWINN, James W., n.a., Baltimorean; died in Paris, December 5, 1893.
GWYNN, Charles R., 83, merchant, Baltimore City, January 7, 1892.
GWYNN, Dr. Henry G., 45, educator, Baltimore City, October 11, 1900.
GWYNN, General Walter, 80, U.S. Eng. (sic), Baltimore City, February 6, 1882.

HAAS, John P., 51, merchant, Baltimore City, December 14, 1900.
HABIGHURST, Conrad J., n.a., U.S. Navy, Baltimore City, March 24, 1901.
HABLE, Joseph, 50, n.a., merchant, Baltimore City, April 4, 1898.
HABLISTON, John M., 61, cashier, The Sun, Baltimore City, March 20, 1882.
HACK, Oliver F., 70, attorney, Baltimore City, August 7, 1894.
HADDAWAY, Arthur F., 30, editor, Easton, Talbot County, April 19, 1901.
HADDAWAY, George E., 62, editor, Easton, Talbot County, July 29, 1904.
HADDAWAY, Thomas D., 47, attorney, Baltimore City, September 3, 1901.
HAGAN, Rev. John P. (R.C.), 63, Baltimore City, June 20, 1897.
HAGAN, Dr. John T., 51, postman, Baltimore City, May 23, 1901.
HAGERTY, James, 86, retired, Baltimore City, April 8, 1884.
HAGERTY, James S., 68, manufacturer, Baltimore City, November 9, 1897.
HAGGERTY, Daniel, 57, clerk, Baltimore City, August 22, 1888.
HAGNER, Richard H., 81, Calvert County, December 19, 1904.
HAGNER, William H., 73, Baltimore City, July 9, 1898.
HAHN, George A., 58, gunsmith, Baltimore City, March 28, 1899.
HAINES, C_____ W_____, 29, Baltimore City, December 26, 1907.
HAINES, Granville S., 78, banker, Westminster, Carroll County, December 9, 1901.
HAINES, Joseph L., 69, Westminster, Carroll County, August 23, 1906.
HAINES, Oakley P., 71, managing editor of The Sun, Baltimore City, March 5, 1909.
HAINES, Mrs. Sophia, 96, Carroll County, July 25, 1902.
HAINES, T_____ Marshall, 63, Elkton, Cecil County, December 5, 1909.
HAIRSTON, Peter W., 65, merchant, Baltimore City, February 17, 1886.
HALBACH, Herman F., 43, attorney, Baltimore City, January 24, 1894.
HALDEMAN, P_____ F_____, n.a., Allegany County, December 16, 1893.
HALE, E_____ W_____, 76, Baltimore City, January 10, 1910.
HALEY, Captain Alexander, 85, mariner, Baltimore City, October 9, 1885.
HALL, Captain B_____ F_____, 54, Baltimore City, December 30, 1912.

HALL, Colonel F_____ M_____, 80, Anne Arundel County, April 18, 1909.
HALL, F_____ Waters, 70, died at Philadelphia, March 26, 1908.
HALL, Dr. Hiram, 62, physician, Baltimore City, March 28, 1895.
HALL, J_____, 68, merchant, Annapolis, Anne Arundel County, August 16, 1893.
HALL, J_____ Bannister, 65, merchant, Baltimore City, February 4, 1902.
HALL, John, 86, Cockeysville, Baltimore County, October 9, 1900.
HALL, Captain John W., 78, Baltimore City, September 22, 1904.
HALL, Dr. Julius, 80, physician, Prince George's County, September 4, 1899.
HALL, Elisha John, 76, teacher, farmer, delegate of the Legislature, Montgomery County, September 10, 1893.
HALL, R_____ C_____, 78, Baltimore City, August 19, 1909.
HALL, Rev. Richard C. (P.E.), 76, Baltimore City, February 23, 1897.
HALL, Robert, 60, musician, Baltimore City, June 29, 1882.
HALL, Dr. Robert J., 76, physician, Baltimore City, September 29, 1895.
HALL, Rev. S_____ D_____ (P.E.), 49, Baltimore City, February 21, 1891.
HALL, Thomas W., 68, lawyer/editor, Baltimore City, July 5, 1901.
HALL, Major Wilburn R., 74, Confederate veteran, educator, Baltimore City, November 18, 1912.
HALL, Colonel Winchester, 90, Pocomoke City, Worcester County, December 10, 1909.
HALLE, Thomas J., 71, British consul, Baltimore City, died durin 1913--no month or day provided.
HALLER, Charles E., 59, Frederick, Frederick City, January 20, 1907.
HALLETT, Captain William A., 77, mariner, Baltimore City, December 1, 1900.
HALLIDAY, Robert, 76, florist, Baltimore City, April 15, 1889.
HALLIDAY, Robert J., 54, florist, Baltimore City, March 11, 1894.
HALLOWELL, Henry C., 70, educator, Montgomery County, August 11, 1899.
HALM, Dr. R_____ J_____, 70, Hagerstown, Washington County, January 8, 1892.
HALSTEAD, E_____ G_____, 66, policeman, Baltimore City, December 24, 1911.
HALYBURTON, William G., 45, journalist, Baltimore City, May 18, 1884.
HAMBLETON, Alfred H., 87, Preston, Caroline County, February 5, 1914.
HAMBLETON, General Frank S., 53, Baltimore City, August 17, 1908.
HAMBLETON, J_____ A_____, 75, financier, Baltimore City, June 1, 1902.
HAMBLETON, T_____ E_____, 77, financier, Baltimore City, September 21, 1906.
HAMBLETON, Samuel, 74, former Congressman, Easton, Talbot County, December 9, 1886.
HAMBURGER, Adolph, 47, Baltimore City, June 17, 1911.
HAMBURGER, Benjamin, 41, artist, Baltimore City, August 6, 1902.
HAMBURGER, Emanuel, 76, Baltimore City, January 13, 1910.

HAMBURGER, Heyman, 87, Baltimore City, July 8, 1912.
HAMBURGER, Isaac, 83, Baltimore City, December 2, 1909.
HAMBURGER, Jacob, 68, merchant, Baltimore City, February 18, 1895.
HAMBURGER, Julius, 38, Baltimore City, February 10, 1907.
HAMBURGER, Lazarus, 70, retired, Baltimore City, April 30, 1896.
HAMBURGER, Solomon, 80, Baltimore City, January 31, 1911.
HAMEL, Dr. E____ F____, 90, physician, Baltimore City, December 8, 1886.
HAMEL, George L., 67, Baltimore City, August 23, 1897.
HAMELL, Henry, 69, Baltimore City, November 10, 1912.
HAMER, William H., n.a., merchant, Baltimore City, May 17, 1881.
HAMILL, Alexander, 77, merchant, Baltimore City, May 17, 1878.
HAMILL, James H., 62, Oil Exchange, Baltimore City, February 5, 1897.
HAMILL, Patrick, n.a., ex-M.C. (sic), Oakland, Garrett County, January 15, 1895.
HAMILTON, Andrew J., 59, Baltimore City, February 24, 1914.
HAMILTON, C____ R____, 56, former member of the House of Delegates, Baltimore City, May 11, 1886.
HAMILTON, Charles, 70, florist, Baltimore City, March 3, 1898.
HAMILTON, Henry, 44, grocer, Baltimore City, November 7, 1882.
HAMILTON, James L., 80, druggist, Baltimore City, October 28, 1879.
HAMILTON, Lewis M., 52, coal operator, Baltimore City, December 24, 1904.
HAMILTON, Matthew A., 63, banker, Baltimore City, December 11, 1898.
HAMILTON, Richard C., 38, lawyer, Baltimore City, December 4, 1886.
HAMILTON, S____ Madison, 78, merchant, Baltimore City, February 3, 1894.
HAMILTON, Major Samuel T., 62, U.S. Army and retired marshall of the Baltimore police force; died at Harrisburg, Pennsylvania, March 30, 1906.
HAMILTON, William, 83, auctioneer, Baltimore City, November 15, 1902.
HAMILTON, Dr. William Augustus, n.a., physician, Baltimore City, May 10, 1888.
HAMILTON, William C., 36, clerk, Baltimore City Council, October 22, 1885.
HAMILTON, W____ L____, 64, machinist, Baltimore City, June 1, 1895.
HAMILTON, William T., 68, former Maryland Governor, Hagerstown, Washington County, September 26, 1888.
HAMLIN, G____ P____, 72, railroad contractor, Baltimore City, November 12, 1893.
HAMMER, Herman, 39, music professor, Baltimore City, December 3, 1885.
HAMMER, Dr. Ludwig, 37, physician, Baltimore City, May 23, 1894.
HAMMER, Peter, 76, millwright, Baltimore City, June 22, 1902.
HAMMERSLEY, David L., n.a., confectioner, Baltimore City, January 8, 1898.
HAMMERSLEY, Rev. James W. (M.E.), 77, Baltimore City, April 21, 1901.

HAMMETT, J_____ R_____, 59, railroad man, Baltimore City, April 29, 1909.
HAMMETT, J_____ R_____, 83, Baltimore City, February 26, 1912.
HAMMOND, G_____ G_____, 66, merchant, Baltimore City, February 6, 1893.
HAMMOND, Henry P., 83, builder, Baltimore City, August 28, 1904.
HAMMOND, Rev. J_____ P_____ (P.E.), 58, Baltimore City, August 9, 1884.
HAMMOND, Dr. Milton, 72, physician, Baltimore City, December 1, 1897.
HAMMOND, Ormond, 71, U.S. Assistant Treasurer at Baltimore; died in Talbot County, May 2, 1897.
HAMMOND, Ormond W., Jr., 24, Baltimore City, January 5, 1907.
HAMMOND, Sebastian, 109, black, Frederick County, _____ __, 1893.
HAMMOND, W_____ A_____, 45, solicitor, Baltimore City, September 28, 1892.
HAMMOND, Rev. W_____ S_____ (M.E.), n.a., Baltimore City, May 13, 1905.
HAMMOND, William R., 46, Baltimore City, December 19, 1909.
HAMNER, Rev. J_____ G_____ (Presbyterian), 89, Baltimore City, January 29, 1887.
HAMNER, Rev. J_____ G_____, 75, Baltimore City, July 13, 1911.
HANCE, Samuel B., 75, attorney, Baltimore City, July 3, 1904.
HANCE, Seth S., 67, druggist, Baltimore City, May 2, 1884.
HANCOCK, Major A_____ M_____, 72, attorney, Baltimore City, August 14, 1904.
HANCOCK, Absalom, 90, realtor, Baltimore City, June 30, 1882.
HANCOCK, John H., 52, druggist, Baltimore City, April 18, 1900.
HANCOCK, J_____ W_____, 28, pharmacist, Baltimore City, October 21, 1902.
HAND, John T., 48, journalist, Baltimore City, February 1, 1883.
HANDLOSER, Robert, 47, brewer, Baltimore City, November 15, 1894.
HANES, Frank W., 64, sexton, Baltimore City, October 24, 1902.
HANNA, George C., 50, merchant, Baltimore City, July 24, 1902.
HANRAHAN, John B., 42, builder, Baltimore City, September 8, 1902.
HANDY, Charles C., n.a., ex-police sergeant, Baltimore City, May 17, 1902.
HANDY, Rev. Henry J., 60, Pocomoke City, Worcester County, February 12, 1907.
HANDY, J_____ A_____, 85, bishop, Baltimore City, October 1, 1911.
HANDY, Luther, 82, Baltimore City, April 20, 1907.
HANDY, Colonel Thomas H., 54, of Maryland died in Louisiana, July 24, 1893.
HANEKE, Rev. August B., 30, of Baltimore died at sea, May 27, 1898.
HANEY, Louis M., n.a., mariner, Baltimore City, October 24, 1900.
HANK, Dr. J_____ W_____ F_____, 55, physician, Baltimore City, November 3, 1881.
HANK, John N., 72, teacher, Baltimore City, December 10, 1899.
HANLINE, Mauritz, 73, retired, Baltimore City, September 4, 1883.
HANLY, T_____ J_____, 55, merchant, Baltimore City, November 21, 1893.
HANNA, Hugh B., 56, Baltimore City, October 21, 1896.
HANSER, Rev. William G. H. (Lutheran), 54, Baltimore City, July 29, 1885.
HANSON, T_____ P_____, 69, merchant, Baltimore City, November 13, 1893.

HANSON, Thomas H., 65, philanthropist, Baltimore City, May 21, 1891.
HANSON, W____ H____, n.a., president, Florida Col'y (sic), December 2, 1878.
HANSON, William H., 51, Baltimore City, July 29, 1898.
HANWAY, W____ E____, 65, Foresthill, Harford County, February 1, 1910.
HANZSCHE, Henry, 85, printer, Baltimore City, September 22, 1905.
HARBAUGH, C____ Leonard, 60, retiree, Baltimore City, July 1, 1900.
HARBAUGH, F____ R____, 56, Baltimore City, December 15, 1911.
HARBURGER, Emmanuel, 88, merchant, Baltimore City, January 11, 1894.
HARBURGER, Sigmund, 70, retired, Baltimore City, May 12, 1905.
HARCOURT, Rev. R____, 70, Baltimore City, March 15, 1911.
HARDCASTLE, General Edmund L. F., 75, Talbot County, August 10, 1899.
HARDCASTLE, Dr. Edward M., 84, Easton, Talbot County, December 27, 1903.
HARDCASTLE, George T., 70, Easton, Talbot County, September 3, 1898.
HARDEN, J____ S____, 67, treasurer, Western Maryland Railroad, March 24, 1890.
HARDEN, James S., Jr., 30, clerk, Baltimore City, January 4, 1881.
HARDESTY, G____ W____, 62, brass founder, presumably Baltimore City, February 7, 1897.
HARDESTY, G____ W____, 62, Baltimore City, December 4, 1908.
HARDESTY, James W., 66, Calvert County, July 1, 1904.
HARDESTY, Richard S., 78, retired, Baltimore City, September 3, 1885.
HARDIE, Captain Robert, 83, merchant, Baltimore City, June 28, 1881.
HARDIN, Dr. James C., 73, Easton, Talbot County, December 17, 1904.
HARDING, Dr. Adam R., 71, Prince George's County, June 1, 1892.
HARDING, Peter, 69, captain, Baltimore City, September 9, 1879.
HARLEY, T____ L____ Walton, 42, Centreville, Queen Anne's County, January 6, 1901.
HARDING, William M. B., 54, printer, Baltimore City, August 14, 1894.
HARDEE, Dr. Albert W., 54, physician, Baltimore City, April 4, 1905.
HARDEN, Thomas J., 69, contractor, Baltimore City, August 22, 1905.
HARDY, John T., 85, Howard County, October __, 1911.
HARFORD, George R., 71, machinist, Baltimore City, September 16, 1883.
HARGETT, Charles N., 53, Frederick, Frederick County, March 19, 1905.
HARGETT, D____ H____, 62, Frederick, Frederick County, September 29, 1908.
HARGETT, John E. W., 52, Frederick, Frederick County, May 9, 1902.
HARGIS, John P., 75, Snow Hill, Worcester County, November 30, 1900.
HARGIS, William T., 80, Somerset County, September 17, 1905.

HARIG, Bernard L., 63, Baltimore City, November 17, 1892.
HARIG, Joseph G., 82, Baltimore City, October 7, 1907.
HARKER, Dr. John F., 40, physician, Baltimore City, April 25, 1887.
HARKER, John J., 75, builder, Baltimore City, November 11, 1892.
HARKER, Dr. Richard M. J., 65, editor, Baltimore City, November 4, 1895.
HARLAN, Dr. David, 84, physician, Bel Air, Harford County, July 12, 1893.
HARLAN, Henry, 50, Harford County, October 27, 1898.
HARLEY, A____ G____, 71, educator, Laurel, Prince George's County, August 3, 1905.
HARLEY, Albert G., 40, teacher, Centreville, Queen Anne's County, August 17, 1898.
HARLEY, James K., 61, artist, Baltimore City, February 4, 1889.
HARLEY, Captain L____ M____, 36, mariner, Baltimore City, November 19, 1882.
HARMAN, Daniel, 71, tailor, Baltimore City, October 24, 1883.
HARMAN, Rev. H____ M____ (M.E.), 75, Baltimore City, July 2, 1897.
HARMAN, William, 74, musician, Baltimore City, March 16, 1881.
HARP, Daniel V., 78, Frederick, Frederick County, ____ __, 1913.
HARPER, Franklin H., 69, Kent County, June 10, 1907.
HARPER, J____ S____, 60, Mansion House, Baltimore City, January 13, 1892.
HARPER, James, 79, ferryboat captain, Baltimore City, November 2, 1893.
HARRIMAN, Horace M., n.a., lumber dealer, Baltimore City, July 23, 1906.
HARRINGTON, Elisha, 89, retired, Baltimore City, November 20, 1882.
HARRIS, Albraham, 59, merchant, Baltimore City, October 20, 1904.
HARRIS, Rev. Alfred (Bapist), n.a., Baltimore City, August 7, 1896.
HARRIS, B____ Hopkins, 79, banker, Baltimore City, May 24, 1901.
HARRIS, Benjamin G., 89, ex-M. C. (sic), St. Mary's County, April 4, 1895.
HARRIS, Benjamin G., 76, insurance, Baltimore City, July 7, 1897.
HARRIS, J____ Morrison, 80, attorney, Baltimore City, July 16, 1898.
HARRIS, James Bailey, 78, builder, Baltimore City, November 13, 1880.
HARRIS, John, 78, contractor, Baltimore City, April 11, 1892.
HARRIS, Joseph, 86, merchant, Baltimore City, December 9, 1905.
HARRIS, Mrs. Mehitabel, 87, Baltimore City, July 15, 1884.
HARRIS, Patrick, 43, theater manager, Baltimore City, August 20, 1890.
HARRIS, W____ A____, 61, surgeon, U.S. Navy, October 26, 1881.
HARRIS, William, 60, manufacturer, Baltimore City, July 14, 1903.
HARRIS, William D., 80, retired, Baltimore City, September 27, 1897.
HARRISON, C____ K____, 60, Baltimore City, April 20, 1908.
HARRISON, Frank A., 55, druggist, Baltimore City, October 23, 1897.
HARRISON, Frederick, 87, surveyor, Baltimore City, January 16, 1892.

HARRISON, George Law, 30, merchant, Baltimore City, June 5, 1902.
HARRISON, Dr. H____ T____, 69, Baltimore City, March 4, 1914.
HARRISON, Rev. Hall (P.E.), 62, Ellicott City, Howard County, February 5, 1900.
HARRISON, J____ G____, 74, Berlin, Worcester County, December 12, 1914.
HARRISON, James P., 45, tavern keeper, Baltimore City, August 7, 1878.
HARRISON, Captain John W., 65, Baltimore City, June 27, 1905.
HARRISON, Rev. Peyton (Presbyterian), 86, Baltimore City, September 10, 1887.
HARRISON, R____ G____, 53, tavern proprietor, Baltimore City, June 25, 1883.
HARRISON, Thomas B., 43, merchant, Baltimore City, February 25, 1885.
HARRISON, W____ E____ C____, 66, bookseller, Baltimore City, January 15, 1898.
HARRISON, William G., 82, retired, Baltimore City, November 18, 1883.
HARRISON, Dr. William G., 53, physician, Baltimore City, August 30, 1895.
HARRISON, Colonel William H., 72, presumably Baltimore City, April 1, 1913.
HARRISS, William C., 81, millwright, Baltimore City, December 27, 1902.
HARRYMAN, J____ G____, 56, merchant, Baltimore City, May 28, 1893.
HART, Captain Benjamin, 79, Cambridge, Dorchester County, November 6, 1905.
HART, Henry B., 55, former member of the Maryland Legislature, Baltimore City, February 5, 1889.
HART, Miss Isabel, 52, Baltimore City, September 6, 1891.
HART, John D., n.a., fruiterer, Baltimore City, November 13, 1900.
HARTLEY, George, 70, manufacturer, Baltimore City, December 3, 1882.
HARTMAN, Dr. Andrew, 66, physician, Baltimore City, December 15, 1884.
HARTMAN, George F., 62, Baltimore City, August 20, 1898.
HARTMAN, Henry C., 60, Baltimore City, May 13, 1898.
HARTMAN, Isaac, 75, banker, Baltimore City, May 22, 1888.
HARTMAN, Jacob P., 68, merchant, Baltimore City, February 16, 1880.
HARTMAN, Wilton H., 39, merchant, Baltimore City, September 12, 1884.
HARMON, Amos R., 73, surveyor, Baltimore City, April 16, 1902.
HARTSOCK, Rev. S____ M____, 69, Laurel, Prince George's County, March 18, 1908.
HARTY, Mrs. Mary, 96, Baltimore City, June 3, 1883.
HARTZ, Sampson, 84, retired, Baltimore City, September 17, 1884.
HARVEY, Alexander, 58, Baltimore City, November 22, 1914.
HARVEY, Charles W., 85, B. & O. Railroad, Baltimore City, December 8, 1905.
HARVEY, James, 76, retired contractor, Baltimore City, January 18, 1901.
HARVEY, Joshua G., 78, banker, Baltimore City, October 19, 1906.
HARVEY, Henry D., 76, merchant, Baltimore City, December 17, 1889.

HARVEY, William, 58, manufacturer, Baltimore City, August __, 1904.
HARVEY, William H., 45, tugboat captain, Baltimore City, September 11, 1881.
HARWOOD, F____ N____, 74, Baltimore City, February 30, 1910.
HARWOOD, Lt. Col. Franklin, n.a., U.S. Army, "well known in Maryland and stationed three years in Baltimore as engineer of the Light House Department"; died at Boston March 26, 1883.
HARWOOD, Major Sprigg, 86, Annapolis, Anne Arundel County, December 17, 1894.
HARWOOD, William, 90, Annapolis, Anne Arundel County, January 21, 1900.
HASLOP, Rev. John S. M. (M.E.), 31 or 37, Baltimore City, May 20, 1887.
HASSENCAMP, Ferdinand, 58, druggist, Baltimore City, April 30, 1885.
HASSON, William F. A., n.a., reporter, Baltimore City, March 6, 1905.
HAST, H____, 63, Cumberland, Allegany County, December 25, 1909.
HASTINGS, Major D____ H____, 68, U.S. Army, Baltimore City, September 22, 1882.
HASTINGS, E____ J____, n.a., builder, Howard County, September 4, 1893.
HASWELL, John, 77, builder, Baltimore City, July 21, 1893.
HATCH, Samuel T., 69, merchant, Baltimore City, July 10, 1881.
HATCHESON, B____ O____, 77, justice of the peace, Baltimore City, March 10, 1879.
HATTER, Charles W., 64, banker, Baltimore City, April 14, 1905.
HATTON, Edward, 67, merchant, Baltimore City, June 3, 1895.
HAUGH, John, 55, contractor, Baltimore City, March 27, 1884.
HAUPT, General Herman, 88, Civil War veteran, Baltimore City, December 14, 1905.
HAUSE, John A., 57, former Baltimore City police sergeant, March 23, 1887.
HAUSER, G____ F____, 81, Baltimore City, May 24, 1910.
HAUSER, Rev. J____ C____ (German Reformed), 52, Baltimore City, November 20, 1890.
HAWKEY, Joseph, 73, coal dealer, Baltimore City, January 14, 1878.
HAWKINS, Joseph, 45, detective, Baltimore City, August 27, 1887.
HAWKINS, Dr. P____ W____, n.a., La Plata, Charles County, September 17, 1908.
HAWLEY, Martin, 57, lumber merchant, Baltimore City, July 10, 1887.
HAWLEY, R____ K____, 77, of Baltimore City at Cleveland, Ohio, June 10, 1898.
HAYDEN, Dr. H____ M____, 83, dentist, Baltimore City, March 7, 1891.
HAYDEN, H____ W____, Sr., 69, bookkeeper, Baltimore City, December 4, 1881.
HAYDEN, Oscar G., 64, St. Mary's County, August 3, 1903.
HAYDEN, William N., 68, former judge, Westminster, Carroll County, September 14, 1885.

HAYES, George, 87, Harford County, March 24, 1893.
HAYES, John S., 82, Baltimore City, October 24, 1898.
HAYES, John S., 78, Baltimore City, December 21, 1913.
HAYES, Timothy, 85, Baltimore City, October 16, 1907.
HAYNES, David F., n.a., Baltimore City, August 24, 1908.
HAYS, Mrs. J____ A____, n.a., died at Colorado Springs, Colorado, July 18, 1909.
HAYS, John Otho, 77, teacher, Frederick County, October 14, 1905.
HAYWARD, Robert R., 65, explorer, Baltimore City, September 18, 1909.
HAYWARD, Dr. William R., 79, Cambridge, Dorchester County, November 7, 1896.
HAZAZER, Joseph, 60, dancing master, Baltimore City, April 27, 1900.
HAZELHURST, Henry R., 64, civil engineer, Baltimore City, February 21, 1900.
HAZELHURST, Samuel, 75, retired, Baltimore City, July 21, 1889.
HAZELTINE, Dr. Silas W., 68, physician, Baltimore City, February 14, 1905.
HAZELTON, William B., 33, journalist, Baltimore City, November 5, 1886.
HEAGY, James, 80, builder, Baltimore City, October 2, 1882.
HEALD, Commander Eugene de F., 50, Annapolis, Anne Arundel County, March 27, 1898.
HEALD, John K., 75, manufacturer, Baltimore City, February 12, 1896.
HEALD, William H., 62, merchant, Baltimore City, February 5, 1882.
HEALY, F____ J____, 74, teacher, Baltimore City, October 20, 1882.
HEALY, J____ Oscar, 64, veteran fire-fighter, Baltimore City, January 22, 1900.
HEBB, H____ C____, 67, Sharpsburg, Washington County, February 13, 1910.
HEBB, Hopewell, 68, former mayor of Cumberland, Allegany County, March 29, 1899.
HEBB, Dr. J____ W____, 71, Ellicott City, Howard County, May 18, 1910.
HEBB, Captain John S., n.a., St. Mary's County, September 28, HEBBEL, Julius, 52, photographer, Baltimore City, November 23, 1905.
HECHHEIMER, Samuel, 50, Baltimore City, February 18, 1897.
HECHT, Jacob, 63, merchant, Baltimore City, December 21, 1891.
HECHT, Mendel, 84, merchant, Baltimore City, November 13, 1899.
HECHT, Moses, 78, retired, Baltimore City, July 16, 1903.
HEDDINGER, D____ C____, 65, Baltimore City, November 14, 1907.
HEDGES, Harry V., 45, civil engineer, Baltimore City, November 25, 1903.
HEDIAN, J____ B____, 48, art collector, Baltimore City, November 25, 1905.
HEDIAN, Thomas, 64, merchant, Baltimore City, October 17, 1899.
HEFFNER, Rev. Edward (M.E.), 76, Baltimore City, August 21, 1886.
HEFFNER, Edward, 42, contractor, Baltimore City, February 4, 1887.

HEFFNER, George R., 65, Baltimore City, October 11, 1912.
HEFT, Dr. H____ J____, 66, Randallstown, Baltimore County, January 10, 1908.
HEHL, Louis, 67, manufacturer, Baltimore City, November 15, 1898.
HEICHEMER, Rev. Charles H., 57, Loyola College, Baltimore City, October 21, 1893.
HEIHLE, Ernst G. A., 84, educator, Baltimore City, February 18, 1904.
HEIMENDAHL, W____ E____, 52, musician, Baltimore City, February 22, 1910.
HEIMILLER, C____, 65, carpenter, Baltimore City, December 24, 1902.
HEIMULLER, William, 54, manufacturer, Baltimore City, March 18, 1902.
HEINE, Henry, 85, cooper, Baltimore City, January 14, 1900.
HEINLEIN, Frederick, 71, Frederick, Frederick County, June 9, 1907.
HEINZ, Charles, 77, machinist, Baltimore City, May 15, 1901.
HEINZ, Sergeant William M., 57, Baltimore City, May 16, 1914.
HEINZMAN, Rev. J____, 60, Baltimore City, January 12, 1908.
HEISE, Ludwig, 95, retired, Baltimore City, September 29, 1897.
HEISKELL, J____ Monroe, n.a., Baltimore City, October 8, 1899.
HEISKELL, Dr. P____ H____, 77, physician, Prince George's County, January 9, 1893.
HEISKELL, Dr. Sydney O., 63, quarantine physician, Baltimore City, June 22, 1906.
HEIZLER, Francis D., 66, bookbinder, Baltimore City, April 2, 1882.
HELDMANN, Dr. Joel A., 77, Baltimore City, March 23, 1898.
HELLBACH, Henry, 54, Baltimore City, October 4, 1895.
HELLDORFER, Sebastian, 57, brewer, Baltimore City, January 29, 1893.
HELLWIG, Justus W., 40, Baltimore City, January 26, 1914.
HELM, C____ G____, 57, December 14, 1911.
HELM, Joseph H., 69, former policeman, Baltimore City, July 9, 1900.
HELM, Wilbur T., 57, merchant, Baltimore City, March 5, 1904.
HEMMETER, John, 70, retired, Baltimore City, February 3, 1899.
HEMMICK, Jacob, 98, veteran of the War of 1812, Baltimore City, June 4, 1888.
HENCKLE, Jennie, 21, seamstress, Front Street Theater panic, December 27, 1895.
HENDERSON, Captain Charles J., n.a., Baltimore City, November 10, 1914.
HENDERSON, Daniel M., 55, poet and bookseller, Baltimore City, September 8, 1906.
HENDERSON, Rev. David (M.E.), 83, Baltimore City, April 18, 1897.
HENDERSON, James A., 73, merchant, Baltimore City, February 13, 1879.
HENDERSON, James G., 70, Sandy Spring, Montgomery County, July 18, 1907.
HENDERSON, William F., 64, Harford County, December 20, 1911.
HENDERSON, William T., 66, merchant, Baltimore City, February 12, 1905.

HENDRICKSON, Dr. William H., 26, physician, Baltimore City, August 22, 1902.
HENKELMAN, Frederick, 74, merchant, Baltimore City, May 11, 1893.
HENKLE, Dr. Eli J., 64, former Congressman, Baltimore City, November 1, 1893.
HENNAMAN, Jesse, 81, manufacturer, Baltimore City, September 8, 1882.
HENNEGEN, William H., 66, jeweler, Baltimore City, June 25, 1901.
HENNICK, Captain J____ C____, 77, retired, Baltimore City, September 19, 1884.
HENNICK, J____ M____, 57, chief engineer, Baltimore City Fire Department, February 1, 1893.
HENNING, F____ W____, 81, merchant tailor, Baltimore City, December 1, 1902.
HENNING, Herman D.A., 51, sculptor and instructor at the Maryland Institute, July 3, 1893.
HENNINGS, Ernest A., n.a., merchant, Baltimore City, August 27, 1881.
HENRIX, F____ A____, 62, former teacher, Baltimore City, February 16, 1902.
HENRY, Charles, 81, mechanic, Baltimore City, January 4, 1883.
HENRY, Daniel Maynadier, 76, lawyer, Cambridge, Dorchester County, August 30, 1899.
HENRY, Francis Jenkins, Jr., 52, Cambridge, Dorchester County, August 5, 1899.
HENRY, Francis Jenkins, 85, Cambridge, Dorchester County, March 18, 1902.
HENRY, John C., 60, Easton, Talbot County, July 15, 1905.
HENRY, Captain Joseph, 68, Baltimore City, July 6, 1909.
HENRY, Dr. Samuel H., 68, physician, Baltimore City, July 12, 1887.
HENRY, William T., 65, Baltimore City, September 13, 1914.
HENRY, Zadok P., 72, Worcester County, January 26, 1904.
HENSLER, John A., 90, retired, Baltimore City, April 21, 1905.
HERBECK, Nicholas, 58, cabinetmaker, Baltimore City, December 2, 1882.
HERBERT, Edward, 55, shipping agent, Baltimore City, October 18, 1886.
HERBERT, J____ B____, 66, justice, Towson, Baltimore County, February 28, 1910.
HERBERT, James R., 51, Baltimore City police commissioner; died near Woodstock, Howard County, August 5, 1884.
HERBERT, Lieutenant Mark A., 26, Baltimore City, December 19, 1899.
HERBERT, Rev. W____ G____, 60, Baltimore City, April 18, 1907.
HERBERT, William H., 67, Hagerstown, Washington County, ____ ____, 1906.
HERFORD, Julius S., 50, restaurateur, Baltimore City, April 28, 1883.
HERING, F____ L____, 74, Finksburg, Carroll County, November 16, 1909.
HERING, Joshua W., n.a., Westminster, Carroll County, September 23, 1913.

HERMAN, Dr. Nathan, n.a., Baltimore City, September 13, 1913.
HERMANN, Peter, 76, retired manufacturer, Baltimore City, December 14, 1901.
HERPEL, Rev. John H., 65, Baltimore City, October 19, 1890.
HERRING, B_____ W_____, 82, former marshal, Baltimore City, June 17, 1892.
HERRING, George W., 77, retired, Baltimore City, December 6, 1897.
HERRING, John Q. A., 71, express, Baltimore City, February 9, 1897.
HERRING, Original, 79, merchant, Baltimore City, September 14, 1899.
HERSPERGER, Tilghman T., 79, Frederick, Frederick County, November 22, 1903.
HERZBERG, Seligman, n.a., merchant, Baltimore City, February 7, 1893.
HERZBURG, Lazarus, 87, weaver, Baltimore City, December 5, 1882.
HERZOG, John, 72, retired merchant, Baltimore City, June 6, 1900.
HESS, Francis A., 84, milk dealer, Baltimore City, February 7, 1883.
HESS, Dr. Frederick, 90, physician, Baltimore City, August 23, 1891.
HESS, John P., 65, Baltimore City, February 20, 1914.
HESS, Louis, 82, Baltimore City, November 7, 1911.
HESS, M_____ S_____, 46, merchant, Baltimore City, January 2, 1879.
HESS, Nathan, 57, manufacturer, Baltimore City, August 29, 1881.
HESS, Solomon N., 46, manufacturer, Baltimore City, February 25, 1903.
HETTCHEN, John, n.a., butcher, Baltimore City, August 22, 1880.
HEUISLER, Mrs. Catherine, 82, presumably Baltimore City, October 9, 1913.
HEUISLER, Joseph S., 67, attorney, Baltimore City, October 15, 1899.
HEUISLER, William G., 44, engineer, Baltimore City, March 17, 1892.
HEWES, James Elliott, 80, retired, Baltimore City, November 23, 1900.
HEWITT, Horatio D., 64, composer, Baltimore City, December 23, 1894.
HEWITT, Professor John H., 89, author, Baltimore City, October 7, 1890.
HEWITT, Captain Joshua, 81, Baltimore City, October 25, 1912.
HEYDE, Rev. George W., 79, Parkton, Baltimore County, January 23, 1913.
HIBBARD, James M., 80, retired, Baltimore City, December 1, 1883.
HIBBARD, Job, 83, banker, New Windsor, Carroll County, August 22, 1901.
HIBN, John B., 60, grocer, Baltimore City, January 10, 1881.
HICKEY, John J., n.a., merchant, Baltimore City, November 27, 1897.
HICKMAN, George S., 84, retired, Baltimore City, August 13, 1895.
HICKMAN, William H., 80, undertaker, Baltimore City, December 22, 1899.

HICKMAN, William H., 62, compositor, Baltimore City, February 5, 1904.
HICKOK, Dr. Charles, 86, Cumberland, Allegany County, December 5, 1906.
HICKS, C____ H____, 55, bridge builder, Baltimore City, September 1, 1902.
HICKS, Dr. George L., 63, Cambridge, Dorchester County, July 13, 1902.
HICKS, Captain John G., 60, mariner, Baltimore City, July 17, 1901.
HIGGENBOTHAM, Edward, 65, musician, Baltimore City, February 27, 1882.
HIGGINS, Asa, 88, captain, Baltimore City, August 27, 1879.
HIGGINS, Edward, Jr., 52, auctioneer, Baltimore City, December 25, 1886.
HIGGINS, Eugene, 61, politician, Baltimore City, January 13, 1899.
HIGGINS, Jesse T., 73, merchant, Baltimore City, October 14, 1887.
HIGHBARGER, William J., 50, Sharpsburg, Washington County, November 21, 1907.
HIGHLY, Rev. Burton S., n.a., Talbot County, March 11, 1904.
HILDEBRANDT, Charles H., 65, manufacturer, Baltimore City, May 16, 1893.
HILDEBRANDT, Henry, 82, cooper, Baltimore City, September 24, 1897.
HILDT, Rev. George (M.E.), 79, Baltimore City, March 7, 1882.
HILGARTNER, Andrew, 48, Towson, Baltimore County, March 21, 1914.
HILGARTNER, Henry, 81, Baltimore City, December 28, 1911.
HILGARTNER, Ludwig, 69, merchant, Baltimore City, January 4, 1902.
HILL, Dr. Alexander S., 38, veterinarian, Catonsville, Baltimore County, January 22, 1906.
HILL, Charles, 78, merchant, Baltimore City, November 4, 1901.
HILL, Dr. Charles I., 36, Baltimore City, February 24, 1914.
HILL, Captain Darius J., 70, retired, Baltimore City, April 4, 1900.
HILL, Captain J____ S____, n.a., Queen Anne's County, March 3, 1893.
HILL, John Harvey, 70, Bsltimore City, November 10, 1913.
HILL, Lewis N., 82, retired, Baltimore City, February 16, 1905.
HILL, Richard, n.a., hatter, Baltimore City, January 8, 1892.
HILL, Lieutenant Richard, n.a., Annapolis, Anne Arundel County, May 8, 1913.
HILL, Samuel E., 58, realtor, Baltimore City, December 19, 1901.
HILL, Samuel J., 77, Kent County, July 23, 1900.
HILL, Thomas, 75, real estate, Baltimore City, September 21, 1909.
HILL, William I., 60, lawyer, Upper Marlboro, Prince George's County, July 17, 1898.
HILL, Dr. William N., 51, Baltimore City, December 25, 1908.
HILL, William J. B., 28, lawyer, Baltimore City, October 11, 1881.
HILL, William R., 51, attorney, Baltimore City, November 16, 1878.
HILLCARY, Dr. J____ W____, 66, physician, Frederick County, January 13, 1897.
HILLEBRAND, August, 79, merchant, Baltimore City, September 15, 1899.

HILTON, Mrs. S____ A____, 94, Baltimore City, February 23, 1910.
HIMMEL, Moses L., 62, manufacturer, Baltimore City, October 9, 1905.
HINCHCLIFFE, Dr. Harry P., 31, Elkton, Cecil County, April 19, 1902.
HINDES, Joseph, n.a., bank officer, Baltimore City, August 16, 1898.
HINDES, S____ J____, 54, bank officer, Baltimore City, September 7, 1893.
HINDS, William S., 81, retired, Baltimore City, October 29, 1901.
HINES, Jesse K., 60, insurance, Baltimore City, September 20, 1889.
HINKLER, George, 72, merchant, Baltimore City, September 24, 1894.
HINKLEY, Charles, 70, broker, Baltimore City, March 17, 1899.
HINKLEY, Edward Otis, 72, lawyer, Baltimore City, July 13, 1896.
HINKS, Lewis E., 52, merchant, Baltimore City, September 19, 1904.
HINKS, Samuel, 72, former mayor of Baltimore City, November 30, 1887.
HINKS, William H., 68, Frederick, Frederick County, December 29, 1912.
HIPKINS, Wiliam, 72, insurance, Baltimore City, November 28, 1888.
HIPSLEY, Levin F., 63, Baltimore City, September 23, 1898.
HIRSHBERG, Henry, 68, retired, Baltimore City, April 14, 1884.
HIRSCHBERG, Natan J., 84, retired, Baltimore City, April 3, 1898.
HISER, James H., 55, baliff, Baltimore City, July 4, 1892.
HISS, Douglas, 46, merchant, Baltimore City, June 27, 1882.
HISS, George, 78, Baltimore City, August 9, 1911.
HISS, George R. A., 30, bank teller, Baltimore City, March 22, 1904.
HISS, Jacob, Jr., 87, merchant, Baltimore City, January 7, 1880.
HISS, John C., 33, merchant, Baltimore City, April 23, 1895.
HISS, Philip, 85, furniture manufacturer, Baltimore City, January 22, 1881.
HISS, William H., 64, purveyor, Bayview, Baltimore City, January 4, 1887.
HITCHCOCK, B. C., 40, Bel Air, Harford County, May 22, 1908.
HITCHCOCK, William H., 71 or 74, proofreader, Baltimore City, December 22, 1898.
HITCHENS, Owens, 61, Forstburg, Allegany County, March 20, 1893.
HITCHINS, Adams H., 74, merchant, Frostburg, Allegany County, October 5, 1906.
HITE, James M., 67, broker, Baltimore City, March 10, 1892.
HITSELBERGER, John A., 77, Baltimore City, November 28, 1896.
HITZEL, Franklin A., 66, Baltimore City, December 10, 1909.
HOBBS, Alexander H., 68, attorney, Baltimore City, January 25, 1888.
HOBBS, Bruce H., n.a., court col. (sic), Baltimore City, March 5, 1903.

HOBBS, Columbus M., 52, justice, Baltimore City, April 23, 1895.
HOBBS, Daniel, 77, retired, Baltimore City, July 7, 1902.
HOBBS, Rev. J____ H____, 79, Howard County, May 5, 1893.
HOBLITZELL, Charles B., 33, broker, Baltimore City, December 31, 1903.
HOBLITZELL, Felter S., 61, attorney, Baltimore City, May 2, 1900.
HOBLITZELL, Rev. S____ A____, 74, Bel Air, Harford County, April 6, 1911.
HOBLITZELL, William, 86, retired, Baltimore City, November 8, 1895.
HOCHHEIMER, Rev. Henry, 93, Baltimore City, January 25, 1912.
HODGES, Benjamin M., Jr., 69, merchant, Baltimore City, March 18, 1881.
HODGES, James, 72, former mayor of Baltimore City, February 15, 1895.
HODGES, William Hanson, 43, architect, Baltimore Coty, May 20, 1908.
HODGES, William R., 62, merchant, Baltimore City, November 7, 1887.
HODSON, James B., 70, retired, Baltimore City, November 22, 1886.
HOECK, Henry, 77, undertaker, Baltimore City, June 26, 1894.
HOEN, Adolph, n.a., Baltimore City, March 29, 1911.
HOEN, August, 65, lithographer, Baltimore City, September 20, 1886.
HOEN, Ernest, 64, lithographer, Baltimore City, June 16, 1893.
HOEN, Henry, 66, lithographer, Baltimore City, March 14, 1893.
HOEN, Irving W., 43, publisher, Baltimore City, December 20, 1903.
HOERR, Rev. John, 63, Baltimore City, January 18, 1907.
HOFF, Rev. John F. (P.E.), 68, Baltimore City, December 19, 1881.
HOFFMAN, Charles T., n.a., Baltimore City, April 11, 1898.
HOFFMAN, Dr. D____ P____, 72, physician, Baltimore City, October 9, 1892.
HOFFMAN, E____ R____, 88, Baltimore City, May 3, 1912.
HOFFMAN, Edmund H., 58, former sheriff, Baltimore City, October 23, 1906.
HOFFMAN, George L., 76, leather dealer, Baltimore City, June 18, 1891.
HOFFMAN, Rev. Henry (R.C.), 52, Baltimore City, July 21, 1882.
HOFFMAN, Henry W., 69, associate judge, Cumberland, Allegany County, July 28, 1895.
HOFFMAN, J____ Latimer, n.a., merchant, Baltimore City, May 29, 1897.
HOFFMAN, John H., 79, Baltimore City, January 30, 1907.
HOFFMAN, John M., 48, merchant, Baltimore City, November 2, 1881.
HOFFMAN, Robert G., 64, retired, Baltimore City, February 8, 1895.
HOFFMAN, Samuel, 89, New Windsor, Carroll County, January 31, 1900.
HOFFMAN, Viet, 74, manufacturer, Baltimore City, February 5, 1882.

HOFFMAN, William Gilmor, 70, retired, Baltimore City, May 16, 1896.
HOFFMANN, Dr. Karl, 57, physician, Baltimore City, April 8, 1895.
HOFFMEISTER, H____, 39, Councilman, Baltimore City, October 3, 1902.
HOFFZUGOTT, James, 81, Roman Catholic priest, Baltimore City, August 18, 1894.
HOGAN, Cornelius R., 38, hotelier, Baltimore City, February 2, 1883.
HOGENDORP, Elias, 80, retired, Baltimore City, May 11, 1884.
HOGG, John S., 58, building inspector, Baltimore City, October 5, 1884.
HOGG, J____ W____, n.a., chief clerk of the Navy Department, Rockville, Montgomery County, November 15, 1893.
HOLBROOK, A____ I____, 68, Baltimore City, December 10, 1907.
HOLBROOK, J____ T____, 78, California pioneer died in Baltimore City, August 10, 1904.
HOLDEN, Caleb T., 84, retired, Baltimore City, December 9, 1896.
HOLDEN, E____ P____, 79, retired, Baltimore City, July 13, 1886.
HOLDEN, Ira S., 76, merchant, Baltimore City, January 4, 1880.
HOLDEN, James, 82, Ellicott City, Howard County, May 26, 1909.
HOLLAND, Albert, 62, music professor, Baltimore City, February 10, 1887.
HOLLAND, Jackson, 76, Baltimore City, October 13, 1908.
HOLLAND, John C., 75, retired, Baltimore City, January 16, 1898.
HOLLIDAY, Daniel, 68, merchant, Baltimore City, November 26, 1892.
HOLLIDAY, Dr. J____ G____, 67, Baltimore City, March 16, 1912.
HOLLIDAY, Rev. William H., 43, Baltimore City, March 23, 1878.
HOLLINGSHEAD, D____ P____, 59, Harford County, January 14, 1907.
HOLLINGSHEAD, David A., 63, school teacher, Baltimore City, April 24, 1880.
HOLLINGSWORTH, Nathaniel T., 64, Harford County, July 22, 1898.
HOLLINS, Cumb(erland?) D., 75, retired, Baltimore City, January 3, 1897.
HOLLINS, Commodore George N., 78, Baltimore City, January 18, 1878.
HOLLINS, Robert S., 86, manufacturer, Baltimore City, August 2, 1882.
HOLLOHAN, Rev. John S., 37, vice-president, Loyola College, S.J., Baltimore City, April 12, 1901.
HOLLOWAY, A____ L____, 45, Baltimore City, October 30, 1913.
HOLLOWAY, Charles T., 70, Baltimore City, March 17, 1898.
HOLLOWAY, J____ Q____ A____, 74, merchant, Baltimore City, January 14, 1904.
HOLLYDAY, George T., 74, Confederate veteran, Baltimore City, August 24, 1907.
HOLLYDAY, George T., 42, insurance, Baltimore City, June 22, 1888.
HOLLYDAY, R____ C____, 73, former Secretary of State of Maryland, January 18, 1885.
HOLMES, J____ B____, 81, farmer, Baltimore County, November 8, 1881.
HOLMES, Dr. Lewis, 53, physician, Baltimore City, October 17, 1883.

HOLMES, Milton W., 44, merchant, Baltimore City, July 4, 1891.
HOLMES, William, 57, merchant, Baltimore City, June 12, 1881.
HOLMES, William, 68, manufacturer, Baltimore City, August 7, 1883.
HOLTER, Lewis, 82, retired, Baltimore City, June 14, 1885.
HOLTER, Samuel B., 73, Frederick, Frederick County, June 3, 1909.
HOLTON, Hart B., 71, Baltimore County, January 4, 1907.
HOLTZMAN, H____ W____, 66, merchant, Baltimore City, June 28, 1882.
HOMER, Charles C., Sr., n.a., died at Bremen, Germany, September 14, 1914.
HOMRIGHAUSEN, George, 71, merchant, Baltimore City, June 20, 1899.
HOOD, General John M., 63, president of United Railways, Baltimore City, December 17, 1906.
HOOD, Joshua, 86, retired, Baltimore City, March 13, 1890.
HOOE, Peter H., 77, Prince George's County, May 12, 1898.
HOOGEWERFF, Mrs. Mary E., 90, Baltimore City, July 17, 1913.
HOOK, John R., 68, mechanic, Baltimore City, August 21, 1884.
HOOK, Richard W., 89, retired, Baltimore City, May 31, 1895.
HOOPER, Edward, 52, shipper, Baltimore City, July 7, 1894.
HOOPER, Eugene H., 38, manufacturer, Baltimore City, December 16, 1901.
HOOPER, J____ E____, 68, Baltimore City, July 5, 1908.
HOOPER, Captain James, 94, Baltimore City, March 14, 1898.
HOOPER, James A., 81, retired merchant, Baltimore City, May 19, 1897.
HOOPER, Captain John B., n.a., Salisbury, Wicomico County, August 1, 1893.
HOOPER, Captain Luther E., 76, Baltimore City, December 22, 1913.
HOOPER, Robert, 72, retired, Baltimore City, December 28, 1884.
HOOPER, T____ H____, 80, retired reporter, Baltimore City, July 9, 1902.
HOOPER, Theodore, 60, manufacturer, Baltimore City, September 11, 1906.
HOOPER, Theodore L., 40, merchant, Baltimore City, May 10, 1899.
HOOPER, Dr. W____ H____, 59, prominent physician and a native of Worcester County, died at Philadelphia, December 18, 1883.
HOOPER, William E., 73, manufacturer, Baltimore City, December 11, 1885.
HOOPES, Franklin B., 83, retired, Baltimore City, August 19, 1883.
HOOPES, Dr. William H., 60, dentist, Baltimore City, January 30, 1895.
HOOVER, Ignatius, 81, retired, Baltimore City, October 24, 1905.
HOOVER, John, 80, Hagerstown, Washington County, June 6, 1909.
HOPKINS, David, 77, retired manufacturer, Baltimore City, July 3, 1901.
HOPKINS, Dr. Edward H., 58, Frederick, Frederick County, June 28, 1906.
HOPKINS, Franklin, 64, manufacturer, Baltimore City, August 28, 1884.
HOPKINS, Gerard, 65, Baltimore City, January 28, 1901.
HOPKINS, Gerard T., 84, retired, Baltimore City, October 10, 1900.
HOPKINS, George W., 51, merchant, Baltimore City, March 22, 1894.
HOPKINS, John G., 53, artist, Baltimore City, June 17, 1891.
HOPKINS, James H., 68, builder, Baltimore City, April 2, 1887.

HOPKINS, John S., 49, merchant, Baltimore City, September 29, 1892.
HOPKINS, Johns, n.a., of Baltimore City, died at Philadelphia, June 7, 1895.
HOPKINS, Joseph, n.a., architect, Baltimore City, June 6, 1892.
HOPKINS, Lambert N., 79, merchant, Baltimore City, June 27, 1891.
HOPKINS, Lewis N., 70, secretary, trustees of Johns Hopkins University, August 19, 1904.
HOPKINS, Thomas, 76, retired, Baltimore City, February 17, 1886.
HOPKINS, Thomas, 83, former pilot, Baltimore City, March 15, 1894.
HOPKINS, William, 67, merchant, Baltimore City, May 28, 1881.
HOPKINS, William, 86, Cambridge, Dorchester County, October 2, 1900.
HOPKINSON, Dr. Moses A., 72, physician, Baltimore City, January 20, 1897.
HOPPER, Daniel C., 83, retired, Baltimore City, February 26, 1899.
HOPPER, S_____ W_____ T_____, 65, insurance, Baltimore City, May 8, 1887.
HORN, General I_____ J_____ W_____, 66, Prince George's County, October 4, 1897.
HORN, John T., 73, former fireman, Baltimore City, April 25, 1884.
HORN, Dr. Louis C., 58, Baltimore City, October 23, 1898.
HORNER, A_____ F_____, 48, merchant, Baltimore City, May 11, 1899.
HORNER, Albert N., 70, Baltimore City, July 3, 1912.
HORNER, J_____ R_____, 70, comptroller, Baltimore City, March 30, 1910.
HORNER, John A., 53, merchant, Baltimore City, June 3, 1885.
HORNER, Joseph H., 82, retired contractor, Baltimore City, March 5, 1901.
HORNER, Joshua, 73, merchant, Baltimore City, February 14, 1879.
HORNER, Joshua, Sr., 67, Baltimore City, March 3, 1913.
HORNER, W_____ Frank, 48, merchant, Baltimore City, March 18, 1902.
HORNER, Rev. William, 81, Baltimore City, January 9, 1892.
HORNER, Captain William L., 46, Solomons Island, Calvert County, February 13, 1913.
HORSEY, George W., 77, merchant, Baltimore City, October 18, 1906.
HORSEY, Outerbridge, 82, Frederick, Frederick County, January 5, 1902.
HORSEY, W_____ Irving, 47, merchant, Baltimore City, December 31, 1906.
HORST, Louis, 91, retired, Baltimore City, October 18, 1894.
HORSTMEIER, E_____ W_____, 70, manufacturer, Baltimore City, February 14, 1902.
HORWITZ, Benjamin F., 68, attorney, Baltimore City, April 27, 1899.
HORWITZ, Mrs. B_____ F_____, n.a., Baltimore City, June 1, 1907.
HORWITZ, Mrs. Debly, 95, Baltimore City, August 4, 1895.
HORWITZ, Dr. Eugene, 39, physician, Baltimore City, November 10, 1893.

HORWITZ, Mrs. Maria G., 70, died at Dinard, Brittany, August 26, 1914.
HORWITZ, Orville, 67, lawyer, Baltimore City, July 30, 1887.
HORWITZ, Theodore B., 75, attorney, Baltimore City, April 5, 1895.
HOROWITZ, Wolf, 32, tailor, Front Street Theater panic, December 27, 1895.
HOTCHKISS, Joseph I., 55, auctioneer, Baltimore City, August 9, 1899.
HOUCK, Dr. H____ J____, 53, physician, Baltimore City, November 22, 1892.
HOUCK, Dr. Jacob, 65, physician, Baltimore City, May 22, 1888.
HOUGH, John E., 53, undertaker, Baltimore City, May 4, 1902.
HOUGH, S____ J____, 72, Baltimore City, January 7, 1911.
HOUGHTON, C____ E____, 81, Baltimore City, January 2, 1908.
HOUSE, Samuel A., 72, agent, Baltimore City, August 23, 1903.
HOUSTON, George Parker, 62, U.S. Army (Ret.), February 7, 1897.
HOWARD, Benjamin, 80, builder, Baltimore City, October 10, 1899.
HOWARD, Dr. Cornelius, 57, physician, Baltimore City, April 13, 1884.
HOWARD, Mrs. E____ P____ Key, 93, Oakland, Garrett County, September 9, 1897.
HOWARD, George W., 74, retired, Baltimore City, November 28, 1888.
HOWARD, J____ T____, 56, pressman, Baltimore City, November 30, 1902.
HOWARD, Rev. J____ W____, 80, Cumberland, Allegany County, October 12, 1906.
HOWARD, Colonel James, 78, Baltimore City, November 1, 1910.
HOWARD, Captain John Eager, 84, Baltimore City, August 15, 1911.
HOWARD, Captain W____ B____, 69, veteran of the Mexican War, Baltimore City, October 16, 1885.
HOWARD, William, 57, officer, Baltimore City jail, June 4, 1883.
HOWARD, William F., 75, manufacturer, Cecil County, November 23, 1893.
HOWARD, William R., 70, Baltimore City, August 2, 1907.
HOWARD, Dr. William T., 86, Baltimore City, July 31, 1907.
HOWELL, Darius, 67, manufacturer, Baltimore City, July 9, 1887.
HOWELL, W____ T____, 50, hotelier, Baltimore City, February 21, 1894.
HOWSER, G____ C____, 47, Baltimore City, December 27, 1907.
HOWSER, Gassaway W., 68, manufacturer, Baltimore City, April 6, 1903.
HOWSER, Jacob R., 68, japanner, Baltimore City, September 19, 1880.
HOY, John F., 68, temperance speaker, Baltimore City, April 3, 1891.
HUBBARD, Charles E., n.a., Elkridge, Howard County, September 12, 1909.
HUBBARD, James W., 87, retired, Baltimore City, September 25, 1905.
HUBBARD, Captain John T., 54, mariner, Baltimore City, September 15, 1897.
HUBBARD, Captain William, 78, mariner, Baltimore City, June 29, 1888.
HUBER, Henry E., 77, printer, Baltimore City, September 21, 1888.

HUCK, Dr. John C.(G?), n.a., Baltimore City, August 13, 1913.
HUFF, Rev. Samuel P. (Baptist), 68, Baltimore City, January 13, 1896.
HUGER, Dr. William E., n.a., physician, Baltimore City, March 29, 1902.
HUGGINS, Ambrose L., 76, transportation agent, Baltimore City, January 2, 1896.
HUGHES, Dr. Alred, 56, physician, Baltimore City, February 25, 1880.
HUGHES, George Wilson, 81, Baltimore City, May 28, 1898.
HUGHES, Jacob, Sr., 62, manufacturer, Baltimore City, June 24, 1905.
HUGHES, James, 72, carpenter, Baltimore City, June 23, 1896.
HUGHES, John, 81, undertaker, Baltimore City, March 15, 1887.
HUGHES, Captain Scott, 79, mariner, Baltimore City, September 2, 1888.
HUGHES, Miss Susan Oliver, 100, Baltimore City, August 23, 1892.
HUGHES, Thomas S., 52, realtor, Baltimore City, December 5, 1885.
HUGHES, William J. S., 50, attorney, Baltimore City, August 14, 1893.
HUGHLETT, John R., 62, Easton, Talbot County, July 27, 1905.
HUGHLETT, Thomas, 69, Easton, Talbot County, March 30, 1896.
HULL, Charles E., 55, manufacturer, Baltimore City, October 10, 1903.
HULL, David, 93, Baltimore City, May 23, 1907.
HULL, J____ Baker T., 45, Baltimore City, January 9, 1912.
HULL, John S., 76, manufacturer, Baltimore City, April 21, 1900.
HULL, Robert, 74, retired, Baltimore City, April 25, 1885.
HULL, Mrs. Susan R., n.a., Baltimore City, April 29, 1913.
HULL, T____ Barling, 71, former judge of the Tax Appeal Court, Baltimore City, February 2, 1906.
HULL, William S., 87, Baltimore City, July 13, 1909.
HULLS, John, 91, merchant, Baltimore City, January 28, 1883.
HUMBIRD, J____ J____, n.a., Cumberland, Allegany County, November 7, 1908.
HUME, Captain Joseph M., 64, Baltimore City, June 30, 1897.
HUMMEL, August M., 68, Baltimore City, May 13, 1897.
HUMMER, Dr. James C., 72, physician, Baltimore City, June 16, 1905.
HUMPHREYS, Dr. Eugene W., 59, Salisbury, Wicomico County, November 24, 1907.
HUMPHREYS, Henry, 79, restaurateur, Baltimore City, October 8, 1882.
HUMPHREYS, Dr. J____ E____, n.a., Baltimore City, August 17, 1897.
HUMPHREYS, Joshua, 60, Wicomico County, January 11, 1900.
HUMPHREYS, Lafayette P., 61, Salisbury, Wicomico County, October 24, 1905.
HUMPHREYS, Leonard, 75, Salisbury, Wicomico County, October 4, 1907.
HUMPHREYS, Thomas, 57, Salisbury, Wicomico County, April 14, 1897.
HUMPHREYS, Thomas W., 78, Baltimore City, January 25, 1897.
HUMRICHOUSE, Charles W., 79, Washington County, March 1, 1903.

HUNCKEL, Otto, 66, lawyer, Baltimore City, December 20, 1897.
HUNGERFORD, James, 68, author, Baltimore City, January 13, 1883.
HUNT, Frank N., 37, bank teller, Baltimore City, August 22, 1885.
HUNT, German H., 77, Baltimore City, June 16, 1907.
HUNT, J____ J____, n.a., Westminster, Carroll County, January 21, 1908.
HUNT, Jesse W., 47, merchant, Baltimore City, April 21, 1883.
HUNT, Samuel, n.a., merchant, Baltimore City, January 7, 1896.
HUNT, William, 59, retired ship joiner, Baltimore City, February 18, 1878.
HUNTER, Mrs. Ellen, 101, Baltimore City, August 26, 1892.
HUNTER, Pleasant, 84, Baltimore County, May 3, 1894.
HUNTER, Robert, Jr., 49, machinist, Baltimore City, March 2, 1899.
HUNTER, William E., n.a., of Baltimore City and a corporal in the U.S. Volunteers; died in Honolulu, Hawaii, October 24, 1900.
HUPFELD, Henry, n.a., retired physician, Baltimore City, November 23, 1880.
HURDLE, George W., n.a., retired engineer, Baltimore City, July 30, 1900.
HURLEY, Benjamin F., 72, lawyer, Hagerstown, Washington County, June 27, 1906.
HURST, Mrs. Ann, 80, Baltimore City, October 20, 1883.
HURST, Henry S., 50, Baltimore City, June 21, 1913.
HURST, John, 73, merchant, Baltimore City, April 12, 1880.
HURST, John E., 71, merchant, Baltimore City, January 6, 1904.
HURST, John J., 38, merchant, Baltimore City, June 29, 1878.
HURT, H____ L____, 84, Baltimore City, November 1, 1909.
HURTT, John M., 27, druggist, Baltimore City, December 3, 1903.
HUDGINS, John R., 64, merchant, Baltimore City, November 3, 1888.
HUSSEY, Martin, n.a., contractor, Baltimore City, April 25, 1900.
HUSSEY, Michael B., 40, detective, Baltimore City, April 12, 1898.
HUSTON, Thomas, 72, Halethorpe, Baltimore County, November 4, 1912.
HUTCHINS, F____ I____, 56, builder, Baltimore City, May 22, 1884.
HUTCHINS, Robert H., 74, retired, Baltimore City, November 25, 1894.
HUTSON, Captain Arthur J., 38, mariner, Baltimore City, September 23, 1902.
HUTSON, N____ Arthur, 64, Denton, Caroline County, August 20, 1905.
HUTTON, Major N____ H____, 73, engineer, Baltimore City, May 8, 1907.
HUTTON, T____ W____, 72, Hagerstown, Washington County, November 16, 1909.
HUTZLER, Charles G., 66, merchant, Baltimore City, April 14, 1907.
HUTZLER, Moses, 88, retired, Baltimore City, January 31, 1889.
HUZZA, Columbus, 77, printer, Baltimore City, April 30, 1900.
HYATT, Edward, 65, distiller, Baltimore City, November 6, 1894.

HYDE, Arnold S., 77, merchant, Baltimore City, December 27, 1906.
HYDE, James, 45, clerk, Baltimore City Council, March 9, 1881.
HYDE, Robert H., 58, retired, Baltimore City, October 26, 1894.
HYDE, William J., 89, retired, Baltimore City, April 21, 1885.
HYLAND, Dr. Henry Ayres, 47, physician, Baltimore City, February 26, 1902.
HYLAND, James, 88, Baltimore City, January 6, 1911.
HYNDS, Professor W_____ C_____, 82, Baltimore City, October 9, 1911.
HYNES, Caleb B., 71, manufacturer, Baltimore City, July 25, 1892.
HYNES, Joshua H., 78, former sheriff, Baltimore City, May 2, 1883.
HYNES, Thomas, 87, retired, Baltimore City, November 10, 1887.
HYNSON, Andrew J., 62, Chestertown, Kent County, June 5, 1903.
HYNSON, J_____ T_____, 55, Queen Anne's County, March 18, 1887.
HYNSON, Stanley, 42, court clerk, Baltimore City, February 28, 1885.
HYSAN, William B., 68, manufacturer, Baltimore City, February 21, 1902.
HYSORE, W_____ F_____, 37, druggist, Baltimore City, January 20, 1879.

IDDINGS, Dr. Caleb E., 74, Sandy Spring, Montgomery County, June 4, 1904.
IGLEHART, John H., 63, manufacturer, Baltimore City, May 7, 1904.
IGLEHART, John W., 56, Baltimore County, February 5, 1901.
IGLEHART, William, 48, Annapolis, Anne Arundel County, March 20, 1896.
IGLEHART, William T., n.a., Annapolis postmaster, Anne Arundel County, December 15, 1886.
IJAMS, Alfred, 74, retired, Baltimore City, April 25, 1905.
IJAMS, John, 91, "Old Defender," Baltimore City, August 31, 1879.
IJAMS, Plummer M., 50, merchant, Baltimore City, November 26, 1901.
IJAMS, William, 79, blacksmith, Baltimore City, July 19, 1892.
IMHOFF, John G., 71, merchant, Baltimore City, April 29, 1901.
ING, John H., 82, attorney, Baltimore City, March 25, 1901.
ING, William, 71, B. & O. Railroad, Baltimore City, October 9, 1901.
INGLE, Dr. J_____ Lowrie, 67, Baltimore City, March 20, 1914.
INGLE, Rev. James A. (P.E.), 36, bishop, Kankow, China, December 7, 1903.
INGLE, Rev. Osborne, n.a., Frederick, Frederick County, September 20, 1909.
INGLE, William P., 79, Baltimore City, May 9, 1907.
INGLIS, Judge John A., 65, Baltimore City, August 26, 1878.
INGMAN, Ambrose, 88, retired, Baltimore City, February 17, 1902.
INGRAM, Charles H., 58, manufacturer, Baltimore City, February 7, 1901.
INGRAM, John M., 32, manufacturer, Baltimore City, April 24, 1904.

INNES, Francis B., 36, merchant, Baltimore City, December 28, 1897.
INLOES, Francis H., 68, Baltimore City, January 29, 1897.
IRELAN, David, 82, retired, Baltimore City, November 9, 1890.
IRELAN, George C., 62, marine engineer, Baltimore City, November 22, 1904.
IRELAN, William S., 41, merchant, Baltimore City, August 18, 1898.
IRELAND, Dr. David C., 56, physician, Baltimore City, January 14, 1901.
IRELAND, Edward H., 74, Calvert County, May 5, 1902.
IRELAND, John, 43, Anne Arundel County, April 28, 1892.
IRELAND, Dr. John F., 68, physician, Calvert County, August 4, 1899.
IRELAND, Ninian L., 57, manufacturer, Baltimore City, May 8, 1902.
IRELAND, Robert, 70, secretary, Maryland Prohibitionist Party, Baltimore City, January 7, 1903.
IRONS, Dr. Edwsrd P., 84, physician, Baltimore City, April 5, 1909.
IRVIN, James H., 60, former jail warden, Baltimore City, August 27, 1887.
IRVING, Rev. John, 70, Carroll County, May 27, 1892.
IRVING, Levin T., 64, judge, Princess Anne, Somerset County, August 24, 1892.
IRWIN, Major P_____ H_____, n.a., Westminster, Carroll County, September 12, 1908.
IRWIN, William L., 33, editor, Boonsboro, Washington County, October 22, 1898.
ISAAC, W_____ M_____, 76, Baltimore City, January 4, 1911.
ISAAC, Z_____ Howard, 44, Towson, Baltimore County, November 7, 1914.
ISAACS, Jonathan, 89, retired, Baltimore City, February 28, 1886.
ISRAEL, Thomas B., 82, lawyer, Baltimore City, November 23, 1903.
ITZEL, Adam, Jr., 28, composer, Baltimore City, September 5, 1893.
ITZEL, George, 66, tailor, Baltimore City, December 26, 1901.
IVES, James H., 32, Baltimore City Councilman, July 10, 1880.
IVES, William M., 76, machinist, Baltimore City, September 12, 1886.

JACKEL, John, 81, dairyman, Baltimore City, June 23, 1879.
JACKSON, Arthur, 76, printer, Baltimore City, September 3, 1898.
JACKSON, Elihu E., 70, former Governor of Maryland, December 27, 1907.
JACKSON, Mrs. Elizabeth, 84, Baltimore City, February 3, 1883.
JACKSON, Hugh, 63, builder, Baltimore City, June 12, 1883.
JACKSON, Isaac N.,. 38, Salisbury, Wicomico County, May 27, 1897.
JACKSON, John J., 66, insurance agent, Baltimore City, April 16, 1904.
JACKSON, Wilbur F., 53, banker, Baltimore Coty, March 12, 1903.
JACOBI, August, 77, silversmith, Baltimore City, May 3, 1902.

JACOBI, George, 82, Annapolis, Anne Arundel County, October 11, 1912.
JACOBS, Dr. James K. H., 45, Centreville, Queen Anne's County, December 18, 1901.
JACOBS, Jesse E., 61, insurance agent, Baltimore City, October 16, 1900.
JAEGER, Dr. E____ A____, 43, physician, Baltimore City, November 11, 1892.
JAKES, Henry, 60, caterer, Caltimore City, June 22, 1881.
JAMES, Mrs. Anna Maria, 93, Baltimore Coty, November 3, 1884.
JAMES, Daniel M, five years old, Cambridge, Dorchester County, April 5, 1905.
JAMES, Edward, n.a., dentist, Baltimore City, July 15, 1880.
JAMES, Rev. Fleming (P.E.), 60, Baltimore City, October 9, 1901.
JAMES, Henry, 76, financier, Baltimore City, July 27, 1897.
JAMES, Henry, 57, merchant, Baltimore City, December 20, 1893.
JAMES, J____ H____, 72, Frederick, Frederick County, December 27, 1908.
JAMES, Thomas C., 61, retired, Baltimore City, November 22, 1888.
JAMESON, Alexander, 55, musician, Baltimore City, February 23, 1880.
JAMESON, Rev. Andrew (M.E.), 75, Baltimore City, May 30, 1885.
JAMIESON, Andrew, 77, retired, Baltimore City, October 13, 1901.
JAMISON, R____ A____, 53, merchant, Baltimore City, August 3, 1893.
JANDORF, Reuben, 71, merchant, Baltimore City, August 15, 1902.
JANNEY, Asbury, 78, veteran, Baltimore City, December 13, 1909.
JANNEY, Mrs. H____ R____, 91, Baltimore City, July 21, 1908.
JANNEY, Henry, 81, retired, Baltimore City, November 5, 1895.
JANNEY, William W., 28, secretary, Canton Company, Baltimore City, March 29, 1903.
JANOWITZ, Simon, 84, jeweler, Baltimore City, July 22, 1899.
JARBOE, John W., 80, retired, Baltimore City, January 10, 1901.
JARMAN, Samuel H., 78, merchant, Baltimore City, February 2, 1904.
JARRETT, A. Lingan, 85, Bel Air, Harford County, February 18, 1894.
JARRETT, Archer H., 55, Baltimore City, November 30, 1914.
JARRETT, Asbury, 89, "Old Defender," Baltimore City, November 10, 1889.
JARRETT, Asbury Bond, 62, Baltimore City, January 11, 1894.
JARRETT, Henry C., 75, Baltimore theatrical manager, died in London, October 13, 1903.
JARRETT, Johnson J., 58, Baltimore County, May 3, 1905.
JARRETT, Captain Samuel, 70, mariner, Baltimore City, January 31, 1900.
JARRETT, Thomas B., 65, Harford County, April 10, 1902.
JARVIS, Amos, 87, mechanic, Baltimore City, March 18, 1883.
JASON, John, 97, mariner, Baltimore City, March 21, 1879.
JAVINS, Harry G., 46, civil engineer, Baltimore City, April 1, 1894.
JEAN, Ichabod, 83, contractor, Baltimore City, August 4, 1898.
JEANNERET, Mrs. L____ P____, 52, Baltimore City, March 27, 1895.

JEFFERS, E____ W____, 31, photographer, Baltimore City, October 15, 1902.
JEFFERS, Madison, 72, retired, Baltimore City, January 18, 1882.
JEFFERSON, Dr. Charles W., 63, physician, Federalsburg, Caroline County, April 27, 1893.
JEFFRIES, John T., 68, judge, Annapolis Junction, Howard County, October 28, 1906.
JELKS, Cincinnatus, 54, printer, Baltimore City, September 20, 1895.
JELLY, Rev. Alexander M., 63, New Windsor College, Carroll County, June 27, 1895.
JENIFER, Colonel Walter H., 58, Baltimore City, April 10, 1878.
JENKINS, Anthony H., 76, retired, Baltimore City, June 20, 1884.
JENKINS, Austin, 82, retired, Baltimore City, November 30, 1888.
JENKINS, Charles E., 34, Orphan's Court, Baltimore City, August 21, 1889.
JENKINS, Cyprian T., 80, Baltimorean, died in Florida, December 28, 1893.
JENKINS, Edward, 68, merchant, Baltimore City, September 20, 1904.
JENKINS, Dr. Felix, 84, Baltimore City, October 9, 1909.
JENKINS, G____ Taylor, 70, merchant, Baltimore City, January 26, 1884.
JENKINS, Captain H____, n.a., Sykesville, Carroll County, February 10, 1912.
JENKINS, Henry W., 64, undertaker, Baltimore City, May 8, 1878.
JENKINS, John W., 72, retired merchant, Baltimore City, October 4, 1901.
JENKINS, Joseph B., 86, retired, Baltimore City, July 6, 1895.
JENKINS, Joseph M., 46, Govanstown, April 18, 1900.
JENKINS, Joseph W., 82, retired, Baltimore City, February 2, 1897.
JENKINS, Michael Wheeler, 68, retired, Baltimore City, May 7, 1896.
JENKINS, Colonel Stricker, 47, merchant, Baltimore City, April 8, 1878.
JENKINS, T____ Meredith, 36, merchant, Baltimore City, May 14, 1890.
JENKINS, T____ Robert, 72, retired, Baltimore City, April 9, 1895.
JENKINS, Thomas, 92, retired, Baltimore City, August 25, 1897.
JENKINS, Thomas C., 80, merchant, Baltimore City, December 24, 1881.
JENKINS, Thomas P., 83, merchant, Baltimore City, October 24, 1899.
JENKINS, Captain W____ H____, 85, mariner, January 14, 1904.
JENNINGS, Samuel, 88, "Old Defender," November 22, 1885.
JENTZ, George B., 74, merchant, Baltimore City, November 29, 1881.
JERNINGHAM, Matilda, 81, author, Baltimore City, February 15, 1891.
JEROME, Rev. John A. (P.E.), 77, Baltimore City, June 18, 1901.
JOBE, Richard McS., 59, merchant, Baltimore City, January 9, 1904.
JOERDENS, Joseph, 71, merchant, Baltimore City, December 27, 1898.
JOHANNES, Allen, 57, jewelry manufacturer, Baltimore City, December 7, 1904.

JOHANNES, John M., 83, jeweler, Baltimore City, June 19, 1883.
JOHNS, Henry VanDyke, 65, lawyer, Baltimore City, July 25, 1897.
JOHNS, Dr. Kensey, 80, Baltimore City, January 3, 1909.
JOHNS, Richard H., 62, builder, Baltimore City, January 1, 1886.
JOHNSON, Abraham, 54, livery stable keeper, Baltimore City, May 20, 1879.
JOHNSON, Bowie, 52, Garrett County, September 29, 1893.
JOHNSON, General Bradley T., 73, Confederate veteran, attorney, and author, October 5, 1903.
JOHNSON, C_____ R_____, 77, marine sur. (sic), September 13, 1902.
JOHNSON, Charles H., 52, black, minister, Baltimore City, July 16, 1894.
JOHNSON, Ezekiel C., 79, merchant, Baltimore City, December 7, 1878.
JOHNSON, George, 74, brother of Reverdy Johnson, Annapolis, Anne Arundel County, July 14, 1892.
JOHNSON, Dr. George, 73, Frederick, Frederick County, October 26, 1905.
JOHNSON, Greenbury, 33, sheriff, Howard County, July 2, 1896.
JOHNSON, Greenleaf, 77, merchant, Baltimore City, September 21, 1897.
JOHNSON, James G., 69, contractor, Baltimore City, September 23, 1900.
JOHNSON, Dr. James M., 68, physician, Baltimore City, June 9, 1896.
JOHNSON, John, 76, merchant, Baltimore City, September 20, 1885.
JOHNSON, Joseph H., 65, Cambridge, Dorchester County, October 10, 1904.
JOHNSON, Julius A., 73, editor, died at Auburn, New York, July 25, 1898.
JOHNSON, Mrs. Mary Elizabeth, 100, Baltimore City, August 31, 1890.
JOHNSTON, R_____ M_____, 76, author, Baltimore City, September 23, 1898.
JOHNSON, Reuben D., 45, Ellicott City, Howard County, January 7, 1900.
JOHNSON, Reverdy, 64, Marley, Anne Arundel County, June 12, 1894.
JOHNSON, Reverdy, Jr., 86, Baltimore City, July 15, 1907.
JOHNSON, Richard D., Sr., 61, merchant, Cumberland, Allegany County, October 21, 1900.
JOHNSON, Ross, 54, lawyer, Baltimore City, January 19, 1883.
JOHNSTON, Thomas Donaldson, 67, retired, Baltimore City, August 13, 1894.
JOHNSON, Thomas W., 69, merchant, Baltimore City, April 18, 1888.
JOHNSON, W_____ R_____, 58, lieutenant of the Baltimore City police, March 29, 1893.
JOHNSON, William, 78, manufacturer, Cecil County, April 14, 1902.
JOHNSON, William A., 67, merchant, Baltimore City, May 15, 1900.
JOHNSTON, Rev. William T., 48, Baltimore City, January 3, 1878.
JOHNSON, William H., 58, retired, Baltimore City, February 25, 1885.
JOHNSON, William H., 61, builder, Baltimore City, October 30, 1899.
JOHNSON, William W., 85, retired, Baltimore City, December 26, 1900.
JOHNSON, Wilmot, 79, Catonsville, Baltimore County, September 9, 1899.

JOHNSTON, Dr. Christopher, 69, Baltimore City, October 11, 1891.
JOHNSTON, Henry E., n.a., banker, Baltimore City, May 5, 1884.
JOHNSTON, Joseph M., 56, printer, Baltimore City, June 25, 1885.
JOHNSTON, Josiah Lee, 70, financier, Baltimore City, October 21, 1904.
JOHNSTON, George J., 77, merchant, Baltimore City, March 29, 1902.
JOHNSTON, Malcolm Hilary, 48, Baltimorean and former member of the Legislature; died at Milledgeville, Georgia, December 26, 1893.
JONES, Albertus C., n.a., physician, Cambridge, Dorchester County, July 5, 1893.
JONES, Alexander, 79, shipowner, Baltimore City, February 14, 1889.
JONES, Alexander F., 59, Baltimore City, March 6, 1914.
JONES, C____ R____, Sr., 62, marine engineer, Baltimore City, August 8, 1902.
JONES, Charles B., 55, postmaster, Rockville, Montgomery County, April 10, 1901.
JONES, Dr. Charles Hyland, 70, physician, December 17, 1897.
JONES, Captain Daniel A., 65, Elkton, Cecil County, April 26, 1909.
JONES, David A., 58, bank cashier, Baltimore City, February 15, 1880.
JONES, Rev. George E. (Presbyterian), 56, Baltimore City, March 17, 1898.
JONES, Dr. George Henry, n.a., physician, Calvert County, October 16, 1899.
JONES, Captain George W., 72, mariner, Baltimore City, July 14, 1897.
JONES, Rev. Hanson, n.a., black, Baltimore City, December 31, 1908.
JONES, Henry C., 70, manufacturer, Baltimore City, October 29, 1901.
JONES, Judge I____ Thomas, 68, Elkridge, Howard County, January 10, 1907.
JONES, Isaac D., 86, former Congressman, Baltimore City, July 5, 1893.
JONES, Captain James, 84, mariner, Baltimore City, December 6, 1891.
JONES, John, 70, compositor, Baltimore City, August 11, 1887.
JONES, John, 83, bricklayer, Baltimore City, May 22, 1902.
JONES, John M., 77, secretary, Odd Fellows, Baltimore City, August 26, 1905.
JONES, Josiah N., 62, clerk, Baltimore City, January 26, 1883.
JONES, Kennon, 41, railway agent, Baltimore City, December 20, 1900.
JONES, Lemuel, 67, merchant, Baltimore City, March 19, 1883.
JONES, Levin, 79, merchant, Baltimore City, September 3, 1878.
JONES, Patrick, 74, retired builder, Baltimore City, November 2, 1897.
JONES, R____ Emmet, 41, lawyer, Baltimore City, March 12, 1883.
JONES, Captain R____ I____ C____, 65, retired, Baltimore City, April 28, 1885.
JONES, Richard H., 48, insurance, Baltimore City, April 26, 1884.
JONES, Captain Roger D., 71, mariner, Baltimore City, March 3, 1883.

JONES, Rev. T____ B____, 76, Brooklyn, Anne Arundel County, October 12, 1909.
JONES, T____ S____, 75, Westminster, Carroll County, March 19, 1911.
JONES, Talbot, 64, Relay, Baltimore County, February 1, 1908.
JONES, Thomas, 64, merchant, Baltimore City, December 25, 1883.
JONES, W____ Edgar, 82, Princess Anne, Somerset County, October 1, 1912.
JONES, William, 86, ropemaker, Baltimore City, August 27, 1881.
JONES, William A., 43, physician, Baltimore City, April 14, 1888.
JONES, William B., 85, shipbuilder, Baltimore City, February 15, 1898.
JONES, William E., 54, Baltimorean, railroad treasurer, died in Cincinnati, Ohio, December 23, 1900.
JONES, Dr. William J., 36, physician, Baltimore City, January 10, 1894.
JORDAN, Hanson J., 84, attorney, Baltimore City, January 10, 1903.
JORDAN, J____ R____, 89, civil engineer, Baltimore City, December 5, 1893.
JORDAN, James W., 71, retired, Baltimore City, July 23, 1896.
JORDAN, Solomon, 76, stock trader, Baltimore City, February 20, 1883.
JORDAN, Rev. William L. (R.C.), 60, Baltimore City, March 19, 1901.
JOSEPH, Sister Mary, 84, Baltimore City, August 1, 1913.
JOSEPH, Solomon, 48, merchant, Baltimore City, April 10, 1902.
JOUETT, James E., 74, Rear-Admiral, U.S. Navy (Ret.), Sandy Spring, Montgomery County, October 1, 1902.
JOYCE, Rev. Charles A., 71, Anne Arundel County, May 9, 1906.
JOYCE, Colonel Eugene T., 64, retired, Baltimore City, November 23, 1903.
JOYCE, Martin R., n.a., attorney, Baltimore City, November 17, 1893.
JOYCE, Stephen J., 76, editor, Baltimore City, October 9, 1905.
JOYNES, Alexander T., 62, Confederate veteran, Baltimore City, June 5, 1907.
JOYNES, J____ T____ R____, 76, retired, Baltimore City, January 13, 1886.
JUDIK, Joseph, 85, livestock dealer, Baltimore City, December 3, 1880.
JUENGER, Sigmund, 60, journalist, Baltimore City, November 13, 1900.
JULLER, William, Sr., 79, cooper, Baltimore City, May 8, 1902.
JUMP, Alfred T., 69, lawyer, Baltimore City, January 21, 1902.
JUMP, John T., 72, Queen Anne's County, May 5, 1899.
JUMP, R____ T____, n.a., Denton, Caroline County, November 14, 1912.
JUNGNICKEL, H____ M____, 72, musician, Baltimore City, November 28, 1892.
JUNKER, Frank, 51, hotelier, Baltimore City, November 6, 1910.
JURGENS, Henry P., 41, mariner, Baltimore City, June 10, 1901.
JURGENS, Captain J____ H____, 76, Baltimore City, June 25, 1912.
JUSTIS, Rev. John, 70, local preacher, Baltimore City, January 7, 1883.

JUSTUS, William S., 87, jeweler, Baltimore City, December 15, 1898.

KABERNAGLE, John, 80, retired merchant, Baltimore City, April 8, 1901.
KAESSMANN, Rev. C____ F____ A___ (Lutheran), 69, Baltimore City, July 5, 1893.
KAHL, George F., 65, artist, Baltimore City, July 26, 1898.
KAHLER, Captain Charles P., n.a., First U.S. Volunteer Engineers, Baltimore City, December 30, 1898.
KAILER, David, 96, Frederick, Frederick County, August 21, 1900.
KAHMER, Professor P____ L____, 41, Baltimore City, February 7, 1905.
KAHN, Aaron, 76, merchant, Baltimore City, June 21, 1902.
KAHN, Samuel, 81, Baltimore City, April 16, 1909.
KAISER, Dr. Alois, 67, Baltimore City, January 5, 1908.
KAISER, Frederick 69, merchant, Baltimore City, August 18, 1898.
KAISER, Henry, 80, Annapolis, Anne Arundel County, October 27, 1901.
KALINE, John H., 48, baliff, Baltimore County, October 7, 1898.
KALISSKY, Abram, 117, Baltimore City, November 17, 1911.
KALLENBACH, Otto, 66, undertaker, Baltimore City, November 3, 1900.
KAMPE, Frank H., 45, merchant, Baltimore City, July 19, 1899.
KANE, Dr. Edward, 27, physician, Baltimore City, December 6, 1898.
KANE, Dr. G____ A____, 74, theater manager, Baltimore City, March 21, 1893.
KANE, Mayor George P., 58, Baltimore City, June 23, 1878.
KANE, Captain Martin, 80, Baltimore City, August 1, 1909.
KANE, Mrs. Mary, 105, Baltimore City, January 27, 1895.
KANN, Solomon, 72, Baltimore City, April 4, 1908.
KAPP, Israel S., 53, potter, Baltimore City, December 27, 1902.
KARSNER, Cecil J., 38, former Councilman, Baltimore City, May 18, 1895.
KATHMAN, Joseph, 71, tailor, Baltimore City, February 24, 1884.
KATZ, Daniel, 85, retired, Baltimore City, June 28, 1899.
KATZ, Kaufman, 75, Baltimore City, December 13, 1909.
KATZ, Louis, 57, grocer, Baltimore City, March 27, 1902.
KATZ, Marcus, 62, Baltimore City, April 25, 1912.
KATZENBERGER, Louis, Sr., 90, retired, Baltimore City, June 23, 1884.
KATZENBERGER, Solomon, 64, merchant, Baltimore City, May 5, 1897.
KAUFFMAN, Marion W., 62, merchant, Baltimore City, July 3, 1902.
KAUFMANN, John C., 81, builder, Baltimore City, July 7, 1895.
KAVANAUGH, Rev. J____ Henry, S.J., 54, Frederick, Frederick County, February 6, 1901.
KAVANAUGH, Joseph M., 68, manufacturer, Baltimore City, December 1, 1904.
KAY, Alexander B., 80, manufacturer, Cecil County, June 3, 1902.
KAYTON, H_____, 93, musician and artist, Baltimore City, May 2, 1902.

KEARNEY, Edward, 77, retired, Baltimore City, February 25, 1899.
KEATING, Thomas J., 69, lawyer, Centreville, Queen Anne's County, June 1, 1898.
KEECH, Henry H., 53, dentist, Baltimore City, April 3, 1884.
KEECH, Rev. James K. (P.E.), 26, Cumberland, Allegany County, December 5, 1900.
KEECH, Dr. James O., 52, Baltimore County, May 12, 1898.
KEELING, John L., 68, builder, Baltimore City, September 7, 1898.
KEECH, William S., 64, attorney, Towson, Baltimore County, February 1, 1900.
KEEDY, Dr. C_____ L_____, 77, Hagerstown, Washington County, March 26, 1911.
KEEDY, C_____ M_____, 77, Hagerstown, Washington County, August 1, 1905.
KEEDY, H_____ H_____, 51, Hagerstown, Washington County, January 22, 1893.
KEEDY, Joseph C., 53, lawyer, Hagerstown, Washington County, March 11, 1906.
KEEDY, Joseph E., 77, Hagerstown, Washington County, May 1, 1909.
KEEN, George V., 75, manufacturer, Baltimore City, January 19, 1897.
KEENAN, James E., 65, manufacturer, Baltimore City, April 23, 1904.
KEENAN, John J., 35, politician, Baltimore City, September 30, 1892.
KEENE, John H., Sr., 87, Lutherville, Baltimore County, June 17, 1894.
KEENE, Robert Goldsborough, 62, lawyer, Baltimore City, December 8, 1900.
KEENER, A_____ D_____, 70, cashier, Baltimore City, May 11, 1905.
KEENER, David, 49, accountant, Baltimore City, January 26, 1888.
KEENER, Bishop John C., 87, Baltimore City, January 20, 1906.
KEENER, William C., 87, "Old Defender," Baltimore City, September 21, 1881.
KEENER, William H., 58, physician, Baltimore City, May 21, 1880.
KEERL, Thomas M., 63, retired, Baltimore City, December 19, 1888.
KEFAUVER, Major Charles M., 76, Baltimore City, January 21, 1914.
KEIDEL, Louis J., 64, merchant, Baltimore City, June 4, 1898.
KEIGHLER, William H., 80, retired, Baltimore City, January 9, 1885.
KEILHOLTZ, George, 81, retired, Baltimore City, March 17, 1889.
KEILHOLTZ, Otis, 46, merchant, Baltimore City, September 13, 1883.
KEILHOLTZ, William, 80, retired, Baltimore City, June 7, 1883.
KEILHOLTZ, William Otis, 34, Baltimore City, March 29, 1902.
KEIM, Charles W., 54, coal company executive, Baltimore City, October 20, 1890.
KEIRLE, Dr. N_____ I_____, Jr., 33, Pasteur Institute, Baltimore City, January 5, 1908.

KEIZER, Lewis R., 69, manufacturer, Baltimore City, March 30, 1902.
KELL, Frederick, 52, butcher, Baltimore City, October 25, 1895.
KELLER, Rev. Joseph E., 59, former Provincial of Maryland, died at Fiesole, Italy, February 4, 1886.
KELLER, Josiah G., 74, butcher, Baltimore City, July 28, 1880.
KELLER, Dr. Josiah G., 58, Baltimore City, April 8, 1897.
KELLER, Dr. William L., 60, Baltimore City, June 27, 1906.
KELLERMAN, Gustav, 73, Baltimore City, December 28, 1909.
KELLEY, Thomas G., 90, Carroll County, January 29, 1902.
KELLNER, Michael, 74, merchant, Baltimore City, March 15, 1894.
KELLOG, F____ Dwight, 64, Baltimore City, June 22, 1894.
KELLOW, William, 68, foundry superintendent, Baltimore City, April 20, 1895.
KELLUM, Captain Lewis, 92, retired, Baltimore City, December 9, 1895.
KELLY, B____ V____, 40, street superintendent, Baltimore City, June 22, 1893.
KELLY, Charles, 64, retired, Baltimore City, April 26, 1899.
KELLY, Charles O., 55, Baltimore City, July 4, 1898.
KELLY, Daniel A., n.a., old-time actor, Baltimore City, August 3, 1906.
KELLY, Edward F., 58, contractor, Baltimore City, April 7, 1900.
KELLY, Francis S., 66, contractor, Baltimore City, December 14, 1893.
KELLY, James, 92, "Old Defender," Baltimore City, January 12, 1883.
KELLY, John W., 43, fireman, Baltimore City, December 23, 1905.
KELLY, Joseph D., 64, builder, Baltimore City, December 27, 1893.
KELLY, Joseph M., 64, merchant, Baltimore City, February 19, 1895.
KELLY, Joseph M., 42, reporter, Baltimore City, February 6, 1894.
KELLY, Michael J., 65, publisher, Baltimore City, January 8, 1879.
KELLY, Dr. Sylvester R., 35, physician, Baltimore City, June 4, 1897.
KELLY, Theophilus J., 49, Baltimore City, April 28, 1892.
KELLY, Captain Thomas, 82, mariner, Baltimore City, December 10, 1882.
KELLY, Thomas, 95, Baltimore City, April 9, 1911.
KELLY, Captain W____ H____ W____, 71, Baltimore City, July 14, 1912.
KELLY, Washington, 50, merchant, Baltimore City, November 17, 1885.
KELLY, William T., 79, retired, Baltimore City, January 7, 1895.
KELSEY, Henry, 79, ship broker, Baltimore City, July 11, 1894.
KELSO, John R., 89, retired merchant, Baltimore City, November 27, 1880.
KELSO, John R., 58, Baltimore City Councilman, July 17, 1895.
KELSO, John T., 74, retired, Baltimore City, August 13, 1887.
KELSO, Mrs. Martha B., 82, Baltimore City, January 14, 1883.
KELSO, Thomas, 94, Baltimore City, July 26, 1878.
KEMP, Alfred, 74, Trappe, Talbot County, November 1, 1911.

KEMP, Rev. Edward L., 77, Baltimore City, April 17, 1914.
KEMP, Rev. John D. (M.E.), 65, Kent County, September 21, 1902.
KEMP, Richard S., 92, Baltimore City, October 13, 1889.
KEMP, Simon I., 83, Baltimore City, February 10, 1914.
KEMP, Thomas, 67, merchant, Baltimore City, June 26, 1892.
KEMP, Dr. William Frederick Amelung, n.a., Baltimore City, July 10, 1913.
KEMP, Dr. William M., 72, physician, Baltimore City, September 6, 1886.
KEMPER, Moses, 68, merchant, Baltimore City, August 13, 1894.
KENDALL, Andrew J., 51, Hagerstown, Washington County, April 6, 1909.
KENDALL, Dr. Thomas, 82, Centreville, Queen Anne's County, July 8, 1906.
KENDALL, William T., 61, merchant, Baltimore City, January 3, 1883.
KENLY, Douglas C., 44, Baltimore City, December 7, 1900.
KENLY, George, 90, retired, Baltimore City, February 23, 1905.
KENLY, General John R., 69, attorney, Baltimore City, December 20, 1891.
KENLY, Major William L., 81, Baltimore City, July 11, 1913.
KENNEDY, A____ P____, 64, Baltimore City, December 28, 1911.
KENNEDY, Anthony, 81, former U.S. Senator, Annapolis, Anne Arundel County, July 31, 1892.
KENNEDY, James, 45, contractor, Baltimore City, February 13, 1902.
KENNEDY, Stephen, 47, Pennsylvania Railroad, Baltimore City, August 24, 1896.
KENNEDY, W____ L____, 38, comedian, Baltimore City, May 21, 1893.
KENNEY, Benjamin F., 62, police captain, Baltimore City, September 29, 1883.
KENNY, Thomas M., 63, reporter, Baltimore City, December 3, 1905.
KENNY, Rev. William John, 50, Baltimore City, October 23, 1913.
KENSETT, John R., 44, packer, Baltimore City, November 4, 1890.
KENT, Captain Enos E., 42, mariner, Baltimore City, April 13, 1886.
KENT, Henry B., 64, merchant, Baltimore City, December 7, 1902.
KENT, Jonathan Y., 74, retired, Baltimore City, May 14, 1901.
KENT, Mrs. Minnie Whitman, n.a., Baltimore City, April 28, 1910.
KENT, Philip E., 85, secretary, University of Maryland Law School, Baltimore City, November 14, 1903.
KEPPLER, Rev. Samuel (M.E.), 79, Baltimore City, August 1, 1884.
KERCHNER, Frederick A., 68, Baltimore City, December 31, 1898.
KERMAN, Owen, 81, merchant, Baltimore City, September 28, 1882.
KERNAN, James L., 74, Baltimore City, December 14, 1912.
KERNAN, James W., n.a., Baltimore City, October 19, 1913.
KERNAN, Michael C., 51, manufacturer, Baltimore City, July 7, 1899.
KERNAN, T____, 74, Baltimore City, February 17, 1910.
KERNAN, Thomas P., 38, merchant, Baltimore City, May 15, 1881.
KERNER, George H., 58, merchant, Baltimore City, March 23, 1899.
KERNEY, James A., 58, auditor, Baltimore City, October 31, 1895.
KERNGOOD, Abraham, 54, Baltimore City, October 26, 1898.
KERNGOOD, Tobias, 72, merchant, Baltimore City, April 24, 1903.
KERR, Andrew S., 59, teacher, Baltimore City, July 21, 1900.

KERR, Charles G., 65, lawyer, Baltimore City, September 19, 1898.
KERR, David, 68, retired, Baltimore City, November 16, 1884.
KERR, Edward L., 48, Baltimore City, December 27, 1884.
KESMODEL, Martin, 78, Baltimore City, March 18, 1908.
KESTLER, John T., 54, brewer, Baltimore City, December 20, 1900.
KETTELL, Rev. George F. (P.E.), 34, Baltimore City, October 28, 1904.
KETTLEWELL, Gover, 51, bank clerk, Baltimore City, March 10, 1903.
KEY, Clarence, 75, Pikesville, Baltimore County, August 13, 1911.
KEY, Horace M., 74, Woodstock, Howard County, May 7, 1893.
KEY, Mrs. Maria Barton, 86, Baltimore City, December 10, 1897.
KEYSER, Moses, 85, retired, Baltimore City, February 3, 1887.
KEYSER, R_____ Fuller, 55, Baltimore City, December 26, 1908.
KEYSER, William, 69, capitalist and manufacturer, Baltimore City, June 3, 1904.
KEYWORTH, Charles B., 90, retired, Baltimore City, March 6, 1897.
KEYWORTH, Charles E., 58, merchant, Baltimore City, May 4, 1895.
KIDD, Captain James H., 86, Conowingo, Cecil County, October 17, 1913.
KIDD, Milton Y., 57, journal clerk, House of Delegates, Baltimore City, February 2, 1884.
KIDD, Oliver G., 76, Cecil County, March 19, 1902.
KIDDER, Henry T., n.a., of Baltimore, died in Italy, July 14, 1902.
KIGER, John P., 87, Catonsville, Baltimore County, June 9, 1907.
KILDUFF, Stephen, 70, horse trainer, Baltimore City, September 19, 1893.
KILGOUR, David, 74, lighthouse proprietor, Baltimore City, January 21, 1883.
KILGOUR, Colonel William, 74, Rockville, Montgomery County, July 14, 1907.
KILLIAN, John M., 72, manufacturer, Baltimore City, December 21, 1903.
KILTY, Augustus H., 73, rear admiral, Baltimore City, November 10, 1879.
KIMBALL, William F., n.a., retired, Baltimore City, August 23, 1905.
KIMBERLY, Henry E., 60, Baltimore City, January 8, 1897.
KIMMEL, Solomon, 66, merchant, Baltimore City, March 25, 1892.
KIMBERLY, Samuel, 50, died at Washington, D.C., December 25, 1893.
KIMMEL, William, 74, former Congressman, Baltimore City, December 28, 1886.
KINES, J_____ G_____, 85, fruit packer, Baltimore City, April 1, 1893.
KING, General Adam B., 76, Civil War veteran and former consul at Paris, November 19, 1910.
KING, Dr. Albert H., 72, dentist, Baltimore City, December 19, 1904.
KING, Calvin G., 62, merchant, Baltimore City, April 29, 1902.

KING, Lieutenant Charles A. E., n.a., of Baltimore City and the U.S. Navy, died at sea on the <u>Asiatic Station</u>, December 25, 1900.
KING, Francis T., 72, banker, Baltimore City, December 18, 1891.
KING, Francis V., 52, Leonardtown, St. Mary's County, February 28, 1913.
KING, Frederick W., 67, superintendent, Baltimore City street lamps, November 1, 1889.
KING, George W., 72, printer, Baltimore City, November 12, 1898.
KING, Henry S., 68, merchant, Baltimore City, March 2, 1890.
KING, J____ C____, 85, former judge, Baltimore City, July 2, 1910.
KING, Jacob, 84, retired, Baltimore City, May 14, 1905.
KING, Dr. John H., 48, Pocomoke City, Worcester County, August 12, 1905.
KING, Joseph, 80, retired, Baltimore City, February 29, 1884.
KING, John, 64, railroader, died at Nice on the Cote d'Azur, March 17, 1897.
KING, Rev. Joshua Y., 59, Denton, Caroline County, November 28, 1906.
KING, Colonel Robert G., 53, retired, Baltimore City, September 24, 1886.
KING, Rufus, 83, Hagerstown, Washington County, February 3, 1910.
KING, Dr. S____ H____, 54, scientist, Baltimore City, June 7, 1902.
KING, Samuel H., 65, realtor, Baltimore City, May 28, 1894.
KING, Sanford, 82, naval veteran, Baltimore City, February 19, 1895.
KING, Solomon, 75, druggist, Baltimore City, May 13, 1898.
KING, Thomas H., 67, builder, Baltimore City, February 20, 1902.
KING, William H., 70, Baltimore City, November 20, 1908.
KING, William J., 77, Baltimore City, September 10, 1897.
KINGDON, Rev. John, n.a., Rockville, Montgomery County, November 8, 1906.
KINGMAN, Eliot, 85, at Washington, D.C., former Washington correspondent ("Ion") for <u>The Sun</u>, February 1, 1883.
KINGSBURY, Henry W., 39, Baltimore City, July 6, 1900.
KINGSLAND, M____ S____, 39, merchant, Baltimore City, died at Chicago, December 7, 1878.
KINNEMON, Charles, 53, Baltimore City, March 28, 1908.
KINNEMON, George S., 36, physician, Baltimore City, December 12, 1884.
KINNER, George, 75, Baltimore City, October 27, 1892.
KINSEY, Albert S., 55, machinist, Baltimore City, September 15, 1883.
KIRBY, George A., 67, retired, Baltimore City, December 18, 1905.
KIRBY, John E., 47, contractor, Baltimore City, March 23, 1903.
KIRBY, Dr. T____ Edward, 60, physician, Baltimore City, April 12, 1894.
KIRK, Alexander C., 23, elevator superintendent, Baltimore City, December 23, 1880.
KIRK, Henry C., 89, Baltimore City, August 1, 1914.
KIRK, James, 75, retired, Baltimore City, June 29, 1885.
KIRK, Jesse A., 82, Rising Sun, Cecil County, August 23, 1903.

KIRK, Richard, 73, Sandy Spring, Montgomery County, March 5, 1893.
KIRK, Samuel, 82, former Councilman, Baltimore City, September 13, 1893.
KIRK, Samuel E., 73, manufacturer, Baltimore City, November 4, 1906.
KIRK, William J., 88, cattle dealer, Baltimore City, December 26, 1904.
KIRKLAND, Albert B., 60, retired, Baltimore City, April 22, 1896.
KIRKLAND, B____ K____, 45, Baltimore City, June 29, 1897.
KIRKLAND, John, 79, retired grocer, Baltimore City, April 28, 1878.
KIRKLAND, Rober R., 89, Baltimore City, May 19, 1909.
KIRKLEY, Rev. John W. (M.E.), 87, Baltimore City, December 29, 1905.
KIRKWOOD, Charles H. W., 62, printer, Baltimore City, December 17, 1900.
KIRKWOOD, Philip, 80, shipwright, Baltimore City, February 15, 1884.
KIRSCHMANN, Rev. Christian (Lutheran), 63, Baltimore City, October 16, 1894.
KIRWAN, J____ Oliver, 64, mariner, Baltimore City, April 20, 1898.
KIRWAN, John H., 74, baliff, Baltimore City, September 15, 1898.
KIRWAN, Captain William E., 65, Dorchester County, June 20, 1904.
KIRWIN, Captain J____ T____, 70, mariner, Baltimore City, September 22, 1886.
KISK, Alfred, 74, Rising Sun, Cecil County, September 15, 1912.
KLAUS, J____, 86, Catonsville, Baltimore County, September 11, 1910.
KLEES, Henry, Sr., n.a., tanner, Baltimore City, December 23, 1879.
KLEIMIEDAM, Rev. Robert (R.C.), 65, Baltimore City, March 31, 1883.
KLEIN, Mrs. Catherine, 104, Baltimore City, August 9, 1907.
KLEIN, George 80, retired tailor, Baltimore City, March 10, 1901.
KLEIN, George P., 73, merchant, Baltimore City, May 3, 1899.
KLEINELBAT, Adolphus, 73, furrier, Baltimore City, July 3, 1902.
KLINGSTINE, George, 59, confectioner, Baltimore City, December 23, 1905.
KLOWMAN, Dr. William C., 72, Baltimore City, June 2, 1907.
KLUNK, Lewis W., 48, builder, Baltimore City, February 6, 1881.
KNABE, Ernest J., 56, piano manufacturer, Baltimore City, April 17, 1894.
KNABE, William, 47, piano manufacturer, Baltimore City, February 5, 1889.
KNACKSTEDT, John T., 80, jeweler, Baltimore City, March 23, 1904.
KNAPP, Frederick, 71, teacher, Baltimore City, January 7, 1893.
KNAPP, Theodor, 68, bookbinder, Baltimore City, June 7, 1896.
KNATZ, Philip, 58, merchant, Baltimore City, March 7, 1898.
KNAUSE, Mrs. Susanna, 100, Baltimore City, April 15, 1903.
KNEASS, Dr. Nicholas W., 56, physician, Baltimore City, November 26, 1896.

KNELL, F_____ L_____, 68, butcher, Baltimore City, May 19, 1910.
KNELL, Joseph, 56, packer, Baltimore City, November 12, 1904.
KNIGHT, Francis J., 84, retired, Baltimore City, April 6, 1883.
KNIGHT, John G., 58, local preacher, Baltimore City, January 26, 1888.
KNIGHT, Dr. Samuel T., 64, physician, Baltimore City, January 20, 1881.
KNIPP, Adam, 75, Baltimore City, December 9, 1909.
KNIPP, George, 65, manufacturer, Baltimore City, July 9, 1904.
KNIPP, Jacob, 77, Baltimore City, December 18, 1909.
KNIPP, John C., 67, manufacturer, Baltimore City, November 25, 1903.
KNOBLOCH, John C., 52, butcher, Baltimore City, March 5, 1878.
KNOOP, John H., 50, merchant, Baltimore City, May 11, 1902.
KNOWLES, Henry, 65, grocer, Baltimore City, November 9, 1882.
KNOX, David, 80, merchant, Baltimore City, March 28, 1902.
KNOX, R_____ T_____, n.a., Confederate veteran, Baltimore City, January 20, 1910.
KOCH, George, 70, lithographer, Baltimore City, June 2, 1895.
KOCH, J_____ Henry, 67, banker, Baltimore City, November 28, 1901.
KOCH, William, n.a., jeweler, Baltimore City, October 4, 1898.
KOHLER, Dr. P_____ W_____, 54, physician, Baltimore City, August 8, 1884.
KOHLSCHNEIDER, Charles, 92, Baltimore City, January 18, 1909.
KOLB, Rev. R_____ T_____, 72, Creagerstown, Frederick County, September 16, 1909.
KONIG, George, n.a., Baltimore City, May 31, 1913.
KONINGS, Rev. Anthony, C.S.S.R., 63, Ilchester, Howard County, June 29, 1884.
KRAFT, John C., 68, retired, Baltimore City, February 11, 1889.
KRAFT, John G., 64, packer, Baltimore City, November 7, 1902.
KRAFT, W_____ A_____, 66, Baltimore City, December 14, 1911.
KRAGER, George W., 58, hotelier, Baltimore City, January 19, 1898.
KRAGER, Henry, 80, builder, Baltimore City, March 29, 1899.
KRAMER, Frederick, 61, jeweler, Baltimore City, November 30, 1895.
KRAMER, Rev. George R. (Baptist), 57, Baltimore City, August 9, 1896.
KRAMER, Rebecca, ten years old, Front Street Theater panic, December 27, 1895.
KRAMER, Samuel, 13, Front Street Theater panic, December 27, 1895.
KRANZ, George N., 80, merchant, Baltimore City, June 17, 1902.
KRAUS, Jacob, 67, packer, Baltimore City, April 25, 1892.
KRAUSE, Rev. August (German Reformed), 53, Baltimore City, April 26, 1885.
KRAUSE, John C., 77, retired, Baltimore City, March 22, 1899.
KRAUSS, J_____ F_____, 48, builder, Baltimore City, June 14, 1893.
KREBS, Charles T., 54, bank teller, Baltimore City, July 11, 1893.
KREBS, George L., 66, packer, Baltimore City, September 24, 1902.

KREBS, George W., 95, retired, Baltimore City, February 23, 1904.
KREBS, Jacob, 49, manufacturer, Baltimore City, April 26, 1892.
KREBS, James W., 71, retired, Baltimore City, June 18, 1901.
KREBS, John W., 75, bank officer, Baltimore City, April 18, 1881.
KREIGH, J____ Frank, 81, Hagerstown, Washington County, May 15, 1913.
KREIS, George J., 64, justice of the peace, Baltimore City, September 13, 1903.
KREIS, Peter, 74, retired, Baltimore City, October 31, 1884.
KREMELBERG, John D., 55, Austrian consul, Baltimore City, May 24, 1882.
KREMER, Christian, 78, Baltimore City, December 6, 1909.
KREMS, John S., 51, agent, Baltimore City, December 23, 1885.
KRETZER, Mrs. Elizabeth, 108, Baltimore City, February 6, 1882.
KREUZER, Christopher, 35, publisher, Baltimore City, July 3, 1878.
KRIEL, Charles G., Sr., 67, pork packer, Baltimore City, February 25, 1903.
KRIETE, August W., 58, packer, Baltimore City, February 18, 1904.
KROEGER, Louis, 67, merchant, Baltimore City, February 17, 1892.
KROH, Dr. William, 46, physician, Baltimore City, December 11, 1905.
KROUT, Adam C., 44, printer, Baltimore City, January 16, 1895.
KROUT, William B., 68, journalist, Baltimore City, April 24, 1910.
KRUG, Captain Lennox, 71, Baltimore City, June 25, 1913.
KUEHN, Louis, 84, retired, Baltimore City, February 5, 1900.
KUHN, S____ J____, 48, merchant tailor, Baltimore City, November 6, 1881.
KUHNE, Hugo G., 44, editor, Baltimore City, February 5, 1882.
KUMMER, Major Arnold, 74, Baltimore City, April 14, 1914.
KUNCZ, Rev. Peter (R.C.), 48, Baltimore City, February 8, 1886.
KUNKEL, August, 71, Baltimore City, December 7, 1904.
KUNKEL, George, 65, actor, Baltimore City, January 25, 1885.
KUNKEL, Philip B., 80, Frederick, Frederick County, January 26, 1900.
KUNKEL, William F., 58, livestock, Baltimore City, May 12, 1902.
KURTZ, Edward, 88, retired, Baltimore City, March 9, 1885.
KURTZ, George J., 74, manufacturer, Baltimore City, January 3, 1901.
KURTZ, T____ Newton, 59, publisher, Baltimore City, January 9, 1881.

LACHENMAYER, Carl, 73, architect, Baltimore City, January 29, 1899.
LAFFERTY, Roy E., n.a., dynamite expert, Baltimore City, June 15, 1905.
LAGARDE, Professor Ernest, 78, Emmitsburg, Frederick County, October 25, 1914.
LAMBDIN, E____ S____, Sr., 76, Baltimore City, September 6, 1879.
LAMBDIN, Thomas J., 66, retired, Baltimore City, March 9, 1882.
LAMBERTON, C____ J____, 83, clerk, Baltimore City, July 10, 1881.

LAMMERT, Frederick W., 66, jeweler, Baltimore City, August 18, 1904.
LAMMRICH, Godfrey, 60, grocer, Baltimore City, June 23, 1881.
LAMPANIUS, Dr. Charles A., 53, Catonsville, Baltimore County, May 16, 1906.
LAMPING, William, n.a., tobacconist, Baltimore City, February 23, 1882.
LAMPLEY, John M., 84, retired, Baltimore City, March 1, 1899.
LANAGAN, M____ J____, 45, actor, Baltimore City, May 16, 1879.
LANAHAN, Rev. John (M.E.), 87, Baltimore City, December 8, 1903.
LANAHAN, Miss Margaret, 97, Baltimore City, March 21, 1914.
LANAHAN, S____ J____, 64, Baltimore City, January 30, 1908.
LANAHAN, Thomas, n.a., Sherwood, Baltimore County, August 24, 1913.
LANAHAN, Thomas M., 79, attorney, Baltimore City, May 17, 1908.
LANCASTER, C____ C____, 72, professor, Baltimore City, April 2, 1883.
LANCASTER, Dr. F____ M____, 70, former Senator, Charles County, January 30, 1899.
LANCASTER, J____ D____, 78, retired, Baltimore City, June 18, 1884.
LANCASTER, Samuel G., 59, LaPlata, Charles County, May 22, 1901.
LANDIS, Benjamin B., 55, Baltimore City, May 20, 1900.
LANDIS, Captain Daniel C., 72, Baltimore City, March 24, 1878.
LANDIS, Henry C., 52, secretary, Baltimore Board of Trade, December 15, 1899.
LANDRETH, Rev. O____ W____ (P.E.), 47, Baltimore City, October 15, 1880.
LANDRY, Rev. John T. (R.C.), 61, Baltimore City, May 25, 1899.
LANDSBERG, Dr. William S., 54, physician, Baltimore City, April 29, 1886.
LANDSTREET, Mrs. Ann V., 92, Baltimore City, May 13, 1883.
LANDWEHR, John, 62, merchant, Baltimore City, February 7, 1895.
LANE, J____ Clarence, 64, Hagerstown, Washington County, May 6, 1914.
LANE, Captain John H., 72, mariner, Baltimore City, November 16, 1884.
LANGDON, Thomas P., 59, drug manufacturer, Baltimore City, November 23, 1903.
LANGE, Frederick, and wife (unnamed), no ages given, murdered in Baltimore City, November 4, 1895.
L'ANGE, John W., 98, Baltimore City, June 12, 1907.
LANGHAMMER, E____, 81, Baltimore City, September 3, 1911.
LANGRILL, Mrs. Elizabeth, 77, Baltimore City, June 22, 1883.
LANIER, Dr. Berwick B., 41, physician, Baltimore City, January 1, 1911.
LANIER, Dr. N____ R____ S____, 25, physician, Baltimore City, December 27, 1881.
LANIER, Sidney, 39, poet and lecturer at Johns Hopkins University, Baltimore City, September 8, 1881.
LANKFORD, Captain B____ F____, 80, Princess Anne, Somerset County, February 23, 1908.
LANKFORD, Henry S., 82, Pocomoke City, Worcester County, November 6, 1905.

LANKFORD, Isaac Smith, 68, judge of the Orphan's Court of Somerset County, died near Princess Anne, November 4, 1883.
LANKFORD, J____ F____, 53, Somerset County, July 14, 1897.
LANKFORD, W____ F____, 47, Princess Anne, Somerset County, July 8, 1909.
LANNAHAN, Charles M., 45, merchant, Baltimore City, February 7, 1901.
LANNAN, J____, 58, deputy policeman, Baltimore City, October 27, 1892.
LANSDOWNE, George E., n.a., Baltimore City, January 20, 1914.
LANTZ, J____ G____, 79, retired Baltimore City manufacturer, December 25, 1902.
LANTZ, Oliver F., 79, Baltimore City, January 5, 1907.
LAPSLEY, T____ J____, 59, Baltimore City, October 26, 1912.
LARKIN, Mrs. Mary, 103, Baltimore City, December 6, 1882.
LARKIN, Rev. William J. (R.C.), 65, Baltimore City, April 23, 1899.
LARNED, Major Frank H., 63, U.S. Army, Baltimore City, January 8, 1891.
LARRABEE, Ephraim, 80, merchant, Baltimore City, May 26, 1883.
LARRABEE, Ephraim F., 61, merchant, Baltimore City, February 13, 1897.
LARRABEE, Harrison C., 58, retired merchant, Baltimore City, June 16, 1900.
LARRABEE, William, 81, merchant, Baltimore City, February 2, 1892.
LASKI, Rev. Dr. Samuel M., 78, rabbi, Baltimore City, January 6, 1899
LASSEN, John C., 60, railroader, Baltimore City, June 18, 1898.
LATANE, Henry W., 30, attorney, Baltimore City, March 31, 1890.
LATANE, James A., 71, bishop, Reformed Episcopal Church, February 21, 1902.
LATIMER, George S., 66, Baltimore City, January 9, 1905.
LATIMER, Dr. Joseph T., 67, Prince George's County, April 28, 1892.
LATIMER, Randolph B., 82, civil engineer, Baltimore City, December 24, 1903.
LATIMER, Dr. Thomas S., 66, Baltimore City, May 16, 1906.
LATROBE, Rev. Benjamin H. (P.E.), 60, Baltimore City, July 7, 1901.
LATROBE, Benjamin H., 71, civil engineer, Baltimore City, October 19, 1878.
LATROBE, C____ H____, 68, civil engineer, Baltimore City, September 19, 1902.
LATROBE, Mrs. Charlotte V., 88, Baltimore City, August 13, 1903.
LATROBE, Ferdinand C., 77, seven-time mayor of Baltimore City, January 13, 1911.
LATROBE, John H. B., 66, attorney, Baltimore City, September 11, 1891.
LATROBE, John H. B., Jr., 35, attorney, Baltimore City, July 22, 1882.
LATROBE, R____ Stuart, 55, attorney, Baltimore City, February 14, 1900.
LATROBE, Thomas Swann, 29, Baltimore City, May 13, 1894.

LAUCHHEIMER, M____ H____, 80, merchant, Baltimore City, November 22, 1902.
LAUER, Ignatius, 77, retired, Baltimore City, February 14, 1896.
LAUER, James M., 31, merchant, Baltimore City, April 8, 1902.
LAUER, Nicholas, 62, Brother Luke of the Christian Brothers, vice-president of Rock Hill College, Ellicott City, Howard County, December 20, 1900.
LAUTERBACH, John H., 46, merchant, Baltimore City, April 1, 1901.
LAURENSON, Francis Beaston, 80, Pikesville, Baltimore County, December 25, 1898.
LAUTENBACH, Joseph, 83, retired, Baltimore City, May 24, 1898.
LAUTENBACH, Dr. R____, 60, druggist, Baltimore City, February 16, 1904.
LAUTS, Henry, 59, Baltimore City, December 30, 1907.
LAUX, Louis. 36, fireman, Baltimore City, December 19, 1892.
LAWFORD, James M., 71, Baltimore City, December 15, 1913.
LAWFORD, Thomas W., 88, retired, Baltimore City, July 13, 1895.
LAWRENCE, Alexander, 61, engineer, Baltimore City, April 29, 1894.
LAWRENCE, Dr. Daniel Howland, 68, physician, Baltimore City, October 27, 1879.
LAWRENCE, Rev. Dr. Edward A. (Congregationalist), 46, Baltimore City, November 10, 1893.
LAWRENCE, F____ L____, 61, grocer, Baltimore City, April 11, 1885.
LAWRENCE, Dr. R____, 70, druggist, Baltimore City, January 27, 1892.
LAWRENCE, William, 70, Baltimore City, June 3, 1881.
LAWRENSON, James, 87, postal official, Baltimore City, June 22, 1890.
LAWS, Captain A____, 39, Salisbury, Wicomico County, April 9, 1908.
LAWS, James, 82, former judge, Salisbury, Wicomico County, March 7, 1906.
LAWSON, Rev. E____ (black, M.E.), 60, Baltimore City, August 16, 1881.
LAWSON, Henry S., 64, shipsmith, Baltimore City, May 25, 1884.
LAWSON, Robert, 79, broker, Baltimore City, September 22, 1894.
LAWSON, Rev. W____ C____ (Baptist), 57, black, Baltimore City, November 16, 1893.
LAWTON, Richard, 93, Baltimore City, December 27, 1898.
LAWYER, William 92, Westminster, Carroll County, May 20, 1903.
LAY, Right Rev. Henry Champlin (P.E.), 62, bishop of the Diocese of Easton, Talbot County; died at the Church Home in Baltimore, September 17, 1885.
LAY, Captain T____ W____, 75, Baltimore City, December 28, 1912.
LAZARUS, Edgar M., 46, merchant, Baltimore City, December 26, 1884.
LAZARUS, Ferdinand, 67, Baltimore City, September 10, 1912.
LEAGUE, Luke, 67, tugboat owner, Baltimore City, July 12, 1879.
LEAKIN, Andrew J., 65, B. & O. Railroad, Baltimore City, July 2, 1898.
LEAKIN, Rev. G____ A____, 94, Baltimore City, July 10, 1912.
LEANE, J____ R____, n.a., justice of the peace, Baltimore City, January 17, 1892.

LEARY, Captain C____ A____, 73, Baltimore City, January 18, 1909.
LEARY, Cornelius L. L., 79, lawyer, Baltimore City, March 21, 1893.
LEARY, William J., 46, attorney, Baltimore City, November 24, 1892.
LEAS, Dr. Charles A., 67, physician, Baltimore City, March 18, 1888.
LEATHAM, C____, 64, Frostburg, Allegany County, April 5, 1909.
LEAVELL, Rev. F____ K____ (P.E.), 30, Baltimore City, December 19, 1887.
LEAVITT, Rev. J____ M____, 85, Annapolis, Anne Arundel County, December 13, 1909.
LE BRUN, Louis A., 71, florist, Baltimore City, June 13, 1898.
LE CATO, E____ F____, 27, wheelman, Baltimore City, October 19, 1891.
LE COMPTE, Edward W., 66, Secretary of Maryland, May 5, 1893.
LE COMPTE, Humphrey B., 43, pilot, Baltimore City, March 2, 1897.
LE COMPTE, Stephen B., 80, Vienna, Dorchester County, February 15, 1908.
LEE, Calvin C., 29, attorney, Baltimore City, September 1, 1898.
LEE, Charles, 76, blacksmith, Baltimore City, May 28, 1882.
LEE, Dr. Charles C., 60, Baltimore City, November 30, 1898.
LEE, Mrs. Elizabeth Blair, 89, Silver Spring, Montgomery County, September 13, 1906.
LEE, Frank M., 48, Baltimore City, January 17, 1900.
LEE, Jacob C., 86, Harford County, October 5, 1905.
LEE, James F., 65, merchant, Baltimore City, February 11, 1884.
LEE, James Fenner, 54, diplomat, St. Mary's County, January 31, 1898.
LEE, John, 77, Elkton, Cecil County, March 20, 1900.
LEE, Colonel John Boykin, 59, Baltimore City, November 4, 1901.
LEE, Major John F., n.a., former judge advocate, U.S. Army and Maryland State Senator, died at Washington, D.C. June 17, 1884.
LEE, John T., 58, distiller, Baltimore City, December 31, 1904.
LEE, John W. M., 49, librarian, Baltimore City, February 10, 1896.
LEE, Joseph A., 32, merchant, Baltimore City, April 13, 1901.
LEE, Rev. Joseph E., 61, Cumberland, Allegany County, August 13, 1912.
LEE, Mrs. Mary S., 88, Baltimore City May 25, 1907.
LEE, Reuben B., 42, Baltimore City, December 21, 1895.
LEE, Richard H., 45, merchant, Baltimore City, March 20, 1883.
LEE, Samuel J., 57, Baltimore City, February 1, 1897.
LEE, Samuel P., 85, rear-admiral, U.S. Navy, Silver Spring, Montgomery County, June 5, 1897.
LEE, Stephen S., 80, merchant, Baltimore City, August 22, 1892.
LEE, Colonel Thomas J., 84, engineer, Baltimore City, December 30, 1891.
LEE, Thomas Sim, 83, Frederick, Frederick County, June 9, 1902.
LEE, William, 75, Bel Air, Harford County, July 19, 1900.
LEE, Dr. William, 54, physician, Baltimore City, April 16, 1898.
LEEDS, Rev. George (P.E.), 68, rector of Grace Church, Baltimore City; died at Philadelphia, April 15, 1885.

LEEF, Henry, 53, druggist, Baltimore City, June 12, 1894.
LEEKE, James, 86, retired, Baltimore City, June 16, 1885.
LE FEVRE, George, 63, pilot, Baltimore City, December 13, 1891.
LE FEVRE, Rev. Dr. Jacob A. (Presbyterian), 77, Baltimore City, February 23, 1905.
LEFFERMAN, William, 85, tanner, Baltimore City, May 24, 1882.
LEFFLER, Albert, 64, Havre de Grace, Harford County, December 6, 1909.
LEFTWICH, Colonel A____ H____, 61, Confederate veteran, Baltimore City, August 11, 1908.
LEFTWICH, Alexander T., 69, Baltimore City, February 5, 1914.
LEFTWITCH, Rev. James T. (Presbyterian), 62, Baltimore City, February 25, 1897.
LEGG, Edgar K., 67, Glen Ellen, Maryland, September 29, 1909.
LEGG, Colonel William H., 76, Baltimore City, May 12, 1908.
LEHMAN, Nathan, 57, retired, Baltimore City, November 25, 1894.
LEHMANN, E____ G____, 75, dancing master, Baltimore City, January 11, 1890.
LEHR, Robert, 67, merchant, Baltimore City, March 10, 1887.
LEIB, Moses, W., 69, merchant, Baltimore City, September 6, 1904.
LEIST, Frederick, Jr., 46, assistant postmaster, Baltimore City, March 22, 1901.
LEIST, Frederick, Sr., 75, retired tailor, Baltimore City, May 26, 1901.
LEISTER, J____ L____, 81, Brummel, Maryland, February 28, 1908.
LEITER, George T., n.a., Hagerstown, Washington County, February 28, 1913.
LEITER, Joseph, 72, Williamsport, Washington County, February 28, 1901.
LEITSCH, Edward G., 55, bookkeeper, Baltimore City, October 9, 1899.
LEITZ, R____, 81, pianos, Baltimore City, April 7, 1909.
LEIZAR, Perry 88, Sandy Spring, Montgomery County, July 14, 1897.
LEMMON, Captain George, 70, Confederate veteran, Baltimore City, August 29, 1905.
LEMMON, William F., 62, Baltimore City, June 5, 1905.
LENAGHAN, Rev. P____ J____, 49, Baltimore City, May 28, 1906.
LENDERKING, Philip H., 57, manufacturer, Baltimore City, February 21, 1902.
LENSCHOW, Professor Charles, 69, musician, Baltimore City, February 27, 1890.
LENTZ, Charles W., 65, merchant, Baltimore City, March 24, 1878.
LEONARD, Dr. Benjamin F., 52, physician, Baltimore City, April 10, 1900.
LEONARD, Charles R., 59, Talbot County, February 27, 1902.
LEONARD, Captain Edmund T., 61, Baltimore City, October 20, 1898.
LEONARD, James M., 71, Talbot County, June 30, 1904.
LEONARD, John J., 55, retired, Baltimore City, March 10, 1901.
LEONARD, Joshua, 80, Talbot County, April 27, 1897.
LEONARD, Nathaniel, 76, farmer and merchant, Oxford, Talbot County, December 15, 1906.
LEONARD, Captain William H., 52, Baltimore City, July 27, 1891.
LEONARD, William J., 85, Salisbury, Wicomico County, October 14, 1901.
LEOPOLD, Lewis, 64, pottery manufacturer, Baltimore City, September 11, 1899.

LEPSON, D____, 68, former police captain, Baltimore City, April 12, 1892.
LESTER, John G., 72, bank cashier, Baltimore City, January 18, 1882.
LESTER, Thomas, 77, educator, Baltimore City, February 11, 1899.
LETZER, Joseph, 61, court interpreter, Baltimore City, October 1, 1899.
LEUTBECHER, Charles W., 64, Baltimore City, August 25, 1897.
LEVERING, Mrs. Ann, 90, Baltimore City, November 21, 1912.
LEVERING, Cassie B., 58, Baltimore City, May 6, 1910.
LEVERING, Joshua, Jr., 23, and WILLIAM T. LEVERING, 24, both of Baltimore City, drowned in the Susquehanna River while canoeing, August 23, 1900.
LEVERING, Madison, 75, merchant, Baltimore City, October 24, 1882.
LEVERING, Thomas W., 83, merchant, Baltimore City, January 7, 1888.
LEVERING, William W., 62, retired, Baltimore City, October 15, 1895.
LEVERWITZ, Joseph, 11, Front Street Theater panic, December 27, 1895.
LEVIN, Morris, 38, grocer, Front Street Theater panic, December 27, 1895.
LEVY, Aaron, 60, retired, Baltimore City, November 26, 1894.
LEVY, C____ V____ S____, 51, lawyer, Frederick County, December 8, 1895.
LEVY, Erastus, 64, retired, Baltimore City, September 13, 1898.
LEVY, Solomon, 73, jeweler, Baltimore City, February 13, 1900.
LEWIN, William H., 62, merchant, Baltimore City, January 26, 1903.
LEWIS, Caleb M., 80, Frederick, Frederick County, May 4, 1909.
LEWIS, George F., 79, reporter, Baltimore City, February 3, 1902.
LEWIS, Captain Henry Howkll (Howell?), 73, Baltimore City, March 17, 1893.
LEWIS, J____ H____, 77, Frederick, Frederick County, December 10, 1912.
LEWIS, J____ Frank, 45, retired, Baltimore City, September 14, 1886.
LEWIS, James, 64, former judge, Orphan's Court, Elkton, Cecil County, September 18, 1893.
LEWIS, Captain James, 60, Baltimore City, March 27, 1908.
LEWIS, Lena, 22, seamstress, Front Street Theater panic, December 27, 1895.
LEWIS, Thomas, 81, pilot, Baltimore City, May 9, 1901.
LEWIS, Thomas, 29, compositor, The Sun, Baltimore City, May 8, 1894.
LEWIS, W____ H____, 51, mariner, Baltimore City, June 1, 1886.
LEWIS, William B., 78, auctioneer, Baltimore City, January 16, 1893.
LEWIS, Captain William C., 78, mariner, Baltimore City, April 10, 1881.
LEWIS, William Penn, n.a., merchant, Baltimore City, October 8, 1897.
LEYBURN, Rev. Dr. John (Presbyterian), 78, Baltimore City, July 13, 1893.

LEYH, Edward, R., 61, editor, Baltimore City, July 2, 1901.
LICKLE, Dr. John D., 56, teacher, Baltimore City, March 20, 1900.
LIEBIG, Dr. Gustav Adolph, 69, Baltimore City, December 17, 1893.
LIEBMAN, Joseph, 74, retired, Baltimore City, July 17, 1898.
LIGHTNER, _____, 85, "Old Defender," Baltimore City, January 24, 1883.
LIGHTNER, Mrs. Fannie, 93, Baltimore City, January 25, 1883.
LIKES, Henry, 67, merchant, Baltimore City, November 14, 1897.
LILIENTHAL, Moses, n.a., Ba;timore City, December 11, 1911.
LILLEY, M_____ S_____, 74, Elkridge, Howard County, June 13, 1910.
LILLY, Alonzo, 89, retired, Baltimore City, January 30, 1890.
LILLY, Channing, n.a., died at Boston, Massachusetts, March 12, 1912.
LILLYBRIDGE, Octavius C., 57, Fifth Regiment, Baltimore City, September 20, 1901.
LINCOLN, William R., 80, Baltimore City, December 2, 1897.
LIND, E_____ G_____, 80, Baltimore City, July 14, 1909.
LINDSAY, George W., 78, former judge, Orphan's Court, Baltimore City, February 25, 1904.
LINDSAY, Dr. James E., 55, Baltimore City, February 7, 1892.
LINDSAY, James L., 50, fireman, Baltimore City, December 13, 1892.
LING, Robert E., 82, pilot, Baltimore City, July 11, 1892.
LINHARD, Andrew, 72, musician, Baltimore City, February 26, 1896.
LINHARD, M_____ A_____, 49, music professor, Baltimore City, February 4, 1883.
LINTHICUM, Dr. A_____ S_____, 78, Jessup, Howard County, March 28, 1909.
LINTHICUM, Dr. Charles G., 78, "vet.," Baltimore City, December 14, 1898.
LINTHICUM, Herbert R., 55, Baltimore City, August 19, 1914.
LINTHICUM, Joshua, 80, retired, Baltimore City, April 17, 1900.
LINTHICUM, S_____ S_____, 50, real estate, Baltimore City, March 10, 1883.
LINTHICUM, Thales Abner, Sr., 49, attorney, Baltimore City, June 28, 1880.
LINTHICUM, Thomas S., 59, dentist, Baltimore City, October 21, 1903.
LINTHICUM, Zachariah Washington, 64, retired, Baltimore City, May 31, 1886.
LIPP, Francis X., 65, clothier, Baltimore City, June 22, 1882.
LIPSCOMB, John D., 55, magistrate, Baltimore City, March 9, 1892.
LIPSCOMB, Rev. Robert M. (M.E.), 82, Baltimore City, February 5, 1890.
LISNER, Abraham, 74, rabbi, Baltimore City, November 15, 1887.
LIST, Rev. F_____ A_____, 85, Ellicott City, Howard County, January 7, 1912.
LITTELL, Dr. Norval W., 62, physician, Baltimore City, February 11, 1897.

LITTIG, A_____ Ward, 59, engineer, Baltimore City, October 14, 1893.
LITTIG, Dr. Thomas, 85, physician, Baltimore City, March 30, 1886.
LITTLE, Anna, 93, Baltimore City, February 8, 1881.
LITTLE, Samuel C., 85, retired hotelier, Baltimore City, December 18, 1898.
LITTLEFIELD, John W., 65, merchant, Baltimore City, April 1, 1894.
LITTLETON, Rev. Charles H. (M.E.), n.a., Baltimore City, January 17, 1905.
LITZ, Henry, 70, merchant, Baltimore City, September 8, 1903.
LLOYD, A_____ Parlett, 46, Baltimore City, September 20, 1908.
LLOYD, Edward, 66, realtor, Baltimore City, July 16, 1901.
LLOYD, Colonel Edward, 82, Easton, Talbot County, October 22, 1907.
LLOYD, J_____ A_____, 91, Baltimore City, August 18, 1912.
LLOYD, James P., 84, retired merchant, Baltimore City, February 16, 1901.
LOANE, George B., 72, educator, Baltimore City, December 29, 1901.
LOANE, J_____ W_____, 70, builder, Baltimore City, April 29, 1893.
LOANE, Jabez W., 82, manufacturer, Baltimore City, December 30, 1901.
LOANE, Joseph R., 60, contractor, Baltimore City, July 25, 1884.
LOANE, William T. V., 56, merchant, Baltimore City, April 9, 1901.
LOCKARD, James, 74, merchant, Baltimore City, August 8, 1904.
LOCKE, Milo W., 63, contractor, Baltimore Coty, October 31, 1894.
LOCKWOOD, Rev. M_____ C_____, 44, Baltimore City, January 8, 1897.
LOCKWOOD, Rev. William F. (P.E.), 73, Baltimore City, April 1, 1883.
LODGE, Dr. William J., 72, physician, Baltimore City, August 21, 1904.
LOGAN, James, Sr., 86, merchant, Baltimore City, March 16, 1883.
LOGAN, Dr. John D., 64, physician, Baltimore City, April 25, 1881.
LOGUE, Peter T., 92, retired, Baltimore City, June 17, 1905.
LOKE, Henry, 52, Baltimore City, May 21, 1907.
LOKER, W_____ A_____, 72, Leonardtown, St. Mary's County, October 31, 1902.
LOMAX, Thomas L., 71, Pikesville, Baltimore County, February 28, 1907.
LONEY, F_____ B_____, 58, merchant, Baltimore City, March 31, 1880.
LONEY, Francis, 43, attorney, Baltimore City, April 27, 1903.
LONEY, Colonel Henry D., 65, attorney, Baltimore City, June 8, 1899.
LONEY, Thomas D., 62, merchant, Baltimore City, August 15, 1889.
LONG, John Ricords, 58, merchant, Baltimore City, March 1, 1896.
LONG, William S., 55, Princess Anne, Somerset County, January 31, 1901.

LONGWELL, J____ K____, 85, Westminster, Carroll County, April 8, 1896.
LOOMIS, Joel P., 63, U.S. Navy, Annapolis, Anne Arundel County, January 12, 1901.
LOOSE, August, 67, Towson, Baltimore County, December 25, 1898.
LORAIN, Major Lorenzo, 48, U.S. Army, Baltimore City, March 6, 1882.
LORD, C____ W____, 81, Baltimore City, January 1, 1909.
LORD, John D., 67, retired, Baltimore City, April 23, 1896.
LORD, Thomas R., 73, packer, Baltimore City, January 5, 1903.
LORD, Willliam E., 72, Denton, Caroline County, June 27, 1907.
LORENTZ, Henry, 86, retired banker, Frederick, Frederick County, March 31, 1899.
LOUD, Granville, 67, merchant, Baltimore City, December 9, 1897.
LOUDERMAN, H____ B____, Sr., 79, retired banker, Baltimore City, December 18, 1878.
LOUGH, Joseph, 75, merchant, Baltimore City, February 9, 1880.
LOVE, Joseph W., n.a., Baltimore City, June 14, 1914.
LOVE, R____ Horace, 68, merchant, Baltimore City, December 7, 1879.
LOVE, Colonel William N., n.a., Reisterstown, Baltimore City, February 14, 1910.
LOWCHAMP, John H., 62, tailor, Baltimore City, April 22, 1883.
LOWE, James, 70, chief judge, Orphan's Court, Talbot County, at Easton, December 18, 1905.
LOWEKAMP, H____, 67, Baltimore City, May 12, 1909.
LOWENKAMP, Rev. William (R.C.), n.a., Baltimore City, July 15, 1899.
LOWENTHAL, A____, 30, merchant, Baltimore City, September 16, 1902.
LOWENTHAL, D____, 70, Baltimore City, June 2, 1912.
LOWENTHAL, Solomon, 54, merchant, Baltimore City, December 12, 1902.
LOWEREE, George E., 59, former Secretary of Maryland; died in Washington, D.C., April 4, 1903.
LOWMAN, Lawrence, 77, retired, Baltimore City, April 17, 1894.
LOWMAN, Matthias, 80, retired, Baltimore City, May 4, 1902.
LOWNDES, Benjamin O., 86, Bladensburg, Prince George's County, July 12, 1897.
LOWNDES, Commodore Charles, 87, U.S. Navy, at his home near Easton, Talbot County, December 14, 1885.
LOWNDES, Charles D., 50, banker, Baltimore City, May 10, 1896.
LOWNDES, Lloyd, 66, clerk, Annapolis, Anne Arundel County, October 27, 1905.
LOWNDES, Lloyd, 59, former Governor of Maryland, Cumberland, Allegany County, January 8, 1905.
LOWNDES, Richard T., Jr., died at Clarksburg, West Virginia, June 29, 1905.
LOWRY, Major Horatio B., 63, U.S. Marine Corps (Ret.), Rockville, Montgomery County, May 22, 1901.
LOWRY, James D., 64, inspector, Baltimore City, October 12, 1882.
LOWRY, Joseph T., 56, photographer, Baltimore City, February 24, 1904.
LOWRY, Captain Thomas, 67, mariner, Baltimore City, June 1, 1883.

LOWRY, William P., 64, court clerk, Baltimore City, March 13, 1904.
LUCAS, G_____ A_____, 85, artist, died at Paris, France, December 17, 1909.
LUCAS, John D., 62, printer, Baltimore County, March 1, 1893.
LUCAS, Richard J., 73, manufacturer, Baltimore City, July 7, 1902.
LUCAS, Samuel, 60, printer, Baltimore City, June 5, 1897.
LUCAS, Captain Thomas, 78, shipmaster, Baltimore City, June 28, 1878.
LUCAS, Thomas B., 73, retired, Baltimore City, January 28, 1901.
LUCAS, William F., 78, retired, Baltimore City, June 15, 1897.
LUCKETT, Horace W., 59, teacher, Baltimore City, December 18, 1894.
LUCKEY, Colonel G_____ R_____, 74, Frederick, Frederick County, February 13, 1912.
LUCY, Professor Thomas, 60, Baltimore City, April 6, 1878.
LUGGER, Otto, 56, entomologist, Baltimore City, May 25, 1901.
LUKE, James L., 45, manufacturer, Cumberland, Allegany County, January 2, 1905.
LUMAN, Theodore, 60, clerk of the Circuit Cout, Allegany County, December 30, 1900.
LURMAN, Charles A., 63, merchant, Baltimore City, November 13, 1902.
LUMBERSON, John, 91, veteran, Baltimore City, February 6, 1898.
LUMLEY, Captain J_____ R_____, 71, Baltimore City, May 11, 1912.
LUMPKIN, Dr. Oscar O., n.a., physician, Baltimore City, July 5, 1898.
LUMSDEN, D_____ L_____, 61, Confederate veteran, Baltimore City, June 5, 1905.
LURSSEN, Charles C., 58, manufacturer, Baltimore City, July 22, 1898.
LUSBY, Alexander F., 37, actuary, Maryland Institute, Baltimore City, April 6, 1884.
LUSBY, James, n.a., Confederate veteran, Pikesville, Baltimore County, December 5, 1908.
LUSBY, John D., 79, builder, Baltimore City, April 9, 1902.
LUSBY, William M., 79, Baltimore City, June 17, 1896.
LYCETT, George, 86, retired, Baltimore City, December 19, 1906.
LYCETT, Michael, 64, Baltimore City, January 18, 1911.
LYCETT, T_____ E_____, n.a., stationer, Thurmont, Frederick County, November 3, 1910.
LYDECKER, Philip, 73, Baltimore City, August 9, 1911.
LYELL, Samuel M., 73, merchant, Baltimore City, September 29, 1885.
LYLES, John T., 75, merchant, Baltimore City, August 5, 1895.
LYMAN, Dr. Albert Benedict, 61, scholar and educator, Baltimore City, August 29, 1907.
LYMAN, Rev. Dwight E. (R.C.), 75, Govanstown, December 29, 1893.
LYMAN, Louisa, 83, Govanstown, December 31, 1893.
LYNAH, James, 56, shipper, Baltimore City, August 6, 1901.
LYNCH, John A., 78, former judge, Frederick, Frederick County, January 31, 1904.
LYNCH, Dr. John S., 60, physician, Baltimore City, September 27, 1888.

LYNCH, Dr. Thomas, 70, physician, St. Mary's County, May 20, 1893.
LYNN, David H., 60, manufacturer, Hagerstown, Washington County, November 9, 1906.
LYON, J____ C____, 59, Baltimore City, January 30, 1912.
LYON, Malcolm J., 70, Baltimore City, August 30, 1909.
LYON, R____ E____, 64, Baltimore City, December 14, 1911.
LYON, William H., 74, retired, Baltimore City, January 6, 1895.
LYON, William L., 75, Baltimore City, June 18, 1907.
LYONS, William B., 71, detective, Baltimore City, July 11, 1905.

MCAFEE, John, 84, retired, Baltimore City, July 27, 1896.
MCAFEE, Willaim C., 42, former Baltimore City Fire Department chief, November 11, 1906.
MCALCER, Hugh, 80, Frederick County, July 2, 1892.
MCALEESE, Charles J., 49, electrician, Baltimore City, March 18, 1899.
MCALEESE, Frank L., 55, electrician, Baltimore City, May 19, 1903.
MCALLISTER, Charles E., 55, merchant, Baltimore City, August 28, 1903.
MCALLISTER, Richard, 60, mariner, Baltimore City, November 19, 1903.
MCATEE, Agnes J., 84, Hagerstown, Washington County, July 30, 1913.
MCATT, Walter B., 63, Baltimore City, August 4, 1898.
MCAVOY, H____ L____, 65, inventor, Baltimore City, October 24, 1891.
MCCABE, James D., 42, historian, formerly of Baltimore City; died at Germantown, Philadelphia, Pennsylvania, February 27, 1883.
MCCAFFREY, Rev. D____ M____ (P.E.), n.a., Baltimore City, December 17, 1885.
MCCAFFREY, Henry, 78, music dealer and publisher, Baltimore City, September 10, 1905.
MCCAFFREY, Jesse T., 56, builder, Baltimore City, March 27, 1883.
MCCAFFREY, Thomas, 62, Baltimore City, February 21, 1898.
MCCAHAN, George L., 64, actuary, Maryland Institute, July 30, 1902.
MCCANDLESS, Rev. John Alfred (M.E.), n.a., near Rock Run, Harford County, August 23, 1883.
MCCANN, Major Charles, 70, Confederate veteran, Baltimore City, October 3, 1905.
MCCANN, Daniel, 83, retired, Baltimore City, July 4, 1899.
MCCARDELL, Captain Thomas F., 75, Cumberland, Allegany County, March 18, 1914.
MCCARTER, James M., 78, Caroline County, June 18, 1900.
MCCARTHY, Florence W., 51, Baltimore City, December 9, 1913.
MCCARTHY, Rev. Jeremiah (R.C.), 51, Annapolis, Anne Arundel County, December 10, 1905.
MCCARTY, Daniel N., 83, Baltimore City, May 3, 1914.
MCCAULEY, Daniel A., 86, Confederate veteran, Pikesville, Baltimore County, April 14, 1910.

MCCAULEY, Rev. James A. (Methodist), 74, Baltimore City, December 12, 1896.
MCCAULEY, Tilliam T., 58, Ellicott City, Howard County, December 19, 1893.
MCCAULL, John A., 50, theater manager, Baltimore City, November 11, 1894.
MCCAY, Professor C_____ F_____, 79, actuary, Baltimore City, March 13, 1889.
MCCAY, Joshua P., 74, merchant, Baltimore City, February 25, 1905.
MCCAY, Robert T., 85, Baltimore City, September 22, 1906.
MCCLEAN, C_____ B_____, n.a., surveyor, Towson, Baltimore County, November 1, 1906.
MCCLEARY, J_____ W_____, Sr., 58, merchant, Baltimore City, Jsnuary 10, 1902.
MCCLEARY, P_____ H_____, 75, Pikesville, Baltimore County, March 12, 1912.
MCCLEAVY, Edward J., Sr., 55, Baltimore City, May 10, 1914.
MCCLELLAN, William W., 80, Baltimore City, August 15, 1897.
MCCLELLAND, Cary, 64, livestock dealer, Baltimore City, July 11, 1879.
MCCLINTOCK, John M., 81, Baltimore City, April 20, 1893.
MCCLINTOCK, Matthew, 78, retired, Baltimore City, December 13, 1885.
MCCLINTOCK, Robert, 57, ex-coun. (sic), Baltimore City, July 18, 1904.
MCCLOSKEY, Rev. John, 63, president of St. Mary's College, December 24, 1880.
MCCLURE, James A. L., 55, lawyer, Baltimore City, April 21, 1890.
MCCOLGAN, Monseigneur Edward, 85, Baltimore City, February 5, 1898.
MCCOLGAN, Charles, 75, retired merchant, Baltimore City, February 6, 1879.
MCCOLGAN, James, 54, attorney, Baltimore City, April 13, 1900.
MCCOLLUM, F_____ A_____, 67, paperhanger, Baltimore City, May 21, 1893.
MCCOMAS, Alexander, 71, gunsmith, Baltimore City, March 12, 1892.
MCCOMAS, C_____, 77, former sergeant of police, Baltimore City, June 24, 1891.
MCCOMAS, F_____ F_____, 46, lawyer, Hagerstown, Washington County, March 27, 1897.
MCCOMAS, George M., 73, Baltimore City, July 7, 1894.
MCCOMAS, James M., 55, builder, Baltimore City, August 5, 1884.
MCCOMAS, James P., 48, clerk, Baltimore City, December 23, 1900.
MCCOMAS, John Emory, 78, merchant, Baltimore City, September 7, 1901.
MCCOMAS, Judge L_____ E_____, 61, Baltimore City, November 10, 1907.
MCCOMAS, Major Winfield S., 59, Baltimore County, June 13, 1908.
MCCOMLEY, William L., 85, Baltimore City, June 3, 1893.
MCCONKEY, Stephen D., 74, retired, Baltimore City, March 12, 1896.

MCCONNELL, Colonel J_____ C_____, 72, retired, Baltimore City, April 14, 1883.
MCCORMICK, Rev. Thomas (M.P.), 92, Baltimore City, February 20, 1883.
MCCORMICK, Rev. Thomas (R.C.), 32, Baltimore City, March 25, 1905.
MCCORMICK, Thomas K., 55, clerk, Baltimore City, November 13, 1904.
MCCORMICK, Thomas M., 62, clerk, Baltimore City, December 23, 1880.
MCCOY, John W., 68, retired, Baltimore City, August 20, 1889.
MCCOY, Rev. Peter (R.C.), 63, Baltimore City, March 2, 1895.
MCCOY, Stephen S., 64, retired, Baltimore City, April 12, 1896.
MCCREARY, John M., 48, printer, Baltimore City, October 21, 1893.
MCCREERY, Samuel, 82, Hagerstown, Washington County, April 15, 1909.
MCCRON, Rev. Dr. John (Lutheran), 76, of Baltimore City; died at Philadelphia, April 25, 1881.
MCCUBBIN, John D., 51, retired, Baltimore City, June 15, 1899.
MCCUEN, Robert J., n.a., Baltimore City, August 30, 1914.
MCCULLEN, John F., n.a., banker, Ellicott City, Howard County, October 1, 1900.
MCCULLOUGH, C_____ F_____, 45, electrician, Baltimore City, June 18, 1884.
MCCULLOUGH, Clinton, 50, former State Senator, Elkton, Cecil County, April 11, 1895.
MCCULLOUGH, Hon. Hiram, 70, former Congressman and Speaker of the Maryland House of Delegates, March 4, 1885.
MCCULLOUGH, Captain J_____ N_____, 79, Port Deposit, Cecil County, May 15, 1912.
MCCULLOUGH, John G., 74, coal dealer, Baltimore City, February 10, 1899.
MCCULLOCH, John S., 86, Glencoe, Baltimore County, July 3, 1900.
MCCUMMINGS, L_____, 83, Rising Sun, Cecil County, April 7, 1912.
MCCURLEY, Felix, 78, retired, Baltimore City, March 8, 1891.
MCCURLEY, James, 73, merchant, Baltimore City, March 8, 1881.
MCCURLEY, Joseph H., 61, Baltimore City, September 2, 1902.
MCCUSKER, Lewis C., 48, builder, Baltimore City, June 5, 1890.
MCDERMOTT, Rev. J_____ J_____ (R.C.), 27, Baltimore City, April 8, 1884.
MCDEVITT, Rev. James (R.C.), 64, August 9, 1895.
MCDONALD, Mrs. Anne, 95, Baltimore City, June 11, 1882.
MCDONALD, Joel W., 90, mariner, Baltimore City, September 9, 1901.
MCDONALD, Dr. Oscar T., 42, physician, Baltimore City, January 1, 1896.
MCDONALD, Rev. William A. (M.E., South), 64, Gaithersburg, Montgomery County, May 14, 1902.
MCDONOUGH, Mrs. Winifred, 91, Baltimore City, July 13, 1884.
MCDOUGALL, James, 72, merchant, Baltimore City, January 25, 1888.
MCDOWELL, Alfred, 37, actor, Baltimore City, May 18, 1891.
MCDOWELL, Dr. C_____ C_____, 60, Baltimore City, January 24, 1912.

MCDOWELL, Hamilton, 51, engraver, Baltimore City, January 17, 1898.
MCDOWELL, Dr. William S., 75, Baltimore City, January 2, 1898.
MCELFRESH, Rev. Charles M. (M.E.), 67, Baltimore City, July 19, 1887.
MCELROY, Charles, 63, B. & O. Railroad, Baltimore City, May 24, 1898.
MCELROY, John M., 63, Baltimore City, June 6, 1896.
MCELROY, William D., 55, Baltimore City, January 19, 1893.
MCELWEE, Robert, 54, Baltimore City, August 31, 1878.
MCEVOY, James, 64, Baltimore City, December 9, 1907.
MCFARLAND, John, 50, merchant, Baltimore City, February 2, 1902.
MCGAHAN, William, 75, plumber, Baltimore City, December 23, 1899.
MCGARIGLE, John, 44, journalist, Baltimore City, December 5, 1882.
MCGEE, Gowin H., 40, auctioneer, Baltimore City, October 4, 1897.
MCGEE, J_____ William, 72, former police officer, Baltimore City, December 18, 1893.
MCGEE, William, 67, sail manufacturer, Baltimore City, November 30, 1893.
MCGILL, Richard G., 65, manufacturer, Baltimore City, October 19, 1895.
MCGINN, Bernard, 54, Baltimore City, August 12, 1888.
MCGINNIS, Frederick, 60, black, former servant of Jefferson Davis, October 11, 1896.
MCGLONE, B_____ F_____, 74, veteran, Westminster, Carroll County, November 18, 1909.
MCGLONE, John T., n.a., member of the Baltimore Bar; died at Demerara, April 7, 1885.
MCGONIGE, James L., 28, athlete, Baltimore City, April 18, 1903.
MCGOVERN, James P., 56, contractor, Baltimore City, March 22, 1901.
MCGRAW, John, 59, athlete, Baltimore City, July 14, 1903.
MCGREGOR, Captain Joseph C., 49, salvage corps, Baltimore City, December 3, 1900.
MCGREGOR, Roderick, 60, surveyor, Prince George's County, October 22, 1903.
MCGUINNESS, Thomas, 63, Highlandtown, Howard County, November 6, 1906.
MCGUIRE, George L., n.a., Confederate veteran, Pikesville, Baltimore County, February 24, 1907.
MCHENRY, Henry, 66, Frederick, Frederick County, April 14, 1901.
MCHENRY, James, 51, civil engineer, Baltimore City, April 14, 1881.
MCHENRY, James Howard, 68, Baltimore City, September 25, 1888.
MCILVAINE, Captain C_____, 69, Cambridge, Dorchester County, August 4, 1909.
MCINERNEY, Rev. Augustine G., 69, Annapolis, Anne Arundel County, July 23, 1914.
MCINTIRE, Dr. James, 81, Baltimore City, April 12, 1879.
MCINTIRE, William W., 62, Baltimore City, April 1, 1912.
MCINTOSH, Vernon A., 57, Baltimore City, March 20, 1901.

MCINTYRE, Mrs. Jane, 90, Baltimore City, January 21, 1879.
MCKAIG, A____ B____, 38, State Senator, Baltimore City, April 9, 1886.
MCKAIG, General William McM., 62, Cumberland, Allegany County, June 6, 1907.
MCKAY, George G., 61, educator, Lonaconing, Allegany County, March 13, 1900.
MCKEE, Charles A., 82, builder, Baltimore City, January 3, 1892.
MCKEE, Dr. Charles E. S., 72, Hagerstown, Washington County, June 30, 1907.
MCKEE, Rev. Joseph F., 52, Baltimore City, January 20, 1914.
MCKEE, William F., n.a., retired merchant, Baltimore City, August 8, 1898.
MCKELLIP, William A., 69, U.S. Consul, Magdeburg, Germany; of Westminster, Carroll County, April 4, 1904.
MCKENNA, Patrick, 62, Baltimore City, October 28, 1898.
MCKENNY, Rev. J____ A____ (P.E.), 74, Baltimore City, November 27, 1880.
MCKENNY, William, 68, Centreville, Queen Anne's County, July 23, 1897.
MCKENZIE, Rev. Elias B. (R.C.), 40, Baltimore City, September 24, 1888.
MCKENZIE, Captain William B., 66, Easton, Talbot County, March 24, 1914.
MCKEW, Dr. Denis I., 56, physician, Baltimore City, February 10, 1885.
MCKEWEN, Thomas Balt(?), 92, retired, Baltimore City, March 31, 1897.
MCKEWEN, William F., 59, forcer court clerk, Baltimore City, April 16, 1891.
MCKIM, Alexander, 24, banker, Baltimore City, January 25, 1884.
MCKIM, Isaac, 27, banker, Baltimore City, June 21, 1898.
MCKIM, Mrs. Catharine L., n.a., Baltimore City, December 30, 1898.
MCKIM, Hollins, 76, Baltimore City, May 17, 1911.
MCKIM, Robert, 77, resident of Baltimore City until 1863; died in New York City, April 23, 1893.
MCKIM, William, 81?, banker, Baltimore City, September 11, 1879.
MCKINLEY, William, 87, retired, Baltimore City, May 16, 1897.
MCKNEW, Dr. Wilberforce Richmond, 64, physician, Baltimore City, May 31, 1904.
MCKNIGHT, James W., 62, Baltimore City, April 13, 1893.
MCLAND, Charles E., n.a., of Baltimore City; died in California, August 24, 1881.
MCLANE, Alan, 69, retired, Baltimore City, December 16, 1891.
MCLANE, Mrs. Georgine, 70, widow of former Governor Robert M. McLane; died in Paris, November 14, 1899.
MCLANE, Louis, 86, financier, Baltimore City, December 13, 1905.
MCLANE, Mrs. Louis, n.a., Baltimore City, April 17, 1906.
MCLANE, Robert M., 36, Mayor of Baltimore City, May 30, 1904.
MCLANE, Robert Milligan, 82, former Governor and minister to France (1885-59); died at Paris, April 16, 1898.
MCLANE, S____ Hoffman, 29, Baltimore City, November 18, 1890.
MCLAUGHLIN, Captain A____, 61, former naval officer, Baltimore City, March 1, 1884.

-150-

MCLAUGHLIN, Professor A_____ B_____, 69, Ellicott City, Howard County, April 15, 1907.
MCLAUGHLIN, Owen C., n.a., Baltimore City, March 27, 1901.
MCLAUGHLIN, Philip S., 73, president, Transfer Company, November 20, 1901.
MCLAUGHLIN, R_____, 62, bank officer, Baltimore City, August 29, 1902.
MCLAUGHLIN, William, 78, contractor, Baltimore City, December 16, 1893.
MCLAURIN, Senator A_____ J_____, n.a., died at Brandon, Mississippi, December 22, 1909.
MCLEAN, Dr. Charles, 75, physician, Baltimore City, August 17, 1883.
MCLEOD, Georgia Hulse, 60, author, Baltimore City, July 2, 1890.
MCMAHON, Michael, 68, manufacturer, Baltimore City, January 20, 1901.
MCMANUS, Rev. B_____ J_____ A_____ (R.C.), 68, Baltimore City, February 28, 1888.
MCMANUS, Dr. F_____ A_____, 45, physician, Baltimore City, April 16, 1885.
MCMANUS, Dr. Felix R., 77, physician, Baltimore City, March 3, 1885.
MCMASTER, Colonel Samuel S., 66, at his home in Worcester County, February 3, 1885.
MCMASTER, William S., 67, lawyer, Princess Anne, Somerset County, December 15, 1906.
MCMILLAN, Elias, 70, veteran of the Mexican War, Baltimore City, December 8, 1883.
MCMULLAN, Rev. A_____ L_____ (R.C.), 64, Baltimore City, July 8, 1884.
MCMURRAY, Louis, 65, packer, Baltimore City, November 3, 1888.
MCMYERS, Dr. Charles, 68, physician, Baltimore City, December 4, 1903.
MCNALLY, Henry, 60, merchant, Baltimore City, April 12, 1887.
MCNALLY, William P., 53, clerk of the court, Baltimore City, February 26, 1900.
MCNAMARA, Patrick, n.a., Baltimore City, December 13, 1896.
MCNAMARA, William J., 26, clerk, Baltimore City, December 15, 1900.
MCNEAL, James, Jr., 72, treasurer, Green Mount Cemetery, August 7, 1887.
MCNULTY, John A., 69, Baltimore City, April 16, 1912.
MCNULTY, John F., 65, B. & O. Railroad, January 30, 1881.
MCNULTY, Thomas, 57, manufacturer, Baltimore City, March 11, 1890.
MCPARLIN, T_____ A_____, n.a., former Surveyor General, U.S. Army (Ret.), Annapolis, Anne Arundel County, January 28, 1897.
MCPHAIL, Colonel Daniel H., 71, formerly of Baltimore City; died at Brooklyn, New York, January 30, 1884.
MCPHERSON, D_____, 73, merchant tailor, Baltimore City, August 29, 1904.
MCPHERSON, Edward J., n.a., Baltimore City, August 31, 1897.
MCPHERSON, Rev. W_____ B_____, 47, Baltimore City, September 7, 1908.
MCPHERSON, William Smith, 88, physician, Baltimore City, November 20, 1879.

MCROBERTS, William, 45, Govanstown, Baltimore County, July 4, 1902.
MCSHANE, Henry, 58, manufacturer, Baltimore City, February 23, 1889.
MCSHANE, James Francis, 54, physician, Baltimore City, August 1, 1905.
MCSHANE, Julian J. G., 37, manufacturer, Baltimore City, December 11, 1906.
MCSHANE, Lawrence, 65, retired, Baltimore City, May 23, 1883.
MCSHERRY, Mrs. Catherine Somerville, 72, Baltimore City, December 2, 1893.
MCSHERRY, Dr. Edward C., 51, Frederick, Frederick County, May 8, 1900.
MCSHERRY, J_____, 25, sergeant, Fifth Regiment, Baltimore City, May 7, 1902.
MCSHERRY, James, 64, chief judge, Court of Appeals, Frederick, Frederick County, October 23, 1907.
MCSHERRY, Dr. Richard, 67, physician, Baltimore City, October 7, 1885; surgeon in the Florida and Mexican Wars.
MCSHERRY, Richard M., 55, lawyer, Baltimore City, June 28, 1898.
MCSWEENEY, Cornelius, 65, shipbuilder, Baltimore City, November 16, 1899.
MCSWEENEY, Miles Benjamin, 64, former governor of South Carolina, at Baltimore City, September 29, 1909.
MCSWYNEY, Rev. Eugene (R.C.), n.a., Charles County, March 23, 1893.
MCVEIGH, William, 75, Cumberland, Allegany County, May 24, 1909.
MCVEY, Harriet, 94, Calvert County, February 23, 1910.

MABLE, John C., 70, Baltimore City, February 22, 1914.
MACCLELLAN, Rufus C., 69, retired, Baltimore City, October 23 or 28, 1884.
MACCOUN, Dr. R_____ T_____, 70, U.S. Navy, March 20, 1890.
MACCUBBIN, Paul W., 53, carpenter, Baltimore City, December 30, 1904.
MACCUBBIN, R_____ W_____, 60, merchant, Baltimore City, January 26, 1904.
MACCUBBIN, Robert W., 90, retired, Baltimore City, March 16, 1903.
MACCULEY, James, 87, Cecil County, January 25, 1897.
MACDERMOTT, W_____ M_____, 45, athlete, Baltimore City, December 17, 1908.
MACDONALD, Frank Y., 64, jeweler, Baltimore City, March 18, 1905.
MACDONALD, Joseph, 81, lawyer, Cumberland, Allegany County, October 26, 1901.
MACGILL, Dr. C_____ S_____, n.a., Catonsville, Baltimore County, April 28, 1907.
MACGILL, Carroll S., n.a., Baltimore City, February 18, 1897.
MACGILL, Dr. Lloyd, 79, Frederick, Frederick County, October 29, 1908.
MACGILL, Oscar V., 21, student, Baltimore City, January 11, 1902.
MACGILL, P_____ H_____, 65, manufacturer, Baltimore City, March 10, 1898.

MACK, John, 51, gardener, Baltimore City, November 8, 1895.
MACKALL, John B., 80, Prince Frederick, Calvert County, June 3, 1913.
MACKALL, Dr. Leonard, 88, Baltimore City, January 1, 1892.
MACKALL, Dr. Richard Covington, 80, Elkton, Cecil County, February 16, 1902.
MACKAY, William, 70, retired, Baltimore City, July 27, 1900.
MACKENZIE, Dr. James S., 65, physician, Baltimore City, May 10, 1886.
MACKENZIE, John P., 40, reporter, Baltimore City, May 4, 1905.
MACKEY, James A., 62, Cecil County, November 12, 1900.
MACKIE, William T., 59, Cecil County, October 29, 1903.
MACKINTOSH, William, 67, Howard County, February 21, 1893.
MACKUBIN, James, 74, lawyer, Howard County, September 11, 1904.
MACMAHON, Michael, 68, bank guard, Baltimore City, December 6, 1893.
MACOMBER, G_____ C_____, 71, stonemason, Baltimore City, November 30, 1880.
MACTIER, Alexander, 88, retired, Baltimore City, July 3, 1886.
MADDOX, Charles T., 83, retired, Baltimore City, September 12, 1890.
MADDOX, J_____ T_____, 68, justice of the peace, Baltimore City, December 24, 1892.
MADDOX, James M., 83, retired, Baltimore City, October 22, 1905.
MADIGAN, D_____ T_____, 68, salesman, Baltimore City, July 4, 1902.
MAGEE, Mrs. Mary, 95, Baltimore City, August 16, 1878.
MAGER, Dr. William, 52, chemist, Baltimore City, March 19, 1901.
MAGNESS, Thomas F., 84, Baltimore City, December 9, 1896.
MAGNIEN, Rev. Dr. A_____ L_____, 65, president emeritus, St. Mary's Seminary, December 21, 1902.
MAGRAW, S_____ C_____, 65, Baltimore City, January 13, 1912.
MAGRUDER, Mrs. Catherine, 109, black, Baltimore City, December 2, 1878.
MAGRUDER, H_____ B_____, 60, Rockville, Montgomery County, September 21, 1909.
MAGRUDER, John Bankhead, 87, Prince George's County, July 25, 1897.
MAGRUDER, Richard H., 43, State Senator, Bladensburg, Prince George's County, September 22, 1884.
MAGRUDER, Thomas J., 67, manufacturer, Baltimore City, July 25, 1891.
MAGUIRE, Christopher P., 77, Baltimore City, September 26, 1900.
MAGUIRE, John E., 56, Baltimore City, April 5, 1897.
MAGUIRE, Miss Mary M., 65, artist, Baltimore City, July 21, 1900.
MAHANEY, Mrs. Bridget, 104, Baltimore City, August 1, 1884.
MAHER, Rev. Daniel, n.a., Baltimore City, May 25, 1906.
MAHON, Dr. Ormsby, 68, physician, Baltimore City, April 3, 1894.
MAIER, Rev. Ludwig D. (Lutheran), 58, Baltimore City, November 10, 1882.
MAIER, Martin L., 34, Hagerstown, Washington County, September 23, 1902.
MAISEL, Andrew, 60, builder, Baltimore City, October 31, 1898.
MAITH, Captain William, 75, Baltimore City, October 9, 1898.
MAITLAND, Benjamin, 84, retired, Baltimore City, April 9, 1884.

MAITLAND, Rev. S____ S____ (P.E.), 39, Baltimore City, April 8, 1884.
MALDEIS, Rev. F____ C____ (Baptist), 39, Baltimore City, December 16, 1888.
MALLALIEU, Edward, 66, retired, Baltimore City, May 3, 1901.
MALLALIEU, Franklin S., 72, retired, Baltimore City, January 4, 1902.
MALLALIEU, Bishop W____ F____, n.a., Auburndale, August 2, 1911.
MALLINCKRODT, William, 67, merchant, Baltimore City, November 13, 1882.
MALLON, Mrs. Isabel A. S., 44, writer, Baltimore City, December 27, 1898.
MALLON, John, 73, ship chandler, Baltimore City, July 21, 1881.
MALLOY, Dr. Charles A., 78, physician, Baltimore City, May 5, 1895.
MALLOY, Rev. L____ S____ (R.C.), 51, Baltimore City, July 25, 1885.
MALONE, T____ J____, 37, Baltimore City employee, November 2, 1881.
MALONEY, J____ M____, 54, bridge builder, Baltimor City, June 16, 1892.
MALONEY, Rev. John A. (R.C.), 65, Baltimore City, February 14, 1901.
MALONEY, Captain M____, 68, mariner, Baltimore City, January 19, 1910.
MALONEY, Timothy, 49, sheriff, Baltimore City, April 25, 1894.
MALLORY, M____ Willard, 68, oyster packer, Baltimore City, September 12, 1878.
MALOY, Rev. William C., 80, Baltimore City, January 21, 1913.
MALSTER, Jeremiah, 84, retired, Baltimore City, April 8, 1895.
MALSTER, William T., 63, former mayor, Baltimore City, March 2, 1907.
MALVANEY, Edward, 61, Cumberland, Allegany County, June 6, 1899.
MANDT, Rev. Olaf, 28, Scandinavian Church, Baltimore City, September 29, 1880.
MANLEY, Rev. Dominic (R.C.), 39, Highland Park, Prince George's County, October 30, 1893.
MANLY, William M., n.a., Ellicott City, Howard County, June 11, 1914.
MANN, Sarah G., n.a., Lutherville, Baltimore County, July 18, 1913.
MANN, Captain T____, 69, mariner, Baltimore City, September 29, 1902.
MANN, Dr. William B., n.a., Baltimore City, May 23, 1913.
MANNING, Charles P., 69, engineer, Baltimore City, April 6, 1886.
MANNING, Lieutenant H____, 29, Fifth Regiment, Baltimore City, December 1, 1880.
MANNING, J____ G____, 72, retired, Baltimore City, June 17, 1884.
MANNING, Joseph C., 41, bank clerk, Baltimore City, February 6, 1889.

MANNING, Rev. Peter M., 53, Baltimore City, September 1, 1906.
MANNING, Richard, 76, Westminster, Carroll County, August 5, 1898.
MANNING, Van H., n.a., Prince George's County, November 3, 1892.
MANNS, John A., 75, tailor, Baltimore City, February 2, 1899.
MANSFIELD, James D., 79, merchant, Baltimore City, May 15, 1904.
MANSFIELD, Dr. Richard W., 58, physician, Baltimore City, June 2, 1898.
MANTZ, Alexander K., 72, merchant, Baltimore City, January 4, 1892.
MANTZ, W____ H____, 49, merchant, Baltimore City, May 13, 1880.
MANYPENNY, Colonel George W., 84, Bowie, Prince George's County, July 15, 1892.
MARAVLANSKY, Annie, seven years old, Front Street Theater panic, December 27, 1895.
MARAVLANSKY, Ida, 13, Front Street Theater panic, December 27, 1895.
MARBURG, Charles L., 64, Baltimore City, February 2, 1907.
MARBURY, F____, 66, Prince George's County, March 17, 1890.
MARBURY, Fendall, Jr., 26, attorney, Baltimore City, May 11, 1887.
MARCH, Philip, 57, Baltimore City, March 25, 1893.
MARCHANT, John R., 47, retired sea captain, Baltimore City, November 5, 1893.
MARDEN, Jesse, Sr., 68, manufacturer, Baltimore City, March 2, 1902.
MARGOLIS, Morris, 21, tailor, Front Street Theater panic, December 27, 1895.
MARINE, Rev. F____ E____ (M.E.), 68, Baltimore City, September 19, 1889.
MARINE, J____ H____, n.a., Baltimore City, January 18, 1912.
MARINE, William M., 61, attorney, Baltimore City, March 2, 1904.
MARIS, Dr. Edward Alexander, 82, physician, Baltimore City, April 20, 1902.
MARKEL, Louis F., 85, retired, Baltimore City, May 28 or 29, 1902.
MARKELL, Charles, 81, Baltimore City, February 22, 1908.
MARKELL, George, 84, financier, Frederick, Frederick County, March 13, 1900.
MARKELL, J____ V____, 46, Baltimore City, September 17, 1908.
MARKELL, Thomas, 84, Frederick, Frederick City, August 9, 1902.
MARKLAND, James H., 75, Baltimore City, October 26, 1896.
MARKLAND, William T., 63, builder, Baltimore City, April 29, 1884.
MARKLAND, William T., 70, educator, Baltimore City, October 27, 1903.
MARKOE, Colonel Frank, 74, Baltimore City, June 4, 1914.
MARLEY, Rev. J____ T____, n.a., Towson, Baltimore County, January 24, 1908.
MARMADUKE, D____, 75, Breathedsville, Washington County, May 7, 1912.
MARR, Andrew, 82, Hagerstown, Washington County, August 29, 1898.

MARRIOTT, George H. M., 53, merchant, Baltimore City, August 13, 1886.
MARRIOTT, Thomas, 62, inspector, Baltimore City, July 8, 1902.
MARRIOTT, Telfair, 49, agent, Baltimore City, May 2, 1882.
MARRIOTT, W____ H____, 73, Baltimore City, December 18, 1912.
MARSH, Andrew M., 60, Baltimore City, January 29, 1897.
MARSH, Captain W____ W____, 64, Confederate veteran, Baltimore City, March 17, 1907.
MARSHAEL, Reuben, 65, costumer, Baltimore City, October 24, 1883.
MARSHALL, Alexander J., 80, attorney, Baltimore City, February 24, 1882.
MARSHALL, Colonel C____, 71, attorney, Baltimore City, April 19, 1902.
MARSHALL, James E., 57, sheriff, Queen Anne's County, September 17, 1893.
MARSHALL, James R., 78, retired pilot, Baltimore City, December 20, 1905.
MARSHALL, John E., 76, builder, Baltimore City, May 1, 1904.
MARSHALL, John L., 71, manufacturer, Baltimore City, October 10, 1893.
MARSHALL, Jerome, 44, contractor, Baltimore City, October 18, 1901.
MARSHALL, Richard H., 84, former judge, Frederick, Frederick County, September 3, 1884.
MARSHALL, Thomas B., 79, builder, Baltimore City, October 20, 1904.
MARSHALL, William A., 49, builder, Baltimore City, March 1, 1905.
MARSHALL, William G., 84, Govanstown, Baltimore County, May 13, 1893.
MARSHALL, William L., n.a., former judge, Baltimore City, October 5, 1879.
MARSTERS, Dr. W____ C____, 85, physician, Wicomico County, August 15, 1893.
MARSTON, Lilcoln W., 79, merchant, Baltimore City, January 13, 1901.
MARTEEN, Susan, 103, Baltimore City, August 23, 1879.
MARTENET, Simon J., 60, surveyor, Baltimore City, November 7, 1892.
MARTENET, Dr. William H., n.a., Baltimore City, December 28, 1909.
MARTIN, C____ W____, 72, Annapolis, Anne Arundel County, January 21, 1908.
MARTIN, Charles A., 52, merchant, Austrian consul at Baltimore City, February 27, 1903.
MARTIN, Charles R., 42, Annapolis, Anne Arundel County, February 7, 1902.
MARTIN, Culbertson, 82, machinist, Baltimore City, April 15, 1883.
MARTIN, David G., 60, merchant, Baltimore City, December 18, 1880.
MARTIN, George A., 61, expressman, Baltimore City, September 27, 1899.

MARTIN, H_____ Newell, 48, Baltimore City, October 29, 1896.
MARTIN, Mrs. Hetty Cary, n.a., Baltimore City, September 27, 1892.
MARTIN, Dr. I_____ J_____, 78, Ellicott City, Howard County, December 15, 1892.
MARTIN, J_____ M_____, 81, Baltimore City, December 11, 1909.
MARTIN, Rev. Dr. J_____ S_____ (M.E., South), 72, Baltimore City, July 8, 1888.
MARTIN, Captain J_____ W_____, 89, Easton, Talbot County, August 7, 1906.
MARTIN, James L., 63, bricklayer, Baltimore City, May 23, 1894.
MARTIN, James Lloyd, 69, physician, Baltimore City, June 29, 1889.
MARTIN, Dr. James S., 76, physician, Baltimore City, April 14, 1900.
MARTIN, John, 57, merchant, Baltimore City, December 15, 1882.
MARTIN, Rev. John (P.E.), 84, Kent County, August 11, 1893.
MARTIN, John Ennalls, n.a., Easton, Talbot County, December 8, 1900.
MARTIN, Lewis, 68, merchant, Baltimore City, April 25, 1887.
MARTIN, Sister Mary, n.a., Baltimore City, November 9, 1913.
MARTIN, Robert K., 58, chief engineer, Baltimore City water department, November 24, 1893.
MARTIN, Samuel, 80, merchant, Baltimore City, April 11, 1901.
MARTIN, Samuel A., 69, contractor, Baltimore City, April 27, 1903.
MARTIN, Dr. T_____ W_____, 82, Easton, Talbot County, February 13, 1906.
MARTIN, Thomas E., 90, Annapolis, Anne Arundel County, April 20, 1902.
MARTIN, Tristam T., 71, Easton, Talbot County, December 23, 1893.
MARTIN, William C., 82, former clerk, Baltimore City, August 29, 1883.
MARTIN, Judge W_____ R_____, 52, Easton, Talbot County, September 5, 1906.
MARTINETTI, Julien, 63, clown, Baltimore City, April 19, 1884.
MARTINI, A_____, 63, superintendent of Bay View, Baltimore City, March 4, 1892.
MARTS, Captain S_____ R_____, 66, ship broker, Baltimore City, February 3, 1905.
MARYE, R_____, 58, Baltimore City, February 1, 1908.
MASINGO, Captain J_____ H_____, 64, mariner, Baltimore City, January 14, 1902.
MASON, Alfrod, 75, architect, Baltimore City, December 31, 1912.
MASON, James D., 62, manufacturer, Baltimore City, August 24, 1887.
MASON, James D., 52, retired merchant and capitalist, Baltimore City, December 10, 1906.
MASON, Dr. John T., 74, surgeon, Baltimore City, June 2, 1891.
MASON, John Thompson (of R_____), 57, attorney, Baltimore City, June 21, 1901.
MASON, Randolph B., 74, contractor, Baltimore City, February 16, 1901.

MASON, Samuel C., n.a., manufacturer, Baltimore City, September 27, 1906.
MASON, Thomas J., 52, Baltimore City, June 18, 1914.
MASSAMORE, Dr. George W., 55, Baltimore City, April 7, 1898.
MASSENBURG, Dr. R____ C____, 68, Towson, Baltimore County, December 30, 1912.
MASSEY, Colonel Joshua, 59, farmer, Kent County, February 22, 1906.
MASSIN, Rev. Louis C., 67, Aberdeen, Harford County, February 22, 1907.
MASTERMAN, Charles A., 75, carpenter, Baltimore City, May 10, 1894.
MATTHAEI, Charles, 50, telegraph manager, Baltimore City, January 26, 1883.
MATTHAI, John C., 77, retired manufacturer, Baltimore City, July 4, 1899.
MATTHAI, Joseph F., 40, manufacturer, Baltimore City, June 12, 1899.
MATTHAEI, Louis, Sr., 64, cooper, Baltimore City, September 25, 1897.
MATTHEW, James W., 76, retired, Baltimore City, November 14, 1901.
MATTHEWS, A____ C____ N____, 84, Baltimore City, March 4, 1909.
MATTHEWS, Mrs. Catherine, 104, Baltimore City, March 29, 1893.
MATTHEWS, George H., 75, builder, Baltimore City, July 22, 1886.
MATTHEWS, I____ T____, 70, bank cashier, Snow Hill, Worcester County, November 22, 1899.
MATTHEWS, J____, 88, lumber merchant, Baltimore City, August 30, 1892.
MATTHEWS, James F., 73, Charles County, June 29, 1908.
MATTHEWS, John N., 68, merchant, Baltimore City, September 24, 1904.
MATTHEWS, R____ Stockett, 60, lawyer, Baltimore City, February 1, 1890.
MATTHEWS, Thomas R., Jr., 67, broker, Baltimore City, January 15, 1898.
MATTHEWS, William B., 70, Charles County, October 3, 1897.
MATTINGLY, Ignatius, 50, St. Mary's County, January 29, 1897.
MAUGHLIN, William W., 69, retired, Baltimore City, October 6, 1885.
MAULSBY, William P., 78, Westminster, Carroll County, October 3, 1894.
MAULSBY, William P., n.a., Frederick, Frederick County, November 14, 1911.
MAUND, George C., 53, lawyer, Baltimore City, May 16, 1884.
MAUPIN, Professor Chapman, 54, educstor, Ellicott City, Howard County, July 25, 1900.
MAURY, J____ S____, 69, former naval officer, Baltimore City, February 4, 1893.
MAUS, Isaac, 92, Rockville, Montgomery County, May 28, 1905.
MAUS, Levi D., Sr., 77, Carroll County, August 25, 1905.
MAXFIELD, William, 66, manufacturer, Baltimore City, December 19, 1899.
MAXWELL, 82, merchant, Baltimore City, November 13, 1879.

MAY, Dominick M. H., 83, music professor, Baltimore City, February 2, 1903.
MAY, Frederick, 46, of Baltimore City; died in England, September 1, 1893.
MAY, Professor James W. A., 65, musician, Baltimore City, December 25, 1889.
MAY, William, 76, retired, Baltimore City, July 9, 1887.
MAYBERRY, J____, 68, register of voters, Baltimore City, September 25, 1881.
MAYBERRY, P____ J____, 69, Customs House, Baltimore City, October 26, 1902.
MAYER, Rev. A____ L____, 70, rabbi, Baltimore City, January 28, 1881.
MAYER, Brantz, 69, author, Baltimore City, February 23, 1879.
MAYER, Charles F., 72, former president, B. & O. Railroad, Baltimore City, February 24, 1904.
MAYER, Charles F., Jr., 58, engineer, Baltimore City, December 18, 1888.
MAYER, Christopher L., n.a., merchant, Baltimore City, May 13, 1880.
MAYER, Elias, 41, manufacturer, Baltimore City, January 15, 1879.
MAYER, Lewis, 50, lawyer, Baltimore City, May 5, 1886.
MAYNADIER, Rev. E____ E____ (R.C.), n.a., Baltimore City, July 31, 1900.
MAYNADIER, George Y., 66, former judge, Bel Air, Harford County, September 5, 1905.
MAYNADIER, John H., 75, retired, Baltimore City, April 15, 1906.
MAYNADIER, William M., 45, merchant, Baltimore City, October 10, 1903.
MAYNARD, James A., 77, merchant, Baltimore City, April 16, 1886.
MAYNARD, Richard F., 81, retired, Baltimore City, January 14, 1897.
MAYNARD, Dr. S____ Sollers, 76, Frederick, Frederick County, August 3, 1913.
MEADE, Rev. F____ A____, 66, Walbrook, Baltimore City, October 13, 1912.
MEADE, Rev. Philip N. (P.E.), n.a., Baltimore City, November 9, 1899.
MEAGHER, George T., 62, florist, Baltimore City, August 26, 1899.
MEAGHER, John, 87, retired, Baltimore City, March 26, 1897.
MEAGHER, Martin, 75, builder, Baltimore City, October 2, 1882.
MEARNS, William L., 75, banker, Rising Sun, Cecil County, October 29, 1903.
MEDAIRY, J____ H____, 82, bookseller, Baltimore City, February 4, 1904.
MEDAIRY, John, 50, Baltimore City, April 20, 1900.
MEDDERS, Albert, 73, merchant, Baltimore City, January 11, 1902.
MEDINGER, John G., 74, retired, Baltimore City, November 6, 1883.
MEEHAN, Patrick, 72, Baltimore City, September 14, 1893.
MEEKER, Cornelius I., 87, financier, Baltimore City, May 13, 1904.
MEEKINS, George A., 37, journalist, Baltimore City, November 5, 1900.

MEEKINS, J____ D____, 72, Taylors Island, Dorchester County, April 21, 1912.
MEEKS, William P., 89, retired, Baltimore City, January 14, 1897.
MEETER, George A., 47, Baltimore City, September 1, 1898.
MEETH, John, 63, veteran of the Mexican War, Baltimore City, March 26, 1897.
MEGENHART, Frederick, 74, Baltimore City, December 4, 1914.
MEHANY, John, 84, Baltimore City, March 18, 1892.
MEISNER, Henry, 64, manufacturer, Baltimore City, February 17, 1905.
MELLIN, Joseph, 72, retired, Baltimore City, October 9, 1903.
MELLINGER, Jacob, 63, chemist, Baltimore City, July 26, 1904.
MELLON, James, 79, musician, Baltimore City, July 24, 1904.
MELVIN, J____ S____, 82, Hagerstown, Washington County, January 28, 1912.
MELVIN, Willard, 71, court clerk, Chestertown, Kent County, November 3, 1906.
MEMMERT, Frederick, 53, salesman, Baltimore City, July 27, 1882.
MENGER, George H., 31, jeweler, Baltimore City, December 17, 1894.
MENTZEL, William M., 68, manufacturer, Baltimore City, October 10, 1893.
MENTZER, Captain J____ M____, 67, editor of the Hagerstown (Washington County) Herald & Torch; died there April 16, 1885.
MENU, Rev. Jean Baptist (R.C.), 67, Baltimore City, March 10, 1888.
MERCER, Charles H., 65, retired, Baltimore City, January 7, 1887.
MERCER, Rev. F____ A____ (M.E.), 73, Baltimore City, January 15, 1902.
MERCER, Dr. William M., 76, physician, Baltimore City, March 24, 1904.
MERCHANT, John O., 93, Boyds, Montgomery County, February 4, 1907.
MEREDITH, Gilmor, 75, merchant, Baltimore City, October 12, 1899.
MEREDITH, Mrs. Hannah, 95, Baltimore City, November 15, 1878.
MEREDITH, Rev. J____ C____ (M.E.), 65, Baltimore City, December 2, 1884.
MEREDITH, J____ F____, 73, federal appraiser, Baltimore City, July 15, 1883.
MEREDITH, William B., 75, Baltimore City, September 12, 1897.
MERGENTHALER, Ottmar, 45, inventor of the linotype, Baltimore City, October 28, 1899.
MERRIAM, Robert W., 64, mariner, Baltimore City, July 23, 1901.
MERLE, Henry A., 74, retired, Baltimore City, December 23, 1902.
MERREFIELD, Joseph, 81, treasurer, Johns Hopkins Hospital, Baltimore City, July 3, 1902.
MERRICK, Charles H. R., 53, Kent County, October 18, 1898.
MERRICK, Mathias, 70, Talbot County, May 29, 1893.
MERRICK, William S., 54, Talbot County, October 9, 1905.

MERRILAT, Dr. J____ C____, 69, physician, Baltimore City, September 18, 1881.
MERRILL, William J., 54, manager, Baltimore City, March 29, 1897.
MERRITT, James A., 58, merchant, Baltimore City, May 2, 1901.
MERRITT, Joseph C., 61, merchant, Baltimore City, May 24, 1883.
MERRITT, William K., 69, merchant, Baltimore City, November 12, 1878.
MERRYMAN, Rev. Charles G. (Baptist), 34, Baltimore City, July 3, 1894.
MERRYMAN, D____ Buchanan, 43, auctioneer, Baltimore City, March 11, 1900.
MERRYMAN, E____ Gittings, n.a., Cockeysville, Baltimore County, April 8, 1913.
MERRYMAN, Dr. George, 74, physician, Baltimore City, September 24, 1885.
MERRYMAN, John, 58, president, Maryland Agricultural Association, November 15, 1881.
MERRYMAN, Joseph, 73, farmer, Baltimore City, May 14, 1880.
MERRYMAN, Dr. Moses W., 75, Baltimore County, January 25, 1904.
MESSERSMITH, Charles, 66, Baltimore City, October 19, 1893.
METHANY, Daniel, 75, pilot, Baltimore City, April 8, 1894.
METTAM, Rev. Joseph (Baptist), 83, Baltimore City, February 1, 1888.
METTEE, Joseph S., 53, postal clerk, Baltimore City, August 26, 1893.
METZ, Augustus H., 59, musician, Baltimore City, March 31, 1879.
METZGER, Francis, 50, druggist, Baltimore City, July 31, 1884.
METZGER, William M., 68, merchant, Baltimore City, March 27, 1899.
MEYER, Barthold, 67, musician, Baltimore City, July 19, 1904.
MEYER, Carl A., 61, Baltimore City, February 4, 1914.
MEYER, Charles, 87, Baltimore City, January 19, 1909.
MEYER, G____ Frederick, 79, Baltimore City, July 20, 1897.
MEYER, George, 86, retired brass founder, Baltimore City, May 17, 1894.
MEYER, Isaac, 56, black, Baltimore City, January 26, 1891.
MEYER, John G., 71, grocer, Baltimore City, December 5, 1879.
MEYER, Solomon, 59, merchant, Baltimore City, April 28, 1902.
MEYER, Captain William, 76, mariner, Baltimore City, October 22, 1883.
MEYERS, Mrs. Anna, 95, Baltimore City, November 20, 1907.
MEYERS, Jacob, 80, merchant, Baltimore City, October 23, 1881.
MEYERS, James H., 84, retired, Baltimore City, May 30, 1896.
MICHAEL, Henry J., 58, merchant, Baltimore City, July 23, 1886.
MICHAEL, Dr. J____ Edwin, 47, Baltimore City physician, December 7, 1895.
MICHAEL, Jacob D., 56, merchant, Baltimore City, October 9, 1897.
MICHAEL, William H., 65, merchant, Baltimore City, March 22, 1878.
MICHEAU, Dr. Theodore J., 71, physician, Baltimore City, March 10, 1895.

MICHELMANN, Henry E., 73, Baltimore City, November 14, 1893.
MICKLE, Robert, 88, bank cashier, Baltimore City, May 10, 1886.
MIDDENDORF, George C., 45, broker, Baltimore City, November 8, 1903.
MIDDLETON, Dr. E____ L____, 73, Upper Marlboro, Prince George's County, January 8, 1906.
MILBOURNE, Charles D., 54, merchant, Baltimore City, January 2, 1879.
MILBOURNE, John M., 93, Baltimore City, May 25, 1905.
MILBOURNE, S____ T____, 76, attorney, Cambridge, Dorchester County, December 24, 1912.
MILBURN, James A., 73, pilot, Baltimore City, March 15, 1882.
MILBURN, Captain John T., 90, Catonsville, Baltimore County, May 20, 1914.
MILBURN, Nicholas P., 60, Cecil County, May 3, 1893.
MILBURN, Thomas, 82, carpenter, Baltimore City, September 11, 1882.
MILES, Augustus W., 100, Baltimore City, January 23, 1907.
MILES, F____ W____, 72, Pocomoke City, Worcester County, April 23, 1893.
MILES, Dr. Francis T., 75, physician, Baltimore City, July 30, 1903.
MILES, Dr. James H., 85, Leonardtown, St. Mary's County, January 26, 1907.
MILES, John T., 74, Somerset County, August 10, 1901.
MILES, Southey F., 78, Somerset County, May 15, 1900.
MILES, William T., 68, merchant, Baltimore City, April 24, 1894.
MILHOLLAND, Robert D., 64, bank clerk, Baltimore City, May 2, 1884.
MILLAR, James, Jr., 51, plumber, Baltimore City, December 31, 1901.
MILLER, Andrew J., 80, merchant, Baltimore City, March 15, 1901.
MILLER, Dr. C____ Edward, 33, Baltimore City, December 1, 1878.
MILLER, Charles, 76, engineer, died at Parkersburg, West Virginia, December 29, 1910.
MILLER, Captain Charles C., n.a., mariner, Baltimore City, March 11, 1892.
MILLER, Columbus A., 65, retired, Baltimore City, May 22, 1883.
MILLER, Daniel, 49, merchant, Baltimore City, December 13, 1898.
MILLER, Decatur H., 69, retired, Baltimore City, December 31, 1890.
MILLER, Edgar G., 83, Baltimore City, December 22, 1910.
MILLER, Edward A., 60, merchant, Baltimore City, June 15, 1900.
MILLER, Edward D., 64, secretary, Builders' Exchange, Baltimore City, February 14, 1900.
MILLER, Edwin A., 75, merchant, Baltimore City, June 28, 1902.
MILLER, G____ W____, 80, manufacturer, Baltimore City, December 18, 1902.
MILLER, George, 75, retired, Baltimore City, May 23, 1897.
MILLER, H____ Clay, 39, merchant, Baltimore City, August 1, 1880.

MILLER, Hartman, 75, contractor, Baltimore City, December 31, 1903.
MILLER, Henry F., 62, manufacturer, Baltimore City, May 20, 1900.
MILLER, Henry W., 51, brewer, Baltimore City, November 2, 1899.
MILLER, Dr. J____ E____, 70, Hagerstown, Washington County, August 25, 1907.
MILLER, J____ M____, 76, former State Senator, Cecil County; died at Wilmington, Delaware, February 1, 1897.
MILLER, J____ Philip, 63, hotelier, Baltimore City, February, 1893.
MILLER, Jacob, 69, merchant, Baltimore City, August 15, 1880.
MILLER, James, 76, retired, Baltimore City, October 20, 1883.
MILLER, Rev. John, 63, Baltimore City, October 10, 1878.
MILLER, John F. W., 83, retired, Baltimore City, August 6, 1905.
MILLER, John R., 67, Hagerstown, Washington County, September 17, 1909.
MILLER, John S., 52, Mayor of Westernport, Allegany County, March 22, 1906.
MILLER, Joseph, 63, retired, Baltimore City, March 21, 1906.
MILLER, Professor Julius, 69, Baltimore City, February 20, 1908.
MILLER, Luke H., 66, manufacturer, Baltimore City, April 24, 1894.
MILLER, Morgan A., 74, Baltimore City, August 1, 1897.
MILLER, O____ J____, 58, police sergeant, Baltimore City, October 16, 1902.
MILLER, Oliver, 68, judge, Ellicott City, Howard County, October, 1892.
MILLER, Oliver M., 75, mechanic, Baltimore City, April 8, 1884.
MILLER, Peter T., 71, realtor, Baltimore City, December 22, 1903.
MILLER, Samuel L., 66, bricklayer, Baltimore City, August 27, 1903.
MILLER, Theodore, 76, retired, Baltimore City, July 31, 1900.
MILLER, W____ D____, 77, merchant, Baltimore City, January 17, 1888.
MILLER, W____ Howard, 24, of Baltimore City; died at Stanford University, in California, March 2, 1893.
MILLER, William C., 68, publisher, Baltimore City, March 30, 1894.
MILLER, Dr. William E., 43, Baltimore City, November 23, 1913.
MILLER, William H., 76, builder, Baltimore City, November 29, 1893.
MILLES, Alphonse L., 72, educator, Baltimore City, December 29, 1901.
MILLIKEN, William H., 69, manufacturer, Baltimore City, August 31, 1901.
MILLS, Ezekiel, Sr., 77, retired, Baltimore City, December 20, 1894.
MILLS, James C., 77, printer, Baltimore City, September 17, 1895.

MILLS, Job, 77, jeweler, Baltimore City, January 28, 1894.
MILLS, John E., 60, ship joiner, Baltimore City, August 18, 1884.
MILLS, John M., 78, printer, Baltimore City, December 30, 1901.
MILLS, Samuel J., 33, merchant, Baltimore City, April 8, 1896.
MILLS, William P., 60, manufacturer, Baltimore City, January 16, 1902.
MILNOR, John P., 65, retired merchant, Baltimore City, May 21, 1899.
MILNOR, Joseph K., 67, insurance, Baltimore City, February 28, 1889.
MILROY, John, 66, police commissioner, Baltimore City, May 22, 1886.
MILTENBERGER, Dr. George Warner, 86, physician, Baltimore City, December 11, 1905.
MILTENBERGER, Mrs. Sarah E., 71, Baltimore City, December 31, 1898.
MINIFIE, William, 75, merchant, Baltimore City, October 24, 1880.
MINNICK, Aloysius B., 42, contractor, Baltimore City, March 19, 1901.
MINNICK, J_____ M_____ E_____, 65, music professor, December 7, 1885.
MITCHELL, Captain C_____ J_____ B_____, n.a., former commander of oyster police steamer Lelia, March 28, 1884.
MITCHELL, Charles E., 61, merchant, Baltimore City, April 3, 1901.
MITCHELL, Dr. Charles H., 41, physician, Baltimore City, July 22, 1898.
MITCHELL, David J., 51, merchant, Baltimore City, October 9, 1897.
MITCHELL, Frank S., 31, merchant, Baltimore City, December 9, 1882.
MITCHELL, G_____ W_____, 65, former policeman, Baltimore City, July 11, 1881.
MITCHELL, Captain George, 76, Havre de Grace, Harford County, January 29, 1913.
MITCHELL, Hugh, 61, Charles County, September 27, 1899.
MITCHELL, Captain J_____ H_____, 52, superintendent, Bayview, October 20, 1884.
MITCHELL, Professor James A., 50, Emmitsburg, Frederick County, October 18, 1902.
MITCHELL, John, 76, superintendent, Bayview, Baltimore City, September 26, 1879.
MITCHELL, John, 86, street preacher, Baltimore City, July 22, 1885.
MITCHELL, John G., 69, attorney, Baltimore City, December 15, 1898.
MITCHELL, John H., 59, Charles County, November 12, 1901.
MITCHELL, Captain Joseph, 72, former police officer, March 22, 1882.
MITCHELL, Joseph C., 71, detective, Baltimore City, July 31, 1898.
MITCHELL, Louisa, 100, Baltimore City, January 7, 1887.

MITCHELL, Captain Richard, 80, retired, Baltimore City, October 17, 1886.
MITCHELL, Stephen D., 82, miller, Baltimore City, September 22, 1901.
MITCHELL, William, 62, gas superintendent, Baltimore City, August 24, 1880.
MITCHELL, William M., 55, Somerset County, July 20, 1893.
MITTEN, Edwin, 70, Westminster, Carroll County, February 25, 1908.
MOALE, Charles H., 71, retired banker, Baltimore City, January 18, 1903.
MOALE, Henry A., n.a., merchant, Baltimore City, January 6, 1890.
MOALE, L____ G____, 70, Baltimore City, December 16, 1912.
MOALE, William A., 81, merchant, Baltimore City, August 15, 1880.
MOBBERLY, William L., 72, Frederick, Frederick County, January 22, 1904.
MOBLEY, Colonel Edward M., 81, Hagerstown, Washington County, April 4, 1906.
MONATH, George, 68, musician, Baltimore City, April 16, 1893.
MONMONIER, Dr. John, n.a., physician, Baltimore City, June 11, 1896.
MONMONIER, Dr. John Francis, 81, physician, Baltimore City, June 8, 1894.
MONMONIER, Dr. Joseph Carroll, 57, physician, Baltimore City, April 6, 1904.
MONROE, Dr. W____ R____, 73, Methodist minister, Baltimore City, February 13, 1894.
MONSARRAT, Oscar, 73, druggist, Baltimore City, March 6, 1887.
MORGAN, Samuel G., 23, Baltimore City; drowned while ice skating, December 28, 1902.
MONTAGUE, Charles P., 67, Howard County, December 26, 1894.
MONTAGUE, William I., 58, insurance broker, Baltimore City, June 4, 1901.
MONTAGUE, W____ L____, 85, Baltimore City, April 4, 1909.
MONTALDO, Pedro, 57, professor of Spanish, U.S.N.A., February 23, 1884.
MONTELIUS, Captain John A., 35, Baltimore City, February 22, 1898.
MONTGOMERY, Dr. James, 88, Baltimore City, April 11, 1878.
MONTGOMERY, Dr. William T., 40, physician, Baltimore City, September 1, 1881.
MOOG, Jacob, 71, brewer, February 12, 1899.
MOONEY, M____ E____, 45, Baltimore City Councilman, April 13, 1883.
MOORE, Cornelius, 85, Cockeysville, Baltimore County, October 30, 1911.
MOORE, Dr. G____ A____, 58, druggist, Baltimore City, December 7, 1881.
MOORE, George H., 72, judge, Orphan's Court, Caroline County, April 9, 1898.
MOORE, Dr. Harrison C., 43, druggist, Baltimore City, December 24, 1883.
MOORE, Herbert F., 56, hotelier, Leonardtown, St. Mary's County, April 16, 1897.

MOORE, Horatio U., 84, merchant, Baltimore City, January 19, 1882.
MOORE, J___ T___, 86, Frederick, Frederick County, May 23, 1907.
MOORE, Dr. J___ Faris, 62, druggist, Baltimore City, February 3, 1888.
MOORE, J___ Wilson, 64, Bel Air, Harford County, June 24, 1909.
MOORE, James O., n.a., railroad builder, Baltimore City, February 2, 1894.
MOORE, Colonel Jesse J., 80, superintendent, House of Correction, Jessup, Howard County, July 3, 1906.
MOORE, John, 71, wharf builder, Baltimore City, April 27, 1893.
MOORE, John, 69, mariner, Baltimore City, July 30, 1901.
MOORE, John, 73, Baltimore City, September 15, 1907.
MOORE, John A., 60, merchant, Baltimore City, November 14, 1899.
MOORE, Philip L., n.a., former reading clerk, Maryland House of Delegates; died at Towson, Baltimore County, July 11, 1886.
MOORE, Robert, 73, merchant, Baltimore City, April 19, 1891.
MOORE, Thomas, 85, dairyman, Baltimore City, April 25, 1883.
MOORE, Thomas B., 79, Salisbury, Wicomico County, August 3, 1902.
MOORE, Thomas H., 59, chief clerk, Maryland House of Delegates; died at Towson, Baltimore County, September 3, 1885.
MOOREHEAD, William H., 68, merchant, Baltimore City, February 2, 1893.
MOORES, John, 82, Bel Air, Harford County, December 20, 1911.
MORAN, Charles S., 73, former policeman, Baltimore City, July 23, 1886.
MORAN, Joseph C., 66, Baltimore City, October 4, 1898.
MORAWETZ, Dr. Leopold Frank, 73, physician, Baltimore City, October 26, 1892.
MORDECAI, David, 80, merchant, Baltimore City, August 22, 1899.
MORDECAI, John R., 60, merchant, Baltimore City, September 25, 1895.
MORDECAI, Moses C., 84, retired, Baltimore City, December 30, 1888.
MORELAND, Margaret L., 21, McDonogh, Baltimore County, October 22, 1912.
MORELAND, James Chamberlain, 91, oldest surviving member of the Old Defenders' Association, Baltimore City, December 17, 1888.
MORGAN, Dr. DeWitt Clinton, 64, Baltimore City, August 23, 1894.
MORGAN, Evan, 32, artist, Baltimore City, February 14, 1886.
MORGAN, George W., 50, Baltimore City, March 13, 1896.
MORGAN, J___ Asbury, 61, teacher, Baltimore City, November 30, 1879.
MORGAN, James B., 64, merchant, Baltimore City, July 21, 1894.
MORGAN, Joseph F., 62, lawyer, Leonardtown, St. Mary's, July 15, 1906.
MORGAN, Rev. L___ A___ (R.C.), 44, Baltimore City, October 5, 1881.

MORGAN, Rev. L_____ F_____ (M.E.), 82, February 28, 1895.
MORGAN, P_____ A_____, 73, Easton, Talbot County, November 8, 1912.
MORGAN, Samuel T., 60, broker, Baltimore City, March 28, 1904.
MORGAN, Rev. T_____ A_____ (M.E.), 71, Baltimore City, April 25, 1887.
MORISON, N_____ H_____, 75, Peabody Institute, Baltimore City, November 14, 1890.
MORLING, F_____ L_____, 62, Baltimore City, March 20, 1896.
MORNINGSTAR, B_____ W_____, n.a., merchant, Westminster, Carroll County, May 21, 1897.
MORRILL, George E., 73, dentist, Baltimore City, May 20, 1880.
MORRIS, C_____ D_____, 60, professor, Johns Hopkins University, February 7, 1886.
MORRIS, Charles M., 75, Confederate veteran, Baltimore City, March 22, 1895.
MORRIS, Elijah J., 48, master mariner, Baltimore City, July 10, 1893.
MORRIS, Rev. George (Presbyterian), 75, Baltimore City, December 10, 1883.
MORRIS, George W., 80, Baltimore City, October 8, 1893.
MORRIS, Dr. John, 79, physician, Baltimore City, January 29, 1903.
MORRIS, John Boucher, 77, Baltimore City, October 8, 1898.
MORRIS, John D., 81, Baltimore City, March 28, 1909.
MORRIS, Rev. John G. (Lutheran), 91, Baltimore City, October 10, 1895.
MORRIS, Joseph ("Fifer Joe"), 48, Baltimore City, April 1, 1893.
MORRIS, Patrick, 52, retired, Baltimore City, October 25, 1884.
MORRIS, Judge T_____ J_____, 75, Baltimore City, June 6, 1912.
MORRISON, Dr. Edwin T., 47, physician, Baltimore City, August 7, 1896.
MORRISON, Frederick D., 67, superintendent, Maryland School for the Blind, Baltimore City, October 8, 1904.
MORRISON, Professor Frederick W., 46, Annapolis, Anne Arundel County, September 8, 1914.
MORRISON, Rev. George (Presbyterian), 67, Baltimore City, August 28, 1898.
MORRISON, George C., n.a., Baltimore City, September 17, 1912.
MORRISON, Dr. James M., 61, physician, Baltimore City, November 13, 1899.
MORRISON, John E., 64, merchant, Baltimore City, October 19, 1885.
MORROW, John B., 62, editor, Ellicott City, Howard County, August 21, 1900.
MORRISON, General Pitcairn, 92, retired, Baltimore City, October 5, 1887.
MORRISON, Robert D., 63, lawyer, Baltimore City, November 23, 1894.
MORROW, Thomas G., 85, Baltimore City, September 16, 1909.
MORSE, Thomas W., 69, former Register of Wills, Baltimore City, April 3, 1899.
MORSE, Dr. William L., 74, physician, Baltimore City, October 19, 1885.

MOSHER, C_____ S_____, 66, prohibitionist, Baltimore City, July 8, 1892.
MORSS, James Southgate, 35, attorney, Baltimore City, October 26, 1882.
MORTON, John I., 26, attorney, Baltimore City, April 21, 1899.
MORTON, Philander, 80, retired, Baltimore City, October 4, 1885.
MOSES, Lieutenant Colonel F_____ J_____, 50, Annapolis, Anne Arundel County, September 26, 1914.
MOTT, George P., 59, hotelier, Baltimore City, April 11, 1895.
MOTTER, Hon. William, 68, former judge, Fourth Judicial Circuit of Maryland; died at Hagerstown, Washington County, August 21, 1885.
MOTTU, Theodore, 75, lumber merchant, Baltimore City, June 5, 1896.
MOWINCKEL, Hans P., 70, clerk, Baltimore City, May 31, 1892.
MOXLEY, Basil, 80, doorman, Baltimore City, March 12, 1906.
MOXLEY, Thomas L., 62, actor, Baltimore City, July 7, 1890.
MOYLAN, John, Sr., 72, merchant, Baltimore City, April 5, 1894.
MUDD, Dr. George D., 73, physician, Baltimore City, December 1, 1899.
MUDD, George D., 26, bookkeeper, Baltimore City, May 2, 1902.
MUDD, Henry L., 63, tobacco inspector, Baltimore City, July 13, 1903.
MUDD, Dr. Samuel, 49, near Bryantown, Charles County, January 10, 1883.
MUDD, Sydney E., 54, former Congressman and political leader, LaPlata, Charles County, October 21, 1911.
MUDD, Mrs. Sydney E., 48, LaPlata, Charles County, June 3, 1907.
MUDGE, Catherine C., 91, Pikesville, Baltimore County, September 6, 1912.
MUELLER, John, 68, cooper, Baltimore City, July 5, 1899.
MUELLER, Julius E., 80, organist, Baltimore City, November 30, 1895.
MUELLER, Rev. Michael (R.C.), 74, Annapolis, Anne Arundel County, August 28, 1899.
MUIRHEAD, Andrew, 80, retired, Baltimore City, February 21, 1884.
MULES, T_____ H_____, 83, Baltimore City, August 22, 1911.
MULAN, Horace E., 66, Annapolis, Anne Arundel County, April 24, 1903.
MULLAN, Dr. James A., 48, surgeon, Baltimore City, October 2, 1882.
MULLAN, Thomas, 40, marble worker, Baltimore City, October 6, 1894.
MULLEN, James S., 77, retired Sun carrier, May 20, 1903.
MULLER, Louis, 84, retired, Baltimore City, April 15, 1899.
MULLER, Professor W_____ M_____ D_____ R_____, 31, musician, Baltimore City, December 12, 1884.
MULLEY, J_____ M_____, 89, manufacturer, Baltimore City, January 22, 1893.
MULLIKIN, Beale D., 64, Prince George's County, December 19, 1901.
MULLIKIN, Clayland, 32, Easton, Talbot County, May 3, 1905.
MULLIKIN, William N., 69, merchant, Baltimore City, April 25, 1885.

MULLIN, Patrick, 53, Baltimore City, February 14, 1897.
MULLINARI, Pietro, 62, merchant, Baltimore City, July 16, 1898.
MUMFORD, William H., 40, merchant, Baltimore City, July 25, 1890.
MUMMA, H____ C____, 76, Hagerstown, Washington County, February 3, 1908.
MUNFORD, Rev. William (P.E.), 75, Annapolis, Anne Arundel County, March 7, 1904.
MUNNICKHUYSEN, Howard, n.a., attorney, Baltimore City, September 6, 1896.
MUNROE, Grafton, 72, Annapolis, Anne Arundel County, December 27, 1908.
MUNROE, J____ Edward, 65, Annapolis, Anne Arundel County, February 7, 1901.
MUNROE, James, 69, Annapolis, Anne Arundel County, September 27, 1896.
MURDOCH, Alexander, 77, merchant, Baltimore City, January 7, 1879.
MURDOCH, Richard, 73, scale-maker, Baltimore City, December 11, 1879.
MURDOCH, Dr. Russell, physician, Baltimore City, March 19, 1905.
MURDOCH, Thomas, 76, merchant, Baltimore City, May 13, 1881.
MURDOCH, Dr. Thomas F., 71, physician, Baltimore City, February 18, 1901.
MURGIONDO, Prudencio de, 79, Uruguayan consul, Baltimore City, March 15, 1910.
MURKLAND, Rev. William U. (Presbyterian), n.a., Baltimore City, May 13, 1899.
MURPHEY, John, 82, Baltimore City, March 17, 1893.
MURPHY, C____ J____, 68, Annapolis, Anne Arundel County, February 24, 1908.
MURPHY, John, 68, bookseller, Baltimore City, May 27, 1880.
MURPHY, Michael J., n.a., compositor, Baltimore City, April 19, 1905.
MURPHY, Rev. Randolph R.(M.E.), 74, Baltimore City, August 20, 1903.
MURPHY, Terence, 101, retired, Baltimore City, December 1, 1901.
MURRAY, Rev. A____ D____ (M.P.), 27, Baltimore City, November 17, 1884.
MURRAY, George, 115, black, Baltimore City, August 9, 1890.
MURRAY, Dr. J____ H____, 77, Anne Arundel County, November 6, 1893.
MURRAY, Rev. Dr. J____ J____ (M.P._, 80, Baltimore City, April 11, 1905.
MURRAY, Rev. J____ Thomas (M.P.), 69, Baltimore City, December 30, 1899.
MURRAY, James B., 85, engraver, Baltimore City, July 12, 1904.
MURRAY, James C., 89, retired, Baltimore City, January 24, 1885.
MURRAY, James D., 77, pay director, U.S. Navy, Annapolis, Anne Arundel County, December 9, 1906.
MURRAY, John, 85, merchant, Baltimore City, October 23, 1892.
MURRAY, John Alexander, 69, representative, Baltimore City, September 29, 1901.
MURRAY, John P., 78, clerk, Baltimore City, December 7, 1888.

MURRAY, General Robert, 91, Baltimore City, January 11, 1913.
MURRAY, Thomas, 58, water engineer, Baltimore City, May 24, 1897.
MURRAY, Thomas C., 29, college professor, Baltimore City, March 20, 1879.
MUSGRAVE, James, 79, retired, Baltimore City, January 26, 1890.
MUTH, John P., 52, merchant, Baltimore City, August 17, 1885.
MUTH, Joseph, 61, druggist, Baltimore City, August 1, 1898.
MUTH, Lewis, 55, brewer, Baltimore City, December 12, 1891.
MUTH, Sebastian A., 65, manufacturer, Baltimore City, March 20, 1900.
MYER, Dr. Abraham, 80, dentist, Baltimore City, May 12, 1892.
MYER, Captain James, 82, retired, Baltimore City, November 7, 1894.
MYERS, James O., 65, merchant, Baltimore City, May 18, 1895.
MYER, Thomas J., 67, packer, Baltimore City, September 29, 1887.
MYERS, A_____ Joseph, 65, merchant, Baltimore City, December 24, 1894.
MYERS, Captain J_____ R_____, 70, former mariner, Baltimore City, February 22, 1884.
MYERS, John B., 68, hotelier, Baltimore City, March 27, 1899.
MYERS, Rev. Thomas (Methodist), 82, Baltimore City, July 27, 1894.
MYERS, William P., 56, merchant, Baltimore City, March 25, 1897.
MYLANDER, Henry, 60, builder, Baltimore City, March 25, 1883.
MYOHL, Charles, 56, merchant, Baltimore City, November 18, 1894.

NACHMAN, Abraham, 75, merchant, Baltimore City, December 20, 1898.
NACHMAN, George G., 76, hotelier, Baltimore City, December 11, 1903.
NALLS, Benjamin F., 80, painter, Baltimore City, October 19, 1892.
NASSAUER, Frederick, 68, Baltimore City, July 23, 1907.
NATHAN, Samuel, 50, merchant, Baltimore City, June 15, 1894.
NAYLOR, Dr. Henry R(?), 76, Baltimore City, November 8, 1913.
NEAL, Charles H., 43, Baltimorean; died at New York City, December 13, 1905.
NEAL, George H. C., 62, merchant, Baltimore City, December 30, 1891.
NEAL, Joseph, 81, retired, Baltimore City, September 27, 1886.
NEAL, Lander, Sr., 63, druggist, Baltimore City, July 3, 1899.
NEAL, Leander, Jr., 32, teacher, Baltimore City, October 26, 1902.
NEALE, Dr. Francis C., 60, of Washington, D.C.; died at New York City, January 17, 1895.
NEALE, Sister Mary Leonard, 81, Order of Visitation Nuns, Baltimore City, September 11, 1901.
NEALE, Mother Mary Regina, n.a., Order of Visitation Nuns, Mount de Sales, Catonsville, Baltimore County, December 16, 1891.
NEARY, Michael, n.a., policeman, Baltimore City, June 20, 1894.
NEEDHAM, Asa, 66, merchant, Baltimore City, November 10, 1902.
NEEDHAM, George F., 59, steamboat agent, Baltimore City, January 15, 1891.
NEEDLES, John, 92, Baltimore City, July 18, 1878.

NEEDLES, John A., 71, merchant, Baltimore City, October 3, 1899.
NEESON, F____ J____, n.a., Frederick, Frederick County, October 15, 1908.
NEFF, Dr. Charles W., 62, physician, Baltimore City, January 17, 1900.
NEFF, Dr. John, 81, former president, Baltimore Medical Association, Baltimore City, June 5, 1913.
NEGLEY, Peter, 66, former U.S. Treasurer at Baltimore; died at Hagerstown, Washington County, June 7, 1884.
NEILSON, J____ Crawford, 84, architect, Baltimore City, December 19, 1900.
NELKER, Christian Frederick, 82, Baltimore City, February 21, 1883.
NELSON, Dr. Edward G., 57, Baltimore City, October 6, 1904.
NELSON, Captain Henry, 85, mariner, Baltimore City, October 26, 1905.
NELSON, Joseph, 70, retired, Baltimore City, May 17, 1896.
NELSON, William B., 78, retired, Baltimore City, April 17, 1896.
NESBITT, Henry C., 81, Port Deposit, Cecil County, December 24, 1903.
NESBITT, Harry A., 47, Port Deposit, Cecil County, November 3, 1905.
NEUDECKER, Leonard H., 75, Baltimore City, September 12, 1912.
NEUHAUS, Dr. Moritz, 57, physician, Baltimore City, September 22, 1902.
NEUMANN, Charles, 70, printer, Baltimore City, December 15, 1902.
NEW, Henry, 91, merchant, Baltimore City, May 27, 1892.
NEW, Marks, 50, cattle dealer, Baltimore City, January 14, 1903.
NEW, Peter, 67, merchant, Baltimore City, January 20, 1897.
NEWBOLD, James F., Sr., 85, merchant, Baltimore City, June 3, 1902.
NEWBOLD, James F., Jr., n.a., merchant, Baltimore City, January 29, 1902.
NEWCOMB, William R., 68, merchant, Baltimore City, December 29, 1883.
NEWCOMER, Alexander, 73, Washington County, September 3, 1903.
NEWCOMER, Benjamin F., 73, financier, Baltimore City, March 30, 1901.
NEWCOMER, D____ F____, n.a., Hagerstown, Washington County, May 12, 1909.
NEWCOMER, J____ D____, 81, Hagerstown, Washington County, January 22, 1912.
NEWCOMER, Knode, 62, Washington County, January 21, 1904.
NEWCOMER, Peter S., 72, Washington County, February 17, 1902.
NEWELL, Alexander McFadden, 68, educator, of Baltimore City; died at Havre de Grace, Harford County, August 4, 1893.
NEWMAN, James J., 80, Baltimore City, September 6, 1897.
NEWMAN, L____ P____ D____, 52, attorney, Baltimore City, May 15, 1885.
NEWMAN, William W., 70, builder, Baltimore City, October 6, 1883.
NEWMAN, Rev. E____ B____ (M.E.), 49, Baltimore City, December 24, 1885.

-171-

NEWTON, William R., 55, Queen Anne's County, August 27, 1900.
NICE, Rev. J____ P____ (Baptist), 72, Baltimore City, November 26, 1890.
NICEWANER, Eph____ B., 66, jeweler, Baltimore City, April 21, 1903.
NICOLAI, John H., 47, oil works, Baltimore City, January 3, 1897.
NICHOLAS, G____ S____, 33; died at Catlett, Virginia, December 16, 1914.
NICHOLAS, John Spear, 85, retired, Baltimore City, January 22, 1887.
NICHOLLS, Dr. William I., 60, physician, Baltimore City, July 1, 1887.
NICHOLS, Dudley, 75, merchant, Baltimore City, March 3, 1904.
NICHOLS, J____ B____, 83, Baltimore City, April 7, 1907.
NICHOLS, Rev. John R. (Methodist), 81, Baltimore City, July 22, 1896.
NICHOLS, Warren, 40, organist, Baltimore City, July 18, 1894.
NICHOLSON, Albert, 47, banker, Baltimore City, October 16, 1895.
NICHOLSON, Andrew, 51, banker, Baltimore City, January 5, 1892.
NICHOLSON, C____ B____, 73, Baltimore City, November 10, 1908.
NICHOLSON, Mrs. Elizabeth, 97, Baltimore City, February 25, 1879.
NICHOLSON, Gustavus, 70, retired, Baltimore City, March 10, 1885.
NICHOLSON, Isaac L., 82, banker, Baltimore City, July 9, 1891.
NICHOLSON, Rev. J____ E____, 70, Baltimore City, December 7, 1913.
NICHOLSON, James A., 66, manufacturer, Baltimore City, December 27, 1902.
NICHOLSON, John, 75, butcher, Baltimore City, April 11, 1883.
NICHOLSON, John H. R., 66, banker, Baltimore City, December 19, 1903.
NICHOLSON, John J., 75, banker, Baltimore City, August 18, 1879.
NICKLE, Alred C., 66, steamboat captain, Baltimore City, April 14, 1899.
NICODEMUS, Jeremiah, 79, retired, Baltimore City, May 20, 1896.
NICODEMUS, Josiah C., 58, merchant, Baltimore City, February 27, 1878.
NICODEMUS, Mary J., 85, Baltimore City, April 11, 1913.
NIEMANN, Henry, 62, manufacturer, Baltimore City, October 26, 1899.
NILES, C____ Rodney, 68, Baltimore City, August 3, 1900.
NIMMO, James R., 64, retired, Baltimore City, March 30, 1896.
NIMMO, Joseph C., 83, retired, Baltimore City, June 17, 1901.
NINER, Charles, 78, Westminster, Carroll County, February 2, 1910.
NITZE, Charles, 80, Baltimore City, October 21, 1909.
NITZE, Henry B. C., 32, Baltimore City, May 25, 1900.
NIXDORF, Samuel, 87, Frederick, Frederick County, January 27, 1907.
NIXDORFF, L____ M____, 80, Frederick, Frederick County, March 8, 1908.
NIXDORFF, T____ S____, 86, Baltimore City, September 8, 1909.

NIXON, Robert, 62, retired, Baltimore City, May 25, 1901.
NOAH, Jacob, 50, merchant, Baltimore City, March 16, 1879.
NOBLE, Dennis, 62, publisher, Baltimore City, June 2, 1904.
NOBLE, Dr. Jacob L., n.a., Preston, Caroline County, May 1, 1913.
NOCK, N_____ N_____, 64, Baltimore City; died at Philadelphia, December 8, 1911.
NOEL, Edgar M., 47, Baltimore City, November 29, 1912.
NOLAN, Captain Joseph, 42, Baltimore City, April 27, 1914.
NORBERG, Lewis, 67, retired, Baltimore City, February 2, 1897.
NORDHOFF, Amandus, 75, pianomaker, Baltimore City, June 11, 1903.
NORDLINGER, Isaac, 73, merchant, Baltimore City, March 8, 1902.
NORFOLK, Joseph J., 68, merchant, Baltimore City, May 22, 1898.
NORMAN, Captain A_____ M_____, 81, former mariner, Baltimore City, April 17, 1881.
NORMAN, Captain W_____ R_____, 92, West River, Anne Arundel County, Msrch 14, 1912.
NORRIS, Andrew J., 84, Baltimore City, July 1, 1909.
NORRIS, Arthur N., 54, merchant, Baltimore City, December 22, 1898.
NORRIS, Edward T., Sr., 60, merchant, Baltimore City, November 27, 1888.
NORRIS, George, 68, Culpeper, Virginia, June 14, 1910.
NORRIS, George S., 83, retired merchant, Baltimore City, March 18, 1900.
NORRIS, George W., 76, retired, Baltimore City, November 25, 1884.
NORRIS, Henrietta, 118, black, Baltimore City, July 10, 1897.
NORRIS, Colonel J_____ C_____, 72, Easton, Talbot County, July 5, 1907.
NORRIS, J_____ Cloud, 55, printer, Baltimore City, December 1, 1882.
NORRIS, J_____ Olney, 69, Baltimore City, October 16, 1912.
NORRIS, John A., 63, hatter, Baltimore City, October 4, 1893.
NORRIS, John B., 62, retired, Baltimore City, February 26, 1897.
NORRIS, John T., 54, African Methodist minister, Baltimore City, September 1, 1894.
NORRIS, Oliver R., 24, manufacturer, Baltimore City, December 12, 1882.
NORRIS, Rev. Scott (M.P.), 62, Baltimore City, April 14, 1897.
NORRIS, Richard, Jr., 61, merchant, Baltimore City, August 1, 1879.
NORRIS, Thomas M., 71, lawyer, Baltimore City, September 20, 1890.
NORRIS, William, 76, Baltimore County, December 29, 1896.
NORRIS, William H., 79, lawyer, Baltimore City, January 31, 1890.
NORRIS, Dr. William H., n.a., physician, Baltimore City, February 8, 1892.
NORRIS, William H., 71, retired, Baltimore City, February 7, 1898.

NORTH, Rev. James, 87, Baltimore City, November 7, 1909.
NORTHROP, General Lucius Bellinger, 82, February 9, 1894.
NORTON, Lewis L., 50, merchant, Baltimore City, April 21, 1899.
NORTON, Dr. Rupert, n.a., Baltimore City, June 19, 1914.
NORTON, T_____ C_____, 43, dentist, Baltimore City, November 10, 1884.
NORVILLE, Captain William, 81, mariner, Baltimore City, August 17, 1886.
NORWOOD, Captain Randolph, 67, U.S. Army (Ret.), Baltimore City, May 24, 1901.
NOWILLE, William 75, retired pilot, Baltimore City, June 23, 1903.
NOYES, B_____ B_____, 92, Baltimore City, March 13, 1910.
NUGENT, James, 76, Baltimore City, January 16, 1909.
NUMSEN, Frederick H., 72, retired, Baltimore City, September 4, 1883.
NUMSEN, John W., 69, retired, Baltimore City, May 7, 1896.
NUMSEN, Nathaniel G., 70, packer, Baltimore City, April 26, 1899.
NUMSEN, W_____ N_____, 75, Baltimore City, June 11, 1911.
NUMSEN, William, 88, packer, Baltimore City, December 16, 1891.
NUNAN, Andrew G., 70, Baltimore City, December 31, 1893.
NUNAN, John, 60, retired, Baltimore City, December 7, 1901.
NUNN, S_____ E_____, 68, mechancial engineer, Baltimore City, November 11, 1904.
NUSBAUM, Meyer A., 87, manufacturer, Baltimore City, September 5, 1900.
NUTTER, Samuel, 79, Baltimore City, July 18, 1909.
NYCE, Jacob R., 64, merchant, Baltimore City, June 17, 1896.
NYBURG, Simon S., 53, merchant, Baltimore City, January 22, 1897.

OBER, Gustave, 62, manufacturer, Baltimore City, January 27, 1881.
OBER, J_____ K_____, 65, Baltimore City, May 4, 1908.
OBER, General Robert, n.a., Baltimore City, September 1, 1912.
OBERHEIM, Christian, 75, tailor, Baltimore City, November 3, 1903.
OBERNDORFF, Abraham, 81, retired, Baltimore City, June 18, 1903.
O'BRIEN, Andrew, 98, retired, Baltimore City, November 27, 1882.
O'BRIEN, Thomas J., 50, Baltimore City, June 21, 1898.
O'BRIEN, William J., 69, judge, Baltimore City Orphan's Court, November 13, 1905.
OCKERMAN, Rev. J_____ F_____ (M.E.), 62, Baltimore City, January 24, 1898.
O'CONNELL, M_____ J_____, 45, hotelier, Annapolis, Anne Arundel County, March 22, 1893.
O'CONNOR, Alexander I., 27, bookkeeper, Baltimore City, December 3, 1901.
O'CONNOR, Rev. Aloysius (R.C.), 27, Baltimore City, March 11, 1899.
O'CONNOR, Hugh, 82, agent, Baltimore City, January 7, 1889.
O'CONNOR, Matthew, 73, builder, Baltimore City, December 6, 1893.

O'CONNOR, William, 65, merchant, Baltimore City, April 24, 1892.
ODOM, John B., 79, prohibitionist, Baltimore City, December 23, 1895.
O'DONNELL, Mrs. Caroline J., n.a., Baltimore City, April 18, 1913.
O'DONNELL, E____ Louis, 65, merchant, Baltimore City, May 7, 1899.
O'DONNELL, John C., 42, Baltimore City, May 29, 1903.
O'DONNELL, William H., 71, Baltimore City, August 17, 1914.
O'DONOGHUE, Sister Mary Louise, 60, superior of the Convent of Visitation, Frederick, Frederick County, August 11, 1891.
O'DONOGUE, Rev. T____ M____, n.a., Baltimore City, March 24, 1908.
O'DONOVAN, Dr. Charles, 60, physician, Baltimore City, December 23, 1889.
O'DONOVAN, John H., 63, real estate, Baltimore City, February 5, 1894.
OEHM, Charles N., 47, merchant, Baltimore City, July 4, 1880.
OEHM, Charles W., 57, Baltimore City, May 10, 1911.
OETTINGER, Solomon, 74, merchant, Baltimore City, September 22, 1894.
O'FERRALL, John, 75, manufacturer, Baltimore City, March 24, 1904.
OFFUT, John F. C., 72, retired, Baltimore City, August 29, 1894.
OFFUTT, James W., 54, Baltimore County, January 5, 1895.
OFFUTT, Milton W., 46, Towson, Baltimore County, August 20, 1903.
OFFUTT, T____ Z____, 82, Granite, Baltimore County, January 30, 1911.
OGLE, Charles, 69, contractor, Baltimore City, December 23, 1894.
OGLE, Dr. George, 74, physician, Baltimore City, November 27, 1890.
OGLE, John, 73, retired, Baltimore City, January 11, 1905.
OGLE, Richard L., 76, retired, Baltimore City, April 4, 1895.
OGLE, The____ A., 76, Cumberland, Allegany County, January 24, 1902.
O'HARA, M____ J____, 34, former member of the Maryland Legislature, Baltimore City, January 12, 1889.
OHLE, Henry, 74, contractor, Baltimore City, June 15, 1899.
OHLENDORF, Christian, 79, retired, Baltimore City, November 17, 1884.
OHM, Henry P., 65, inventor, Baltimore City, September 13, 1885.
OHM, Dr. Charles H., 92, Cumberland, Allegany County, March 3, 1903.
O'KEEFE, Rev. M____, 78, Towson, Baltimore County, January 28, 1906.
O'KEENE, Captain Thomas D., n.a., fireman, Baltimore City, June 21, 1899.
O'LAUGHLIN, Francis, 75, blacksmith, Baltimore City, November 5, 1882.
OLER, William G., 45, merchant, Baltimore City, April 2, 1902.
OLER, William Goerge, 34, ice dealer, Baltimore City, February 6, 1881.

OLER, W____ M____, 70, merchant, Baltimore City, July 19, 1889.
OLIVER, John B., 66, agent, B. & O. Railroad, Baltimore City, July 15, 1896.
OLIVER, David, 65, hotel clerk, Baltimore City, September 1, 1890.
OLIVER, Dr. E____ S____, 30, physician, Baltimore City, March 18, 1902.
OLIVER, Dr. James H., 67, Baltimore City, December 8, 1878.
OLIVER, Captain John S., 67, mariner, Baltimore City, August 18, 1885.
OLIVER, Lydia, 109, black, Baltimore City, March 25, 1879.
OLIVER, Professor Marshall, U.S. Naval Academy, November 25, 1900.
OLIVER, Thomas V., 63, merchant, Baltimore City, November 5, 1882.
OLIVER, William B., 75, Hagerstown, Washington County, March 9, 1907.
ONDERDONK, Andrew, 50, civil engineer, Cumberland, Allegany County, November 29, 1901.
ONDERDONK, Henry, n.a., educator, St. James (Baltimore County?), August 14, 1895.
O'NEAL, T____ H____, 72, former Secretary of State of Maryland, August 19, 1884.
O'NEILL, Captain James M., 43(?), mariner, Baltimore City, October 24, 1900.
O'NEILL, Captain John, 68, ship chandler, Baltimore City, July 20, 1896.
O'NEILL, Joseph, 43, merchant, Baltimore City, February 18, 1900.
O'NEILL, Michael, 59, hackman, Baltimore City, December 22, 1887.
O'NEILL, Michael J., 40, contractor, Baltimore City, October 10, 1901.
ONION, John W., 85, Baltimore City, August 5, 1879.
ONION, Lewis G., 47, merchant, Baltimore City, October 13, 1901.
ONLEY, Henry T., 73, Snow Hill, Worcester County, April 15, 1901.
OPIE, Dr. Thomas, 74, Washington (D.C.?), October 6, 1914.
OPPELT, Edward J., 50, cigar manufacturer, Baltimore City, October 19, 1884.
OPPENHEIMER, David, 62, jeweler, Baltimore City, April 3, 1902.
OPPENHEIMER, Herman, 55, merchant, Baltimore City, August 3, 1901.
OPPENHEIMER, M____, 47, salesman, Baltimore City, May 4, 1902.
OPPENHEIMER, Martin, 57, Baltimore City, June 22, 1914.
OPPENHEIMER, Morris, 64, Baltimore City, January 17, 1913.
OPPENHEIMER, Moses T., 65, Baltimore City, April 21, 1907.
OPPENHEIMER, R____, 68, importer, Baltimore City, April 1, 1892.
OREM, Calvert, 62, Cambridge, Dorchester County, December 22, 1907.
OREM, Mrs. Caroline P., 80, Baltimore City, December 25, 1911.
OREM, Daniel T., 66, Baltimore City, November 2, 1897.
OREM, George W., Jr., 57, merchant, Baltimore City, April 5, 1904.

OREM, J____ H____, 74, Baltimore City, February 8, 1910.
OREM, Captain J____ Bailey, 83, Baltimore City, June 16, 1911.
OREM, Mrs. Mary, 105, Baltimore City, February 26, 1881.
OREM, Perry C., 62, bank cashier, Baltimore City, May 3, 1889.
ORLANDO, Valentine, 56, decorator, Baltimore City, September 5, 1904.
ORNDROFF, W____ W____, 63, Baltimore City, April 18, 1892.
ORR, Captain William, 51, mariner, Baltimore City, December 31, 1902.
ORRICK, Rev. W____ P____, 74, Cumberland, Allegany County, May 22, 1910.
OSBORN, Dr. William H., 46, druggist, Baltimore City, June 16, 1881.
OSBORNE, Rev. J____ W____ (P.E.), 70, Baltimore City, April 22, 1881.
OSBORNE, Thomas J., 54, contractor, Baltimore City, September 6, 1879.
OSBORNE, Rev. W____ M____, 85, Baltimore City, November 4, 1908.
OSLER, William Van B., 61, Thurmont, Baltimore City, March 1, 1901.
OSTENDORF, Clemens, 47, merchant tailor, Baltimore City, January 15, 1881.
OSTER, Jacob, 74, builder, Baltimore City, August 3, 1895.
OSTERLING, Walter, 48, merchant, Baltimore City, August 20, 1902.
OSWALD, G____ B____, 65, Hagerstown, Washington County, April 26, 1908.
OSWALD, John D., n.a., Hagerstown, Washington County, April 9, 1913.
OTTO, Frederick A., n.a., druggist, Baltimore City, January 16, 1904.
OUDESLUYS, Charles L., 67, merchant, Baltimore City, January 24, 1886.
OULD, Marion H., 74, Baltimore City, April 24, 1909.
OULD, Rev. W____ (Presbyterian), 46, Baltimore City, January 22, 1899.
OUTRAM, Benjamin, 72, Talbot County, February 16, 1893.
OWEN, Rev. Elisha D., n.a., Baltimore City, December 17, 1892.
OWEN, John T., 59, realtor, Baltimore City, November 20, 1901.
OWEN, Robert D., 76, retired, Baltimore City, April 27, 1901.
OWENS, Ambrose B., 64, merchant, Baltimore City, April 22, 1883.
OWENS, Captain F____ B____, 60, mariner, Baltimore City, November 17, 1882.
OWENS, Captain H____ F____, 91, Perryville, Cecil County, March 26, 1892.
OWENS, Henry, 84, merchant, Baltimore City, September 15, 1906.
OWENS, John E., 63, comedian, near Towson, Baltimore County, December 7, 1886.
OWENS, Robert R., 58, merchant, Baltimore City, March 5, 1901.
OWENS, Samuel W., 71, Catonsville, Baltimore County, September 27, 1909.
OWENS, Dr. Thomas F., 78, physician, Baltimore City, July 23, 1899.

OWINGS, Dr. Harry W., 53, physician, Baltimore City, November 15, 1890.
OWINGS, John H., 68, veteran, Oakland Mills, Howard County, June 24, 1909.
OWINGS, Dr. Thomas Boyle, 72, Ellicott City, Howard County, August 28, 1914.
OZMAN, John H., 74, Queen Anne's County, August 14, 1902.

PACA, John P., 55, Baltimore City, January 4, 1893.
PACETTI, Dr. Louis B., 51, physician, Baltimore City, November 20, 1901.
PACKARD, T_____ J_____, 58, Rockville, Montgomery County, January 9, 1912.
PADELFORD, A_____, 37, Baltimorean; died at Paris, June 7, 1896.
PADGETT, W_____ W_____, 80, Port Tobacco, Charles County, September 17, 1900.
PADGETT, William A., 64, merchant, Baltimore City, November 4, 1886.
PAGE, Henry, 84, Baltimore City, September 10, 1910.
PAGE, Judge Henry, 70, Princess Anne, Somerset County, January 7, 1913.
PAGE, Walker G., 86, educator, Baltimore City, April 16, 1903.
PAGELS, Christopher, 97, farmer, Baltimore City, August 24, 1882.
PAGON, William H., 61 or 68, merchant, Baltimore City, February 21, 1906.
PAINE, Rev. R_____ H_____, 64, Baltimore City, June 4, 1908.
PAINE, R_____ Treat, 55, died at Waltham, Massachusetts, August 11, 1910.
PAINTER, Nathan, 75, corn doctor, Baltimore City, December 21, 1881.
PAINTER, William, 67, inventor, Baltimore City, July 15, 1906.
PALMER, B_____ D_____, 65, Sandy Spring, Montgomery County, December 13, 1912.
PALMER, George S., 76, Centreville, Queen Anne's County, March 12, 1900.
PALMER, General Innis, n.a., U.S. Army (Ret.), Chevy Chase, Montgomery County, September 9, 1900.
PALMER, Dr. John W., 80, poet and writer, Baltimore City, February 26, 1906.
PALMER, Rev. Joseph D. (R.C.), n.a., Baltimore City, September 10, 1886.
PALMER, Levin, 62, Cambridge, Dorchester County, June 27, 1912.
PALMER, Pennell, 86, retired, Baltimore City, July 19, 1883.
PALMER, William C., 74, philanthropist, Baltimore City, May 7, 1904.
PANCOAST, J_____ K_____, 79, former police captain, Baltimore City, November 7, 1892.
PANCOAST, Joseph T., 66, merchant, Baltimore City, January 11, 1882.
PANGHORN, Major J_____ G_____, 70, Baltimore City, August 15, 1914.
PAPE, Dr. George W., 34, physician, Baltimore City, January 7, 1882.
PARET, Mrs. Maria G., n.a., Baltimore City, February 1, 1897.
PARET, Bishop William, 84, Baltimore City, January 18, 1911.
PARKE, Joseph M., 88, attorney, Westmister, Carroll County, February 18, 1898.

PARKER, Edward L., n.a., merchant, Baltimore City, October 6, 1906.
PARKER, Dr. James H., 55, physician, Baltimore City, February 26, 1887.
PARKER, Mrs. Susanna, 103, Oakland, Baltimore County?, May 27, 1892.
PARKHURST, George T., 76, merchant, Baltimore City, June 21, 1898.
PARKHURST, Jared, Jr., 83, merchant, Baltimore City, July 14, 1881.
PARKHURST, Mrs. Mary D., 75, Baltimore City, December 12, 1909.
PARKHURST, Sophia E., 76, Baltimore City, February 15, 1910.
PARKS, Boyer, 78, contractor, Baltimore City, March 8, 1903.
PARKS, Caleb, 82, retired, Baltimore City, September 17, 1884.
PARKS, Rev. John W. (M.P.), 73, Baltimore City, September 20, 1899.
PARLETT, Benjamin F., 60, merchant, Baltimore City, September 3, 1884.
PARLETT, John T. B., 57, president, Board of Baltimore County Commissioners, January 18, 1885.
PARLETT, William J., 57, Baltimore City, June 2, 1896.
PARR, David Preston, 82, retired, Baltimore City, November 14, 1900.
PARR, Israel M., 78, merchant, Baltimore City, August 1, 1901.
PARRAN, Charles S., n.a., senior editor, Calvert Journal; died near Prince Frederick, Calvert County, January 30, 1884.
PARRAN, William A., 76, Calvert County, February 14, 1902.
PARRAN, William J., n.a., merchant, Baltimore City, August 30, 1898.
PARRISH, William B., 81, retired, Baltimore City, October 24, 1898.
PARROTT, Joseph J., 86, retired, Baltimore City, February 24, 1901.
PARSON, W_____ Irving, 59, banker, Frederick, Frederick County, November 20, 1900.
PARSONS, Thomas C., 77, Kent County, August 30, 1893.
PARSONS, Rev. William D. (R.C.), 79, Baltimore City, December 24, 1899.
PARTRIDGE, Dr. Frank E., 57, physician, Baltimore City, March 16, 1883.
PARTRIDGE, John, 88, Elkton, Cecil County, July 23, 1898.
PASCAULT, Hettie, 35, of Baltimore City; died at San Francisco, June 17, 1893.
PASSANO, Joseph, 65, merchant, Baltimore City, June 29, 1904.
PASSANO, Leonard, 88, merchant, Baltimore City, February 21, 1904.
PASSANO, Louis Durbin, 65, Baltimore City, May 6, 1908.
PASTERFIELD, William H., 76, plumber, Baltimore City, February 16, 1891.
PASTORIUS, Samuel, 86, "Old Defender," Baltimore City, September 11, 1880.
PATERSON, J_____ W_____, 64, Annapolis, Anne Arundel County, March 19, 1908.
PATERSON, Thomas H., 43, Baltimore City, April 15, 1913.
PATIENCE, Captain James, 51, mariner, Baltimore City, November 24, 1905.

PATTERSON, Abram B., 75, broker, Baltimore City, April 4, 1893.
PATTERSON (Bonaparte), Elizabeth, 94, Baltimore City, April 4, 1879.
PATTERSON, Gilbert H., 84, florist, Baltimore City, July 1, 1904.
PATTERSON, Dr. John H., 76, physician, Baltimore City, May 25, 1893.
PATTERSON, Rev. J_____ H_____ T_____ (Baptist), 49, Baltimore City, October 3, 1882.
PATTERSON, John T., 68, manufacturer, Baltimore City, May 13, 1902.
PATTERSON, Joseph, 64, contractor, Baltimore City, April 6, 1884.
PATTERSON, Matthew M., 81, retired, Baltimore City, September 10, 1901.
PATTERSON, Robert, 50, florist, Baltimore City, May 26, 1887.
PATTERSON, Robert J., 72, retired, Baltimore City, October 24, 1905.
PATTERSON, S_____ C_____, 73, merchant, Baltimore City, July 27, 1906.
PATTERSON, Thomas N., 59, merchant, Baltimore City, February 19, 1887.
PATTISON, Samuel, 70, mechanic, Baltimore City, October 13,
PATTISON, Rev. T_____ E_____, 75, Baltimore City, March 3, 1909.
PATTISON, Thomas, 58, wholesale grocer, Baltimore City, November 28, 1880.
PAUL, August H., 73, lithographer, Baltimore City, June 19, 1904.
PAUL, D'Arcy, 36, attorney, Baltimore City, January 7, 1890.
PAUL, Captain J_____, 92, Baltimore City, February 8, 1909.
PAUL, William, 82, retired merchant, Baltimore City, August 17, 1901.
PAULET, Dr. Stuart E., 35, physician, Baltimore City, November 20, 1895.
PAULUS, John P., 64, undertaker, Baltimore City, March 27, 1894.
PAYANT, Edward, 68, contractor, Baltimore City, February 12, 1903.
PAYNE, J_____ J_____, 96, Baltimore City, May 9, 1912.
PAYNE, Dr. J_____ P_____, 75, Baltimore City, October 1, 1914.
PAYNE, Joseph F., 76, Frederick, Frederick County, January 3, 1907.
PAYNTER, Nathan W., 81, merchant, Baltimore City, September 22, 1903.
PEACOCK, James, 77, veteran fireman, Baltimore City, February 21, 1901.
PEARRE, Hon. George A., 64, of Cumberland, Allegany County, associate judge, Fourth Judicial Circuit; died at Hagerstown, May 22, 1883.
PEARSON, Professor George, 87, Washington County, June 18, 1897.
PEARSON, Levi, 84, manufacturer, Baltimore City, November 2, 1891.
PECK, Elizabeth A., 100, Baltimore City, October 26, 1881.
PECOR, Alfred C., 70, retired, Baltimore City, December 7, 1901.
PEED, Captain James R., 89, Baltimore City, March 21, 1913.

PEIRCE, Thomas, 81, importer, Baltimore City, July 24, 1887.
PEIRSON, Henry, 68, accountant, Baltimore City, September 28, 1899.
PELS, Moses, 61, Baltimore City, March 22, 1907.
PFEFFER, Charles, 68, merchant, Baltimore City, April 21, 1902.
PFEFFER, D_____ Charles, 40, Baltimore City, September 22, 1906.
PFIEL, Frederick, 69, merchant, Baltimore City, December 22, 1904.
PEMBROKE, Dr. George W., 58, Anne Arundel County, May 12, 1901.
PENDERGAST, Charles H., 69, Baltimorean; died in New York City, March 5, 1898.
PENN, Jacob, 71, mechanic, Baltimore City, January 6, 1883.
PENNIMAN, E_____ J_____, 59, Fiduciary Company, Baltimore City, February 21, 1904.
PENNIMAN, Nicholas G., 72, manufacturer, Howard County, September 17, 1895.
PENNINGTON, Eugene, 43, Queen Anne's County, March 6, 1893.
PENNINGTON, Josias, 49, broker, Baltimore City, March 10, 1882.
PENNINGTON, Ross T., 72, Baltimore City, June 20, 1892.
PENNINGTON, William C., n.a., Baltimore City, April 12, 1913.
PENNINGTON, Yates, 43, Baltimore City, December 17, 1913.
PENTLAND, James, 80, florist, Baltimore City, March 19, 1902.
PENTLAND, Robert E., 58, florist, Baltimore City, June 30, 1878.
PENTZ, George L., n.a., Baltimore City, December 4, 1911.
PENTZ, Henry B., 69, butcher, Baltimore City, February 11, 1894.
PENTZ, John W. D., 72, retired, Baltimore City, October 29, 1899.
PENTZ, William F., 65, retired, Baltimore City, June 6, 1885.
PENTZ, William H., Sr., 73, Baltimore City, November 29, 1909.
PENZKOFER, Joseph, 58, musician, Baltimore City, April 23, 1900.
PEPPER, Wilson S., 70, hotelier, Baltimore City, July 4, 1891.
PERCIVAL, Dr. Charles F., 70, teacher, Baltimore City, April 2, 1887.
PERDUE, Kendall, 94, Parsonsburg, Wicomico County, December 28, 1898.
PEREGOY, Charles, 65, retired, Baltimore City, August 6, 1883.
PEREGOY, Charles, 95, retired, Baltimore City, March 19, 1900.
PERIN, Nelson, 50, financier, Baltimore City, May 12, 1904.
PERIN, Oliver, 69, B. & O. Railroad, Baltimore City, August 12, 1898.
PERKINS, Dr. B_____ B_____, 82, Chestertown, Kent County, December 23, 1909.
PERKINS, Eben F., 72, Chestertown, Kent County, March 17, 1902.
PERKINS, Dr. Elisha H., 76, druggist, Baltimore City, June 24, 1888.
PERKINS, James, 60, Baltimore City inventor, January 17, 1892.
PERKINS, James H., 71, druggist, Baltimore City, September 28, 1879.
PERKINS, James T., Sr., 73, Prince George's County, May 16, 1898.
PERKINS, Dr. James T., 47, Prince George's County, February 10, 1901.
PERKINS, Martin J., 57, Cambridge, Dorchester County, November 13, 1904.
PERKINS, Palmer L., 76, Baltimore City, October 1, 1900.

PERKINS, Thatcher, 71, machinist, Baltimore City, January 8, 1883.
PERKINS, Captain William G., 67, Anne Arundel County, June 23, 1908.
PERKINS, William H., 75, merchant, Baltimore City, July 1, 1897.
PERKY, Henry D., 63, educator, manufacturer, and farmer, Glencoe, Baltimore County, June 29, 1906.
PERLICH, Herman, 74, florist, Baltimore City, May 8, 1903.
PEROT, William H., 77, merchant, Baltimore City, June 8, 1903.
PERRIGO, James L., 79, merchant, Baltimore City, July 6, 1899.
PERRIN, John T., 66, Old Bay Line, Baltimore City, February 25, 1904.
PERRIN, Peter, 63, merchant, Baltimore City, September 3, 1893.
PERRY, Ancel C., 46, merchant, Baltimore City, September 28, 1880.
PERRY, J_____ P_____, 81, Frederick, Frederick County, December 2, 1909.
PERRY, James St. L., 70, Baltimore City Councilman, January 2, 1889.
PERRY, John B., 88, retired merchant, Baltimore City, December 3, 1893.
PESSAGNO, Giacomo, 69, merchant, Baltimore City, May 16, 1902.
PETER, George, 63, Montgomery County, August 9, 1893.
PETER, John A., 77, grocer, Baltimore City, March 29, 1900.
PETER, Robert, 88, Montgomery County, November 17, 1903.
PETER, William B., 60, former Senator, Ellicott City, Howard County, April 15, 1907.
PETERS, C_____ George, 49, florist, Baltimore City, May 7, 1895.
PETERS, Colonel Clarence, 49, Baltimore City, October 10, 1892.
PETERS, Peter F., 77, retired, Baltimore City, May 9, 1898.
PETERSON, John, 107, black, Baltimore City, January 25, 1894.
PETHERBRIDGE, Major E_____ R_____, 78, retired, Baltimore City, December 18, 1891.
PETHERBRIDGE, Dr. J_____ F_____, 86, Annapolis, Anne Arundel County, October 28, 1897.
PETIT LE BRUN, Dr. Alphonse, 62, Baltimore City, October 25, 1892.
PETTICORD, John, 91, "Old Defender," Baltimore City, October 11, 1887.
PETTS, Rev. James H. (Methodist), 25, Baltimore City, September 27, 1896.
PHELAN, Nicholas, 84, retired, Baltimore City, January 12, 1885.
PHELPS, Almira H. L., 91, educator and author, Baltimore City, July 15, 1884.
PHELPS, Judge C_____ E_____, 85, Baltimore City, December 27, 1908.
PHELPS, Rev. E_____ P_____ (M.E.), 72, Baltimore City, April 24, 1887.
PHELPS, Edwin, 73, manufacturer, Baltimore City, December 14, 1902.
PHELPS, Dr. Francis P., 87, died at Cambridge, Dorchester County, November 18, 1886.

PHELPS, Dr. Francis P., Cambridge, Dorchester County, September 17, 1904.
PHELPS, George D., 89, retired, Baltimore City, November 14, 1905.
PHILLIPS, Q____ W____, 60, Salisbury, Wicomico County, August 10, 1908.
PHILLIPS, R____ A____, n.a., Baltimorean; died in Washington, D.C., August 30, 1881.
PHILLIPS, Rev. W____ H____ (P.E.), 63, Anne Arundel County, March 17, 1900.
PHILPOT, George, 57, attorney, Baltimore City, December 3, 1899.
PHILPOT, Thomas, 56, Baltimore County, November 29, 1896.
PHOEBUS, William A., 71, Somerset County, October 27, 1901.
PHIPPS, Colonel Joseph B., 61, insurance, Baltimore City, May 11, 1906.
PICK, Dr. C____ H____, 80, physician, Baltimore City, August 10, 1893.
PICKETT, Nelson, 26, black giant (387 lbs., 8' 1"), Baltimore City, January 19, 1892.
PIERCE, Dr. James J., 86, physician, Baltimore City, July 18, 1897.
PIERCE, William H., 88, "Old Defender," Baltimore City, January 15, 1883.
PIET, Ambrose, 52, salesman, Baltimore City, September 12, 1893.
PIGOTT, Michael R., 35, former assistant surgeon, U.S. Navy, Annapolis, Anne Arundel County, January 31, 1901.
PIGGOT, Rev. Robert, 92, oldest minister in the P.E. Church, Sykesville, Carroll County, July 24, 1887.
PIKE, Abraham, 51, merchant, Baltimore City, September 19, 1897.
PILES, W____ H____, 98, Montgomery County, September 16, 1908.
PILLING, James C., 49, ethnologist, Montgomery County, July 26, 1895.
PINKNEY, Campbell W., 74, former judge, Baltimore City, June 28, 1903.
PINKNEY, Captain Robert F., 66, Baltimore City, March 14, 1878.
PINKNEY, Rev. William, n.a., Bishop of the Episcopal Diocese of Maryland; died at Cockeysville, Baltimore County, July 4, 1883.
PIPER, E____ Balton, 82, retired, Baltimore City, May 25, 1898.
PIPER, Dr. Jackson, 79, Baltimore City, October 11, 1907.
PIPITONE, Vito, 54, manufacturer, Baltimore City, May 18, 1894.
PIPPIN, Solomon, 55, Easton, Talbot County, August 5, 1902.
PIQUETT, J____ T____, 62, former street commissioner, Baltimore City, April 20, 1878.
PISTEL, Lawrence, 54, captain, Baltimore City Fire Department, April 28, 1904.
PITCHER, Rev. William H. (Methodist), 69, Baltimore City, December 27, 1893.
PITT, Charles Faris, 64, died at Blue Ridge Summit, Franklin County, Pennsylvania, October 16, 1908.
PITT, George, 73, butcher, Baltimore City, December 31, 1911.
PITTMAN, Edward, 82, merchant, Baltimore City, December 28, 1881.
PITTS, Charles H., 44, bank cashier, Baltimore City, November 10, 1887.

PITTS, Edward R., 52, clerk, Baltimore City, November 13, 1902.
PITTS, Dr. J____ W____, 69, Berlin, Worcester County, December 27, 1910.
PITTS, John G., 49, attorney, Baltimore City, October 31, 1902.
PLACK, Jacob, 72, merchant, Baltimore City, March 2, 1900.
PLANTEVIGNE, Rev. John A., n.a., Baltimore City, January 27, 1913.
PLASKITT, Joshua, 73, former school board member, Baltimore City, October 15, 1903.
PLATER, John R., 73, Talbot County, November 8, 1896.
PLATT, L____ B____, 75, packer, Baltimore City, February 26, 1887.
PLATT, William D., 59, Baltimore City, December 23, 1913.
PLEASANTS, Brooke, 72, merchant, Baltimore City, August 4, 1901.
PLEASANTS, J____ Hall, 79, merchant, Baltimore City, August 20, 1901.
PLEASANTS, John T., 50, The Sun, Baltimore City, March 7, 1911.
PLEASANTS, Richard Hall, 75, merchant, Baltimore City, February 28, 1894.
PLEASANTS, Samuel S., 40, attorney, Baltimore City, January 9, 1892.
PLOWMAN, Jacob H., 61, Harford County, October 5, 1897.
PLUMMER, Dr. Edward, 60, veterinarian, Baltimore City, September 27, 1896.
PLUMMER, Rev. Dr. William S. (Baptist), 88, Baltimore City, October 22, 1880.
PLUNKERT, H____ D____, 69, Ellicott City, Howard County, February 26, 1914.
PLUNKETT, Lieutenant Michael H., 80, Baltimore City, October 1, 1914.
POE, George, 71, merchant, Baltimore City, January 10, 1879.
POE, George, 104, St. George's Island, St. Mary's County, November 1, 1907.
POE, John P., 73, lawyer, Ruxton, Baltimore County, October 14, 1909.
POE, Neilson, 75, former judge, Orphan's Court, Baltimore City, January 3, 1884.
POE, Neilson, Jr., n.a., Baltimore City, April 1, 1913.
POE, Dr. William C., 62, Baltimore City, January 20, 1906.
POISAL, Rev. John, 75, Baltimore City, June 25, 1882.
POISAL, Thomas B., 67, auditor, Baltimore City, June 9, 1902.
POISAL, Rev. W____ M____, 70, Baltimore City, November 30, 1911.
POLACK, Sarah, 17, seamstress, Front Street Theater panic, December 27, 1895.
POLACK, Simon, eight years old, Front Street Theater panic, December 27, 1895.
POLK, Ephraim, 58, editor, Princess Anne, Somerset County, October 16, 1899.
POLK, J____ B____, 60, actor and manufacturer, Baltimore City, January 5, 1902.

POLK, Dr. J_____ P_____, Sr., 80, physician, Baltimore City, June 21, 1904.
POLK, Nathaniel W., 54, insurance, Baltimore City, January 16, 1901.
POLK, Robert M., 78, retired, Baltimore City, October 1, 1896.
POLK, Captain Trusten, 61, gauger, Baltimore City, July 12, 1902.
POLK, William Causey, n.a., Carroll County, December 28, 1893.
POLLARD, James, 55, attorney, Baltimore City, September 14, 1898.
POLLARD, Percival, 42, author, Baltimore City, December 28, 1911.
POLMYER, Frederick, 43, journalist, Baltimore City, August 16, 1891.
PONTIER, Edward F., 67, Fifth Regiment, Baltimore City, February 23, 1895.
PONTIER, John S., 63, detective, Baltimore City, July 3, 1899.
PONTIER, L_____ E_____, 81, merchant, Baltimore City, December 8, 1880.
POOLE, George, 74, Myersville, Frederick County, April 2, 1910.
POOLE, James, 85, merchant, Baltimore City, July 10, 1893.
POOLE, Robert, 85, manufacturer, Baltimore City, January 4, 1903.
POOLE, Rev. Robert A., 77, Ellicott City, Howard County, February 14, 1913.
POOR, Major R_____ L_____, 68, Bay Line, Baltimore City, March 20, 1908.
POPE, Franklin F., 84, retired merchant, Baltimore City, April 28, 1893.
POPE, Rudolph, 81, manufacturer, Baltimore City, December 29, 1893.
POPE, William H., 61, superintendent, Pikesville Home, Baltimore County, December 6, 1904.
POPPLEIN, George J., 60, chemist, Baltimore City, March 31, 1901.
POPPLEIN, Nicholas, 77, retired, Baltimore City, July 23, 1885.
PORTER, George U., 63, editor, Baltimore City, July 5, 1886.
PORTER, Major J_____ C_____, 64, Annapolis, Anne Arundel County, November 20, 1912.
PORTER, William, 80, Elkton, Cecil County, June 23, 1909.
PORTER, William F., 54, attorney, Baltimore City, June 10, 1907.
POSEY, John V., 68, Baltimore City, January 30, 1900.
POSKE, Herman F., 71, merchant, Baltimore City, January 10, 1900.
POSNER, Elias, 39, merchant, Baltimore City, February 15, 1885.
POST, Eugene, 73, retired, Baltimore City, August 7, 1884.
POST, J_____ E_____ Howard, n.a., Baltimore City, December 27, 1911.
POSTILL, Dobson, 82, retired merchant, Baltimore City, April 12, 1902.
POTEE, Peter P., 71, detective, Baltimore City, May 12, 1881.
POTTER, Dr. Charles H., 50, physician, Baltimore City, November 9, 1904.
POTTER, Martin, 50, ferry engineer, Baltimore City, June 28, 1894.

POTTER, William S., 54, clerk, Baltimore City, December 14, 1902.
POTTS, Arthur, 79, Frederick, Frederick County, October 10, 1914.
POTTS, Edward, 54, B. & O. Railroad, Baltimore City, January 27, 1881.
POTTS, Jesse N., 59, Baltimore City, August 4, 1900.
POTTS, Robert, 75, engineer, Baltimore City, March 21, 1883.
POULTNEY, S_____ Eugene, 53, Baltimore City, April 18, 1894.
POULTNEY, Thomas, 61, retired, Baltimore City, April 20, 1887.
POULTNEY, Thomas, 61, merchant, Baltimore City, December 26, 1893.
POULTON, John, 68, maintenance man, Baltimore City, August 18, 1894.
POWELL, Dr. Albert H., 73, physician, Baltimore City, November 4, 1904.
POWELL, Dr. Samuel F., 53?, physician, Baltimore City, April 21, 1894.
POWELL, Captain Sidney, n.a., Baltimorean; died at Brazil, February 27, 1894.
POWELL, William H., 60, merchant, Baltimore City, September 17, 1900.
POWLES, Henry, 82, realtor, Baltimore City, September 17, 1884.
PRACHT, August C., 80, retired, Baltimore City, December 15, 1894.
PRACHT, Charles A., 68, merchant, Baltimore City, January 15, 1893.
PRAG, Isiah, 78, retired, Baltimore City, May 12, 1894.
PRATT, Mrs. Adaline Kent, 82, Baltimore City, May 31, 1897.
PRATT, Enoch, 88, philanthropist, Baltimore City, September 17, 1896.
PRATT, Thomas St. George, 58, Baltimore City, January 7, 1895.
PRENDERGAST, Patrick F., 52, ship chandler, Baltimore City, November 24, 1901.
PRENTISS, Dr. John H., 61, physician, Baltimore City, January 26, 1888.
PRENTISS, T_____ Melville, 71, retired merchant, Baltimore City, September 29, 1901.
PRESBURY, George G., 69, retired, Baltimore City, June 8, 1883.
PRESSTMAN, Benjamin C., 71, attorney, Baltimore City, July 15, 1889.
PRESSTMAN, George, 74, realtor, Baltimore City, September 18, 1880.
PRESTON, Dr. George Jenkins, 50, Baltimore City, June 17, 1908.
PRESTON, J_____ Alexander, 68, lawyer, Baltimore City, January 12, 1904.
PRESTON, James B., 76, Bel Air, Harford County, December 20, 1902.
PRESTON, John F., 59, attorney, Baltimore City, September 14, 1900.
PRESTON, Mrs. Margaret J., 74, poetess, Baltimore City, March 28, 1897.
PRESTON, Robert L., 34, attorney, Baltimore City, January 7, 1904.
PRESTON, William P., 69, attorney, Baltimore City, October 25, 1880.

PRETTYMAN, Dr. E____ B____, 77, Rockville, Montgomery County, December 9, 1907.
PRETTYMAN, Ebenezer P., 77, retired, Baltimore City, July 10, 1894.
PRETTYMAN, Rev. Wesley (M.E.), 73, Baltimore City, May 18, 1901.
PRETZOLD, Louis, 82, retired, Baltimore City, February 4, 1900.
PREVOST, Professor Aime, 89, retired, Baltimore City, February 12, 1885.
PREVOST, Clarence, 67, retired, Baltimore City, August 4, 1899.
PREVOST, Francis A., 64, court clerk, Baltimore City, July 26, 1882.
PRICE, Dr. Abram H., 66, Baltimore County, March 1, 1904.
PRICE, Captain Benjamin, 64, Lutherville, Baltimore County, April 3, 1909.
PRICE, Rev. Benjamin F., 85, Elkton, Cecil County, March 22, 1901.
PRICE, Edward, 63, bank cashier, Baltimore City, November 24, 1902.
PRICE, Dr. Elias C., 76, physician, Baltimore City, June 16, 1902.
PRICE, John H., 84, former judge, Harford County, August 3, 1892.
PRICE, John S., 71, merchant, Baltimore City, November 26, 1899.
PRICE, John W., 8_, retired, Baltimore City, June 8, 1899.
PRICE, Dr. Mordecai, 80, Govanstown, Baltimore County, March 5, 1902.
PRICE, Oliver Perry, 63, fruit merchant, Baltimore City, March 3, 1894.
PRICE, Samuel D., 76, builder, Baltimore City, November 29, 1895.
PRICE, William T., 53, Baltimore City, July 22, 1898.
PRICE, Winfield Scott, 61, Baltimore City, December 29, 1908.
PRICHARD, Dr. John E., 64, physician, Baltimore City, March 1, 1899.
PRIMROSE, Harry C., 48, baritone, Baltimore City, December 15, 1908.
PRIMROSE, William D., 51, president, Loudon Park Cemetery Company, Baltimore City, August 28, 1904.
PRIMROSE, William G., 66, engineer, Baltimore City, February 11, 1893.
PRINCE, Lemuel S., 87, Baltimore City, April 19, 1893.
PRIOR, Edward A., 53, merchant, Baltimore City, January 7, 1895.
PRITCHARD, Richard, 62, sea captain, Baltimore City, July 24, 1880.
PRITCHETT, Elmer H., 54, Havre de Grace, Harford County, October 2, 1907.
PRITCHETT, Captain John M., 82, Cambridge, Dorchester County, May 8, 1906.
PROCTOR, Charles W., 60, Bel Air, Harford County, December 30, 1904.
PROCTOR, R____ S____, 91, War of 1812 veteran, Baltimore City, January 22, 1883.
PROSPERI, Augustus, n.a., pharmacist, U.S.N.A., Annapolis, Anne Arundel County, December 8, 1900.

-187-

PROUD, John G., 70, insurance, Baltimore City, August 28, 1883.
PROUD, Robert M., 72, retired, Baltimore City, April 20, 1890.
PROUDFIT, Rev. Alexander (Presbyterian), n.a., Baltimore City, April 2, 1897.
PRY, Emory A., 64, Keedysville, Washington County, April 4, 1913.
PRYOR, Edward W., 80, mechanic, Baltimore City, October 8, 1883.
PRYOR, Stephen, 80, realtor, Baltimore City, August 30, 1881.
PUE, Edward H. D., 64, Confederate veteran, Bel Air, Harford County, December 23, 1905.
PUGH, Dr. T____ C____, 74, Confederate veteran, Baltimore City, December 29, 1911.
PUHL, Frederick, 45, compositor, Baltimore City, June 10, 1896.
PULLMAN, Rev. Dr. Royal H. (Universalist), 74, Baltimore City, August 26, 1900.
PUMPHREY, Edwin J., 47, architect, Baltimore City, September 19, 1894.
PUMPHREY, Greenbury A., 62, Baltimore City, August 2, 1893.
PUMPHREY, J____ H____, 68, Baltimore City, November 30, 1912.
PUMPHREY, John T., 68, farmer, Baltimore City, November 27, 1881.
PUNDT, John T., 50, manufacturer, Baltimore City, January 9, 1906.
PURCHELL, Rev. James B. (P.E.), 60, Sykesville, Carroll County, September 24, 1901.
PURCELL, John J., 75, builder, Baltimore City, August 20, 1893.
PURNELL, Dr. F____ Jenkins, n.a., Worcester County, May 19, 1896.
PURNELL, George W., 58, lawyer, Snow Hill, Worcester County, May 8, 1899.
PURNELL, John R., 70, Worcester County, August 3, 1902.
PURNELL, L____ B____, 60, merchant, Baltimore City, May 5, 1898.
PURNELL, Levi A., 62, Snow Hill, Worcester County, August 20, 1903.
PURNELL, Rev. Dr. William H., 76, commander of the Purnell Legion during the Civil War, March 31, 1902.
PURVIANCE, Mrs. Elizabeth R., 81, Baltimore City, May 21, 1893.
PURVIANCE, Admiral Hugh Y., 83, U.S. Navy, October 21, 1882.
PURVIANCE, Margaret, 71, Baltimore City, April 17, 1879.
PUTTS, John W., 58, merchant, Baltimore City, February 5, 1910.
PUTTS, W____ E____, 32, Baltimore City, December 21, 1910.
PUTZEL, Lewis, 47, Baltimore City, May 30, 1914.
PUTZEL, Selig G., 77, merchant, Baltimore City, December 27, 1898.
PYLE, Ebenezer, 67, manufacturer, Baltimore City, November 30, 1885.

QUAID, Thomas S., 33, attorney, Baltimore City, January 31, 1901.
QUANDT, Dr. E____, 45, Baltimore City, January 17, 1911.
QUANDT, John H., 78, retired, Baltimore City, February 20, 1904.

QUARLES, Giles W., 49, merchant, Baltimore City, September 21, 1898.
QUARTERLY, Charles, 68, photographer, Baltimore City, December 11, 1904.
QUIGLEY, James, 84, Baltimore City, August 2, 1912.
QUIGLEY, William S., 69, superintendent, Baltimore City, August 23, 1894.
QUINAN, Dr. John Russell, 68, physician, Baltimore City, November 11, 1890.
QUINN, Charles, 90, Texas, Baltimore County, June 6, 1899.
QUINN, Daniel, 87, Baltimore City, December 6, 1878.
QUINN, John, 67, former sheriff, Baltimore City, December 6, 1899.
QUINN, M____ E____, 50, police lieutenant, Baltimore City, March 23, 1892.

RABILLON, Leonce, n.a., professor of Baltimore City; died at Cape May, New Jersey, August 11, 1886.
RABINOWITZ, R____ S____, 43, rabbi, Baltimore City, January 5, 1892.
RABORG, Goddard, n.a., packer, Baltimore City, June 7, 1879.
RADCLIFFE, George W., 55, Ellicott City, Howard County, August 17, 1914.
RADCLIFFE, Joseph L., 52, Talbot County, February 18, 1907.
RADCLIFFE, William H., 79, Cambridge, Dorchester County, July 31, 1902.
RADDATZ, Professor Charles F., n.a., Baltimore City, January 14, 1914.
RADECKE, J____ F____, 96, Baltimore City, December 9, 1907.
RAINE, Edward, 77, editor, Baltimore City, April 23, 1911.
RAINE, Edwsrd, Jr., 42, Baltimore City, November 1, 1896.
RAINE, Frederick, 71, publisher, German *Correspondent*, Baltimore City, February 26, 1893.
RAINE, William, 80, wood inspector, Baltimore City, January 15, 1879.
RAINE, William, 76, editor of Baltimore City; died at St. Joseph, Missouri, November 14, 1898.
RAISIN, James M., 70, merchant, Baltimore City, February 21, 1880.
RALEY, James T., 68, Leonardtown, St. Mary's County, March 19, 1895.
RAMSBURG, L____ P____, 78, Frederick, Frederick County, December 23, 1908.
RAMSEY, J____ W____, 54, Baltimore City, February 14, 1909.
RAMSEY, Robert H., 58, shipmaster, Baltimore City, August 1, 1882.
RAMSEY, Thomas L., 40, merchant, Baltimore City, January 14, 1895.
RANDALL, Dudley A., 75, manufacturer, Baltimore City, February 6, 1881.
RANDALL, Mrs. Elizabeth Philpot Blanchard, 67, Annapolis, Anne Arundel County, July 9, 1895.
RANDALL, J____ Wirt, lawyer, banker, and churchman, Roland Park, Baltimore City, August 17, 1912.
RANDALL, John K., 76, clerk, Baltimore City, August 29, 1883.
RANDALL, John K., 32, librarian, Baltimore City, February 8, 1886.

RANDALL, Miss Sarah A., 102, Baltimore City, September 14, 1887.
RANDLE, Richard, 72, merchant, Baltimore City, November 27, 1902.
RANDOLPH, A_____, 32, journalist, Baltimore City, December 16, 1892.
RANDOLPH, Innes, 49, journalist, Baltimore City, April 28, 1887.
RANDOLPH, James L., n.a., engineer, Baltimore City, September 17, 1888.
RANDOLPH, Richard, 60, engineer, Baltimore City, February 9, 1893.
RANDOLPH, Miss Sarah N., n.a., teacher, Baltimore City, April 25, 1892.
RANK, Henry C., 34, editor, Cumberland, Allegany County, March 25, 1904.
RANKIN, Rev. Alexander T. (Presbyterian), 81, Baltimore City, April 30, 1885.
RANKIN, Rev. Dr. C_____ R_____ (P.E.), 67, Baltimore City, October 19, 1886.
RANKIN, Dr. Robert G., 70?, physician, Baltimore City, September 26, 1897.
RANKIN, Rev. Robert J. (Presbyterian), 28, Baltimore City, June 5, 1894.
RANSTEAD, Charles, 69, Baltimore City, April 25, 1885.
RANSTEAD, Charles F., 52, merchant, Baltimore City, September 13, 1896.
RASIN, I_____ Freeman, 74, politician, Baltimore City, March 9, 1907.
RASIN, Robert W. T., 68, manufacturer, Baltimore City, March 18, 1905.
RASIN, Philip Freeman, 75, Kent County, March 5, 1900.
RATCLIFF, Daniel, 75, lawyer, Baltimore City, December 13, 1882.
RAU, Christopher F., 69, retired, Baltimore City, May 27, 1901.
RAU, Captain John, 70, Highlandtown, Baltimore County, April 21, 1899.
RAUSCHENBERG, Louis, 61, sea captain, Baltimore City, May 12, 1892.
RAWLINGS, John W., 60, clerk of court, Hyattsville, Prince George's County, November 20, 1906.
RAWLINGS, R_____ C_____, 37, merchant, Baltimore City, May 7, 1881.
RAWLINGS, William P., 82, merchant, Baltimore City, August 7, 1905.
RAY, Benjamin F., 75, manufacturer, Baltimore City, January 4, 1895.
RAY, John I., 90, Ellicott City, Howard County, September 20, 1907.
RAYMO, Louis, 85, hatter, Baltimore City, November 12, 1906.
RAYNER, Isidor, 62, Maryland Senator, Baltimorean; died at Washington, D.C., November 25, 1912.
RAYNER, William S., 78, financier, Baltimore City, March 1, 1899.
RAYNER, Mrs. William S., 80, Baltimore City, May 30, 1900.
REA, John H., 82, retired, Baltimore City, July 27, 1884.
REA, Joseph B., 52, former Councilman, Baltimore City, March 27, 1893.

READ, Larkin, 82, miller, Baltimore City, April 6, 1893.
READ, Robert, 77, retired, Baltimore City, December 9, 1896.
READ, Samuel McK., 72, lumber inspector, Baltimore City, April 20, 1896.
READ, Sophia Catherine, 81, Baltimore City, November 22, 1880.
READ, William George, 50, attorney, Baltimore City, February 19, 1878.
READ, William H., n.a., druggist, Baltimore City, February 10, 1900.
READ, Rev. William S. (Baptist), 32, Baltimore City, November 20, 1881.
REANEY, William B., marine contractor, Baltimore City, March 27, 1901.
REARDON, Daniel, n.a., contractor, Baltimore City, December 15, 1900.
REARDON, George E., 45, attorney, Baltimore City, August 23, 1898.
REAY, Henry P., 65, druggist, Baltimore City, August 7, 1905.
REBHAN, Rev. John, 29, Baltimore City, February 19, 1879.
RECKEFUS, William K., n.a., judge, Orphan's Court, Cecil County; died at Port Deposit there, January 29, 1898.
RECKFORD, J____ H____, 53, Bel Air, Harford County, February 26, 1908.
REDGRAVE, John B., 85, Baltimore City, December 15, 1892.
REDWOOD, Francis T., 50, stock broker, Baltimore City, November 29, 1906.
REED, Bernard C., 75, educator, Baltimore City, October 9, 1902.
REEDER, Charles, 83, shipbuilder, Baltimore City, December 1, 1900.
REEDER, Charles F., 39, Baltimore City, November 5, 1898.
REEDER, Oliver, 59, ship chandler, Baltimore City, February 23, 1904.
REESE, ____, 93, merchant, Baltimore City, August 31, 1897.
REESE, Rev. Aquilla A., 65, Baltimore City, March 7, 1878.
REESE, George D., 71, retired, Baltimore City, July 28, 1899.
REESE, Gerard H., n.a., merchant, Baltimore City, August 31, 1879.
REESE, Henry D., 47, teacher, Baltimore City, July 22, 1881.
REESE, John E., 81, bank teller, Baltimore City, January 26, 1880.
REESE, Rev. Thomas M., 60, Baltimore City, March 26, 1882.
REESE, Thomas S., 55, Baltimore City, May 16, 1896.
REESE, Thomas M., 89, Baltimore City, August 1, 1909.
REESE, William H., 70, possibly Carroll County, October 2, 1900.
REESE, Dr. William S., 71, chemist, Baltimore City, October 21, 1890.
REGESTER, Joshua, 89, foundryman, Baltimore City, July 3, 1906.
REGESTER, Joshua J., 56, manufacturer, Baltimore City, March 1, 1904.
REGESTER, Rev. S____ (M.E., South), 64, Baltimore City, October 17, 1881.
REGESTER, Dr. Wilson G., 37, Baltimore City, April 22, 1882.
REIBETANTZ, Dr. Carl J., 68, editor, Baltimore City, December 20, 1894.
REICHE, Dr. Peter H., 68, physician, Baltimore City, December 10, 1905.

-191-

REID, Andrew, 77, Baltimore City, January 4, 1896.
REID, Captain James, 68, Cumberland, Allegany County, November 6, 1913.
REID, Thomas N., 87, realtor, Baltimore City, September 3, 1899.
REID, William, 65, builder, Baltimore City, July 20, 1882.
REIFSNIDER, Charles T., 63, former judge, Westminster, Carroll County, October 11, 1903.
REIFSNIDER, Jesse, 71, merchant, Carroll County, January 2, 1882.
REIFSNIDER, John L., 68, Westminster, Carroll County, July 17, 1905.
REIGERT, H____ F____, 68, bank teller, Baltimore City, March 7, 1882.
REILEY, P____ E____, 66, hatter, Baltimore City, August 20, 1882.
REILLEY, George 80, retired, Baltimore City, October 25, 1901.
REILLY, Bernard, 109, Baltimore City, June 29, 1888.
REILLY, John W., 68, restaurateur, Baltimore City, April 25, 1905.
REILLY, Patrick, 80, Baltimore City, November 2, 1900.
REILLY, William P., 60, livery, Baltimore City, November 29, 1901.
REIMAN, Dr. G____, 84, physician, Baltimore City, February 9, 1902.
REINDOLLAR, Jacob T., 86, Baltimore City, September 8, 1898.
REINDOLLAR, Dr. William, 85, Westminster, Carroll County, April 29, 1906.
REINHARD, Harry E., 62, manufacturer, Baltimore City, November 15, 1902.
REINHARD, John, 57, merchant, Baltimore City, December 15, 1903.
REINHARD, Meyer E., 45, manufacturer, Baltimore City, November 5, 1882.
REINHARDT, Bernardt, 86, merchant, Baltimore City, March 21, 1901.
REINHARDT, Charles, 64, police sergeant, Baltimore City, August 16, 1905.
REINHARDT, Charles W., 56, musician, Baltimore City, November 21, 1882.
REINHARDT, Melchior, 67, merchant tailor, Baltimore City, April 29, 1904.
REINHART, George, 83, contractor, Baltimore City, July 9, 1903.
REINICKER, George A., 85, retired, Baltimore City, November 1, 1899.
REINICKER, John F., 73, contractor, Baltimore City, January 25, 1903.
REIP, Margsret, 97, Baltimore City, January 29, 1880.
REITSNIDER, John, 62, merchant, Baltimore City, February 5, 1879.
REITZ, Herman J., Sr., 62, merchant, Baltimore City, February 19, 1879.
REITZ, Herman J., 52, hatter, Baltimore City, November 6, 1905.
REITZ, Philip, 67, manufacturer, Baltimore City, January 23, 1898.

RELLEY, Rev. John McK. (M.E.), 80, Baltimore City, June 2, 1897.
RENNERT, Robert, 61, hotelier, Baltimore City, October 3, 1898.
RENSHAW, Joseph, 61, manufacturer, Baltimore City, December 10, 1893.
RENSHAW, William, n.a., Baltimorean; died in France, May 4, 1900.
RENTCH, Andrew, 85, one of the largest landowners in Washing- County; died there, May 8, 1883.
RENWICK, Frank, 57, Baltimore City, February 22, 1903.
RENWICK, Robert, 41, furniture dealer, Baltimore City, July 17, 1884.
REQUARDT, J____ F____, 64, Baltimore City, December 15, 1907.
REQUARDT, John Jacob, 75, retired, Baltimore City, June 25, 1894.
RESLER, Arthur, 47, musician, Baltimore City, July 20, 1900.
RESLEY, Horace, 87, Cumberland, Allegany County, April 13?, 1902.
REUTER, Charles, 59, merchant, Baltimore City, January 7, 1900.
REVELL, Dr. Henry M., n.a., Anne Arundel County, July 2, 1901.
REVELL, Judge James, n.a., Annapolis, Anne Arundel County, March 21, 1908.
REVELLE, Benjamin, 44, Baltimore City, murdered on September 22, 1895.
REYNOLDS, Byron, 37, attorney, Baltimore City, July 5, 1898.
REYNOLDS, Charles, Jr., 28, journalist, Baltimore City, March 28, 1886.
REYNOLDS, Dr. George B., 70?, Baltimore City, October 2, 1914.
REYNOLDS, Captain James J., 52, Baltimore City, February 5, 1913.
REYNOLDS, Jesse K., 71, watchman, Baltimore City, June 20, 1891.
REYNOLDS, Dr. Joseph W., 74, Rising Sun, Cecil County, November 25, 1909.
REYNOLDS, Luther M., 83, attorney, Baltimore City, December 12, 1901.
REYNOLDS, Owen, 66, merchant, Baltimore City, January 22, 1899.
RHETT, Charles H., 72, retired, Baltimore City, December 4, 1894.
RHETT, General Thomas Grimke, 56, Baltimore City, July 28, 1878.
RHETT, Thomas S., 68, Confederate officer; died at Washington, D.C., December 26, 1893.
RHOADS, John R., 65, ship broker, Baltimore City, October 25, 1884.
RICARDS, John R., 68, merchant, Baltimore City, September 1, 1899.
RICAUD, Laurence H., 33, pharmacist, Baltimore City, April 4, 1901.
RICE, Frederick, 71, builder, Baltimore City, July 29, 1893.
RICE, Rev. M____ J____ (R.C.), 26, Baltimore City, December 23, 1881.
RICE, Miss Sara S., n.a., teacher, Baltimore City, October 30, 1909.
RICE, Rev. U____ F____ B____, n.a., Baltimore City, January 17, 1913.
RICE, William T., n.a., shipmaster, Baltimore City, May 8, 1893.

RICH, Rev. A_____ J_____ (P.E.), 63, Baltimore County, July 5, 1893.
RICH, Arthur, Jr., 65, physician, Baltimore City, April 25, 1880.
RICH, Thomas R., 67, retired financier, Baltimore City, July 8, 1900.
RICHARDS, John T., 83, Cumberland, Allegany County, February 2, 1907.
RICHARDSON, Benjamin V., 83, retired, Baltimore City, October 24, 1894.
RICHARDSON, Caleb, 71, shipbuilder, Baltimore City, August 10, 1893.
RICHARDSON, Charles H., 49, clerk, Baltimore City, November 23?, 1889.
RICHARDSON, Charles M., 50, actor, Baltimore City, February 29, 1898.
RICHARDSON, E_____ D_____, 83, surveyor, Baltimore City, September 11, 1893.
RICHARDSON, Dr. E_____ H_____, n.a., Bel Air, Harford County, March 7, 1908.
RICHARDSON, Dr. E_____ Hall, 67, Bel Air, Harford County, January 12, 1893.
RICHARDSON, Edward A., 76, insurance agent, Baltimore City, August 26, 1904.
RICHARDSON, Rev. Ezekiel (M.E.), 63, Baltimore City, January 10, 1900.
RICHARDSON, H_____ G_____, 55, Confederate veteran, Baltimore City, November 26, 1902.
RICHARDSON, J_____ S_____, 78, Bel Air, Harford County, March 18, 1908.
RICHARDSON, J_____ V_____, n.a., lieutenant, Fourth Regiment, Baltimore City, February 22, 1904.
RICHARDSON, Rev. J_____ T_____, 84, Baltimore City, February 6, 1905.
RICHARDSON, John T., 73, machinist, Baltimore City, October 16, 1894.
RICHARDSON, S_____ McD., 59, bank president, Baltimore City, June 13, 1892.
RICHARDSON, William H., 78, veteran of the Mexican War, Baltimore City, May 29, 1882.
RICHARDSON, William H., 67, editor, Baltimore City, September 2, 1905.
RICHARDSON, W_____ L_____, 73, bank officer, Baltimore City, August 14, 1882.
RICHARDSON, Dr. William S., n.a., physician, Bel Air, Harford County, April 23, 1894.
RICHTER, Dr. Adolph, 44, druggist, Baltimore City, June 11, 1883.
RICKARDS, J_____ S_____, 78, manufacturer, Ridgely, (Caroline County?), October 23, 1906.
RICKERD, Caleb B., 85, Baltimore City, July 7, 1900.
RICKETTS, Benjamin, 48, merchant, Baltimore City, November 9, 1879.
RICKETTS, George B., 51, type founder, Baltimore City, October 19, 1881.
RICKETTS, Wesley, 67, retired, Baltimore City, September 20, 1889.

RICKETTS, Wesley, Jr., 30, merchant, Baltimore City, October 22, 1882.
RICKEY, Harry, 52, Chestertown, Kent County, February 11, 1901.
RICKEY, Mrs. Mary, 93, Baltimore City, August 24, 1882.
RIDENOUR, Silas, 71, Mapleville, Washington County, September 2, 1912.
RIDER, Elizabeth, 113, Baltimore City, January 14, 1879.
RIDER, Moses, 75, retired, Baltimore City, February 9, 1886.
RIDER, Thomas F. J., 69, Salisbury, Wicomico County, September 13, 1905.
RIDGELY, Dr. A____ T____, 68, physician, Baltimore City, November 15, 1892.
RIDGELY, Charles W., 81, lawyer, Baltimore City, May 31, 1896.
RIDGELY, David W., 77, retired, Baltimore City, January 27, 1896.
RIDGELY, Howard, n.a., Baltimore County, September 28, 1900.
RIDGELY, J____ L____, 76, Baltimore City, May 17, 1909.
RIDGELY, James L., 75, secretary, Odd Fellows, Baltimore City, November 16, 1881.
RIDGELY, John, 57, Baltimore City, December 10, 1899.
RIDGELY, John Randolph, n.a., retired, Baltimore City, December 21, 1896.
RIDGELY, Lot W., 58, property agent, Baltimore City, October 10, 1883.
RIDGELY, Captain Samuel, 57, Baltimore City, July 16, 1897.
RIDGELY, Thomas G., 72, retired, Baltimore City, July 25, 1898.
RIDGELY, Thomas H., 56, lawyer, Lutherville, Baltimore County, June 7, 1904.
RIDGELY, Dr. William S., 84, physician, Baltimore City, December, 1885.
RIDOUT, Addison, 75, Annapolis, Anne Arundel County, January 29, 1902.
RIDOUT, Rev. Dr. Samuel (P.E.), 68, rector of St. Margaret's Church, Anne Arundel County, September 8, 1885.
RIDOUT, Weems, 61, Annapolis, Anne Arundel County, September 7, 1913.
RIEHL, Captain James L., 68, Baltimore City, July 21, 1913.
RIEHL, John H., 62, boatbuilder, Baltimore City, February 22, 1900.
RIEMAN, Joseph H., 65, merchant, Baltimore City, December 3, 1897.
RIEMAN, Joseph H., 42, Baltimore City, July 16, 1900.
RIFFLE, Thomas, 50, merchant, Baltimore City, November 29, 1882.
RIGBY, Henry J., 78, retired, Baltimore City, February 5, 1884.
RIGBY, J____ Arthur, 40, insurance, Baltimore City, April 19, 1882.
RIGGER, Lawrence, Sr., 71, marine engineer, Baltimore City, October 19, 1886.
RIGGS, Edward, 77, retired, Baltimore City, November 18, 1900.
RIGGS, Elisha, 59, banker, Baltimore City, July 8, 1881.
RIGGS, G____ W____, 66, Rockville, Montgomery County, July 25, 1912.
RIGGS, Joshua W., 53, merchant, Baltimore City, January 10, 1898.
RIGGS, Lawrason, 69, retired, Baltimore City, October 13, 1884.

RIGNEY, Patrick, 45, former Baltimore City Councilman, December 30, 1883.
RILEY, Elihu S., Jr., 65, associate editor of the Anne Arundel Advertiser, Annapolis, July 22, 1883.
RILEY, James, 77, Baltimore City, February 18, 1900.
RILEY, John H., 55, manufacturer, Baltimore City, January 24, 1898.
RILEY, John D., Sr., 79, retired, Baltimore City, March 18, 1901.
RILEY, Patrick, 82, retired, Baltimore City, June 27, 1883.
RILEY, Patrick, 54, merchant, Baltimore City, July 10, 1891.
RILEY, Dr. William, 80, physician, Baltimore City, August 15, 1887.
RILEY, William B., 37, Baltimore City, February 23, 1896.
RILEY, William L., 62, painter, Baltimore City, December 1, 1882.
RINEHART, Evan T., 63, merchant, Baltimore City, June 1, 1891.
RINEHART, Henry, 72, Westminster, Carroll County, December 31, 1893.
RINEHART, William H., 29, insurance agent, Baltimore City, July 16, 1902.
RING, G_____ M_____, 69, hermit, Relay, Baltimore County, December 12, 1911.
RINGGOLD, J_____ Edwin, 71, pharmacist, Baltimore City, November 2, 1901.
RINGGOLD, James T., attorney, Baltimore City, January 17, 1898.
RINN, John S., 70, retired, Baltimore City, March 19, 1899.
RIORDON, Timothy, 71, merchant, Baltimore City, July 17, 1899.
RITCHIE, Albert, 69, judge, Baltimore City, September 14, 1903.
RITCHIE, Hon. John, 56, chief judge, Sixth Judicial District, Frederick, Frederick County, October 27, 1887.
RITTENHOUSE, Dr. George S., 49, Elkton, Cecil County, September 22, 1906.
RITTER, George J., 69, contractor, Baltimore City, January 25, 1900.
RITTLER, W_____ H_____, 55, merchant, Baltimore City, October 7, 1892.
RIVERA, J_____ B_____, 70, confectioner, Baltimore City, November 9, 1902.
RIVERS, Albert W., 32, attorney, Baltimore City, March 17, 1901.
ROANE, Henry W., 73, manufacturer, Baltimore City, April 15, 1901.
ROBB, John A., 81, register, Walbrook, Baltimore, December 27, 1910.
ROBB, Joseph, 75, retired, Baltimore City, December 11, 1894.
ROBBINS, Horace W., 64, manufacturer, Baltimore City, August 11, 1878.
ROBERTS, Charles B., 57, judge, Court of Appels, Westminister, Carroll County, September 10, 1899.
ROBERTS, Edward, 57, merchant, Baltimore City, June 18, 1880.
ROBERTS, Colonel Ed_____, n.a., Baltimore City, May 26, 1910.
ROBERTS, John W., 71, merchant, Baltimore City, March 1, 1904.
ROBERTS, Joseph, 64, druggist, Baltimore City, January 31, 1888.
ROBERTS, Joseph K., 48, collector of internal revenue, Upper Marlboro, Prince George's County, October 1, 1888.

ROBERTS, Rev. Dr. Stephen C. (P.E.), 68, Baltimore City, September 5, 1899.
ROBERTS, William, 70, mechanic, Baltimore City, February 21, 1883.
ROBERTSON, Elias J., 60, Salisbury, Wicomico County, September 5, 1909.
ROBERTSON, N____ C____, 43, court clerk, Baltimore City, July 21, 1880.
ROBERTSON, William, 65, Baltimore City, November 25, 1895.
ROBERTSON, Dr. William W., 60, Baltimore City, January 31, 1906.
ROBINSON, Adoniram J., 44, lawyer, Baltimore City, November 23, 1904.
ROBINSON, Edward A., 63, merchant, Baltimore City, February 28, 1900.
ROBINSON, Edward W., 84, manufacturer, Baltimore City, July 22, 1893.
ROBINSON, Francis J., 80, retired, Baltimore City, January 3, 1888.
ROBERTSON, G____ S____, 43, athlete, Baltimore City, December 23, 1908.
ROBINSON, George, 45, clerk, Maryland Supreme Court, Baltimore City, February 8, 1878.
ROBINSON, George W., 57, merchant, Baltimore City, July 25, 1878.
ROBINSON, George W., 53, manufacturer, Baltimore City, July 5, 1894.
ROBINSON, James R., 32, Baltimore City, January 1, 1898.
ROBINSON, John, Sr., 76, retired, Baltimore City, January 28, 1883.
ROCHE, John L., n.a., Baltimore City, December 6, 1878.
ROBINSON, John M., 57, rd. presdt (sic), Baltimore City, February 14, 1893.
ROBINSON, John R., 82, financier, Talbot County, May 9, 1892.
ROBINSON, Joseph J., 72, manufacturer, Baltimore City, February 7, 1888.
ROBINSON, Lewis H., Jr., 65, attorney, Baltimore City, October 12, 1904.
ROBINSON, William, 90, retired, Baltimore City, March 31, 1902.
ROBINSON, William, 82, retired, Baltimore City, April 2, 1900.
ROBINSON, William H., 77, mariner, Baltimore City, January 16, 1883.
ROBINSON, William Wirt, 49, lawyer, Baltimore City, April 24, 1890.
ROBSON, John Q. A., 66, police commissioner, Baltimore City, November 17, 1894.
ROBSON, Stuart, 67, comedian of Baltimore; died in New York City, April 29, 1903.
ROCHE, James, 81, Mount Washington, Baltimore County, May 9, 1911.
ROCHE, John, 52, hotelier, Baltimore City, September 9, 1903.
ROCHE, John H., 76, teacher, Baltimore City, July 24, 1880.
ROCHE, Joseph I., n.a., journalist, Baltimore City, January 5, 1890.
ROCHE, Michael, 85, retired builder, Baltimore City, July 7, 1897.
ROCHESTER, William, 59, merchant, Baltimore City, September 28, 1899.

ROCK, J_____ J_____, 47, tax department, Baltimore City, May 29, 1902.
RODEMYER, Ernest, 86, retired, Baltimore City, September 29, 1901.
RODENMAYER, A_____ E_____, 71, musician, Baltimore City, March 16, 1905.
RODGERS, George H., 77, retired, Baltimore City, March 12, 1905.
RODGERS, John, Sr., 74, fisherman, Baltimore City, January 17, 1883.
RODGERS, John J., n.a., U.S. Shipping Commission, Baltimore City, March 4, 1891.
RODGERS, Dr. Samuel, 65, Methodist minister, Baltimore City, November 1, 1894.
RODOWICZ, Rev. John (R.C.), 68, Baltimore City, May 9, 1896.
ROE, Andrew D., 67, Greensboro, Caroline County, October 28, 1897.
ROE, James A., 77, Easton, Talbot County, December 18, 1903.
ROEDER, Fritz, 67, Baltimore City, April 16, 1896.
ROETH, Frederick A., 34, salesman, Baltimore City, August 2, 1882.
ROGERS, Alexander M., 65, lawyer, Baltimore City, December 26, 1889.
ROGERS, C_____ Lyon, Sr., 79, Baltimore City, April 30, 1907.
ROGERS, Edmund Law, 45, actor; died in New York City (stage name: Leslie Edmunds), December 19, 1893.
ROGERS, Edmund Law, 80, Baltimore City, January 21, 1896.
ROGERS, Dr. H_____ C_____, 44, physician, Baltimore City, November 28, 1881.
ROGERS, Henry J., 69, telegrapher, Baltimore City, August 20, 1879.
ROGERS, Henry W., 71, realtor, Baltimore City, July 12, 1901.
ROGERS, James C., 55, pharmacist, Baltimore City, March 24, 1883.
ROGERS, James S., 74, merchant, Baltimore City, February 19, 1903.
ROGERS, Rev. Jason (Presbyeterian), 59, Baltimore City, September 26, 1882.
ROGERS, Jonathan C., 56, Baltimore City, September 22, 1914.
ROGERS, Joseph, Jr., 73, Baltimore City, February 22, 1893.
ROGERS, Martin, 83, Baltimore City, March 8, 1910.
ROGERS, Philip, 53, druggist, Baltimore City, January 7, 1889.
ROGERS, R_____ L_____, 83, Baltimore City, October 8, 1909.
ROGERS, William, 86, merchant, Baltimore City, December 25, 1892.
ROGERS, William, 73, broker, Baltimore City, July 27, 1897.
ROGERSON, Robert, 64, gardener, Baltimore City, August 27, 1903.
ROGGE, Christian, 64, importer, Baltimore City, June 12, 1894.
ROHE, Dr. George H., 48, physician, Baltimore City, February 6, 1899.
ROHR, Henry, 74, merchant, Baltimore City, October 26, 1904.
ROHRER, Josiah C., 89, Washington County, April 13, 1902.
ROKES, Emerson, 58, shipowner, Baltimore City, May 23, 1887.
ROLLINS, Solomon A., 87, miller, Baltimore City, September 6, 1894.
ROLOSON, Frederick, 73, manufacturer, Baltimore City, August 22, 1891.
ROLOSON, Hugh, 76, merchant, Baltimore City, November 2, 1881.
ROMOSER, John, 72, retired, Baltimore City, October 30, 1896.
ROOT, Calvin S., 80, musician; died at Denver, Colorado, September 27, 1893.

ROOT, J_____, 78, Thurmont, Frederick County, January 31, 1910.
ROSE, Dr. C_____ H_____, 79, "Grand Old Man of Talbot County"; died at Centreville, Queen Anne's County, August 23, 1912.
ROSE, Isaac, 61, merchant, Baltimore City, December 6, 1880.
ROSE, Rev. J_____, 76, Baltimore City, December 4, 1907.
ROSE, John T., 39, inspector, Baltimore City, July 28, 1902.
ROSE, Peter, 69, merchant, Baltimore City, October 5, 1882.
ROSE, William B., 42, merchant, Baltimore City, March 9, 1902.
ROSEMAN, G_____ W_____, 68, deputy sheriff, Baltimore City, May 26, 1895.
ROSEN, Sarah, 18, seamstress, Front Street Theater panic, December 27, 1895.
ROSENAUR, Levi, 62, merchant, Baltimore City, July 18, 1902.
ROSENBERG, Morris, 56, merchant, Baltimore City, June 21, 1894.
ROSENBERGER, Francis, 78, retired, Baltimore City, April 9, 1897.
ROSENBERGER, John A., 52, musician, Baltimore City, November 1, 1884.
ROSENBLATT, Samuel A., 55, merchant, Baltimore City, January 21, 1903.
ROSENDALE, Henry, 77, retired, Baltimore City, October 28, 1897.
ROSENFELD, Simon, 84, merchant, Baltimore City, October 30, 1883.
ROSENON, Theodore, 84, riding master, Baltimore City, December 18, 1904.
ROSENSTEEL, Theodore, 46, merchant, Baltimore City, June 27, 1881.
ROSENSTOCK, Gerson, 71, retired merchant, Baltimore City, September 14, 1880.
ROSENSTOCK, S_____ I_____, 66, merchant, Baltimore City, November 17, 1902.
ROSENSTOCK, Samuel, 77, merchant, Baltimore City, March 27, 1901.
ROSENTHAL, Jacob, 21, tailor, Front Street Theater panic, December 27, 1895.
ROSENTHAL, Levi, 83, retired, Baltimore City, April 8, 1905.
ROSENTHAL, Moses, 85, retired merchant, Baltimore City, June 19, 1899.
ROSENTHAL, Samuel, 60, merchant, Baltimore City, October 25, 1893.
ROSEWALD, Judah, 89, Baltimore City, June 4, 1894.
ROSS, Oscar E., 39, pharmacist, Baltimore City, April 5, 1906.
ROSS, Richard L., 70, contractor, Baltimore City, December 16, 1891.
ROSS, General W_____ F_____ W_____, 69, G.A.R., Baltimore City, November 12, 1907.
ROSSITER, John F., 62, boatbuilder, Baltimore City, May 20, 1893.
ROTHROCK, T_____ M_____, 74, Baltimore City manufacturer, February 14, 1902.
ROUND, Rev. Dr. J_____ Emory, 56, Baltimore City, January 10, 1892.
ROUTSON, Jesse H., 45, Buckeystown, Frederick City, April 28, 1914.
ROUTZAHN, D_____ Henry, 57, Frederick County, February 11, 1898.
ROUTZAHN, Joseph L., 62, Frederick, Frederick County, July 22, 1904.
ROUZER, Colonel John R., 75, Thurmont, Frederick County, March 25, 1914.

ROWE, C____ M____, 67, Cockeysville, Baltimore County, June 2, 1910.
ROWE, Thomas, 93, taxidermist, Jessup, Howard County, November 7, 1904.
ROWE, Lieutenant W____ B____, 70, Baltimore City, November 10, 1910.
ROWE, William T., 62, Baltimore City merchant, January 25, 1898.
ROWLAND, Henry A., 32, professor of physics, Baltimore City, April 16, 1901.
ROWLAND, J____ H____, 89, Cecil County, May 24, 1908.
ROWLAND, Dr. William B., 74, of Cecil County; died at Philadelphia, September 6, 1885.
ROYCROFT, J____ A____, 58, police sergeant, Baltimore City, December 23, 1902.
ROYER, John, 73, retired, Baltimore City, October 1, 1883.
ROYER, Dr. Levi, 61, New Windsor, Carroll County, February 10, 1901.
ROYSTON, Elijah B., 55, retired, Baltimore City, August 18, 1894.
ROYSTON, Joshua, 82, merchant, Baltimore City, December 22, 1883.
RUARK, Edward W., 80, merchant, Baltimore City, January 25, 1898.
RUBENSTEIN, Dr. W____, 60, physician, Baltimore City, July 1, 1903.
RUBY, William H., 75, editor, Towson, Baltimore County, February 26, 1905.
RUCKLE, George, 88, retired, Baltimore City, April 20, 1887.
RUDDACH, Joseph H., 59, retired, Baltimore City, October 29, 1884.
RUDOLPH, Ernest B., 69, retired, Baltimore City, October 19, 1897.
RUDOLPH, William, 61, Baltimore City, August 22, 1901.
RUDY, T____ C____, 66, Middletown, Frederick County, October 2, 1903.
RUFF, J____ Frederick, 52, merchant tailor, Baltimore City, August 6, 1882.
RUHL, Conrad, Sr., 69, merchant, Baltimore City, January 25, 1901.
RULAND, Rev. George, 68, rector of the Redemptorist Seminary, Ilchester, Howard County, November 21, 1885.
RUMBOLD, Captain H____ E____ W____, 74, August 27, 1911.
RUSH, Campion, 50, hotelier, Baltimore City, March 6, 1902.
RUSH, Dr. Charles W., n.a., physician, Annapolis, Anne Arundel County, November 9, 1893.
RUSK, George W., 83, retired, Baltimore City, May 4, 1901.
RUSK, Lemuel J., 76, Baltimore City, February 2, 1892.
RUSK, Thomas J., 90, retired, Baltimore City, May 28, 1891.
RUSSELL, A____ H____, 69, Baltimore City, May 6, 1909.
RUSSELL, E____ Walton, 60, druggist, Baltimore City, October 5, 1892.
RUSSELL, Eugene J., 79, druggist, Baltimore City, August 26, 1899.
RUSSELL, Henry J., 81, Baltimore City, November 5, 1898.
RUSSELL, J____, 65, packer, Annapolis, Anne Arundel County, February 6, 1893.
RUSSELL, Thomas, 69, merchant, Baltimore City, April 9, 1878.
RUSSELL, William T., 72, pilot, Baltimore City, September 27, 1900.
RUSSELL, Dr. William L., 65, physician, Baltimore City, December 21, 1899.
RUSSUM, George M., 67, attorney, Denton, Caroline County, October 21, 1901.

RUST, John, 78, retired, Baltimore City, April 1, 1884.
RUTH, Francis, 73, merchant, Baltimore City, February 27, 1900.
RUTHERFORD, Alexander, 62, retired, Baltimore City, December 19, 1894.
RUTHERFORD, Allan, 59, clerk, Maryland Cort of Appeals, April 28, 1900.
RUTLEDGE, Dr. E_____ Hall, 38, physician, Baltimore City, November 7, 1888.
RUTTER, John H., 51, contractor, Baltimore City, April 30, 1901.
RUYTER, Frank, 26, compositor, The Sun, Baltimore City, April 8, 1894.
RYAN, John, 68, type founder, Baltimore City, May 8, 1888.
RYAN, Rev. John J., 70, Baltimore City, December 16, 1913.
RYAN, Timothy, 58, superintendent, Baltimore City Hall, December 9, 1887.
RYAN, William H., 68, broker, Baltimore City, April 6, 1878.

SACHSE, Theodore, 76, lithographer, Baltimore City, February 10, 1891.
SADLER, Professor W_____ H_____, 67, Baltimore City, January 8, 1909.
SADTLER, C_____ C_____, 70, merchant, Baltimore City, February 10, 1902.
SADTLER, Ernest T., 34, Baltimore City, July 15, 1898.
SADTLER, George T., 66, optician, Baltimore City, April 18, 1888.
SADTLER, John P., 74, retired, Baltimore City, January 6, 1888.
SADTLER, Rev. Philip B. (Lutheran), 77, Baltimore City, April 28, 1901.
SADTLER, William J., 68, retired, Baltimore City, February 16, 1888.
SALZBERG, Kate, seven years old, Front Street Theater panice, December 27, 1895.
SALZBERG, Moses, 11, Front Street Theater panic, December 27, 1895.
SALZER, Dr. Henry, 55, physician, Baltimore City, June 19, 1896.
SAMMANI, Louis P., 45, Baltimore City, February 3, 1914.
SAMS, Judge Conway W., 47, Baltimore City, September 5, 1909.
SAND, Rev. J_____ A_____ (United Brethren), 69, Baltimore City, September 15, 1880.
SANDER, Dr. A_____ R_____, 69, physician, Baltimore City, February 7, 1879.
SANDER, Hender, 66, mortician, Baltimore City, April 4, 1892.
SANDERS, Henry, 81, Cumberland, Allegany County, February 27, 1901.
SANDERS, J_____ J_____, 90, Hamilton, Maryland, November 25, 1909.
SANDERS, James W., n.a., merchant, Baltimore City, January 29, 1901.
SANDERS, John W., 87, pressman, Baltimore City, June 30, 1891.
SANDS, Mrs. Elizabeth, 101, Baltimore City, August 3, 1890.
SANDS, Samuel, 92, publisher, Baltimore City, July 28, 1891.
SANDS, Dr. William, 76, physician, Baltimore City, June 24, 1879.
SANFORD, J_____ L_____, 83, mariner, Baltimore City, August 17, 1893.
SANFORD, Joseph B., 75, contractor, Baltimore City, July 4, 1906.
SANGSTON, George E., 77, merchant, Baltimore City, November 5, 1884.

SANNER, George I., 71, builder, Baltimore City, January 16, 1893.
SANNER, Isaac D., 72, Baltimore City, November 12, 1911.
SANNER, Isaac S., 88, pilot, Baltimore City, December 12, 1898.
SANTOS, Mary D., n.a., Baltimore City, February 4, 1913.
SANTOS, T____ A____, 33, Baltimorean; died in New York City, September 12, 1898.
SAPPINGTON, C____ F____, 61, Baltimore City, January 4, 1910.
SAPPINGTON, Dr. John, 57, Darlington, Harford County, February 10, 1905.
SAPPINGTON, N____ J____, 86, Baltimore City, January 28, 1912.
SAPPINGTON, Dr. Richard, 84, Baltimore City, May 14, 1911.
SAPPINGTON, Dr. T____ P____, 62, Libertytown, Frederick County, December 9, 1909.
SAPPINGTON, Dr. Thomas, 84, Baltimore City, August 11, 1901.
SARGENT, Rev. Thomas B., 75, Baltimore City, August 14, 1879.
SASSEER, P____ A____, 67, Waldorf, Charles County, September 30, 1898.
SATTERFIELD, J____ M____, 43, auctioneer, Baltimore City, December 23, 1881.
SAUER, Dr. Andrew J., 30, physician, Baltimore City, May 20, 1903.
SAUERHOFF, J____ F____, 81, shipbuilder, Baltimore City, October 16, 1892.
SAUERS, Henry A., 30, clerk, Baltimore City, March 5, 1900.
SAUERWEIN, F____ D____, 75, Baltimore City, July 15, 1907.
SAUERWEIN, John, 84, retired, Baltimore City, November 21, 1901.
SAUERWEIN, Peter G., 70, retired, Baltimore City, August 10, 1886.
SAUL, Joseph W., 86, manufacturer, Baltimore City, February 20, 1900.
SAULSBURY, Charles, 87, Talbot County, August 11, 1900.
SAULSBURY, James K., 87, Ridgely, Caroline County, November 19, 1900.
SAUMENIG, J____ William, 82, builder, Baltimore City, January 12, 1899.
SAUNDERS, James M., 64, engineer, Baltimore City, April 7, 1880.
SAUNDERS, John S., 67, State Adjutant General, Annapolis, Anne Arundel County, January 19, 1904.
SAUNDERS, Dr. William N., 74, LaPlata, Charles County, October 6, 1910.
SAUNER, J____ C____, 78, Confederate veteran, Pikesville, Baltimore County, December 1, 1908.
SAVAGE, Charles E., 74, realtor, Baltimore City, December 19, 1908.
SAVAGE, Judge George, 65, Towson, Baltimore County, November 6, 1909.
SAVILLE, John, 71, machinist, Baltimore City, May 16, 1887.
SAVIN, F____ Augustus, n.a., broker, Baltimore City, March 6, 1899.
SAVAGE, Professor Robert T., 73, Easton, Talbot County, February 9, 1907.
SAVIN, William F., 72, merchant, Baltimore City, July 3, 1881.
SAXTON, J____ A____, 65, Cambridge, Dorchester County, May 12, 1909.
SAYLOR, John, 71, merchant, Baltimore City, April 7, 1883.
SCAGGS, Pinknew A., 50, Prince George's County, December 7, 1901.

SCARLETT, Robert, n.a., veteran, Baltimore City, April 15, 1897.
SCARLETT, William G., n.a., attorney, Baltimore City, September 26, 1900.
SCHAD, Andrew, 70, musician, Baltimore City, August 9, 1882.
SCHAEFER, Henry, 55, undertaker, Baltimore City, November 10, 1899.
SCHAEFER, Jean H., 63, musician, Baltimore City, November 10, 1892.
SCHAEFFER, Milton, 48, Westminster, Carroll County, September 13, 1902.
SCHAEFFER, William C., n.a., scenic artist, Baltimore City, April 17, 1893.
SCHAFER, Rev. J____, 49, local preacher, Baltimore City, March 5, 1881.
SCHAFER, J____ Frederick, 62, fireman, Baltimore City, November 21, 1900.
SCHAIDT, John, 54, civil engineer, Cumberland, Allegany County, September 9k 1904.
SCHALL, Thomas, 53, merchant, Baltimore City, November 3, 1897.
SCHARF, J____ Thomas, 54, Baltimorean and historian of Maryland; died in New York City, February 28, 1898.
SCHARFF, Rev. T____ C____ (M.E.), 32, Baltimore City, November 20, 1880.
SCHEFFER, John, 76, mechanic, Baltimore City, Mary 19, 1883.
SCHEFFER, William J., 48, stereotyper, Baltimore City, July 9, 1881.
SCHEFFLER, Rev. Albert (R.C.), 81, Baltimore City, October 12, 1890.
SCHEIB, Rev. Henry (Lutheran), 89, Baltimore City, November 15, 1897.
SCHEIDLER, Charles A., 63, musician, Baltimore City, March 26, 1879.
SCHENUIT, H____ J____, Sr., 65, musician, Baltimore City, February 29, 1888.
SCHERER, John, 73, manufacturer, Baltimore City, January 11, 1896.
SCHEURMAN, G____, 83, retired, Baltimore City, January 10, 1902.
SCHEURMAN, G____ C____, 50, manufacturer, Baltimore City, January 10, 1902.
SCHARF, Thomas G., 70, retired, Baltimore City, August 10, 1886.
SCHIEVE, L____ B____, 40, lieutentant, Baltimore City Fire Department, March 26, 1893.
SCHILLER, Charles, 81, manufacturer, Baltimore City, August 15, 1894.
SCHILLING, Frank A., 31, undertaker, Baltimore City, August 13, 1901.
SCHIRMER, George M., 81, retired, Baltimore City, June 17, 1898.
SCHLEGEL, Frederick, 79, retired, Baltimore City, November 11, 1897.
SCHLEGEL, Henry, 61, Baltimore City, December 14, 1900.
SCHLEIFER, Joseph E., 55, confectioner, Baltimore City, August 24, 1905.
SCHLEY, Alfred, 81, Liberty, Frederick County, March 15, 1900.
SCHLEY, Eugene L, 53, compositor, Baltimore City, June 22, 1889.
SCHLEY, Dr. Fairfax, 79, Frederick, Frederick County, February 1, 1903.

SCHLEY, Colonel James M., 68, Cumberland, Allegany County, November 15, 1883.
SCHLEY, William C., 48, attorney, Baltimore City, December 14, 1888.
SCHLEY, William Louis, 75, attorney, Baltimore City, December 15, 1898.
SCHLEY, Admiral Winfield Scott, 72; died in New York City, October 2, 1911.
SCHLOGEL, Rev. C_____ A_____, 64, Baltimore City, January 27, 1892.
SCHLOSS, Joseph, 73, tailor, Baltimore City, October 9, 1900.
SCHLOSS, Moses, 50, merchant, Baltimore City, August 31, 1902.
SCHLOSS, Seligman, 69, retired, Baltimore City, August 25, 1897.
SCHLOSS, William, 65, merchant, Baltimore City, December 10, 1894.
SCHMALZ, Matthew, 63, music professor, Baltimore City, May 5, 1888.
SCHMIDT, A_____, Sr., 67, musician, Baltimore City, September 29, 1902.
SCHMENNER, Daniel, 72, baker, Baltimore City, November 24, 1881.
SCHMIDT, Charles F., 71, lithographer, Baltimore City, March 29, 1894.
SCHMIDT, Christopher, 47, barber, Baltimore City, November 22, 1884.
SCHMIDT, Edwin B., n.a., Cockeysville, Baltimore County, July 3, 1914.
SCHMIDT, Rev. F_____ X_____ (R.C.), 51, Baltimore City, February 21, 1899.
SCHMIDT, Henry D., 53, carriage maker, Baltimore City, January 31, 1891.
SCHMIDT, Dr. Jacob, 68, physician, Baltimore City, March 21, 1880.
SCHMIDT, John N., 58, editor, Baltimore City, May 23, 1893.
SCHMIDT, P_____ D_____, 52, carriage maker, Baltimore City, July 8, 1884.
SCHMIDT, W_____ J_____, 82, Baltimore City, December 18, 1911.
SCHMUCKER, Judge Samuel D., 67, Baltimore City, March 3, 1911.
SCHNAUFFER, Mrs. Elise, 61, publisher, Baltimore City, February 14, 1895.
SCHNAUFFER, William 54, publisher, Baltimore City, November 19, 1889.
SCHNEEBERGER, Louis, 48, postal cashier, Baltimore City, December 20, 1899.
SCHNEIDER, Adam, 66, contractor, Baltimore City, June 29, 1882.
SCHNEIDER, Peter, 63, contractor, Baltimore City, March 3, 1878.
SCHOENER, John P., 52, manufacturer, Baltimore City, December 30, 1900.
SCHOFIELD, Henry, 71, Baltimore City, April 3, 1900.
SCHOMANN, John, 44, musician, Baltimore City, February 9, 1881.
SCHOOLHERR, Samuel, n.a., merchant, Baltimore City, January 29, 1882.
SCHORR, Rev. Henry G. (P.E.), 29, Baltimore City, May 26, 1889.
SCHOTT, Christopher, 84, retired, Baltimore City, December 6, 1895.
SCHREIER, Joseph, 65, brewer, Baltimore City, August 19, 1884.
SCHROEDER, Andrew F., 53, manufacturer, Baltimore City, June 18, 1882.

SCHROEDER, G_____ W_____, 33, manufacturer, Baltimore City, January 27, 1902.
SCHROEDER, Henry A., 58, lithographer, Baltimore City, October 31, 1896.
SCHROEDER, Captain Henry B., 83, Frederick County, December 21, 1904.
SCHRYVER, James M., n.a., B. & O. Railroad, October 29, 1900.
SCHULTE, W_____ F_____, 92, Baltimore City, December 21, 1912.
SCHULTZ, Kendall H., n.a., pilot, Baltimore City, July 8, 1900.
SCHULZE, Ferdinand, 60, manufacturer, Baltimore City, April 3, 1893.
SCHULTZ, Dr. H_____ M_____, 68, Baltimore City, July 6, 1898.
SCHULTZ, Richard, 32, musician, Baltimore City, September 3, 1898.
SCHULZ, Alfred J., 71, Baltimore City, February 26, 1914.
SCHULZE, J_____ Albert, 48, druggist, Baltimore City, December 4, 1893.
SCHUMANN, Valentine, 78, retired, Baltimore City, November 25, 1882.
SCHWANNCKE, Herman C., n.a., U.S. Artillery; died at Honolulu, Hawaii, December 16, 1900; interred Baltimore City.
SCHWARTZ, Rev. Andrew (Lutheran), 75, Baltimore City, December 29, 1894.
SCHWARTZ, Dr. William H., 51, druggist, Baltimore City, April 2, 1896.
SCHWARTZMAN, G_____ A_____, 67, retired, Baltimore City, February 20, 1882.
SCHWARTZE, Dr. Edward, 82, physician, Baltimore City, March 12, 1886.
SCHWSRTZE, Dr. John, 63, druggist, Baltimore City, November 18, 1893.
SCHWARZ, Charles W. H., 78, merchant, Baltimore City, October 11, 1903.
SCHWARZ, J_____ D_____, 76, Hagerstown, Washington County, December 22, 1907.
SCHWARZ, William, Sr., 62, merchant, Baltimore City, June 22, 1884.
SCHWATKA, J_____ A_____, 78, Baltimore City, June 2, 1912.
SCOFIELD, James, 81, Sun carrier, Baltimore City, April 7, 1881.
SCOPINICH, Marco A., 43, interpreter, Baltimore City, March 23, 1887.
SCOTT, Daniel, 75, attorney, Bel Air, Harford County, July 29, 1900.
SCOTT, George, 78, merchant, Baltimore City, August 16, 1898.
SCOTT, Rev. Hugh B., 80, Baltimore County, August 22, 1905.
SCOTT, Jacob, 94, Cecil County, November 4, 1902.
SCOTT, Job, 72, bank cashier, Baltimore City, February 13, 1902.
SCOTT, John, 40, attorney, Baltimore City, November 6, 1882.
SCOTT, John, 71, inventor, Baltimore City, November 2, 1890.
SCOTT, Jonathan W., 50, printer, Baltimore City, August 30, 1886.
SCOTT, Dr. Martin P., 81, Hagerstown, Washington County, December 30, 1904.
SCOTT, Norman B., 86, Hagerstown, Washington County, September 21, 1905.
SCOTT, Rossieter S., 70, banker, Baltimore City, June 6, 1898.
SEBOLD, C_____ W_____, 62, Hagerstown, Washington County, December 15, 1907.

SEEBOLD, Dr. Charles S., 51, Baltimore City, June 12, 1901
SEEGER, John Jacob, 72, brewer, Baltimore City, February 18, 1883.
SEEMULLER, John R., 61, merchant, Baltimore City, August 1, 1891.
SEEMULLER, W_____, n.a., auctioneer, Baltimore City, December 23, 1898.
SEEMULLER, William, 27, journalist, Baltimore City, March 20, 1883.
SEIBERT, Adam, 72, Cumberland, Allegany County, November 20, 1907.
SEIBERT, J_____ E_____, 71, cabinetmaker, Baltimore City, July 7, 1902.
SEIBERT, Samuel, 87, merchant, Hagerstown, Washington County, March 8, 1900.
SEIBOLD, Michael, 94, merchant, Baltimore City, February 7, 1903.
SEIDELL, Henry G., n.a., Baltimore City, October 10, 1913.
SEIDENSTRICKER, Abraham, 65, grocer, Baltimore City, November 25, 1903.
SEIDENSTRICKER, Albert, 63, railroad man, Baltimore City, January 13, 1897.
SEIDENSTRICKER, John B., 84, Baltimore City, June 24, 1894.
SEIM, Henry, 75, manufacturer, Baltimore City, December 14, 1898.
SEIPP, Charles, 46, merchant, Baltimore City, July 28, 1903.
SELDNER, Lewis, 51, merchant, Baltimore City, September 8, 1881.
SELIGER, Joel, 83, merchant, Baltimore City, July 3, 1893.
SELIGER, Joseph, 85, retired, Baltimore City, March 17, 1898.
SELLMAN, Alexander, 81, merchant, Baltimore City, November 17, 1904.
SELLMAN, James C., 85, retired, Baltimore City, August 20, 1884.
SELLMAN, Lew W., 30, manufacturer, Baltimore City, February 28, 1901.
SELLMAN, Richard P., 65, Anne Arundel County, October 15, 1903.
SEMMES, Sister Mary Gabriel, 85, Baltimore City, May 28, 1883.
SENFT, Louis, 44, druggist, Baltimore City, May 13, 1881.
SESSIONS, Augustus D., 80, Baltimore City, March 31, 1900.
SETH, Dr. James, 58, Talbot County, January 26, 1901.
SETH, T_____ Alexander, 39, attorney, Baltimore City, January 13, 1889.
SETH, Judge William H., 68, Easton, Talbot County, April 9, 1907.
SEWSRD, Alexander, 73, Cambridge, Dorchester County, April 23, 1909.
SEXTON, Henry, 66, U.S. Army (Ret.), Baltimore City, September 6, 1904.
SEXTON, Samuel B., 79, stove manufacturer, Baltimore City, June 3, 1890.
SEXTON, Samuel B., Jr., 52, Baltimore City manufacturer, November 22, 1904.
SHAFER, George H., 68, clerk, Land Office, Annapolis, Anne Arundel County, January 21, 1906.
SHAFER, Jacob C., 65, packer, Baltimore City, June 24, 1901.
SHAEFFER, O_____ W_____, 45, Cumberland, Allegany County, June 15, 1901.

SHAFFER, William H., 68, Westminster, Carroll County, November 27, 1905.
SHANKS, Thomas, 68, Baltimore City, July 4, 1898.
SHANAHAN, Charles E., 59, attorney, Baltimore City, September 23, 1903.
SHANE, John H., 63, publisher, Baltimore City, February 19, 1901.
SHANNON, James P., 57, hotelier, Baltimore City, April 28, 1901.
SHARE, Philip T., 72, retired, Baltimore City, July 30, 1883.
SHARE, Richard, 68, hotelier, Baltimore City, June 16, 1881.
SHARP, Alpheus S., 86, druggist, Baltimore City, October 10, 1909.
SHARP, Judge George Matthews, 59, Baltimore City, July 7, 1911.
SHARP, Captain James T., n.a., master mariner, Baltimore City, December 12, 1898.
SHARETTS, William L., 67, retired, Baltimore City, December 3, 1885.
SHARRETTS, Jacob, 83, Carroll County, March 2, 1900.
SHARRETTS, John F., 82, retired, Baltimore City, April 18, 1898.
SHAW, Major Alexander, 65, capitalist, Baltimore City, December 13, 1902.
SHAW, Alexander J., 54, undertaker, Baltimore City, July 20, 1891.
SHAW, Isaiah, Sr., 93, builder, Baltimore City, January 23, 1879.
SHAW, J____ L____, 71, furnace builder, Baltimore City, February 23, 1893.
SHAW, James W., n.a., salvage corps, Baltimore City, May 22, 1893.
SHAW, James F., 64, florist, Baltimore City, March 20, 1895.
SHAW, Dr. Joseph S., 56, professor at Rock Hill College, June 27, 1895.
SHAW, John K., 60, coal operator, Baltimore City, August 26, 1905.
SHAW, Joseph M., 84, pilot, Baltimore City, February 8, 1901.
SHAW, Robert H., 59, printer, Baltimore City, March 4, 1901.
SHAW, Samuel H., 93, bank officer, Baltimore City, August 3, 1881.
SHEAHAN, James Washington, n.a., leading editorial writer for the Chicago Tribune; formerly of Baltimore, June 17, 1883.
SHECKELLS, B____ T____, 75, retired, Baltimore City, March 29, 1902.
SHECKELLS, John, 73, merchant, Baltimore City, May 21, 1879.
SHEEHAN, Cornelius, 61, builder, Baltimore City, March 13, 1899.
SHEEHAN, Maurice, 67, contractor, Baltimore City, August 9, 1894.
SHEEKS, E____ A____, 70, Confederate veteran, Pikesville, Baltimore County, January 3, 1908.
SHEIVE, G____ W____, 37, Masonic lecturer, Baltimore City, December 27, 1886.
SHELLEY, William H., 59, educator, Baltimore City, August 11, 1900.
SHEPHERD, George Goodridge, 40, Baltimore City, August 13, 1912.
SHEPHERD, J____ E____, 64, judge, Baltimore City, February 7, 1910.
SHEPPARD, John T., 67, engineer, Baltimore City, March 4, 1900.

SHERIFF, Dionysius T., 63, chief judge, Orphan's Court, Prince George's County, November 7, 1904.
SHEWELL, Mrs. Olivia Rand, 50, actress and Baltimorean; died at New York City, June 23, 1898.
SHERIDAN, John, 57, mine owner and capitalist, Mount Savage, Allegany County, February 4, 1902.
SHERIDAN, Thomas, 75, Cumberland, Allegany County, March 6, 1893.
SHERIFF, Benjamin R., 62, publisher, Baltimore City, May 20, 1904.
SHIMEK, Joseph, 73, organ builder, Baltimore City, May 30, 1890.
SHIPLEY, Dr. Benjamin F., 69, Alpha, Howard County, June 13, 1913.
SHIPLEY, Charles, 89, realtor, Baltimore City, June 18, 1904.
SHIPLEY, Cornelius H., 75, Baltimore City, January 14, 1901.
SHIPLEY, Daniel E., 75, merchant, Baltimore City, April 1, 1885.
SHIPLEY, Francis M., 60, Baltimore City, July 26, 1896.
SHIPLEY, J____ S____, 67, lawyer, Baltimore City, April 14, 1886.
SHIPLEY, Robert H., 74, retired, Baltimore City, October 14, 1894.
SHIPLEY, Robert L., 68, Baltimore City, September 24, 1896.
SHIPPEN, Dr. Edward, 67, physician, Baltimore City, April 22, 1895.
SHIRK, Henry Sr., 86, realtor, Baltimore City, June 18, 1891.
SHIRLEY, William, 84, merchant, Baltimore City, December 19, 1900.
SHOCK, DeWitt C., 48, solicitor, Baltimore City, May 29, 1882.
SHOCKLEY, U____ F____, 77, Snow Hill, Worcester County, April 12, 1908.
SHOEMAKER, Mrs. Rachel, 94, Baltimore City, April 10, 1883.
SHOEMAKER, Samuel M., 63, retired, Baltimore City, May 31, 1884.
SHOOK, Henry, 90, watchman, *The Sun*, Baltimore City, March 3, 1894.
SHOWELL, Lemuel, 75, Ocean City, Worcester County, March 1, 1902.
SHRECK, George E. W., 67, Baltimore City, December 21, 1899.
SHREEVES, Benjamin B., 44, Baltimore City, October 22, 1911.
SHRIVER, Albert, 57, retired, Baltimore City, December 30, 1895.
SHRIVER, Andrew K., 60, merchant, Baltimore City, May 21, 1897.
SHRIVER, Anthony, 62, Cumberland, Allegany County, October 3, 1902.
SHRIVER, Calvin S., 65, manufacturer, Baltimore City, June 13, 1901.
SHRIVER, David K., n.a., banker, Westminster, Carroll County, April 19, 1906.
SHRIVER, E____ T____, 80, Cumberland, Allegany County, February 7, 1896.
SHRIVER, Edward, 83, retired postman, Baltimore City, February 24, 1896.
SHRIVER, Harry Courtney, n.a., electrician, Baltimore City, February 21, 1896.
SHRIVER, Howard, 76, Cumberland, Allegany County, February 15, 1901.
SHRIVER, J____ Alexander, 70, president, steamboat line, Baltimore City, March 1, 1891.

SHRIVER, James, 66, Westminster Carroll County, May 1, 1893.
SHRIVER, Robert, 75, Cumberland, Allegany County, March 18, 1912.
SHRIVER, Rev. Samuel S. (Presbyeterian), 76, Baltimore City, February 25, 1898.
SHRIVER, William, 79, Baltimore City, April 9, 1911.
SHRYOCK, Henry S., 75, retired, Baltimore City, December 6, 1882.
SHRYOCK, J____ S____, 70, master mechanic, Baltimore City, April 9, 1882.
SHRYOCK, William H., 67, banker, Baltimore City, April 19, 1902.
SHULTZ, J____ A____ G____, n.a., policeman, Baltimore City, March 22, 1911.
SHUTER, James, 55, express agent, Baltimore City, October 22, 1890.
SHUTT, A____ P____, 66, merchant, Baltimore City, July 10, 1881.
SHUTT, Captain John, 72, mariner, Baltimore City, December 7, 1885.
SIEBOLD, H____ C____, n.a., policeman, Baltimore City, December 22, 1909.
SIEGEL, Emmanuel, 46, merchant, Baltimore City, December 22, 1904.
SIEGEL, Samuel, 77, retired, Baltimore City, April 11, 1884.
SIEGAL, Sarah, ten years old, Front Street Theater panic, December 27, 1895.
SIGMUND, Albert, 77, merchant, Baltimore City, January 26, 1896.
SILVER, Benjamin, Sr., 85, Harford County, April 25, 1894.
SILVER, George B., 64, Harford County, December 13, 1902.
SILVERWOOD, William, 79, retired, Baltimore City, November 18, 1905.
SIMERING, John C., 60, secretary, Republican Committee, Baltimore City, October 22, 1906.
SIMMERS, Thomas, 59, Smithsburg, Washington County, December 2, 1907.
SIMMONS, Dr. Oliver D. Bowens, n.a., Baltimore City, November 25, 1913.
SIMMONS, R____ L____, 63, veteran, Baltimore City, January 13, 1908.
SIMMONS, Robert D., 69, retired, Baltimore City, January 25, 1897.
SIMMONS, Dr. Thomas Warfield, n.a., Hagerstown, Washington County, December 30, 1905.
SIMMS, Benjamin, 51, caterer, Baltimore City, December 15, 1897.
SIMMS, William C., 61, manufacturer, Baltimore City, April 10, 1881.
SIMON, A____ J____ L____, 86, Baltimore City, December 12, 1912.
SIMON, E____, 79, Baltimore City, March 28, 1912.
SIMON, F____ W____, 55, merchant, Baltimore City, October 6, 1893.
SIMON, Herman, 68, merchant, Baltimore City, August 5, 1887.
SIMON, Moses, 64, merchant, Baltimore City, February 12, 1899.
SIMONS, Dr. James, 68, surgeon, U.S. Army, Baltimore City, November 11, 1885.

SIMPSON, Achilles, 90, merchant, Baltimore City, March 12, 1882.
SIMPSON, Andrew, 93, retired, Baltimore City, February 16, 1904.
SIMPSON, Dr. G____ W____, 71, Baltimore City, March 18, 1912.
SIMPSON, James A., n.a., artist, Baltimore City, May 4, 1880.
SIMPSON, James T., 83, Baltimore City, August 17, 1898.
SIMPSON, John A., 67, printer, Baltimore City, December 31, 1901.
SIMPSON, R____, 51, granite cutter, Baltimore City, December 17, 1881.
SIMPSON, William A., 69, merchant, Baltimore City, January 31, 1901.
SINCLAIR, Dr. William B., 76, physician, Baltimore City, September 27, 1895.
SINDALL, D____ P____, 78, Evergreen Lawn (sic), October 7, 1911.
SINDALL, Samuel, 54, merchant, Baltimore City, February 17, 1879.
SINGEWALD, Traugott, 68, retired, Baltimore City, March 30, 1884.
SINGLETON, Philip, n.a., merchant, Baltimore City, November 30, 1896.
SINN, Charles W., n.a, Frederick, Frederick County, April 30, 1893.
SINN, Edward, 83, Frederick, Frederick County, July 19, 1902.
SINSKEY, J____ Frederick, 47, police sergeant, Baltimore City, June 1, 1886.
SISSON, Hugh, 73, marble manufacturer, Baltimore City, August 31, 1893.
SISSON, J____ B____, n.a., Baltimore City, August 8, 1910.
SISSON, William P., 91, retired, Baltimore City, July 7, 1891.
SKINNER, George W., 75, shipbuilder, Baltimore City, January 16, 1894.
SKINNER, J____ A____, 90, shipbuilder, Baltimore City, February 25, 1908.
SKINNER, Trueman, 52, merchant, Baltimore City, November 14, 1882.
SKINNER, Walter, 68, St. Michaels, Talbot County, February 14, 1913.
SKINNER, Washington H., 75, Cambridge, Dorchester County, February 25, 1901.
SKINNER, Dr. Wilbur F., 54, physician, Baltimore City, November 16, 1893.
SKINNER, William H., 68, shipbuilder, Baltimore City, April 9, 1891.
SKINNER, Captain William J., 59, mariner, Baltimore City, May 8, 1899.
SLACK, William D., 44, superintendent, House of Correction, Baltimore City, January 26, 1898.
SLADE, Christopher, 81, former, Baltimore County, July 3, 1906.
SLADE, Louis, F., 75, Baltimore County, September 29, 1905.
SLADE, Nelson W., 79, merchant, Baltimore City, May 25, 1881.
SLADE, William, 83, Baltimore County, August 17, 1905.
SLAGLE, Charles W., 77, financier, Baltimore City, May 7, 1905.
SLAGLE, David W., 56, merchant, Baltimore City, November 13, 1893.

SLARROW, Rev. J____ M____, 49, Baltimore City, June 5, 1906.
SLATER, "Gus," 55, Baltimore City, October 19, 1910.
SLATER, R____ J____, 64, Baltimore City, May 3, 1902.
SLATER, Robert, 75, retired, Baltimore City, November 18, 1896.
SLATER, Thomas W., 64, railroad conductor, Baltimore City, December 14, 1890.
SLAVIN, Robert, 39, minstrel, Baltimore City, December 29, 1892.
SLEMERS, William J., 51, lawyer, Baltimore City, January 29, 1905.
SLEMMER, Captain Lloyd, 79, mariner, Baltimore City, September 5, 1890.
SLESINGER, Moses, 73, merchant, Baltimore City, January 14, 1900.
SLICER, Edward A., 90, retired merchant, Baltimore City, February 3, 1901.
SLINGLUFF, Charles Bohn, 68, manufacturer, Baltimore City, July 1, 1899.
SLINGLUFF, Dr. Frank, 68, Baltimore City, June 13, 1914.
SLINGLUFF, Jesse, 68, bank president, Baltimore City, June 20, 1882.
SLINGLUFF, Josiah H., 59, merchant, Baltimore City, January 31, 1895.
SLINGLUFF, R____ Sewell, 34, Baltimore City, December 27, 1901.
SLIVER, A____ P____, 55, Harford County, September 24, 1905.
SLOAN, David, 62, Cumberland, Allegany County, April 16, 1908.
SLOAN, Judge David W., 52, Cumberland, Allegany County, August 9, 1902.
SLOAN, James, 88, retired, Baltimore City, February 17, 1885.
SLOAN, James, 66, merchant, Baltimore City, September 1, 1891.
SLOAN, James, Jr., 66, bank president, Baltimore City, May 13, 1900.
SLOAN, John J., 59, manufacturer, Baltimore City, July 11, 1901.
SLOTHOWER, George E., 68, retired, Baltimore City, December 10, 1897.
SMALL, George, 65, merchant, Baltimore City, April 11, 1891.
SMALL, John, Jr., 69, attorney, Baltimore City, October 26, 1878.
SMALL, Josiah, 84, merchant, Baltimore City, November 24, 1881.
SMALL, W____ H____, 85, Baltimore City, February 13, 1909.
SMALL, William H., 56, attorney, Baltimore City, June 27, 1879.
SMEDLEY, Enos, n.a., Towson, Baltimore County, January 8, 1892.
SMILEY, Robert, 84, retired, Baltimore City, March 8, 1886.
SMITH, A____ J____, 67, Elkton, Cecil County, December 28, 1908.
SMITH, A____ K____, 76, Trego, Washington County, January 31, 1910.
SMITH, Dr. Alan Penniman, 58, surgeon, Baltimore City, July 18, 1898.
SMALL, Albert, 58, attorney, Hagerstown, Washington County, December 23, 1898.
SMITH, Albert G., Ridgely, Caroline County, October 10, 1901.
SMITH, Andrew, 57, editor, Baltimore City, March 8, 1879.
SMITH, Asa H., 77, manufacturer, Baltimore City, February 5, 1901.
SMITH, Benjamin F., 85, banker, Baltimore City, February 25, 1899.

SMITH, C_____ Hart, 68, manufacturer, Baltimore City, June 29, 1895.
SMITH, Chandler P., 54, broker, Baltimore City, March 15, 1900.
SMITH, Charles G., n.a., druggist, Baltimore City, November 3, 1898.
SMITH, Edward P., 70, Cambridge, Dorchester County, May 8, 1905.
SMITH, Dr. F_____ B_____, 85, Frederick Frederick County, November 5, 1912.
SMITH, Dr. Francis F., 72, banker, Westminster, Carroll County, September 17, 1900.
SMITH, Frederick H., n.a., civil engineer, Baltimore City, December 24, 1898.
SMITH, G_____ W_____, Jr., 74, Hagerstown, Washington County, February 28, 1908.
SMITH, G_____ W_____ W_____, Sr., 71, butcher, Baltimore City, December 19, 1902.
SMITH, George A., 60, merchant, Baltimore City, October 25, 1903.
SMITH, George L., n.a., teacher, Baltimore City, June 25, 1892.
SMITH, H_____ Tillard, 45, attorney, Baltimore City, May 27, 1881.
SMITH, Henry, Sr., 59, builder, Baltimore City, September 22, 1890.
SMITH, Henry C., 59, merchant, Baltimore City, January 26, 1886.
SMITH, Henry C. A., 31, attorney, Baltimore City, March 23, 1882.
SMITH, Henry G., 53, editor, Baltimore City, September 17, 1880.
SMITH, Major J_____ C_____, 78, Baltimore City, March 12, 1912.
SMITH, J_____ Hume, 57, merchant, Baltimore City, September 5, 1904.
SMITH, James, 78, builder, Baltimore City, April 5, 1902.
SMALL, Jesse W., 86, Baltimore City, October 17, 1897.
SMITH, John W., 57, organist, Baltimore City, February 27, 1894.
SMITH, Joseph H., 58, Baltimore City, December 28, 1911.
SMITH, Rev. Dr. Joseph T., 87, Baltimore City, April 11, 1906.
SMITH, Dr. Josiah F., 69, Hagerstown, Washington County, October 3, 1883.
SMITH, Mrs. Julietta, 85, Baltimore City, April 12, 1883.
SMITH, Lewis, 83, ship joiner, Baltimore City, April 17, 1883.
SMITH, Lewis C., 43, former president of C. & O. Canal, Hagerstown, Washington County, November 20, 1886.
SMITH, Dr. Lloyd H., 45, Easton, Talbot County, April 3, 1898.
SMITH, Marshall P., 52, retired, Baltimore City, February 7, 1884.
SMITH, Nelson R., 65, produce dealer, Baltimore City, June 1, 1883.
SMITH, Mrs. R_____, 97, Harford County, August 30, 1881.
SMITH, Rev. R_____ H_____ (M.E.), 78, Baltimore City, December 29, 1902.
SMITH, Richards C., 83, retired, Baltimore City, December 26, 1897.
SMITH, Robert M., 80, druggist, Baltimore City, February 1, 1893.
SMITH, Robert T., 85, conveyancer, Baltimore City, November 22, 1899.
SMITH, Rodney B., 75, merchant, Baltimore City, April 3, 1902.

SMITH, Dr. Rudolph, 42, Annapolis, Anne Arundel County, June 29, 1914.
SMITH, Samuel R., 70, pork packer, Baltimore City, October 5, 1879.
SMITH, Samuel W., 87, retired, Baltimore City, December 16, 1887.
SMITH, Seabury, 51, merchant, Baltimore City, September 8, 1892.
SMITH, Sylvester, 76, Ridgely, Caroline County, March 28, 1898.
SMITH, T_____ W_____, 82, journalist, Baltimore City, May 4, 1909.
SMITH, Thomas, 54, merchant, Baltimore City, November 23, 1881.
SMITH, Thomas T., 49, bank cashier, Baltimore City, July 23, 1880.
SMITH, Sergeant W_____ D_____, 59, Baltimore City, April 20, 1913.
SMITH, W_____ P_____, 63, detective, Baltimore City, November 16, 1891.
SMITH, Dr. W_____ P_____, 34, physician, Baltimore City, July 18, 1902.
SMITH, Walter N., n.a., druggist, Baltimore City, November 13, 1905.
SMITH, William C., 65, sea captain, Baltimore City, February 18, 1880.
SMITH, Dr. William G., n.a., Salisbury, Wicomico County, January 31, 1913.
SMITH, William J., 55, former postmaster, Elkton, Cecil County, June 13, 1906.
SMITH, Willoughby N., 60, Baltimore City, April 22, 1910.
SMOOT, Dr. Andrew Jackson, 77, LaPlata, Charles County, April 11, 1906.
SMOOT, Charles B., 71, merchant, Baltimore City, July 30, 1882.
SMOOT, Colonel L_____ R_____, 69, secretuary, utility company, Baltimore City, April 28, 1892.
SMULL, David B., 87, veteran, War of 1812, December 20, 1886.
SMYRK, Alfred E., 77, retired, Baltimore City, April 7, 1903.
SMYTHE, Rev. Herbert V. (P.E.), n.a., Baltimore City, July 21, 1881.
SNEBLEY, H_____ Chew, 90, retired, Baltimore City, March 13, 1905.
SNEERINGER, William J., 76, Baltimore City, December 12, 1913.
SNEIDER, C_____ E_____, 63, firearms manufacturer, Baltimore City, February 17, 1892.
SNOUFFER, George W., 79, Frederick County, December 3, 1893.
SNOW, Captain C_____ F_____, 68, Baltimore City, November 29, 1908.
SNOWDEN, Charles Alexander, 68, civil engineer, Baltimore City, February 15, 1899.
SNOW, E_____ J_____, 81, Baltimore City, February 28, 1910.
SNOWDEN, Harry W., 73, Baltimore City, March 2, 1914.
SNOWDEN, Henry, 73, manufacturer, Baltimore City, January 16, 1894.
SNOWDEN, Rev. John B. (M.E.), 84, black, Westminster, Carroll County, September 8, 1885.
SNOWDEN, John Thomas, 71, Baltimore City, March 9, 1894.
SNOWDEN, Philip L., 40, merchant, Baltimore City, April 11, 1904.

SNOWDEN, Colonel Philip M., 79, Towson, Baltimore County, March 27, 1910.
SNOWDEN, Samuel, 61, attorney, Baltimore City, November 9, 1894.
SNOWDEN, Dr. Wilton, 80, Laurel, Prince George's County, November 25, 1897.
SNYDER, Rev. George W., 72, Hagerstown, Washington County, November 18, 1913.
SNYDER, Henry, 77, merchant, Baltimore City, May 27, 1879.
SNYDER, John H., 70, builder, Baltimore City, December 12, 1898.
SNYDER, William C., 88, bank employee, Baltimore City, November 12, 1881.
SOHL, J_____ Adam, 59, retired, Baltimore City, March 2, 1906.
SOHL, John, 64, druggist, Baltimore City, August 4, 1905.
SOLDEN, G_____ C_____, 63, civil engineer, Baltimore City, January 26, 1902.
SOLLERS, Basil, 56, educator, Baltimore City, July 8, 1909.
SOLLERS, G_____ L_____, 69, Hamilton, Maryland, November 20, 1908.
SOLLERS, Thomas O., 74, bookkeeper, Baltimore City, July 22, 1881.
SOLLIDAY, A_____ C_____, 75, Hagerstown, Washington County, December 1, 1907.
SOLOMON, Isaac, 76, Solomons Island, St. Mary's County, September 15, 1895.
SOMERVELL, William C., 39, Calvert County, January 21, 1901.
SOMMER, J_____ W_____, n.a., scenic painter, Baltimore City, November 27, 1902.
SOMMERFIELD, John, 68, brewer, Baltimore City, April 29, 1899.
SOMMERLOCK, J_____ F_____, 63, former Councilman, Baltimore City, April 11, 1896.
SONNEBORN, Myer, 83, Baltimore City, November 5, 1912.
SONNEBORN, Samuel, 72, retired, Baltimore City, January 26, 1897.
SOPER, Edward, 75, auctioneer, Baltimore City, November 3, 1894.
SOPER, Horace, 70, registrar, Agricultural College, Baltimore City, October 25, 1889.
SOPER, Samuel J., n.a., auctioneer, Baltimore City, April 16, 1889.
SOPER, Captain William T., 54, mariner, Baltimore City, August 29, 1894.
SOTHORON, J_____ H_____, 85, St. Mary's County, April 12, 1893.
SOURIN, Rev. Edward J. (R.C.), 77, Baltimore City, May 20, 1888.
SOUTHERLAND, Rev. S_____ B_____, 90, Baltimore City, September 5, 1907.
SOUTHGATE, Rev. Dr. William S. (P.E.), 66, Annapolis, Anne Arundel County, May 21, 1899.
SPALDING, Dr. A_____ J_____, 71, physician, Leonardtown, St. Mary's County, October 6, 1897.
SPALDING, Mrs. Charity M., 73, Baltimore City, February 26, 1885.
SPALDING, Rev. E_____ W_____ (P.E.), 68, Baltimore City, October 3, 1902.
SPALDING, Dr. John T., 50, Leonardtown, St. Mary's County, July 24, 1892.

SPANGLER, Rev. J____ N____ (M.E.), 67, Baltimore City, December 20, 1887.
SPANGLER, James D., 38, police sergeant, Baltimore City, August 19, 1878.
SPARKS, Mrs. C____ R____, 74, Baltimore City, December 31, 1912.
SPARLIN, Samuel, 80, clergyman, Baltimore City, July 10, 1880.
SPATES, Alfred, 79, Cumberland, Allegany County, November 17, 1892.
SPEAKE, Rev. William F., 61, Baltimore City, May 15, 1892.
SPEAR, Alexander L., 67, jeweler, Baltimore City, April 3, 1891.
SPEAR, P____ F____, 59, merchant, Baltimore City, September 28, 1898.
SPRECHER, Dr. Samuel, 85, Hagerstown, Washington County, January 16, 1906.
SPEDDEN, John L., 64, Cambridge, Dorchester County, October 24, 1911.
SPEDDEN, Oliver W., 63, Baltimore City, July 4, 1897.
SPEDDEN, Captain R____ M____, 60, Baltimore City, April 21, 1911.
SPEDDEN, Rufus, 77, Cambridge, Dorchester County, January 30, 1912.
SPENCE, Carroll, 78, Baltimore City, August 9, 1896.
SPENCE, Charles L. S., 66, retired, Baltimore City, July 20, 1887.
SPENCE, Charles R., 40, financier, Baltimore City, January 31,
SPENCE, Charles W., 44, steamboat captain, Claiborne, Talbot County, October 22, 1904.
SPENCE, John S., 71, Cambridge, Dorchester County, March 4, 1905.
SPENCER, A____, n.a., animal trainer, Baltimore City, October 24, 1902.
SPENCER, Rev. C____ S____, 72, Annapolis, Anne Arundel County, October 20, 1906.
SPENCER, Edward, 49, author, Baltimore City, July 17, 1883.
SPENCER, John M., 65, merchant, Baltimore City, November 29, 1881.
SPERRY, William, n.a., merchant, Baltimore City, September 2, 1881.
SPICER, Dr. Hiram L., 57, Baltimore City, February 12, 1898.
SPICER, Hiram Louis, n.a., Baltimore City, September 29, 1914.
SPICER, John, 84, retired, Baltimore City, December 13, 1884.
SPICKNALL, John W., n.a., Dunkirk, Calvert County, December 22, 1893.
SPIELMAN, Louis, 51, merchant, Baltimore City, June 29, 1904.
SPIER, Andrew, 60, president, coal company, Baltimore City, December 8, 1886.
SPIES, Charles L., 83, dancing master, Baltimore City, December 7, 1894.
SPIES, George L., 50, dancing master, Baltimore City, July 26, 1890.
SPIES, John G., 75, brickmaker, Baltimore City, September 1, 1882.
SPIES, Ludwig W., 85, merchant tailor, Baltimore City, January 26, 1901.

SPILCKER, George H., 73, merchant, Baltimore City, February 26, 1889.
SPILLER, Robert M., 70, merchant, Baltimore City, January 10, 1878.
SPILLMAN, Henry, 82, Baltimore County, February 11, 1901.
SPONSLER, Charles R., 56, printer, Baltimore City, December 28, 1880.
SPRAGINS, S. Bolling, 74, merchant, Baltimore City, July 5, 1904.
SPRANKLING, Dr. C_____ W_____, 61, veterinarian, Baltimore City, June 23, 1892.
SPRIGG, Frederick, 64, bank president, Baltimore City, December 23, 1886.
SPRINGER, Thomas H., 70, broker, Baltimore City, September 20, 1897.
SPURRIER, G_____ D_____, 64, conveyancer, Baltimore City, September 21, 1879.
SPURRIER, Harry R., 43, merchant, Baltimore City, January 31, 1902.
SPURRIER, John, 64, engineer, Baltimore City, December 15, 1908.
STAB, George, 66, brewer, Baltimore City, November 8, 1895.
STABLER, Alban G., 77, retired, Baltimore City, May 7, 1903.
STABLER, Caleb, 84, Alloway, Montgomery County, October 26, 1883.
STABLER, Edmund, 59, Baltimore County, June 3, 1905.
STABLER, Edward, 89, postmaster for more than 50 years at Sandy Spring, Montgomery County, September 4, 1883.
STABLER, Thomas S., 73, Baltimore City, March 29, 1909.
STABLER, Warwick M., 79, Sandy Spring, Montgomery County, November 25, 1912.
STABLER, William H., 80, near Sandy Spring, Montgomery County, February 22, 1883.
STACK, Mrs. J_____ K_____, n.a., actress, Baltimore City, June 12, 1910.
STACK, John, 75, Baltimore City, May 7, 1907.
STAFFORD, Dr. Andrew, 60, Caroline County, May 27, 1892.
STAFFORD, W_____ J_____, 60, merchant tailor, Baltimore City, November 15, 1902.
STAKE, Judge Edward, 56, Hagerstown, Washington County, November 16, 1902.
STALLINGS, Albert K., 50, Annapolis, Anne Arundel County, March 3, 1905.
STALLO, Frank C., 31, Baltimore City, March 20, 1914.
STANDIFORD, Edward P., 74, contractor, Baltimore City, January 24, 1903.
STANHOPE, L_____ G_____, 79, Hagerstown, Washington County, April 5, 1898.
STANLEY, Charles H., n.a., Laurel, Prince George's County, December 20, 1913.
STANLEY, Rev. Harvey (P.E.), 75, Glendale, Prince George's County, January 25, 1885.
STANSBURY, Abraham, 90, Baltimore City, May 6, 1897.
STANSBURY, Colonel Elijah, 93, former mayor of Baltimore and president, Old Defenders Association, December 19, 1883.
STANSBURY, Thomas, 80, physician, Baltimore City, July 6, 1883.
STANSBURY, W_____ T_____, 78, compositor, The Sun, February 18, 1894.
STAPLETON, John, 74, retired, Baltimore City, May 28, 1902.
STARKEY, Rev. J_____ T_____ M_____ (R.C.), 36, Baltimore City, April 19, 1881.

STARR, Benjamin F., 63, manufacturer, Baltimore City, January 26, 1882.
STARR, Edward G., 72, justice, Baltimore City, November 28, 1882.
STARR, George W., n.a., Baltimore City, October 8, 1898.
STARR, Dr. Hezekiah, 82, Baltimore City, October 23, 1898.
STARR, Rev. Jesse C., 72, Westminster, Carroll County, February 26, 1914.
STARR, William H., 69, banker, Westminster, Carroll County, September 17, 1900.
STARTZMAN, Daniel R., 50, Hagerstown, Washington County, April 26, 1903.
STAUF, Frederick 58, tailor, Baltimore City, September 6, 1886.
STAUFFER, D_____ Edward, 35, teacher, Baltimore City, September 30, 1898.
STAYLOR, John F., 59, cattle dealer, Baltimore City, November 9, 1885.
STAYMAN, Dr. J_____ A_____, 70, physician, Baltimore City, January 31, 1897.
STAYMAN, John K., 58, musician, Baltimore City, July 4, 1882.
STEARNS, George, 78, retired, Baltimore City, January 13, 1896.
STEELE, Isaac Nevett, 82, Baltimore City attorney, April 11, 1891.
STEELE, Joseph H., 77, Chesapeake City, Cecil County, December 13, 1913.
STEELE, Dr. Thomas B., 83, Cambridge, Dorchester County, June 22, 1905.
STEEVER, Daniel, 60, turfman, Baltimore City, July 24, 1887.
STEEVER, Edward W., 64, collector, Baltimore City, May 18, 1883.
STEFFENS, Captain Henry, 73, mariner, Baltimore City, October 8, 1906.
STEHL, John. 66, druggist, Baltimore City, June 29, 1882.
STEIN, Dr. A_____ E_____, 46, physician, Baltimore City, November 16, 1884.
STEIN, Christopher, 95, Baltimore City, January 18, 1908.
STEIN, Joseph, 76, merchant, Baltimore City, July 11, 1892.
STEIN, Levi, 44, merchant, Baltimore City, December 11, 1882.
STEIN, Mayer, 74, banker, Baltimore City, June 16, 1897.
STEIN, Michael, 48, banker, Baltimore City, January 24, 1903.
STEIN, Samuel, 65, banker, Baltimore City, August 14, 1893.
STEINBRENNER, George F., 77, Baltimore City, November 11, 1897.
STEINER, General John A., 86, Frederick County, April 20, 1902.
STEINER, Lewis, 79, retired merchant, Baltimore City, May 20, 1903.
STEINER, Dr. Lewis H., 65, librarian, Baltimore City, February 18, 1892.
STEINER, Mathews, 95, retired merchant, Baltimore City, September 12, 1880.
STEMBLER, John V., 60, shoemaker, Baltimore City, March 8, 1883.
STENERNAGLE, J_____ H_____, n.a., policeman, Baltimore City, December 24, 1909.
STEPHENS, John A., 87, merchant, Baltimore City, November 6, 1895.
STEPHENSON, Alfred W., n.a., insurance, Baltimore City, July 30, 1882.

STERN, Joseph, 80, retired, Baltimore City, January 17, 1896.
STERN, Simon, 72, merchant, Baltimore City, August 1, 1903.
STERNBERG, Alexander, 52, retired, Baltimore City, May 30, 1905.
STERRETT, Samuel, 46, cotton broker, Baltimore City, September 28, 1879.
STEUART, General George H., 76, Anne Arundel County, November 22, 1903.
STEUART, Dr. J____ H____, 57, physician, Baltimore City, October 8, 1892.
STEUART, Dr. James A., 75, physician, Baltimore City, March 27, 1903.
STEVENS, Dr. E____ T____, 77, physician, Baltimore City, November 19, 1904.
STEVENS, Colonel Francis Putnam, 63, attorney, Baltimore City, September 16, 1906.
STEVENS, George O., 63, manufacturer, Baltimore City, May 9, 1898.
STEVENS, John C., 52, undertaker, Baltimore City, September 6, 1905.
STEVENS, John W., 65, Denton, Caroline County, December 21, 1894.
STEVENS, Thomas H., 77, rear admiral, U.S. Navy, Rockville, Montgomery County, May 15, 1896.
STEVENS, Colonel William H., 65, Ocean City, Worcester County, August 9, 1914.
STEVENSON, Dawson H., 60, merchant, Baltimore City, November 16, 1900.
STEVENSON, Dr. James S., 67, physician, Baltimore City, August 2, 1882.
STEVENSON, Dr. John M., 37, Union surgeon who was wounded at Gettysburg, Baltimore City, March 6, 1879.
STEVENSON, John M., 85, merchant, Baltimore City, January 28, 1904.
STEWART, Arthur, 56, Marylander who died at New York City, January 22, 1912.
STEWART, Charles, 93, railroad veteran, Baltimore City, July 7, 1897.
STEWART, Charles Morton, 72, merchant, Baltimore City, August 13, 1900.
STEWART, Columbus J., 79, merchant, Baltimore City, March 15, 1887.
STEWART, Columbus, n.a., merchant, Baltimore City, July 8, 1900.
STEWART, Ebenezer, C., 64, Baltimore City, September 20, 1879.
STEWART, Mrs. Elizabeth, 101, Baltimore City, October 1, 1882.
STEWART, Frederick A., 58, Confederate veteran, Baltimore City, September 10, 1900.
STEWART, J____ J____, Sr., 87, retired merchant, Baltimore City, October 22, 1880.
STEWART, James M., 77, journalist, Baltimore City, October 27, 1899.
STEWART, John, 72, stonecutter, Baltimore City, February 13, 1879.
STEWART, John, 74, attorney, Baltimore City, February 26, 1901.
STEWART, Joseph J., 52, lawyer, Baltimore City, January 19, 1882.
STEWART, Perry W., 75, former chief judge of the Talbot County Orphan's Court, at Easton, January 23, 1885.

STEWART, Richard B., 81, retired merchant, Baltimore City, August 15, 1900.
STEWART, Captain T____ R____, 78, Confederate veteran, Baltimore City, November 26, 1908.
STEWART, Thomas, 76, dentist, Baltimore City, August 11, 1880.
STEWART, William A., 66, judge, Baltimore City, August 26, 1892.
STEWART, William E., 88, Baltimore City, December 20, 1906.
STEWART, Dr. William F., 74, physician, Baltimore City, December 10, 1889.
STICKNEY, J____ Henry, 81, manufacturer, Baltimore City, May 3, 1893.
STIEBLER, Charles, 54, musician, Baltimore City, December 7, 1881.
STIEFF, John L., 69, piano manufacturer, Baltimore City, June 29, 1901.
STINE, C____ R____, 37, Baltimore City, December 28, 1912.
STINE, Joseph, 73, retired, Baltimore City, April 30, 1890.
STINSON, Captain R____ J____, n.a., Baltimore City, April 7, 1912.
STIRLING, Archibald, Sr., 89, retired, Baltimore City, February 16, 1888.
STIRLING, Archibald, 60, Baltimore City, May 30, 1892.
STIRLING, William, 56, merchant, Baltimore City, July 12, 1881.
STITT, Rev. Joseph B. (M.E.), 66, Hagerstown, Washington County, April 3, 1904.
STOCKBRIDGE, Henry, 62, attorney, Baltimore City, March 11, 1895.
STOCKBRIDGE, Sylvester L., 54, Baltimore City, February 11, 1897.
STOCKETT, F____ H____, 75, Annapolis, Anne Arundel County, November 22, 1896.
STOCKETT, J____ Shaaff, 69, Annapolis, Anne Arundel County, April 6, 1896.
STOCKLEY, Albert A., 64, merchant, Baltimore City, November 24, 1904.
STOCKSDALE, F____ G____, 58, merchant, Baltimore City, May 1, 1902.
STOCKSDALE, H____ C____, 30, clerk, Baltimore City, January 19, 1898.
STODDARD, G____ W____, 73, died at Atlantic City, New Jersey, December 26, 1912.
STOKES, Rev. George C. (P.E.), 80, Baltimore City, April 3, 1904.
STOKES, Dr. W____ H____, 81, physician, Baltimore City, May 7, 1893.
STOLEL, Captain William, 71, G.A.R. veteran, Baltimore City, August 20, 1908.
STONE, Frederick, 79, former judge, Maryland Court of Appeals; died in Charles County, October 17, 1899.
STONE, James H., 76, retired, Baltimore City, January 14, 1897.
STONE, Dr. James M., 80, physician, Baltimore City, June 5, 1901.
STONEBRAKER, Joseph R., 59, financier, Baltimore City, October 25, 1903.
STONESTREET, Benjamin G., 76, LaPlata, Charles County, December 10, 1905.

STORCK, Adolph, 75, manufacturer, Baltimore City, July 10, 1892.
STOREY, Norman H., 67, packer, Baltimore City, March 28, 1899.
STORK, Dr. Charles A., 46, former pastor of St. Mark's Lutheran Church in Baltimore; died at Philadelphia, December 17, 1883.
STORK, Captain W____ T____, 67, builder, Baltimore City, February 28, 1908.
STORM, Jeremiah, 81, retired, Baltimore City, May 30, 1883.
STORY, James W., 80, retired, Baltimore City, March 11, 1899.
STOTT, John, 71, merchant, Baltimore City, May 13, 1903.
STOUFFER, Daniel, 59, Washington County, March 7, 1898.
STOUFFER, Wilford R., 70, Hagerstown, Washington County, November 27, 1913.
STRASBURGER, Charles, 79, retired, Baltimore City, March 12, 1890.
STRASSBURGER, K____, 71, merchant, Baltimore City, July 10, 1892.
STRAUGHN, Dr. William D., 49, Snow Hill, Worcester County, July 29, 1913.
STRAUS, Henry, 71, brewer, Baltimore City, November 25, 1881.
STRAUS, Henry L., 61, Baltimore City, September 24, 1914.
STRAUS, Joseph H., 66, Baltimore City, May 23, 1914.
STRAUS, Levi, 87, maltster, Baltimore City, January 14, 1902.
STRAUS, Martin L., 70, merchant, Baltimore City, December 17, 1891.
STRAUS, Moses, 65, merchant, Baltimore City, September 22, 1902.
STRAUS, Moses, 74, retired, Baltimore City, June 20, 1905.
STRAUS, Solomon, 59, maltster, Baltimore City, July 13, 1903.
STRAUSS, George L., 92, retired, Baltimore City, January 28, 1894.
STRAUSS, Juda, 74, manufacturer, Baltimore City, November 8, 1904.
STRAUSS, Louis, 62, merchant, Baltimore City, June 3, 1904.
STRAUSS, Mayer, 65, Baltimore City, March 24, 1912.
STREAKER, E____, 80, Carroll County, January 23, 1908.
STREET, Charles W., 50, manufacturer, Baltimore City, February, 1905.
STREET, John C., 76, butcher, Baltimore City, October 6, 1881.
STREETT, David, 67, retired, Baltimore City, November 3, 1887.
STRETT, Dr. Frank C., 32, dentist, Baltimore City, November 25, 1901.
STRINGER, Rev. W____ R____ (M.E.), 54, Baltimore City, November 12, 1888.
STROBEL, Charles, 55, butcher, Baltimore City, July 19, 1878.
STROEBEL, Charles C., 46, postman, Baltimore City, December 25, 1900.
STROHMER, Andrew, 67, manufacturer, Baltimore City, December 20, 1899.
STROHMEYER, George L., 71, tailor, Baltimore City, January 31, 1884.
STRONG, Edward R., 68, retired, Baltimore City, September 12, 1897.
STRONG, Joseph McF., 97, coroner of Cumberland, Allegany County, December 6, 1899.

STRONG, Norton, 51, surgeon, U.S. Army (Ret.), Baltimore City, March 23, 1903.
STROUSE, Isaac, 77, wholesale clothier, Baltimore City, December 12, 1912.
STROUSE, Leopold, 60, merchant, Baltimore City, February 22, 1904.
STROUSE, Samuel, 75, Baltimore City, September 15, 1909.
STRUVE, Rev. A____ M____ (Lutheran), 23, Baltimore City, January 14, 1895.
STRYKER, Rev. Augustus P. (P.E.), 61, Baltimore City, December 25, 1891.
STUART, Henry F., 55, merchant, Baltimore City, February 19, 1903.
STUBBS, Edward S., 54, merchant, Baltimore City, February 17, 1905.
STUMP, Judge Frederick, 64, Cecil County, September 12, 1901.
STUMP, Henry, 81, June 2, 1910.
STURGEON, Edward G., 74, shipbuilder, Baltimore City, July 16, 1882.
STURGIS, John J., n.a., merchant, Snow Hill, Worcester County, November 5, 1898.
SUDLER, Dr. Thomas, n.a., coroner, Baltimore City, November 14, 1911.
SUDSBURG, General Joseph M., 76, retired, April 8, 1901.
SULLIVAN, Dr. John J., 41, physician, Baltimore City, October 4, 1895.
SULTZER, Thomas D., 74, compositor, Baltimore City, March 17, 1891.
SULLIVAN, Dr. John McKew, 50?, physician, Baltimore City, April 28, 1881.
SUMMERSON, Seth, 85, retired, Baltimore City, January 20, 1886.
SUMPTION, Thomas M., n.a., Havre de Grace, Harford County, January 13, 1897.
SUMWALT, David S., 59, ice dealer, Baltimore City, November 4, 1878.
SUMWALT, George W., 66, builder, Baltimore City, February 24, 1893.
SUMWALT, Samuel, 83, retired, Baltimore City, April 11, 1883.
SUMWALT, W_____ F_____, 56, Baltimore City, February 11, 1912.
SUNDERLAND, Daniel H., 42, manufacturer, Baltimore City, December 6, 1901.
SUNSTROM, Calvin, n.a., police lieutenant, Baltimore City, April 15, 1888.
SUPER, Frederick, 72, provision dealer, Baltimore City, October 24, 1883.
SUTER, Alexander G., 88, manufacturer, Baltimore City, August 10, 1902.
SUTER, Henry, 88, veteran, Baltimore City, October 25, 1882.
SUTER, John H., 61, court clerk, Baltimore City, February 27, 1894.
SUTHERLAND, Dr. D_____ Cameron, Jr., n.a., Baltimore City, July 11, 1914.
SUTRO, Otto, 62, merchant, Baltimore City, January 19, 1896.
SUTTON, Robert M., 74, merchant, Baltimore City, February 7, 1906.

SWAIN, Rev. Charles P. (M.E.), 41, Somerset County, May 22, 1900.
SWAIN, Edward, 62, merchant, Baltimore City, May 23, 1903.
SWAISE, Captain J____ J____, 72, died at Cascade, Virginia, December 30, 1911.
SWAN, Donnell, 56, died at Atlantic City, New Jersey, September 13, 1911.
SWANN, James, 53, Denton, Caroline County, December 5, 1901.
SWANN, Hon. Thomas, 77, former Governor of Maryland; died near Leesburg, Virginia, July 24, 1883.
SWANN, Thomas, 31, Baltimore City, March 16, 1896.
SWARTZ, Rev. Dr. Joel, 87, Baltimore City, March 16, 1914.
SWEENEY, Alfred, 62, builder, Baltimore City, June 18, 1887.
SWENTZELL, Rev. F____ (P.E.), 58, Baltimore City, October 26, 1880.
SWICK, William A., 83, police sergeant, Baltimore City, September 15, 1881.
SWINDELL, James E., 65, Baltimore City, May 28, 1895.
SWINDELL, William, 70, glass manufacturer, Baltimore City, September 27, 1891.
SWINDELL, William E., 37, manufacturer, Baltimore City, October 16, 1901.
SWINNEY, E____, 68, attorney, Baltimore City, February 26, 1902.
SWITZER, George 83, butcher, Baltimore City, September 4, 1881.
SWITZER, William, 65, butcher, Baltimore City, March 10, 1898.
SYESTER, Andrew K., 64, associate judge, Fourth Judicial Circuit of Maryland, March 25, 1891.
SYKES, James, 61, hotelier, Baltimore City, March 7, 1881.
SYLVESTER, Edward C., 66, merchant, Baltimore City, May 12, 1899.
SYLVESTER, Dr. Leo, 79, physician, Baltimore City, September 18, 1895.
SYLVESTER, S____ R____, n.a., druggist, Govanstown, October 6, 1881.
SYMINGTON, Lieutenant John, died at Monterey, California, June 28, 1914.
SYMINGTON, Thomas A., 58, insurance, Baltimore City, January 19, 1900.
SYMINGTON, Major W____ Stuart, 73, Confederate veteran, Baltimore City, June 9, 1912.
SYMINGTON, William N., 58, mining engineer, Baltimore City, December 24, 1899.
SZEMELYENI, Ernest, 64, musician, Baltimore City, March 1, 1888.
SZOLD, Rev. B____, 73, rabbi, Baltimore City, July 31, 1902.

TABB, Rev. John Bannister, 64, poet, Ellicott City, Howard County, November 19, 1909.
TABLER, A____ J____ P____, 72, merchant, Baltimore City, July 28, 1902.
TABLER, Rev. T____ F____, n.a., Cambridge, Dorchester County, January 15, 1913.
TAFEL, Rev. Louis, 69, Baltimore City, November 29, 1909.
TAGART, Enoch D., n.a., Baltimore City, June 26, 1898.
TAGART, S____ H____, 80, lawyer, Baltimore City, March 19, 1892.

TAGGART, Calvin, 71, steamboat, Baltimore City, March 18, 1887.
TAIT, John R., 75, artist and critic, Baltimore City, July 29, 1909.
TALBOT, Hattersley W., 70, Rockville, Montgomery County, May 1, 1912.
TALBOTT, Alvin, 48, ticket agent, Baltimore City, April 7, 1891.
TALBOTT, Benson, 83, Gaithersburg, Montgomery County, December 30, 1902.
TALBOTT, Captain C_____ M_____, 55, mariner, Baltimore City, August 2, 1888.
TALBOTT, Charles A., 56, printer, Baltimore City, April 25, 1881.
TALBOTT, E_____ N_____, 74, Forest Park, February 20, 1912.
TALBOTT, George F., 29, printer, Baltimore City, December 24, 1880.
TALBOTT, John A., n.a., compositor, The Sun, May 2, 1894.
TALBOTT, Leon, n.a., fireman, Baltimore City, February 24, 1892.
TALBOTT, Mrs. J. F. C., 73, Lutherville, Baltimore County, February 15, 1913.
TALBOTT, Senator Joseph Francis, 41, Calvert County, February 24, 1892.
TALBOTT, N_____ B_____, 63, printer, Baltimore City, March 25, 1892.
TALBOTT, William R., 69, piano maker, Baltimore City, April 21, 1881.
TALL, Dr. R_____ J_____ H_____, 59, physician, Baltimore City, May 12, 1902.
TALLEY, B_____ N_____, 49, insurance agent, Baltimore City, October 15, 1898.
TALLMAN, William, 66, supervisor of immigration, Baltimore City, August 11, 1891.
TANEY, Joseph A., 73, Montgomery County, December 22, 1894.
TANEYHILL, Professor J. E. W., 54, Baltimore City, December 31, 1906.
TANKERSLEY, Hiram D., 72, Baltimore City, December 23, 1913.
TANNEYHILL, J_____ E_____, 61, Baltimore City, December 2, 1912.
TARBUTTON, William A., 68, professor of music, Baltimore City, July 7, 1885.
TARR, Major F_____ C_____, 71, Baltimore City, April 22, 1911.
TATE, James E., 62, merchant, Baltimore City, December 11, 1897.
TATE, John L., 40, Baltimore City, January 24, 1900.
TATE, Robert W., 65, crier, Circuit Court, Annapolis, Anne Arundel County, June 23, 1906.
TAW, Abraham, 82, druggist, Baltimore City, October 25, 1897.
TAWNEY, George H., 54, hotelier, Baltimore City, September 13, 1896.
TAYLOR, A_____ K_____, 42, hatter, Baltimore City, March 19, 1902.
TAYLOR, Colonel A_____ S_____, 82, Confederate veteran, Baltimore City, May 26, 1899.
TAYLOR, Charles F., 70, retired, Baltimore City, February 26, 1901.

TAYLOR, Charles R., 85, banker, Baltimore City, March 15, 1900.
TAYLOR, Clark, 96, Chestertown, Kent County, May 16, 1912.
TAYLOR, Edward John, 73, manufacturer, Baltimore City, April 1, 1903.
TAYLOR, Edward W., 51, merchant, Baltimore City, October 6, 1901.
TAYLOR, G_____ B_____ S_____, 79, Pikesville, Baltimore County, July 21, 1908.
TAYLOR, Lieutenant Harry L., 35, Rev. Marine., Baltimore City, January 23, 1901.
TAYLOR, Henry, 75, bookseller, Baltimore City, December 3, 1898.
TAYLOR, General Henry S., 62, retired, Baltimore City, December 12, 1886.
TAYLOR, Hezekiah, 83, retired, Baltimore City, May 16, 1883.
TAYLOR, Hezekiah, 80, newsdealer, Baltimore City, December 6, 1897.
TAYLOR, Isaiah, 62, retired, Baltimore City, February 12, 1884.
TAYLOR, Captain James Frisby, 77, mariner, Baltimore City, April 18, 1897.
TAYLOR, Joseph J., 70, banker, Baltimore City, February 12, 1894.
TAYLOR, Dr. Melville, 33, physician, Baltimore City, September 16, 1884.
TAYLOR, Dr. Milton N., 79, physician, Baltimore City, February 25, 1895.
TAYLOR, Mortimer, 77, conductor, Baltimore City, April 5, 1887.
TAYLOR, Rev. Riley T., 83, Baltimore City, November 2, 1909.
TAYLOR, Robert A., 89, retired, Baltimore City, July 23, 1901.
TAYLOR, Rev. Robert H. (P.E.), 62, Baltimore City, December 7, 1903.
TAYLOR, Robert Q., 76, hatter, Baltimore City, June 23, 1895.
TAYLOR, Captain S_____ M_____, 70, Gratitude, Kent County, July 23, 1912.
TAYLOR, Samuel W., 62, cigar manufacturer, Baltimore City, August 13, 1894.
TAYLOR, Talbot J., 47, merchant, Baltimore City, January 19, 1879.
TAYLOR, Thomas I., 47, Sun correspondent, Annapolis, Anne Arundel County, May 13, 1901.
TAYLOR, William, 105, Baltimore City, May 31, 1896.
TAYLOR, Captain William, 66, Civil War veteran, April 6, 1902.
TAYLOR, William H., 48, merchant, Baltimore City, November 5, 1901.
TAYLOR, Captain William H., 70, Brooklandville, Baltimore County, April 3, 1914.
TAYLOR, William W., 75, banker, Baltimore City, March 15, 1898.
TEACKLE, Dr. St. George W., 53, physician, Baltimore City, August 30, 1902.
TEGMEYER, John H., 79, civil engineer, Baltimore City, July 4, 1901.
TEMPLEMAN, James A., 55, physician, Baltimore City, October 27, 1894.
TERRELL, John M., 62, Elkton, Cecil County, July 30, 1902.

TERRELL, Joseph S., 87, Elkton, Cecil County, January 18, 1904.
TERRY, T_____ W_____, 47, former Councilman, Baltimore City, May 7, 1890.
TEUFEL, John, 60, undertaker, Baltimore City, November 2, 1894.
TEWES, Rev. Francis J. (R.C.), 35, Baltimore City, June 24, 1889.
THAYER, Professor N_____ H_____, 76, Baltimore City College, January 17, 1883.
THELIN, William T., 59, auditor, B. & O. Railroad, Baltimore City, November 17, 1894.
THEOPHILIA, Mother Mary (Crescentia Baur), 75, superioress, Notre Dame College, Baltimore City, July 11, 1904.
THIEDE, W_____ F_____, 89, Baltimore City, 23, 1911.
THIEMEYER, William E., 71, accountant, Baltimore City, January 12, 1903.
THIENEMAN, Charles, 38, druggist, Baltimore City, December 7, 1882.
THIES, Henry W., n.a., artist, Baltimore City, November 5, 1897.
THIRSTON, John B., 86, builder, Hagerstown, Washington County, January 4, 1898.
THOM, J_____ Pembroke, 71, physician, Baltimore City, August 21, 1899.
THOM, Mrs. J_____ Pembroke, 72, Baltimore City, March 26, 1912.
THOM, Pembroke L., 40, Baltimore City, July 3, 1901.
THOMAS, Captain Charles, 78, U.S. Navy, Baltimore City, February 24, 1891.
THOMAS, Dr. Charles H., 52, physician, Baltimore City, May 13, 1900.
THOMAS, Rev. David (Methodist), 87, Baltimore City, January 3, 1895.
THOMAS, E_____, 54, trustee, almshouse, Baltimore City, January 11, 1879.
THOMAS, Edward L., 77, retired, Baltimore City, May 7, 1898.
THOMAS, Dr. Edwin S., 72, physician, Baltimore City, October 17, 1900.
THOMAS, Francis W., 41, manufacturer, Baltimore City, February 23, 1897.
THOMAS, Dr. George, 39, physician, Baltimore City, June 3, 1897.
THOMAS, George P., 58, insurance, Baltimore City, November 17, 1887.
THOMAS, J_____ Hanson, 47, railway treasurer, Baltimore City, December 20, 1888.
THOMAS, Dr. Jacob D., 67, Frederick County, November 22, 1894.
THOMAS, Dr. James, 70, physician, Baltimore City, October 18, 1892.
THOMAS, John Henry, 74, attorney, Baltimore City, July 15, 1898.
THOMAS, J_____ R_____ D_____, 65, realtor, Baltimore City, March 18, 1889.
THOMAS, Dr. James Carey, 64, physician, Baltimore City, November 9, 1897.
THOMAS, Dr. James H., 82, Cambridge, Dorchester County, June 20, 1909.

THOMAS, John H., 69, former mayor of Annapolis; died there, Anne Arundel County, March 9, 1904.
THOMAS, John L., Sr., 85, merchant, Baltimore City, July 27, 1880.
THOMAS, Joseph A., 71, attorney, Baltimore City, April 12, 1900.
THOMAS, Sister Mary, 76, Mount de Sales Convent, Catonsville, Baltimore County, December 23, 1891.
THOMAS, Morris A., 59, broker and agent, Baltimore City, June 12, 1903.
THOMAS, Philip Francis, 80, former Governor of Maryland, October 2, 1890.
THOMAS, R____ M____, 75, merchant, Frostburg, Allegany County, July 13, 1900.
THOMAS, R____ W____, 48, appraiser, Baltimore City, April 22, 1902.
THOMAS, Richard, n.a., Elkton, Cecil County, November 1, 1892.
THOMAS, General Richard, 90, bank cashier, Easton, Talbot County, October 14, 1906.
THOMAS, Dr. Richard Henry, 51, physician, Baltimore City, October 3, 1904.
THOMAS, Dr. S____ F____, 66, Frederick County, November 22, 1907.
THOMAS, Captain W____ N____, 55, mariner, Baltimore City, April 20, 1904.
THOMAS, William Lansdale, 71, St. Mary's County, January 27, 1900.
THOMPSON, Albert E., 57, pharmacist, Baltimore City, August 25, 1906.
THOMPSON, Albert W., 56, historical painter; died at Summit, New Jersey, August 30, 1896.
THOMPSON, George R., 59, retired, Baltimore City, December 15, 1887.
THOMPSON, Goerge W., 59, hotelier, Baltimore City, June 20, 1901.
THOMPSON, H____ F____, 80, Baltimore City, October 10, 1910.
THOMPSON, Hedge, 65, Talbot County, August 5, 1900.
THOMAS, Dr. J____ Hanson, 68, banker, Baltimore City, July 15, 1881.
THOMAS, James P., 62, broker, Baltimore City, August 29, 1881.
THOMPSON, Charles, 81, retired, Baltimore City, April 3, 1884.
THOMPSON, Gustavus A., 82, retired, Baltimore City, January 9, 1883.
THOMPSON, John, 55, agent for the poor, Baltimore City, June 1, 1896.
THOMPSON, John T., n.a., lawyer, Howard County, April 18, 1906.
THOMPSON, John W., 39, merchant, Baltimore City, November 30, 1881.
THOMPSON, Joshua A., 86, retired, Baltimore City, October 21, 1905.
THOMPSON, Marcellus, 60, Charles County, November 16, 1898.
THOMPSON, Peter, 82, retired, Baltimore City, January 22, 1900.
THOMPSON, R____ H____, 52, railroad superintendent, Baltimore City, February 3, 1889.

THOMPSON, R____ W____, 60, dentist, Baltimore City, August 30, 1886.
THOMPSON, S____ Chapman, 63, merchant, St. Mary's County, October 15, 1900.
THOMPSON, Samuel P., 57, Baltimore City Collector, January 8, 1887.
THOMPSON, William, 71, silver merchant, Baltimore City, October 31, 1894.
THOMPSON, William, 64, Hyattsville, Prince George's County, December 8, 1911.
THOMPSON, William H., 66, captain, Baltimore City, March 14, 1879.
THOMPSON, William H., 74, teacher, Annapolis, Anne Arundel County, June 11, 1893.
THOMSEN, John Jacob, n.a., druggist, Baltimore City, November 22, 1892.
THOMSON, C____ H____, 34, paymaster, U.S. Navy, Baltimore City, July 13, 1881.
THOMSON, Edward H., 88, retired, Baltimore City, February 21, 1899.
THOMSON, Edward H., 53, banker, Baltimore City, December 27, 1906.
THOMSON, Henry A., 80, banker, Baltimore City, March 2, 1880.
THOMSON, Dr. I____ Davis, n.a., physician, Baltimore City, June 14, 1881.
THOMSON, Lawrence, 70, merchant, Baltimore City, September 27, 1889.
THOMSON, William, 70, journalist, Baltimore City, January 29, 1887.
THORBURN, H____ C____, 57, attorney, Baltimore City, October 15, 1898.
THORNE, Rev. Levi, 53, Baltimore City, January 21, 1879.
THORNTON, Benaijah, 72, Baltimore City, April 14, 1900.
THORNTON, James M., 60, stewsrd, Baltimore City, November 1, 1886.
THORNTON, Stephen, 81, retired, Baltimore City, December 17, 1884.
THORNTON, William E., 40, druggist, Baltimore City, February 11, 1888.
THURSBY, David U., 68, shipbuilder, Baltimore City, April 21, 1900.
THURSTON, Captain G____ A____, 58, U.S. Army, Baltimore City, July 13, 1892.
THURSTON, James, 63, storage business, Baltimore City, April 13, 1904.
THURSTON, Mary Jane, n.a., Catonsville, Baltimore County, November 1, 1911.
TIDY, John B., 43, lawyer, Baltimore City, December 2, 1884.
TIDY, John B., 79, former Baltimore City Councilman, November 13, 1893.
TIEPEL, Charles K., 60, druggist, Baltimore City, September 23, 1900.
TIERNAN, C____ B____, 72, Baltimore City, October 31, 1912.
TIERNAN, Charles, 87, retired, Baltimore City, January 12, 1886.

TIERNAN, Luke, 68, retired, Baltimore City, December 29, 1890.
TIERNAN, Mary Spear, 56, author, Baltimore City, January 13, 1891.
TIERNEY, Michael, V., 52, former mayor of Hyattsville, Prince George's County, September 12, 1906.
TIFFANY, George P., 58, retired, Baltimore City, September 1, 1886.
TIFFANY, Rev. Dr. O____ H____, 66, Baltimore City, October 24, 1891.
TIFFANY, Osmond, 72, retired, Baltimore City, November 18, 1895.
TILGHMAN, C____ C____, 43, Centreville, Queen Anne's County, January 14, 1907.
TILGHMAN, Dr. Charles H., 60, Baltimore City, April 25, 1906.
TILGHMAN, Peregrine, 75, Centreville, Queen Anne's County, October 26, 1897.
TILGHMAN, S____ H____, 67, Baltimore City, November 23, 1911.
TILLMAN, Professor Nicholas, 64, musician, Baltimore City, July 8, 1894.
TILTON, Colonel McLane, 77, Annapolis, Anne Arundel County, January 2, 1914.
TILTON, Lieutenant Palmer, 52, Baltimore City, March 5, 1905.
TILYARD, A____ H____, 67, clerk, Baltimore City, July 4, 1892.
TIMANUS, Jacob H., 66, builder, Baltimore City, March 1, 1891.
TIMANUS, John T., 56, miller, Baltimore City, June 14, 1879.
TIMMONS, Thomas 69, broker, Baltimore City, January 30, 1883.
TIMMONS, William E., 84, Snow Hill, Worcester County, March 15, 1902.
TINGES, George W., 72, realtor, Baltimore City, September 21, 1887.
TINSLEY, Tipton L., 70, retired, Baltimore City, July 28, 1887.
TIPPETT, George R., 52, Baltimore City, April 20, 1900.
TISCHMYER, Levi, 62, retired, Baltimore City, May 9, 1884.
TITCOMB, Dr. Benaiah, 67, physician, Baltimore City, February 23, 1882.
TOADVINE, A____ G____, 62, Salisbury, Wicomico County, March 28, 1894.
TODD, Rev. Robert W., 75, Baltimore City, January 28, 1906.
TODD, Captain William H., 60, mariner, Baltimore City, June 20, 1897.
TODHUNTER, C____ H____, 56, streetcar superintendent, Baltimore City, August 3, 1884.
TOLSON, Stonewall J., 49, Baltimore City, March 1, 1912.
TOMAY, Sylvester C., 56, journalist, Towson, Baltimore County, January 31, 1901.
TOME, Jacob, 87, financier, Port Deposit, Cecil County, March 16, 1898.
TOME, Jacob E., 47, Port Deposit, Cecil County, March 21, 1903.
TOME, Peter, 83, Port Deposit, Cecil County, January 5, 1901.
TOMLINSON, Henry W., 60, broker, Baltimore City, June 23, 1895.
TOMS, Joshua, 78, Hagerstown, Washington County, August 21, 1913.
TONER, Frank, 46, police captain, Baltimore City, January 7, 1896.

TONER, George M., 76, California pioneer; died in Baltimore City, May 12, 1901.
TONGUE, Harrison W., n.a., Baltimore City, June 17, 1913.
TONRY, Professor William P., 65, chemist, Baltimore City, October 3, 1905.
TOOGOOD, Nicholas, 92, black, Baltimore City, January 12, 1879.
TORMEY, Francis, D., 65, broker, Baltimore City, August 3, 1891.
TORMEY, Frank A., 71, retired, Baltimore City, February 5, 1905.
TORMEY, Leonard J., 53, broker, Baltimore City, July 23, 1883.
TORSCH, Henry F., 83, retired, Baltimore City, December 23, 1886.
TORSCH, Captain John W., 64, engraver, Baltimore City, October 1, 1898.
TOTEBUSCH, Henry W., 51, manufacturer, Baltimore City, December 20, 1884.
TOWLES, James, 68, Baltimore City, March 22, 1898.
TOWNER, John F., 68, merchant, Baltimore City, January 19, 1879.
TOWNSEND, Lemuel P., 65, manufacturer, Baltimore City, November 3, 1896.
TOWNSEND, Samuel, 75, minister, Baltimore City, January 17, 1883.
TOWNSEND, Rev. Sylvanus, 69, Baltimore City, February 1, 1906.
TOWNSEND, Walter, 54, Baltimore City, October 8, 1911.
TOWNSEND, William P., 58, ship agent, Baltimore City, February 7, 1901.
TOWSON, Charles, 73, hatter, Baltimore City, October 23, 1881.
TOWSON, Jacob Tolley, 75, Smithsburg, Washington County, March 17, 1907.
TRACEY, Richard C., 77, Baltimore County, October 5, 1900.
TRAPP, Dr. Charles P., 48, druggist, Baltimore City, October 19, 1903.
TRAUERMAN, Charles, 78, merchant, Baltimore City, January 28, 1882.
TRAUTFELTER, John H., 52, Baltimore City, August 29, 1914.
TRAVERS, John 92, retired, Baltimore City, August 25, 1882.
TRAVERS, Judge Levi D., 79, Dorchester County, May 26, 1907.
TRAVERS, Captain Robert M., 58, mariner, Baltimore City, May 2, 1881.
TRAVERS, Captain Thomas K., 63, mariner, Baltimore City, December 24, 1900.
TREADWAY, Mrs. Susan, 87, granddaughter of President of John Adams, at her residence in Baltimore, January 21, 1884.
TREGELLAS, Samuel R., 49, merchant, Baltimore City, June 29, 1904.
TREGO, William H., 61, expressman, Baltimore City, November 18, 1899.
TREGOE, G_____ W_____, 80, Baltimore City, November 29, 1907.
TREGOR, M_____ A_____, 72, Baltimore City, August 9, 1912.
TRENT, John W., 47, clerk, Baltimore City, April 15, 1898.
TREUSCH, Charles, 75, manufacturer, Baltimore City, February 9, 1903.
TREW, Dr. Bartus, 33, physician, Baltimore City, December 12, 1902.

TRICON, Paul F., 51, Confederate veteran, Hyattsville, Prince George's County, December 28, 1893.
TRIMBLE, David C., n.a., retired, Baltimore City, December 11, 1888.
TRIMBLE, General Isaac R., 86, retired, Sandy Spring, Montgomery County, January 2, 1888.
TRIMBLE, Dr. Isaac Ridgeway, 48, surgeon, Baltimore City, February 23, 1908.
TRIMBLE, Thomas, 82, merchant, Baltimore City, February 21, 1892.
TRIMBLE, William H., 89, retired, Baltimore City, May 30, 1899.
TROEGER, Andrew, 53, librarian, Baltimore City, June 4, 1903.
TROTTEN, John, 74, merchant, Baltimore City, July 3, 1903.
TROUP, Dr. H_____ N_____, 75, physician, Baltimore City, October 7, 1884.
TRUESCHLER, Rev. J_____ M_____ (R.C.), 30, Baltimore City, November 29, 1881.
TRUMBO, Charles H., 78, builder, Baltimore City, March 19, 1902.
TRUMBO, George W., 50, Baltimore City, February 21, 1900.
TRUNDLE, W_____ Burns, 78, Baltimore City, April 19, 1914.
TRUST, Herman, 73, baker, Baltimore City, January 26, 1879.
TRUST, Jacob, 75, merchant, Baltimore City, February 16, 1882.
TSCHUDY, Cornelius H., 79, retired, Baltimore City, July 30, 1899.
TUCK, W_____ Clement, 79, Annapolis, Anne Arundel County, May 8, 1898.
TUCK, Dr. W_____ G_____, 77, Annapolis, Anne Arundel County, February 5, 1908.
TUCK, William H., 75, former judge, Annapolis, Anne Arundel County, March 17, 1884.
TUCKER, Dr. J_____ H_____, 53, physician, Baltimore City, July 11, 1902.
TUCKER, Enoch G., 76, retired merchant, Baltimore City, January 12, 1894.
TUCKER, Joseph F., 56, broker, Baltimore City, March 9, 1893.
TUCKER, N_____ Summerfield, 48, Methodist minister, Baltimore City, November 3, 1894.
TUCKER, Thomas, 58, merchant, Baltimore City, August 9, 1901.
TULLEY, Alfred H., 75, express, Baltimore City, June 20, 1902.
TUMBLESON, Charles, H., 56, Baltimore City merchant, March 9, 1880.
TUNIS, Albert D., 30, Talbot County, August 26, 1903.
TURNBULL, William C., 68, Baltimore City merchant, September 25, 1892.
TURNER, A_____ Frank, 63, Salisbury, Wicomico County, December 9, 1905.
TURNER, Harry F., 60, merchant, Baltimore City, April 14, 1904.
TURNER, J_____ S_____, 58, steamboat, Baltimore City, August 25, 1902.
TURNER, J_____ Berry, 48, supervisor of elections, Baltimore City, January 12, 1899.
TURNER, Dr. John, 84, Calvert County, November 9, 1896.
TURNER, Joshua J., 80, banker, Baltimore City, October 17, 1889.

TURNER, Lewis, Jr., 44, butcher, Baltimore City, November 25, 1879.
TURNER, Robert, 79, merchant, Baltimore City, January 3, 1898.
TURNER, Thomas B. H., 89, Saint Leonard, Calvert County, July 27, 1913.
TURNER, Thomas K., 89, frescoer, Baltimore City, November 19, 1900.
TURPIN, Mrs. Sarah, 112, black, Baltimore City, December 2, 1884.
TURPIN, W____ W____ T____, 69, Centreville, Queen Anne's County, June 1, 1914.
TUTTTLE, I____ O____ B____, 65, liveryman, Baltimore City, April 23, 1902.
TUTTLE, William H., 56, merchant, Baltimore City, January 11, 1897.
TWAMLEY, William P., 62, Baltimore City, December 16, 1913.
TWIGG, S____, 62, Cumberland, Allegany County, October 23, 1912.
TYLER, Captain Alexander T., 76, mariner, Baltimore County, July 5, 1888.
TYLER, Charles, Sr., 83, merchant, Baltimore City, July 15, 1881.
TYLER, Charles, 68, manufacturer, Baltimore City, December 14, 1903.
TYLER, E____ B____, 70, former postmaster, Baltimore City, January 2, 1891.
TYLER, Rev. James J. (Methodist), 76, Baltimore City, March 10, 1896.
TYLER, Joseph E., 49, manufacturer, Baltimore City, February 17, 1893.
TYSON, Alva H., n.a., Baltimore City, March 13, 1913.
TYSON, Charles R., 78, retired, Bsltimore City, November 15, 1884.
TYSON, Frederick, 75, merchant, Baltimore City, June 16, 1901.
TYSON, James, 83, retired, Baltimore City, July 26, 1900.
TYSON, James E., 88, merchant, Bsltimore City, September 4, 1904.
TYSON, Mrs. James E., n.a., Ellicott City, Howard County, July 2, 1893.
TYSON, James Wood, 72, capitalist, Baltimore City, December 3, 1900.
TYSON, Jesse, 80, capitalist, Baltimore City, November 28, 1906.
TYSON, John S., n.a., attorney, Baltimore City, July 26, 1890.
TYSON, Mordecai T., 45, manufacturer, Baltimore City, June 6, 1901.
TYSON, Robert, 80, Baltimore City, July 15, 1911.
TYSON, Walter J., 26, Fifth Regiment, Baltimore City, November 5, 1901.

UHLER, Dr. H____ N____, n.a., physician, Cecil County, March 25, 1893.
UNDERWOOD, J____ A____, 73, veteran, Baltimore City, June 26, 1902.
UHLER, H____ I____, 25, clerk, Baltimore City, March 21, 1902.

UHLER, Dr. J_____ R_____, n.a., Baltimore City, October 9, 1911.
UHLER, Dr. Philip R., 78, Baltimore City, October 21, 1913.
ULMAN, Benjamin F., 59, merchant, Baltimore City, May 12, 1885.
ULLMAN, Henry, 42, cattle broker, Baltimore City, October 24, 1878.
ULMAN, Albert J., 78, distiller, Baltimore City, October 14, 1906.
ULMAN, Simon, 61, merchant, Salisbury, Wicomico County, September 5, 1904.
ULRICH, Seth S., 46, surgeon, Fourth Regiment, Baltimore City, November 20, 1904.
UNDUCH, John, n.a., Fourth Regiment, Baltimore City, February 21, 1904.
UNDUCH, Nicholas H., 82, retired merchant, Baltimore City, June 18, 1900.
UNGER, E_____ C_____, 40, editor, Brunswick, Frederick County, October 17, 1897.
UPDEGRAFF, Joseph B., 81, Hagerstown, Washington County, August 19, 1904.
UPHAM, Alfred E., n.a., Loch Raven, Baltimore County, February 16, 1914.
URBAN, Rev. Anthony (R.C.), 69, March 6, 1882.
URBAN, Charles, 72, manufacturer, Baltimore City, January 10, 1902.
URNER, William J., n.a., died at Savannah, Georgia, November 30, 1912.
URSPRUCH, Thomas, 52, merchant tailor, Baltimore City, June 20, 1903.
URQHARDT, Dr. Richard A., 41, Baltimore City, April 22, 1914.

VAIL, Horatio N., 40, oyster packer, Baltimore City, August 20, 1878.
VAIN, Edward, 91, butcher, Baltimore City, November 13, 1901.
VALENTINE, Brother, 45, Baltimore City, October 30, 1914.
VALENTINE, Ezra, 78, Baltimore City, May 30, 1898.
VALENTINE, Levi, 86, Carroll County, February 4, 1903.
VALIANT, Thomas J., 70, Poplar Island, Dorchester County, January 22, 1899
VALIENT, William Thomas, 72, merchant, Baltimore City, January 2, 1891.
VALLE, C_____ A_____, 60, manufacturer, Baltimore City, February 24, 1902.
VALLIANT, Sam Macubbin, n.a., Talbot County, September 14, 1897.
VAN BIBBER, Dr. Claude, 57, physician, Baltimore City, July 11, 1910.
VAN BIBBER, Judge G_____ L_____, 64, Bel Air, Harford County, October 5, 1911.
VAN BIBBER, Dr. John Pierre, 42, Baltimore City, May 5, 1892.
VAN BIBBER, Washington Chew, 68, physician, Baltimore City, December 14, 1892.
VANDEGRIFT, John M., 55, manufacturer, Baltimore City, February 1, 1882.
VAN DE KAMP, Rev. Henry (R.C.), 59, June 21, 1888.

VAN DEUSEN, Rev. E____ M____ (P.E.), 75, August 8, 1890.
VANDERFORD, Henry, 82, journalist, Westminster, Carroll County, January 27, 1894.
VANDERFORD, William H., 65, manager, **Advocate**, Westminster, Carroll County, June 23, 1906.
VANDIVER, J____ T____, 76, Cecil County, February 13, 1910.
VAN EMSTEDE, Rev. Francis (R.C.), 57, Baltimore City, August 4, 1886.
VANHORN, J____ E____, 75, contractor, Baltimore City, August 18, 1902.
VAN LEER, Solomon, 75, retired, Baltimore City, February 7, 1898.
VANNAMAN, R____ K____, 59, Havre de Grace, Harford County, July 8, 1912.
VAN NESS, Eugene, 58, Baltimore City, March 31, 1900.
VANSANT, James H., 61, Annapolis, Anne Arundel County, April 15, 1905.
VANSANT, Joshua, 80, former mayor of Baltimore; died there, April 8, 1884.
VANSANT, Joshua R., 25, musician, Baltimore City, September 12, 1903.
VANSANT, Nicholas, 85, retired, Baltimore City, August 27, 1902.
VANSANT, William J., 28, Baltimore City, June 13, 1903.
VAN TROMP, John, 82, watchmaker, Baltimore City, November 24, 1905.
VEAZEY, James W., 83, Cecil County, June 20, 1897.
VEAZEY, Captain W____ F____, 71, Salisbury, Wicomico County, March 26, 1908.
VEES, Dr. Charles H., 33, physician, Baltimore City, May 27, 1892.
VEITCH, John W., n.a., lawyer, Garrett County, October 11, 1892.
VICKERS, B____ Albert, 66, bank president, Baltimore City, April 16, 1882.
VICKERS, Henry C., 89, retired, Baltimore City, April 25, 1904.
VICKERS, William M., 78, merchant, Baltimore City, March 18, 1899.
VICKERY, Hazeltine G., 76, banker, Baltimore City, December 21, 1904.
VICKERY, Jacob, 71, retired, Baltimore City, November 3, 1887.
VICKERY, William H., 69, merchant, Baltimore City, March 1, 1897.
VIESSMAN, John C., 48, merchant, Baltimore City, February 9, 1903.
VIGER, Rev. G____ E____, 69, Ellicott City, Howard County, November 11, 1908.
VINCENTE, Edward P., 52, deputy clerk, Baltimore City, March 28, 1887.
VINSON, John T., 78, former judge, Rockville, Montgomery County, February 7, 1903.
VINSON, Napoleon B., 82, Rockville, Montgomery County, March 24, 1904.
VINSON, William B., 82, Montgomery County, May 20, 1902.
VINTON, O____ P____, n.a., clergyman, Baltimore City, June 15, 1880.
VIRDIN, Dr. William Ward, 67, physician, Harford County, May 20, 1897.

VIRTUE, Charles W., 31, teacher, Baltimore City, September 20, 1882.
VOCKE, Claas, 88, consul of the Netherlands; died in Baltimore City, December 20, 1903.
VODERY, Rev. W____ H____ B____ (M.E.), 28, black, Baltimore City, September 20, 1884.
VOGELER, Charles A., 31, manufacturer, Baltimore City, August 5, 1882.
VOGELL, Charles L., 83, retired, Baltimore City, May 7, 1899.
VOGLE, Dr. Bernhard, 57, physician, Baltimore City, April 14, 1904.
VOGLE, Henry, 77, tailor, Baltimore City, April 30, 1899.
VOGT, Ambrose, 66, pharmacist, Baltimore City, March 8, 1901.
VOGLE, Leonard, 76, Smithsburg, Washington County, September 16, 1909.
VOGT, Joseph C., 48, auctioneer, Baltimore City, March 24, 1899.
VOGTMANN, Rev. Ludwig (R.C.), 60, Baltimore City, February 18, 1890.
VOIGT, Henry, 50, jeweler, Baltimore City, August 10, 1897.
VOLCK, Dr. A____ J____, 84, artist, Baltimore City, March 26, 1912.
VOLKERT, Nicholas H., 71, retired merchant, Baltimore City, December 1, 1901.
VOLKMAN, William H., 58, Baltimorean and U.S. Consul, Puerto Cabello, Venezuela, April 19, 1904.
VOLKMAR, Charles, 84, artist, Baltimore City, December 18, 1892.
VOLTZ, George, 80, Howard County, June 3, 1900.
VOLZ, John, 37, artist, Baltimore City, March 30, 1895.
VOLZ, Peter, Sr., 70, grocer, Baltimore City, November 14, 1879.
VON DER HORST, Harry R., 54, baseball manager, Baltimore City, July 28, 1905.
VONDERHORST, J____ H____, 64, Baltimore City, January 28, 1898.
VONEIFF, Edward W., 44, Baltimore City, November 6, 1897.
VON LINGEN, G____ A____, 68, Baltimore City, June 26, 1907.
VONDERHORST, John H., 69, brewer, Baltimore City, July 4, 1894.
VONDERHORST, John H., 42, brewer, Baltimore City, March 4, 1895.
VONSPRECHELSON, G____ H____, 56, merchant, Baltimore City, July 11, 1881.
VORDEMBERGE, William F., 67, retired, Baltimore City, November 27, 1896.
VOSHELL, J____ C____, 75, hotelier, Salisbury, October 9, 1893.

WACHTER, August E., 79, retired, Baltimore City, March 5, 1904.
WACHTER, Frank C., 49, Baltimore City, July 1, 1910.
WACKER, Philip, 57, teacher, Baltimore City, September 15, 1884.
WADDELL, Captain James I., 61, commander, Maryland Fishing Force, Annapolis, Anne Arundel County, March 15, 1886.
WADDELL, William 82, gardener, Baltimore City, August 13, 1883.
WADE, John J., 73, lawyer, Baltimore City, November 24, 1897.
WADE, William H., 44, editor, Baltimore City, April 14, 1882.
WAGGNER, George E., 42, park commissioner, Baltimore City, July 6, 1888.

WAGGNER, Lewis, 70, ship joiner, Baltimore City, February 19, 1883.
WAGNER, Dr. Albert S., 23, physician, Baltimore City, February 23, 1893.
WAGNER, Alfred, 72, Baltimore City, November 16, 1897.
WAGNER, Francis M., 75, manufacturer, Baltimore City, February 17, 1899.
WAGNER, Frederick, 72, retired, Baltimore City, May 29, 1905.
WAGNER, George, 76, restaurateur, Baltimore City, May 31, 1882.
WAGNER, Henry G., 59, shipbuilder, Baltimore City, March 18, 1904.
WAGNER, Isaiah, 69, retired, Baltimore City, April 22, 1889.
WAGNER, James V., 54, Venezuelan consul, Baltimore City, January 31, 1903.
WAGNER, John, 58, Green House, Baltimore City, July 19, 1894.
WAHL, Jacob, 67, manufacturer, Baltimore City, November 17, 1882.
WAILES, John B., 79, Arlington, Baltimore County, March 10, 1913.
WAITE, S____ M____, 65, merchant, Baltimore City, December 24, 1912.
WAKEFIELD, John, 82, retired shipmaster, Baltimore City, January 3, 1893.
WAKELY, James P., 78(73?), retired, Baltimore City, January 29, 1884.
WALBACH, James DeB., 43, Charles County, May 23, 1905.
WALDEN, R____ W____, 60, Middleburg, Carroll County, April 28, 1905.
WALDRON, Rev. E____ Q____ S____ (R.C.), 77, Baltimore City, April 16, 1888.
WALKER, Henry, 69, merchant, Baltimore City, July 25, 1881.
WALKER, J____ L____, n.a., Easton, Talbot County, April 17, 1908.
WALKER, Mrs. Mary, 102, Baltimore City, August 6, 1884.
WALLACE, Captain William, 40, U.S.M.C., native of Baltimore, December 11, 1883.
WALKER, William F., 76, retired manufacturer, Baltimore City, March 30, 1901.
WALLACE, David M., 63, printer, Baltimore City, May 1, 1901.
WALLACE, George F., 59, salesman, Baltimore City, November 1, 1884.
WALLACE, James, 69, lawyer, Baltimore City, February 12, 1887.
WALLACE, James, 53, Cambridge, Dorchester County, January 7, 1903.
WALLACE, Joseph W., 68, bookkeeper, Baltimore City, September 27, 1899.
WALLACE, Rebecca, 101, black, Baltimore City, December 14, 1878.
WALLACE, Richard M., 55, merchant, Baltimore City, August 30, 1897.
WALLACE, Samuel A., 74, merchant, Baltimore City, October 10, 1904.
WALLACE, Thomas, 26, billiard player, Baltimore City, December 27, 1887.
WALLACE, William A., 57, master carpenter, Baltimore City, January 7, 1882.
WALLACH, Richard L., 52, Laurel, Prince George's County, January 4, 1896.

WALLER, C____ C____, 57, Princess Anne, Somerset County, March 10, 1908.
WALLIS, John S., 73, Baltimore City, October 6, 1897.
WALLIS, Severn Teakle, 77, lawyer and litterateur, Baltimore City, April 11, 1894.
WALSH, Francis, 81, Araby, Frederick County, August 28, 1909.
WALSH, Henry E., 42, agent, Baltimore City, March 21, 1883.
WALSH, John Carroll, 77, Harford County, December 1, 1894.
WALSH, John J., 58, manufacturer, Baltimore City, June 1, 1899.
WALSH, Rev. Michael J. (R.C.), 49, Baltimore City, April 29, 1901.
WALSH, Patrick, 80, retired, Baltimore City, March 2, 1898.
WALSH, Philip, Jr., 45, builder, Baltimore City, July 1, 1894.
WALSH, William, 64, former Congressman, Cumberland, Allegany County, May 17, 1892.
WALSHE, David J., 55, hotelier, Baltimore City, March 26, 1891.
WALTER, Ambrose, 66, choir master, Baltimore City, June 20, 1894.
WALTER, Andrew J., 60, fireman, Baltimore City, September 25, 1897.
WALTER, E____ T____ H____, 63, claim agent, Baltimore City, December 24, 1880.
WALTER, Edwin, 53, merchant, Baltimore City, April 19, 1897.
WALTER, Gustav, 58, manufacturer, Baltimore City, April 2, 1902.
WALTER, J____ A____, n.a., Confederate veteran, Emmitsburg, Frederick County, September 10, 1908.
WALTER, Joseph, 49, insurance agent, Baltimore City, December 6, 1899.
WALTER, Rev. Joseph M., 31, Baltimore City, March 20, 1898.
WALTERS, William J. H., 71, merchant, Baltimore City, February 15, 1906.
WALTERS, William T., 75, merchant, Baltimore City, November 22, 1894.
WALTJEN, Andrew S., 79, manufacturer, Baltimore City, October 26, 1901.
WALTJEN, J____ H____, 68, confectioner, Baltimore City, January 24, 1902.
WALTON, Robert J., 51, Baltimore City, October 7, 1898.
WALTON, Dr. Thomas O., 66, Annapolis, Anne Arundel County, December 21, 1900.
WALTON, W____ V____, 54, teacher, Baltimore City, December 5, 1883.
WALTZ, Jacob, 41, druggist, Baltimore City, April 26, 1881.
WALZ, G____, 70, brass founder, Baltimore City, April 17, 1902.
WALZL, Julius, 45, photographer, Baltimore City, January 20, 1897.
WALZL, Richard, n.a., photographer, Baltimore City, May 10, 1899.
WAMBECK, Charles, 52, Baltimore City, July 9, 1897.
WANSTALL, Dr. Emma S., 28, physician, Baltimore City, September 10, 1882.
WARD, George W., 74, retired, Baltimore City, April 13, 1886.
WARD, J____ Harry, 49, merchant, Baltimore City, August 15, 1890.
WARD, Dr. James R., 77, physician, Baltimore City, April 29, 1884.
WARD, Rev. James T., 76, president, Westminster Theological Seminary, March 4, 1897.

-236-

WARD, John, 73, machinist, Baltimore City, November 3, 1884.
WARD, James R., Sr., 82, contractor, Baltimore City, January 31, 1903.
WARD, Josephus C., 75, Hagerstown, Washington County, February 25, 1913.
WARD, R____ P____, 68, Baltimore City, May 21, 1909.
WARD, Dr. Robert, 70, veterinarian, Baltimore City, March 24, 1905.
WARD, Thomas, 50, merchant, Baltimore City, August 26, 1897.
WARD, Thomas Cooksey, 110, Charlotte Hall, St. Mary's County, August 11, 1903.
WARD, Thomas H., 86, Barnesville, Montgomery County, October 19, 1913.
WARD, William, 78, broker, Baltimore City, January 20, 1882.
WARD, Rev. William F. (M.E.), 51, Baltimore City, January 30, 1889.
WARD, William S., 80, sea captain, Baltimore City, February 9, 1892.
WARE, Elias, 66, former Speaker, Maryland House of Delegates; died at Portsmouth, Kentucky; word received at Ellicott City, Howard County, January 13, 1885.
WARE, Robert G., 78, retired, Baltimore City, August 5, 1884.
WAREHEIM, Dr. W____ W____, 50, Hampstead, Carroll County, December 2, 1892.
WARFIELD, A____ G____, n.a., civil engineer; died at his home in Howard County, December 26, 1883.
WARFIELD, Augustus, 75, Ellicott City, Howard County, February 21, 1905.
WARFIELD, Beale, 77, Baltimore City, October 19, 1910.
WARFIELD, Caleb M., 56, Montgomery County, March 20, 1895.
WARFIELD, Ella L., n.a., Sykesville, Carroll County, July 22, 1913.
WARFIELD, Dr. Evan W., 78, Howard County, February 17, 1904.
WARFIELD, G____ T____, 77, Anne Arundel County, June 17, 1898.
WARFIELD, G____ Watkins, n.a., Howard County, September 25, 1892.
WARNER, George W., 71, marine engineer, Baltimore City, December 7, 1904.
WARFIELD, Henry M., 59, retired, Baltimore City, January 17, 1885.
WARFIELD, Henry W., 68, merchant, Baltimore City, November 23, 1899.
WARFIELD, Israel G., 74, Rockville, Montgomery County, February 27, 1907.
WARFIELD, Dr. Jesse L., 86, physician, Baltimore City, February 9, 1887.
WARFIELD, Magruder, 64, bank officer, Baltimore City, March 7, 1900.
WARFIELD, Dr. Milton W., 78, Howard County, November 26, 1905.
WARFIELD, Oliver C., 60, attorney, Baltimore City, August 25, 1906.
WARFIELD, Thomas J., 66, merchant, Baltimore City, June 28, 1903.
WARFIELD, Thomas O., 69, Howard County, May 14, 1902.
WARING, B____ H____, 72, died at Atlantic City, New Jersey, November 20, 1911.

WARING, David E., 58, insurance, Baltimore City, February 6, 1897.
WARING, Robert K., 65, Baltimore City, January 17, 1913.
WARINGTON, William, Sr., 65, Ocean City, Worcester County, September 8, 1897.
WARNER, Brinton, 31, dentist, Baltimore City, April 6, 1886.
WARNER, George K., 74, coal dealer, Baltimore City, January 2, 1879.
WARNER, Dr. John E., 64, physician, Baltimore City, February 6, 1888.
WARNER, John H., 45, lawyer, Baltimore City, July 26, 1880.
WARNER, Dr. M____ K____, 49, physician, Baltimore City, July 22, 1905.
WARNER, Michael, 80, Baltimore City, August 29, 1879.
WARNER, Rev. Dr. T____ C____ (M.E.), n.a., Baltimore City, July 19, 1899.
WARREN, Leander, 64, reporter, Baltimore City, June 24, 1881.
WASHBURN, Wyman F., 78, Baltimore City, November 4, 1898.
WATERHOUSE, William E., 70, druggist, Baltimore City, June 21, 1885.
WATERMAN, William J., 70, lawyer, Baltimore City, February 17, 1893.
WATERS, Asa, 93, carpenter, Baltimore City, January 1, 1883.
WATERS, Professor C____ Dorsey, 40, Baltimore City, July 14, 1908.
WATERS, C____ E____, 95, Ellicott City, Howard County, October 11, 1912.
WATERS, Charles A., 92, retired, Baltimore City, March 15, 1882.
WATERS, Charles E., 75, retired, Baltimore City, December 25, 1896.
WATERS, Charles E., 43, merchant, Baltimore City, September 6, 1879.
WATERS, G____ W____, 65, Laurel, Prince George's County, June 12, 1912.
WATERS, James, 62, gardener, Baltimore City, June 13, 1902.
WATERS, Levin L., 71, attorney, Somerset County, January 8, 1900.
WATERS, R____ Frank, 38, pharmacist, Baltimore City, July 24, 1901.
WATERS, Richard R., 90, near Gaithersburg, Montgomery County, January 5, 1885.
WATERS, Richard T., 82, merchant, Baltimore City, April 21, 1900.
WATERS, Robert C. J., 81, retired merchant, Baltimore City, October 20, 1880.
WATHEN, F____ Eugene, 47, school superintendent, Annapolis, Anne Arundel County, November 7, 1905.
WATKINS, General J____ Wesley, 79, retired, Baltimore City, September 18, 1887.
WATKINS, James, 82, retired, Baltimore City, October 24, 1896.
WATKINS, James S., 60, writer, Baltimore City, July 20, 1899.
WATKINS, John N., 71, magistrate, Baltimore City, January 7, 1884.
WATKINS, Joseph P., 87, merchant, Baltimore City, March 5, 1899.
WATKINS, Mortimer S., 62, Baltimore City, January 26, 1897.
WATKINS, N____ W____, 62, Confederate veteran, Baltimore City, February 7, 1905.

WATKINS, Rudolph, 65, Rockville, Montgomery County, November 8, 1909.
WATKINS, Samuel, 84, local preacher, Baltimore City, January 29, 1882.
WATKINS, Spencer, 59, Montgomery County, November 6, 1904.
WATKINS, Lieutenant William McK., 63, policeman, Baltimore City, November 28, 1890.
WATTERS, Judge J____ D____, 73, Bel Air, Harford County, March 29, 1908.
WATTS, Rev. John, 49, local preacher, Baltimore City, April 17, 1883.
WATSON, Dr. Arthur G., 53, Councilman, Baltimore City, September 29, 1904.
WATSON, John, 66, gardener, Baltimore City, April 8, 1898.
WATTENSCHEIDT, August, 81, jeweler, Baltimore City, April 7, 1891.
WATTS, Henry A., 78, pilot, Baltimore City, March 27, 1894.
WATTS, Nathaniel, 94, "Old Defender," Baltimore City, October 28, 1888.
WATTS, Philip, 61, Pikesville, Baltimore County, August 7, 1912.
WATTS, Theodore A., 80, printer, Baltimore City, December 15, 1905.
WATTS, Thomas M., 82, pilot, Baltimore City, January 28, 1902.
WATTY, Hiram, 60, black politician, Baltimore City, October 20, 1905.
WAUGH, Rev. John W., n.a., physician and local preacher, Baltimore City, July 6, 1881.
WAY, A____ J____ H____, 62, artist, Baltimore City, February 7, 1888.
WAY, Dr. E____ J____, 75, physician, Baltimore City, July 5, 1886.
WAYMAN, A____ W____, 74, bishop (A.M.E.), Baltimore City, November 30, 1902.
WAYMAN, Rev. Robert F., 60, black, Baltimore City, August 2, 1891.
WAYS, Charles E., 75, Baltimore City, January 2, 1914.
WEANT, John W., 68, Carroll County, August 30, 1904.
WEATHERBY, J____ Emory, 63, retired, Baltimore City, June 3, 1899.
WEATHERBY, Jeremiah, 89, retired, Baltimore City, October 6, 1894.
WEAVER, Dr. Jacob J., Sr., 73, Uniontown, probably Frederick County, December 27, 1895.
WEAVER, John W., 66, undertaker, Baltimore City, August 20, 1886.
WEBB, Albert L., 69, merchant, Baltimore City, August 26, 1882.
WEBB, Charles, 71, manufacturer, Baltimore City, June 19, 1891.
WEBB, Charles J., 34, clerk, Baltimore City, December 4, 1882.
WEBB, Charles W., 68, Baltimore City, April 1, 1913.
WEBB, E____ J____, 60, insurance agent, Baltimore City, January 11, 1879.
WEBB, George R., 68, retired, Baltimore City, January 20, 1890.
WEBB, George W., 78, jeweler, Baltimore City, March 12, 1890.
WEBB, Henry W., 58, merchant, Baltimore City, December 17, 1881.
WEBB, J____ A____, 71, Forest Park, December 9, 1911.

WEBB, William B., 64, insurance, Baltimore City, December 23, 1895.
WEBB, Rev. H_____ H_____, 74, black, Baltimore City, December 12, 1878.
WEBB, Herbert L., 42, merchant, Baltimore City, December 26, 1899.
WEBB, John M., 71, retired, Baltimore City, December 14, 1899.
WEBB, R_____ Walton, 60, Dorchester County, January 4, 1901.
WEBB, William George, 66, merchant, Baltimore City, December 17, 1899.
WEBB, Dr. William Kelso, 45, physician, Baltimore City, July 12, 1895.
WEBER, A_____, 76, merchant, Baltimore City, December 24, 1902.
WEBER, Charles, 63, banker, Baltimore City, November 9, 1884.
WEBER, Frederick A., 72, brewer, Baltimore City, February 27, 1899.
WEBER, Henry, Sr., 69, Garrett County, January 21, 1904.
WEBER, J_____ Henry, 49, clerk, Baltimore City, April 3, 1886.
WEBER, Rev. Joseph, 61, Baltimore City, March 10, 1913.
WEBER, William, 77, editor, Cumberland, Allegany County, January 14, 1885.
WEBER, William F., 55, architect, Baltimore City, January 23, 1893.
WEBNER, Dr. Henry W., 62, Baltimore City, July 14, 1914.
WEBSTER, Rev. Augustus, 83, Ind_____ M_____, Baltimore City, October 26, 1890.
WEBSTER, E_____ H_____, 64, ex-coll_____, Bel Air, Harford County, April 24, 1893.
WEBSTER, George S., 77, Harford County, June 9, 1903.
WEBSTER, Henry Worthington, Jr., 64, physician, Baltimore City, August 29, 1894.
WEBSTER, J_____ T_____, 70, Harford County, November 4, 1912.
WEBSTER, James R., 57, professor, Baltimore City, March 15, 1882.
WEBSTER, Dr. Warren, 60, physician, Baltimore City, January 13, 1896.
WEBSTER, Captain William, n.a., veteran mariner, Baltimore City, June 19, 1897.
WEDGE, Simon, 87, retired, Baltimore City, May 23, 1887.
WEED, Henry T., 83, Allegany County, July 28, 1893.
WEEDON, Austin R., n.a., Centreville, Queen Anne's County, February 10, 1900.
WEEDON, James H., 78, merchant, Baltimore City, December 30, 1901.
WEEKS, John L., 66, retired, Baltimore City, August 28, 1888.
WEEMS, Alexander Bellington, 78, Baltimore City, March 8, 1893.
WEEMS, Edwin D., 36, steamboat manager, Baltimore City, March 11, 1903.
WEER, Leonard, 75, Rockville, Montgomery County, March 26, 1893.
WEGLEIN, Louis, 69, merchant, Baltimore City, March 13, 1906.
WEHAGE, J_____ G_____, 65, musician, Baltimore City, August 12, 1912.
WEHR, Frederick, 77, builder, Baltimore City, April 11, 1893.
WEHRHANE, Henry, 83, retired, Baltimore City, December 25, 1886.
WEIDEMANN, Gottfried, 85, Baltimore City, June 1, 1898.

WEIDMAN, Melchior, 44, Baltimore City, July 11, 1905.
WEIDMEYER, Adam, 64, mechanic, Baltimore City, June 6, 1883.
WEIGANDT, Charles F., 80, artist, Baltimore City, March 29, 1892.
WEIL, Albert, 54, publisher, Baltimore City, November 18, 1904.
WEIL, Jacob, n.a., merchant, Baltimore City, May 17, 1881.
WEILER, Alexander, 60, merchant, Baltimore City, October 25, 1897.
WEILER, Jacob, 60, Baltimore City, July 10, 1898.
WEILLER, Charles, 60, merchant, Baltimore City, October 31, 1881.
WEINBERG, Bernard, 40, Baltimore City, March 28, 1898.
WEISHAMPLE, Rev. J_____ F_____, Sr., 76, Baltimore City, November 20, 1883.
WEISHAMPLE, John F., 64, publisher, Baltimore City, May 5, 1904.
WEISKITTEL, Anton, Sr., 59, iron founder, Baltimore City, April 18, 1884.
WEITZEL, Jacob, 88, Baltimore City, February 27, 1898.
WELCH, Charles S., 84, Annapolis, Anne Arundel County, April 24, 1899.
WELCH, Dr. Warren, 54, dentist, Baltimore City, May 28, 1883.
WELCOME, Dr. John B., 71, physician, Baltimore City, November 13, 1897.
WELD, William George, 51, attorney, Baltimore City, December 30, 1906.
WELFLEY, Dr. D_____ P_____, 54, physician and author, Cumberland, Allegany County, December 19, 1886.
WELL, W_____ Starr, 58, lawyer, Baltimore City, August 23, 1905.
WELLENER, B_____ S_____, 70, shipbuilder, Baltimore City, February 1, 1892.
WELLING, David O., 72, Point of Rocks, Frederick County, February 5, 1914.
WELLMORE, Edward, 75, artist, native of Montgomery County; died at Philadelphia, January 23, 1883.
WELLS, George, 81, banker, Annapolis, Anne Arundel County, October 21, 1881.
WELLS, Joseph, 91, retired, Baltimore City, October 7, 1900.
WELLS, Richard, 70, Annapolis, Anne Arundel County, September 21, 1914.
WELLS, Richard P., 71, mariner, Baltimore City, July 22, 1895.
WELLS, William, Sr., 74, carpenter, Baltimore City, July 29, 1887.
WELLS, William, 52, bank cashier, Baltimore City, January 4, 1892.
WELLSLAGER, W_____ W_____, 26, teacher, Baltimore City, September 25, 1902.
WELSH, David, 87, retired, Baltimore City, March 26, 1884.
WELSH, E_____ H_____, 74, Cumberland, Allegany County, January 21, 1914.
WELSH, Michael, 58, hotelier, Baltimore City, December 5, 1891.
WELSH, Napoleon B., 77, fox hunter, Baltimore City, April 3, 1902.
WELSH, Robert, 82, retired, Baltimore City, December 30, 1901.
WELSH, Thomas, 70, jeweler, Baltimore City, January 28, 1904.
WELSH, William, 94, "Old Defender," Baltimore City, June 1, 1894.
WELSH, William H., 77, journalist, Baltimore City, December 2, 1903.

WELSH, William H., 77, merchant, Baltimore City, October 23, 1904.
WELSH, Dr. William P., 70, Baltimore City, November 3, 1907.
WELTY, Rev. Dr. Elias (Reformed), 69, Baltimore City, September 4, 1890.
WENTZ, Henry C., 70, retired attorney, Baltimore City, May 22, 1899.
WENTZ, Lieutenant James H., 38, Baltimore City, September 15, 1914.
WENTZ, John B., 66, Baltimore City, September 25, 1897.
WERBER, Rev. Paul (Lutheran), 52, Baltimore City, September 9, 1896.
WERDEBAUGH, H_____ J_____, 62, merchant, Baltimore City, October 9, 1882.
WERDER, John F. Von, 90, soldier, Baltimore City, November 16, 1879.
WERGER, Peter, 71, former Sun carrier, Baltimore City, April 21, 1883.
WERHANE, William H., n.a., Baltimore City, October 24, 1895.
WERNER, August F., 67, club superintendent, Baltimore City, August 4, 1901.
WERNER, Rev. Laurence, 71, faculty, Ilchester College, December 31, 1908.
WERT, J_____ S_____, 52, attorney, Elkton, Cecil County, May 17, 1904
WERTHEIM, Henry, 90, merchant, Baltimore City, February 19, 1902.
WEST, Christopher, 89, retired, Baltimore City, August 13, 1890.
WEST, D_____ Pinkney, 63, detective, Baltimore City, January 2, 1899.
WEST, Dr. Frank, 48, physician, Baltimore City, November 18, 1899.
WEST, George F., 61, telegraph manager, Baltimore City, June 23, 1900.
WESTCOTT, C_____ T_____, 63, Baltimore City, December 15, 1911.
WEST, Erasmus, 66, druggist, Baltimore City, August 15, 1903.
WEST, Rev. W_____ A_____, 84, Hagerstown, Washington County, September 26, 1909.
WESTCOTT, George B., 86, bank president, Chestertown, Kent County, March 22, 1887.
WESTERMAN, Joshua S., 58, banker, Baltimore City, September 20, 1900.
WESTPHAL, Henry, 62, contractor, Baltimore City, August 11, 1900.
WETHERALL, William G., 88, importer, Baltimore City, April 21, 1888.
WETHERED, George Yates, 86, Baltimore City, August 17, 1892.
WHALEY, J_____ B_____, 75, Methodist minister, Baltimore City, October 14, 1894.
WHEAT, John B., 79, collector, Baltimore City, March 26, 1880.
WHEEDEN, Edward L., 63, sailmaker, Baltimore City, August 2, 1899.
WHEEDEN, James C., 87, merchant, Baltimore City, December 18, 1892.

WHEELER, Arthur W., 21, fellow, Johns Hopkins University, Baltimore City, January 7, 1881.
WHEELER, Caleb C., 59, shipowner, Caroline County, April 20, 1899.
WHEELER, Darius, 85, "Old Defender," Baltimore City, January 21, 1884.
WHEELER, F____ I____, 64, warden, Baltimore City, December 10, 1884.
WHEELER, Captain John M., 98, Leonardtown, St. Mary's County, February 12, 1913.
WHEELER, Mrs. Rachel, 97, Baltimore City, December 22, 1881.
WHELAN, Edmund J., 43, bank officer, Baltimore City, December 3, 1899.
WHELAN, Captain James, 70, Baltimore City, April 27, 1914.
WHELAN, Matthew J., 30, clerk, Baltimore City, November 17, 1880.
WHELAN, T____, 77, Baltimore City, December 31, 1909.
WHELAN, Thomas, 66, lawyer, Baltimore City, August 14, 1890.
WHELOCK, S____, 87, sea captain, Baltimore City, July 29, 1892.
WHERRETT, R____ M____, 55, secretary, pilots association, Baltimore City, February 3, 1894.
WHISNER, Rev. Dr. P____ H____, n.a., Baltimore City, April 21, 1906.
WHITAKER, Dr. J____ S____, 56, Cecil County, March 12, 1904.
WHITAKER, Lemuel D., 55, Baltimore City, November 26, 1914.
WHITE, Dr. A____ A____, 73, physician, Baltimore City, December 18, 1904.
WHITE, Alexander J., 78, insurance, Baltimore City, December 28, 1885.
WHITE, Ambrose A., 76, retired, Baltimore City, September 25, 1885.
WHITE, Benjamin R., 84, Glen Echo, Montgomery County, February 10, 1913.
WHITE, Captain E____ T____, 78, Baltimore City, July 14, 1914.
WHITE, Dr. Edward H., 70(?), physician, Baltimore City, June 2, 1897.
WHITE, Francis, 79, capitalist, Baltimore City, September 11, 1904.
WHITE, George A., 68, mariner, Baltimore City, April 30, 1901.
WHITE, George B., 66, retail merchant, Baltimore City, December 11, 1901.
WHITE, Gideon, n.a., shipowner, Baltimore City, September 14, 1894.
WHITE, Rev. H____ F____, 77, Baltimore City, October 23, 1912.
WHITE, Henry, 89, Baltimorean; died in Paris, December 25, 1882.
WHITE, John, 95, merchant, Salisbury, Wicomico County, December 27, 1898.
WHITE, John C., 47, broker, Baltimore City, January 12, 1884.
WHITE, Dr. John D., 68, Worcester County, October 22, 1901.
WHITE, Rev. John P. (R.C.), 44, Baltimore City, August 15, 1904.
WHITE, Dr. John W., 74, Glyndon, Baltimore County, July 22, 1913.

WHITE, Captain L_____, S_____, 84, Confederate veteran, Baltimore City, December 12, 1908.
WHITE, Samuel W., 50, mariner, Baltimore City, May 29, 1901.
WHITE, T_____ B_____, 61, manufacturer, Baltimore City, January 3, 1902.
WHITE, T_____ H_____, 64, merchant, Baltimore City, May 30, 1902.
WHITE, Dr. Walter W., 61, physician, Baltimore City, November 2, 1904.
WHITEFORD, Dr. Aloyius X., 53, Parkville, Baltimore County, February 28, 1901.
WHITEFORD, Dr. C_____ R_____, 35, State Legislator, Baltimore City, January 9, 1888.
WHITEFORD, James, 67, retired merchant, Baltimore City, October 3, 1878.
WHITEFORD, Dr. James E., 50, Baltimore City, December 20, 1898.
WHITEFORD, Dr. Lingard I., n.a., Parkville, Baltimore County, August 2, 1913.
WHITELY, General Robert H. K., 88, Baltimore City, June 9, 1896.
WHITELOCK, R_____ J_____, builder, Baltimore City, July 10, 1879.
WHITELOCK, William, 77, Mount Washington, Baltimore County, June 28, 1893.
WHITELY, Dr. Benjamin, 64, Baltimore City, September 26, 1908.
WHITELY, James S., n.a., Baltimore City, February 24, 1909.
WHITESIDE, John, 86, Baltimore City, November 15, 1913.
WHITING, James, 68, merchant, Baltimore City, January 4, 1883.
WHITMAN, Ezra, 75, editor and manufacturer, Baltimore City, July 13, 1887.
WHITNEY, Joseph C., 68, retired, Baltimore City, March 2, 1886.
WHITRIDGE, Dr. G_____ H_____, 41, Baltimore City, March 20, 1912.
WHITRIDGE, J_____ A_____, 72, Baltimore City, May 24, 1907.
WHITRIDGE, James H. B., 42, Baltimore City, August 28, 1904.
WHITRIDGE, Dr. John, 85, physician, Baltimorean; died at Tiverton, Rhode Island, July 23, 1878.
WHITESIDE, John, 93, Brookville, Montgomery County, December 25, 1893.
WHITRIDGE, Thomas, 82, merchant, Baltimore City, October 27, 1883.
WHITRIDGE, Thomas and wife (unnamed), no ages, Baltimore City, January 15, 1895.
WHITRIDGE, Dr. William, 70, physician, Baltimore City, February 6, 1910.
WHITTAKER, Edmund S., 60, manufacturer, Principio Furnace, Cecil County, December 13, 1898.
WHITTINGHAM, Mrs. Hannah, 90, Baltimore City, October 17, 1885.
WHITTINGHAM, William R., 74, cleric, Baltimore City, October 17, 1879.
WHITTINGTON, Joseph S., 72, Baltimore City, December 25, 1913.
WHYTE, Mrs. Louisa, n.a., Baltimore City, October 28, 1885.
WHYTE, Mrs. Mary McDonald, 49, wife of former Governor William Pinkney Whyte, Baltimore City, May 13, 1900.
WHYTE, W_____ H_____, 40, lawyer, Baltimore City, February 4, 1888.
WHYTE, Senator William Pinkney, 83, Baltimore City, March 17, 1908.

WICKES, Charles H., 73, Chestertown, Kent County, December 11, 1893.
WICKES, Thomas W., 50, druggist, Chestertown, Kent County, January 24, 1898.
WIDDEFIELD, Thomas E., 53, policeman, Baltimore City, May 30, 1883.
WIDENER, J_____ B_____, 90, Cumberland, Allegany County, July 13, 1908.
WIDERMAN, Ezra T. G., 59, Baltimore City, January 27, 1898.
WIEGAND, Carl H., 77, piano manufacturer, Baltimore City, August 23, 1903.
WIEGEL, Henry H., 62, Baltimore City, October 17, 1900.
WIEL, H_____, 35, merchant, Baltimore City; died at Goldsboro, North Carolina, December 8, 1878.
WIENER, Dr. George W., n.a., physician, Baltimore City, November 15, 1882.
WIENER, Dr. Morris, 94, author, Baltimore City, October 12, 1905.
WIESENFELD, David, 66, Baltimore City, October 20, 1914.
WIESNER, John F., 65, brewer, Baltimore City, January 1, 1897.
WIESSNER, J_____ Frederick, 46, manufacturer, Baltimore City, March 7, 1904.
WIGET, Rev. Bernard F. (S.J.), 63, Charles County, January 2, 1883.
WILCOX, Henry, 76, merchant, Baltimore City, October 23, 1905.
WILCOX, John H., 83, retired, Baltimore City, August 11, 1900.
WILCOX, Louis E., 50, merchant, Baltimore City, September 12, 1893.
WILCOX, Thomas S., 89, merchant, Baltimore City, March 4, 1901.
WILCOX, William L., Sr., 77, merchant, Baltimore City, February 25, 1881.
WILCOX, William L., 73, Baltimore City, May 10, 1910.
WILDERMUTH, John H., 56, Baltimore City, June 15, 1898.
WILEY, Hugh, 69, journalist, Baltimore City, October 1, 1903.
WILEY, Dr. William W., 64, Cumberland, Allegany County, August 26, 1913.
WILFSON, David, 70, manufacturer, Baltimore City, September 14, 1906.
WILFSON, Joseph, 56, merchant, Baltimore City, June 24, 1902.
WILFSON, Moritz, 60, distiller, Baltimore City, June 30, 1891.
WILHELM, George W., 81, builder, Baltimore City, March 5, 1893.
WILHELM, John C., n.a., florist, Baltimore City, November 26, 1897.
WILKENS, Julius C., 60, merchant, Baltimore City, March 10, 1898.
WILKENS, William, 57, manufacturer, Baltimore City, November 29, 1902.
WILKES, David J., 55, photographer, Baltimore City, September 12, 1905.
WILKES, James K., 50, merchant, Baltimore City, January 30, 1881.
WILKINS, Bartus, 77, saddler, Baltimore City, June 6, 1884.
WILKINS, Dr. J_____, 79, physician, Baltimore City, February 5, 1902.
WILKINS, George T., 67, merchant, Baltimore City, August 19, 1901.
WILKINS, Dr. John, 50, physician, Baltimore City, September 20, 1879.

WILKINS, Louis, 62, merchant, Baltimore City, February 7, 1893
WILKINS, Willard C., 61, merchant, Baltimore City, February 11, 1888.
WILKINS, William, 62, manufacturer, Baltimore City, July 12, 1879.
WILKINSON, Alexander, 71, watchman, Fort Carroll, Baltimore City, November 12, 1897.
WILKINSON, James E., 45, stenographer, Baltimore City, April 5, 1905.
WILKINSON, Captain John, 70, former naval officer, Annapolis, Anne Arundel County, December 29, 1891.
WILKINSON, Thomas S., 66, contractor, Baltimore City, March 2, 1901.
WILKINSON, Walter S., 72, Baltimore City, July 30, 1912.
WILLIAMS, E_____ Calvin, 45, attorney, Baltimore City, September 6, 1893.
WILLIAMS, Dr. Elijah, 55, Anne Arundel County, July 5, 1904.
WILLIAMS, Lieutenant Ferdinand, 24, U.S. Army, Annapolis, Anne Arundel County, June 1, 1906.
WILLIAMS, George, 72, Mount Washington, Baltimore County, June 7, 1912.
WILLIAMS, George H., 70, lawyer, Baltimore City, March 7, 1889.
WILLIAMS, Dr. George H., 38, Baltimore City, July 12, 1894.
WILLIAMS, George M., 31, attorney, Baltimore City, February 19, 1880.
WILLIAMS, Hallock B., 57, contractor, Baltimore City, July 19, 1901.
WILLIAMS, Henry V., 79, Baltimore City, June 17, 1894.
WILLIAMS, J_____ P_____, 74, shipbuilder, Baltimore City, July 23, 1904.
WILLIAMS, J_____ Savage, 77, Baltimore City, January 16, 1907.
WILLIAMS, J_____ W_____ M_____, 74, Baptist minister, Baltimore City, August 28, 1894.
WILLIAMS, John, 82, notary public, Baltimore City, October 27, 1885.
WILLIAMS, John B., 61, retired, Baltimore City, September 4, 1899.
WILLIAMS, John F., 50, manufacturer, Baltimore City, December 14, 1883.
WILLIAMS, John F., 76, manufacturer, Baltimore City, January 6, 1883.
WILLIAMS, John F., 64, Baltimore City, May 11, 1913.
WILLIAMS, Dr. L_____ J_____, 69, U.S. Medical Director, Baltimore City, April 8, 1888.
WILLIAMS, Nathaniel F., 84, retired, Baltimore City, August 19, 1884.
WILLIAMS, Otho Holland, Jr., 40, Baltimore City, October 31, 1896.
WILLIAMS, Otho Holland, 83, banker, Baltimore City, February 23, 1903.
WILLIAMS, Dr. Philip C., 68, physician, Baltimore City, November 21, 1896.
WILLIAMS, R_____ A_____, 70, journalist, Baltimore City, May 12, 1893.
WILLIAMS, Rev. Robert H. (Presbyterian), 70, Baltimore City, August 18, 1904.
WILLIAMS, Theodore W., 80, chief judge, Worcester County Orphan's Court; died at Snow Hill, January 20, 1884.

WILLIAMS, Thomas C., 72, retired, Baltimore City, August 22, 1897.
WILLIAMS, Dr. Thomas H., 82, Cambridge, Dorchester County, September 22, 1904.
WILLIAMS, Rev. Dr. Walter W., 60, Baltimore City, June 29, 1892.
WILLIAMS, William S., 67, merchant, Baltimore City, October 8, 1884.
WILLIAMS, William T., 70, bookkeeper, Baltimore City, December 1, 1899.
WILLIAMSON, A____ M____, 81, retired manufacturer, Baltimore City, March 22, 1897.
WILLIAMSON, C____ A____, 78, retired merchant, Baltimore City, December 14, 1878.
WILLIAR, Andrew J., 65, grocer, Baltimore City, June 9, 1894.
WILLIAR, George P., 68, merchant, Baltimore City, May 30, 1890.
WILLIG, Henry, 74, musician, Baltimore City, September 2, 1909.
WILLIS, Dr. E____ W____, 28, physician, Baltimore City, August 7, 1893.
WILLIS, James H., 73, Oxford, Talbot County, December 2, 1913.
WILLMS, J____ Harry, 28, lawyer, Baltimore City, July 21, 1905.
WILLNER, Samuel H., 65, rabbi, Baltimore City, June 19, 1894.
WILLS, John, 74, journalist, Baltimore City, April 26, 1888.
WILMER, Charles, 63, Baltimore City, December 10, 1893.
WILMER, Colonel Edwin, 68, Baltimore City, January 27, 1888.
WILMER, Peregrine, 62, retired, Baltimore City, January 12, 1886.
WILMER, Skipwith, 58, attorney, Baltimore City, July 12, 1901.
WILMER, Dr. William R., 60, Baltimore City, April 25, 1890.
WILSON, C____ Webster, 65, Captain, U.S. Navy (Ret.), Baltimore City, May 28, 1903.
WILSON, Charles A., 64, Annapolis, Anne Arundel County, May 20, 1902.
WILSON, Charles L., 48, politician, Baltimore City, April 21, 1904.
WILSON, Clarissa, 107, black, Baltimore City, December 16, 1878.
WILSON, David, 70, retired, Baltimore City, February 12, 1890.
WILSON, David E., 79, Harford County, February 27, 1901.
WILSON, David S., 80, merchant, Baltimore City, October 19, 1882.
WILSON, Edward DeL., 62, manufacturer, Baltimore City, February 28, 1902.
WILSON, Rev. Dr. Franklin (Baptist), 74, Baltimore City, October 14, 1896.
WILSON, George W., 64, Upper Marlboro, Prince George's County, March 16, 1907.
WILSON, Dr. H____ P____ C____, 70, physician, Baltimore City, December 27, 1897.
WILSON, Mrs. Hannah, 95, Baltimore City, August 9, 1878.
WILSON, Henry C., 51, retired, Baltimore City, March 9, 1897.
WILSON, Henry P. C., Jr., 29, manufacturer, Baltimore City, April 18, 1896.
WILSON, Ignatius, 47, editor, Upper Marlboro, Prince George's County, October 8, 1897.
WILSON, Rev. J____ P____, 72, Baltimore City, September 13, 1908.

WILSON, James G., 74, banker, Baltimore City, June 1, 1904.
WILSON, Rev. James P., n.a., Sparrows Point, Baltimore City, July 27, 1914.
WILSON, James S., 87, master mariner, Baltimore City, January 25, 1893.
WILSON, Jane Marshall, n.a., Catonsville, Baltimore County, June 15, 1913.
WILSON, John, 56, coal operator, Baltimore City, November 1, 1899.
WILSON, John D'Arcy, 52, Baltimore City, December 22, 1900.
WILSON, John E., 41, hotel clerk, Baltimore City, December 17, 1883.
WILSON, John E., 51, attorney, Elkton, Cecil County, September 30, 1892.
WILSON, John F., Sr., 93, farmer, Baltimore City, August 22, 1881.
WILSON, Captain John G., 63, mariner, Baltimore City, May 1, 1891.
WILSON, John L., 60, railroad officer, Baltimore City, March 19, 1880.
WILSON, John W., 69, mariner, Baltimore City, February 10, 1898.
WILSON, Joseph S., 47, Senator, Prince George's County, August 18, 1904.
WILSON, Leroy M., 46, merchant, Baltimore City, December 28, 1881.
WILSON, Olin A., 23, teacher, Chestertown, Kent County, September 8, 1900.
WILSON, P_____ B_____, 66, chemist, Baltimore City, November 3, 1902.
WILSON, Rev. Peter L. (M.P.), 60, Baltimore City, January 10, 1883.
WILSON, Richard C., 56, bank teller, Baltimore City, October 7, 1903.
WILSON, Rev. Samuel A. (M.E.), 77, Baltimore City, September 27, 1903.
WILSON, Samuel G., 69, auctioneer, Baltimore City, February 16, 1895.
WILSON, Thomas, 91, merchant, Baltimore City, September 2, 1879.
WILSON, Thomas J., 58, journalist, Baltimore City, February 28, 1886.
WILSON, Thomas J., 79, retired, Baltimore City, August 7, 1894.
WILSON, Dr. William Griffith, 38, Baltimore City, December 31, 1908.
WILSON, William J., 64, grocer, Baltimore city, July 8, 1878.
WILSON, William Sidney, 45, Snow Hill, Worcester County, November 14, 1897.
WILSON, Young O., 70, manufacturer, Baltimore City, February 17, 1897.
WINANS, C_____ DeWitt, 56, Baltimorean; died in London, November 27, 1892.
WINANS, Ross R., 62, Baltimore City, April 25, 1912.
WINANS, Thomas, 57, Baltimore City, June 10, 1878.
WINANS, William Louis, 73, Baltimorean; died in England, June 22, 1897.

WINCHESTER, Dr. Benjamin T., 61, Baltimore City, January 14, 1913.
WINCHESTER, Lycurgus, 32, broker, Baltimore City, August 2, 1906.
WINDER, Charles H., 71, attorney, Baltimore City, April 10, 1881.
WINDER, George W., 60, merchant, Baltimore City, December 17, 1905.
WINDER, Dr. Richard B., 66, dentist, Baltimore City, July 18, 1894.
WINDER, William H., 71, broker, Baltimore City, October 18, 1879.
WINDERS, Dr. John K., 82, physician, Baltimore City, November 28, 1886.
WINDSOR, C____ Hall, 63, Confederate veteran, Baltimore City, April 11, 1907.
WINEBRENER, David C., 69, Frederick, Frederick County, October 10, 1903.
WINGO, Dr. Charles E., n.a., Baltimore City, December 20, 1914.
WINSLOW, Dr. Caleb, 72, physician, Baltimore City, June 13, 1895.
WINTER, Florenz, 78, merchant, Baltimore City, July 28, 1903.
WINTER, George, 94, Cumberland, Allegany County, July 23, 1914.
WINTER, Dr. Philip, Sr., 70, physician, Baltimore City, June 28, 1899.
WINTERS, Charles, 53, mariner, Baltimore City, October 1, 1901.
WIRTH, Rev. Joseph (R.C.), 63, December 14, 1895.
WISE, Henry, 85, manufacturer, Baltimore City, May 22, 1901.
WISE, Henry A., 56, merchant, Baltimore City, May 29, 1899.
WISE, John J., 79, piano maker, Baltimore City, October 27, 1879.
WISONG, William A., 72, retired, Baltimore City, April 14, 1891.
WITHERS, D____ A____, 83, Pikesville, Baltimore County, November 2, 1912.
WITMER, Edmund F., 85, merchant, Baltimore City, October 16, 1904.
WITMER, George K., n.a., merchant, Baltimore City, March 6, 1901.
WITMER, Peter A., 64, Hagerstown, Washington County, August 2, 1898.
WITTERS, Thomas D., 58, former policeman, Baltimore City, December 1, 1900.
WITTLER, Christopher F., 88, veteran of the Battle of Waterloo, Baltimore City, September 12, 1883.
WOHLLEBER, Jacob, 74, brewer, Baltimore City, July 10, 1882.
WOLF, Christian, 62, tailor, Baltimore City, August 9, 1899.
WOLF, Edmund, 68, manufacturer, Baltimore City, January 16, 1886.
WOLF, Rev. Ferdinand, 80, Plains, March 9, 1914.
WOLF, Moses, 81, insurance agent, Baltimore City, March 13, 1899.
WOLFERSBERGER, Isaiah, 53, editor, *American Progress*, Ellicott City, Howard County, September 12, 1884.
WOLFF, Alexander, 52, attorney, Baltimore City, May 14, 1880.
WOLFF, Colonel William, 83, Baltimore City, January 17, 1913.
WOLLE, Alexander, Sr., 81, taxidermist, Baltimore City, December 10, 1886.

WOOLEN, William Z., 49, mariner, Baltimore City, April 11, 1901.
WOOLFORD, J_____ W_____ W_____, 68, Centreville, Queen Anne's County, January 24, 1908.
WOOLFORD, Roger, 57, Princess Anne, Somerset County, February 4, 1908.
WOOLFORD, Thomas T. C., 72, mariner, Baltimore City, November 18, 1900.
WOMBLE, Dr. J_____ G_____, 43, physician, Baltimore City, March 13, 1889.
WOMBLE, Dr. Pembroke M., 76, physician, Baltimore City, January 30, 1903.
WONDERLY, J_____ C_____ T_____, n.a., merchant, Baltimore City, November 11, 1882.
WOOD, Charles W., 64, Baltimore City, February 23, 1914.
WOOD, H_____ G_____, n.a., auditor, Baltimore City, April 13, 1895.
WOOD, John P., 87, retired, Baltimore City, August 25, 1901.
WOOD, Oliver, 66, retired, Baltimore City, November 11, 1886.
WOOD, Rufus K., 60, steel company, Sparrows Point, Baltimore City, May 16, 1909.
WOOD, Rev. Thomas, 62, Baltimore City, August 19, 1906.
WOOD, William, 82, merchant, Baltimore City, March 31, 1901.
WOOD, William E., 72, manufacturer, Baltimore City, December 17, 1898.
WOOD, William H., 76, merchant, Baltimore City, January 3, 1889.
WOOD, William M., 72, naval surgeon, Baltimore City, March 1, 1880.
WOODALL, Captain Andrew, 87, farmer, Kent County, May 19, 1906.
WOODALL, H_____ E_____, 82, Baltimore City, December 20, 1909.
WOODALL, Captain Washington, 78, Millington, Kent County, March 21, 1914.
WOODALL, William E., 47, shipbuilder, Baltimore City, June 20, 1884.
WOODCOCK, Amos W., 76, merchant, Salisbury, Wicomico County, February 25, 1906.
WOODLAND, John C., n.a., mariner, Baltimore City, February 19, 1900.
WOODLAND, Wesley, 70, marine engineer, Baltimore City, December 27, 1903.
WOODROW, Miss Lydia, 100, Cecil County, November 1, 1903.
WOODS, Andrew, 63, Laurel, Prince George's County, April 15, 1900.
WOODS, Mrs. Ann, 104, Baltimore City, June 24, 1885.
WOODS, Dr. Benjamin W., 67, physician, Baltimore City, August 19, 1883.
WOODS, Charles L., 84, retired, Baltimore City, April 1, 1896.
WOODS, D_____ C_____, 81, realtor, Baltimore City, November 10, 1910.
WOODS, Frank, 50, attorney, Baltimore City, August 17, 1900.
WOODS, Hiram, 75, realtor, Baltimore City, December 7, 1901.
WOODS, John W., 81, retired, Baltimore City, November 27, 1886.
WOODSIDE, Edmund L., n.a., yachtsman, Baltimore City, November 16, 1906.

WOODSIDE, W____ G____, 67, B. & O. Railroad officer, Baltimore City, September 8, 1893.
WOODWARD, Professor D____ A____, 86, artist, Relay, Baltimore County, November 29, 1909.
WOODWARD, Dr. J____ S____, 60, Baltimore City, May 28, 1914.
WOODWARD, N____ R____, 73, livery, Baltimore City, July 25, 1882.
WOODWARD, Reginald T., 65, Anne Arundel County, March 29, 1904.
WOODWARD, William, 94, retired merchant, Baltimore City, May 21, 1896.
WOODYEAR, W____ E____, 82, manufacturer, Baltimore City, August 11, 1893.
WOOTEN, Dr. E____, 70, Rockville, Montgomery County, April 1, 1910.
WOOTERS, James Marion, 54, Talbot County, August 22, 1897.
WOOTERS, John T., 45, druggist, Baltimore City, January 28, 1890.
WOOTTEN, Henry Edgar, 56, lawyer, Howard County, April 13, 1894.
WOOTTON, Colonel Richard, 66, Baltimore City, December 3, 1901.
WORLEY, John, 85, mechanic, Baltimore City, January 14, 1887.
WORTHINGTON, Alexander C., 70, financier, Baltimore City, April 17, 1904.
WORTHINGTON, Daniel D., 26, clerk, Baltimore City, November 16, 1882.
WORTHINGTON, Dr. Eugene, 72, Annapolis, Anne Arundel County, January 27, 1914.
WORTHINGTON, Rev. George F. (P.E.), 75, Baltimore City, August 16, 1887.
WORTHINGTON, J____ L____, 23, cadet, U.S.N.A., Annapolis, Anne Arundel County, July 14, 1881.
WORTHINGTON, John T., 79, Frederick, Frederick County, March 28, 1905.
WORTHINGTON, John Toddy, n.a., Baltimore City, March 22, 1894.
WORTHINGTON, Nicholas Brice, 67, former agricultural editor, Baltimore Weekly, Annapolis, Anne Arundel County, June 18, 1884.
WORTHINGTON, Colonel Thomas, 80, died at Washington, D.C., February 23, 1884.
WORTHINGTON, Dr. Thomas C., 80, Laurel, Prince George's County, September 15, 1899.
WRIGHT, Benjamin N., 59, Annapolis, Anne Arundel County, July 8, 1900.
WRIGHT, C____ C____, 55, professor, Baltimore City College, June 25, 1897.
WRIGHT, George F., 60, painter, Baltimore City, January 26, 1905.
WRIGHT, Gustavus G., 62, merchant, Baltimore City, July 21, 1903.
WRIGHT, Henry S., 70, Baltimore City, May 22, 1907.
WRIGHT, Isaac H., 75, retired merchant, Baltimore City, December 26, 1900.
WRIGHT, Dr. J____ J____, 73, Elkton, Cecil County, March 26, 1910.
WRIGHT, James, 70, merchant, Baltimore City, September 4, 1881.

WRIGHT, Joel, 78, retired, Baltimore City, March 8, 1882.
WRIGHT, John S., 68, merchant, Baltimore City, January 23, 1883.
WRIGHT, John W., 68, merchant, Baltimore City, July 21, 1882.
WRIGHT, Dr. Robert, 86, thought to be the oldest living graduate of West Point; died at Centreville, Queen Anne's County, April 21, 1884.
WRIGHT, Robert Clinton, 67, merchant, Baltimore City, November 12, 1879.
WRIGHT, Robert T., 67, fireman, Baltimore City, March 2, 1883.
WRIGHT, Solomon, 76, Baltimore City, November 21, 1914.
WRIGHT, Thomas, 80, Baltimore County, July 20, 1900.
WRIGHT, Major W_____ A_____, 59, Elkton, Cecil County, February 19, 1906.
WRIGHTSON, Francis A., 86, Talbot County, March 12, 1898.
WRIGHTSON, Dr. S_____ Byron, n.a., Baltimore City, May 25, 1913.
WRIGHTSON, W_____ W_____, n.a., Baltimore City, December 15, 1911.
WRIGHTSON, William D., 70, Queenstown, Queen Anne's County, March 16, 1903.
WRIGHTSON, William L., 84, Talbot County, December 4, 1897.
WRIGHTSON, William T., 64, Talbot County, August 25, 1903.
WROTH, Dr. Peregrine, 94, physician and native of Kent County; died in Baltimore City, June 13, 1879.
WUNDER, Dr. Joseph C., 47, Sabillasville, Frederick County, July 20, 1913.
WURZBURGER, Simon, 74, merchant, Baltimore City, January 19, 1903.
WYAND, Caleb, 72, Keedysville, Washington County, August 21, 1913.
WYATT, Charles H., 68, attorney, Baltimore City, August 2, 1904.
WYLIE, G_____ M_____, 65, dyer, Baltimore City, February 17, 1902.
WYATT, John F., 68, mariner, Baltimore City, April 22, 1901.
WYATT, Rev. Thomas J. (P.E.), 77, Reisterstown, Baltimore County, March 13, 1895.
WYE, Rev. Philip, 74, black, Baltimore City, November 10, 1885.
WYETH, Charles, 92, retired, Baltimore City, January 27, 1891.
WYETH, William N., 52, merchant, Baltimore City, April 15, 1890.
WYLIE, Douglas M., 59, Baltimore City, March 9, 1914.
WYLIE, Robert M., 64, merchant, Baltimore City, June 20, 1902.
WYLIE, Samuel F., 55, dyer, Baltimore City, February 4, 1881.
WYLIE, William, 84, Baltimore City, November 23, 1878.
WYMAN, Samuel G., 74, merchant, Baltimore City, March 6, 1883.
WYMAN, William, 78, capitalist, Baltimore City, November 26, 1903.
WYNN, Christopher, 87, "Old Defender," Baltimore City, June 22, 1883.
WYSHAM, Dr. W_____ E_____ W_____, 70, Catonsville, Baltimore City, December 23, 1896.

YAKEL, Louis, 49, manufacturer, Baltimore City, February 27, 1902.
YATEMAN, Henry, 79, Baltimore merchant; died at Catonsville, Baltimore County, January 17, 1904.

YATES, Arthur C., 32, printer, Baltimore City, August 8, 1901.
YATES, Dr. C____ M____, 86, physician, Baltimore City, May 15, 1891.
YATES, Thomas F., 70, Chestertown, Kent County, May 7, 1914.
YEAGER, John P., 76, woodcarver, Baltimore City, March 23, 1899.
YEAKEL, Charles L., 65, jeweler, Baltimore City, August 13, 1903.
YEAKEL, Conrad, 70, Baltimore City, December 17, 1911.
YESRLEY, Thomas C., 68, realtor, Baltimore City, November 26, 1887.
YEATON, J____ Southgate, 61, Baltimore City, November 12, 1911.
YELLOTT, George, 83, former judge, Baltimore County, November 13, 1902.
YELLOTT, Jeremiah, 83, Baltimore County, June 20, 1894.
YELLOTT, John, 44, Long Green, Baltimore County, April 8, 1914.
YERBY, W____ H____, 68, Confederate veteran, Baltimore City, August 6, 1910.
YINGLING, J____ D____, 81, Pikesville, Baltimore County, October 31, 1911.
YINGLING, Dr. Joel B., 65, Baltimore City, April 14, 1913.
YOE, Benjamin R., 49, merchant, Baltimore City, September 30, 1882.
YOST, Dr. G____ P____, 62, Baltimore City, June 12, 1910.
YOUNG, Alexander, 64, manufacturer, Baltimore City, June 5, 1901.
YOUNG, Benjamin, 85, Confederate veteran, Baltimore City, March 31, 1905.
YOUNG, Captain E____ S____ L____, 78, mariner, Baltimore City, February 24, 1885.
YOUNG, Frederick, 87, retired, Baltimore City, January 18, 1886.
YOUNG, Frederick B., 75, printer, Baltimore City, May 21, 1886.
YOUNG, J____ M____, 39, court clerk, Baltimore City, December 7, 1878.
YOUNG, James, 64, printer, Baltimore City, November 26, 1895.
YOUNG, John, Sr., 70, retired, Baltimore City, July 17, 1883.
YOUNG, Josepha H., 81, McDonough, April 22, 1911.
YOUNG, Joshua T., 71, shipbuilder, Baltimore City, August 15, 1904.
YOUNG, Rev. Martin L. (Lutheran), n.a., Cumberland, Allegany County, December 12, 1904.
YOUNG, Mortimer, 74, veteran, Pikesville, Baltimore County, May 26, 1909.
YOUNG, Rev. S____ A____ (United Brethren), 57, Baltimore City, January 20, 1888.
YOUNG, Rev. Thomas J., n.a., Baltimore City, October 14, 1913.
YOUNG, Rev. W____ G____ (Methodist), 76, Baltimore City, March 1, 1884.
YOUNG, William H., 70, Frederick, Frederick County, May 2, 1909.
YOUNG, William S., 77, merchant, Baltimore City, June 30, 1902.
YOUNGER, D____ K____, 73, lumber inspector, Baltimore City, March 14, 1883.
YOUNGHEIM, J____, 65, manufacturer, Baltimore City, February 10, 1902.
YOUSE, Christian J., 54, manufacturer, Baltimore City, October 13, 1901.

YOUSON, George P., 52, Hagerstown, Washington County, February 10, 1907.

ZACHARIAS, John F., 63, chemist, Cumberland, Allegany County, August 16, 1904.
ZACHARIUS, Miss Jane, n.a., Frederick, Frederick County, October 8, 1906.
ZEIGLER, Daniel, 66, Baltimore City, April 4, 1900.
ZELL, G_____ A_____, 74, Baltimore City, October 22, 1912.
ZELL, Louis A., 83, Lake Shore, Anne Arundel County, June 29, 1911.
ZELL, Oliver C., 49, manufacturer, Baltimore City, October 22, 1884.
ZELLERS, John, 66, compositor, Baltimore City, March 18, 1904.
ZELLNER, John, 72, retired, Baltimore City, May 19, 1902.
ZIEGLER, John, 68, musician, Baltimore City, August 9, 1903.
ZIEGLER, John M., 71, printer, Baltimore City, November 21, 1898.
ZIMMER, Rev. Peter (R.C.), 70, Annapolis, Anne Arundel County, October 26, 1901.
ZIMMERMAN, Benjamin F., 84, bank officer, Baltimore City, October 2, 1903.
ZIMMERMAN, Dr. C_____ F_____, 56, Frederick, Frederick County, March 5, 1908.
ZIMMERMAN, Charles L. B., 79, Union veteran, Baltimore City, September 30, 1901.
ZIMMERMAN, G_____ H_____, 63, former police officer, Baltimore City, February 20, 1883.
ZIMMERMAN, Rev. George H., 60, Baltimore City, November 3, 1898.
ZIMMERMAN, George W., 70, Frederick, Frederick County, December 16, 1896.
ZIMMERMAN, J_____ N_____, 76, Frederick, Frederick County, August 23, 1909.
ZIMMERMAN, Captain L_____ M_____, n.a., Baltimore City, December 18, 1909.
ZIMMERMAN, W_____ F_____, 82, Frederick, Frederick City, December 14, 1911.
ZIMMERMANN, Rev. A_____ H_____, n.a., Baltimore City, July 24, 1900.
ZIMMERMANN, George R., 65, Savage, Howard County, April 6, 1913.
ZINK, Louis, 58, Baltimore City, December 10, 1898.
ZIRKLER, Henry, 69, ship carpenter, Baltimore City, June 5, 1903.
ZITZER, Dr. John J., 57, physician, Baltimore City, October 30, 1883.
ZLEGLER, Edward B., 35, confectioner, Baltimore City, January 25, 1902.
ZOLLER, Dr. Frederick C., 49, physician, Baltimore City, February 2, 1896.
ZOLLICKOFFER, H_____ F_____, 61, physician, Baltimore City, September 30, 1885.
ZOLLICOFFER, Dr. Henry, 78, Baltimore City, August 23, 1895.
ZURMEHL, C_____ H_____, 23, Baltimore City, October 5, 1910.
ZWANZGER, John, 50, druggist, Baltimore City, December 14, 1892.